2022

Tax Preparation Course

©2022 Latino Tax Pro

Table of Contents

Chapter 1 Due Diligence and Penalties 7

Chapter 2 Compiling Taxpayer Information 53

Chapter 3 Filing Status, Dependents, and Deductions 53

Chapter 4 Income 136

Chapter 5 Adjustments to Income 212

Chapter 6 Other Taxes 237

Chapter 7 Payments and Tax Credits 261

Chapter 8 Itemized Deductions 303

Chapter 9 Schedule C 333

Chapter 10 Schedule E 372

Chapter 11 Farm Income 397

Chapter 12 Depreciation 415

Chapter 13 Capital Gains and Losses 433

Chapter 14 Electronic Filing 448

Chapter 15 Extensions and Amendments 472

Quick Start Guide

WELCOME to the most advanced tax learning system in the United States: Prendo365 powered by Latino Tax Professionals! Our tax education is a powerful, user-friendly e-learning system. An optional textbook is available. The following instructions will provide the steps to create and/or login to your Prendo365 account.

First-Time User Purchased Online or Through Sales Rep

Step 1: After purchasing your course, you will receive an email from edsupport@latinotaxpro.com with the subject line "Welcome to Prendo365" — open the email, it contains a password and username to access your account. Check your spam/junk folder if you do not see it.

Step 2: At login, you MUST complete and save the required fields marked with a red asterisk to continue to the user dashboard.

Step 3: On the top left side of the user dashboar next to the word PRENDO, you will see three bars, clic on them, and scroll down to "My Courses." You will see the list of courses in your account. Click on the course you purchase and start learning!

First-Time User Purchased Through Instructor or Office Manager

Step 1: To create an account, enter www.prendo365.com into your preferred browser then hit enter. (We recommend Google Chrome or Firefox for best user experience.)

Step 2: Click on the "Register" button on the top right corner.

Step 3: Use your email as your username*. Remember the email and password you used. Complete all required fields on the two registration pages.

Step 4: If you have an instructor, click on the drop-down menu, "*do you have an instructor*" and select your instructor. Otherwise, click on the "I Accept the terms of the privacy policy" and click "Next." You will receive an email from edsupport@latinotaxpro.com. If you do not receive the email within 15 minutes, check your spam folder. Click next to continue your registration. Make sure to complete all required fields.

Step 5: Enter your PTIN and State information for Continuing Education Credits, if applicable. If you do not have a PTIN, type "N/A". Complete all required fields indicated by a red asterisk.

Step 6: Open the email you received from edsupport@latinotaxpro.com — it contains your temporary password. Click the link to confirm your registration and use the temporary password provided to sign in. When you do, click "Save Changes t

Step 7: Enter the temporary password and then create a new password that you will remember. Click "Save Changes." Click on the word PRENDO on the top left corner to view your dashboard and the course in your account. Click on the course and start learning!

*If you receive a message that your email is already in the system, an account has been created by a staff member, instructor, or by purchasing online. Click on "Forgot your password?" to reset your password or call or text support at 866.936.2587 for assistance.

Returning User

Step 1: Enter Prendo365.com in your preferred browser. Hit enter.

Step 2: Click the "Sign In" button on the top right corner.

Step 3: Enter your username and password. You user name is your email. Forgot your password? Click "Forgot your password?" and follow the prompts.

Step 4: Click "Sign In."

Step 5: In the user dashboard, click on the three bars on the top left corner next to the word PRENDO, then click on "My Courses" to find your course — open your course by clicking on the thumbnail. Then click on "Start Learning Now".

Step 6: Started your course already? Find your course once again on the dashboard under "Courses" and click on the thumbnail to open. Then choose "Resume Where You Left Off" to go to the last section completed. If you still have questions, call or text support at 866.936.2587 or email questions to edsupport@latinotaxpro.com.

How to Use This Textbook

LTP has organized this study material to give line-by-line instructions for Form 1040. It is our editorial staff's belief that you, the student, should understand theory before putting it into practice. Therefore, we recommend that all practice returns be prepared by hand first. Our course is designed to explain where tax information is reported on the individual tax return. Yes, you will most likely preparer tax return using a software, but you still have to understand how the process works so you can identify what you need to know. The software will not tell you what form to use for certain tax items.

Chapter Introduction

Each chapter begins with an introductory paragraph that will give the student an overview of what is covered in the chapter.

Chapter Objectives

Each chapter is designed to build upon the others. The chapter objectives state the framework for the material presented in the chapter.

Chapter Resources

The chapter resources serve as a guide for students when more research may be needed on a particular topic. Our editorial team has created this list of resources to make it easier to begin researching.

Part Questions

The content of each chapter is divided into several parts. You will find review questions at the end of each chapter part. LTP encourages the student not to skip these but read and learn from the answers and feedback.

Chapter Questions "To Test Your Knowledge"

There is a short quiz at the end of each chapter. The online review questions are designed to help the student recall subject matter from the chapter. These review questions are not graded and are not part of the final grade you need to pass this course.

Final Exams

Per regulations, this course does not include the final federal tax law exam. It does include chapter exams, chapter practice tax return quizzes and a Practice Tax Return Final Exam which you Must pass with a 70% or better to complete the course and receive your certificate.

Practice Tax Returns

LTP has created practice tax returns (PTR) to assist the student in understanding tax preparation. Each PTR is based on a scenario encompassing the course content that has been included up to that point. For example, if a lesson covers income, the tax calculations will not reflect any credits that have not yet been discussed in the course, even if the taxpayer in the scenario would have qualified for them. Ideally, the student would prepare the PTR by hand and then answer the PTR review questions on the website. LTP does not discourage software preparation.

When preparing a Schedule A, there are 2 choices for Taxes You Paid; State Tax Withheld or Sales Tax. PTR instructions will use a fixed Sales Tax when preparing the tax return. Be aware that individual states, and county and city could vary in rate and tax withheld.

Textbook Updates

The digital version of the textbook is updated throughout the year to always contain the most recent information. The physical copy of the textbook will also be updated periodically. Notifications are inside Prendo365 indicated by the bell in the upper right of the screen.

LTP Mission

LTP promotes entrepreneurship, education, diversity, and knowledge among tax preparation businesses across the nation — a number that is growing every year. Not only do we provide education, we provide support for tax professionals who pursue opening their own tax preparation businesses or for current business owners who strive to expand their businesses.

- Our **GOAL** is to help you grow your practice and increase your profits.
- Our **VISION** is to give you the best education, leadership, and business-skill training available.
- Our **MISSION** is to give tax professionals a unified, powerful voice on a national level.

LTP believes the best way to begin tax preparation is by understanding Form 1040 efficiently. The chapters in this textbook are designed to give the student basic instructions. When the chapter is completed, the student will go online and complete multiple-choice review questions with feedback for review.

LTP Commitment

This publication is designed to provide accurate and authoritative information on the matter covered. It is presented with the understanding that Latino Tax Professionals is not engaged in rendering legal or accounting services or other professional advice and assumes no liability in connection with its use. Pursuant to Circular 230, this text has been prepared with due diligence; however, the possibility of mechanical or human error does exist. The text is not intended to address every situation that may arise. Consult additional sources of information, as needed, to determine the solution of tax questions.

Tax laws are constantly changing and are subject to differing interpretation. In addition, the facts and circumstances of a particular situation may not be the same as those presented here. Therefore, the student should do additional research to understand fully the information contained in this publication.

Federal law prohibits unauthorized reproduction of the material in this manual. All reproduction must be approved in writing by Latino Tax Professionals. This is not a free publication. Illegal distribution of this publication is prohibited by international and United States copyright laws and treaties. Any illegal distribution by the purchaser can subject the purchaser to penalties of up to $100,000 per copy distributed. No claim is made to original government works; however, within this product or publication, the following are subject to LTP's copyright:

1. Gathering, compilation, and arrangement of such government materials
2. The magnetic translation and digital conversion of data if applicable
3. The historical statutory and other notes and references
4. The commentary and other materials

Authors: Kristeena S. Lopez, MA Ed, EA
Carlos C. Lopez, MDE, EA

Editor: Fernando Cabrera, MA

Contributing Staff: Niki Young, BS, EA
Fernando Cabrera, MA
Andres Santos, EA
Timur Taluy, BS
Roberto Pons, EA
Ricardo Rivas, EA
Pascual Garcia, EA

Graphic Designers: Susan Espinoza, BS
David Lopez

ISBN: 9798828547197

Made in California, USA

Published Date: June 7, 2022

Chapter 1 Due Diligence and Penalties

Prerequisite

This course is designed for tax preparers with zero to basic tax knowledge and about Form 8867. A novice tax preparer needs to know the taxpayer's questions to determine if they qualify for any credits on Form 8867.

Objectives

At the end of this lesson, the student will:

- ➢ Identify the due diligence requirements of the tax preparer when completing a tax return with refundable credits.
- ➢ Explain what documentation must be maintained by the IRS when preparing refundable credits tax returns.
- ➢ Understand what documents the tax preparer should maintain for their records.

Resources

Form 886	Instructions Form 8867
Form 8867	Publication 596
Circular 230	

Table of Contents

Prerequisite 7
Introduction 10
Part 1 Ethics and Due Diligence 10
    Purpose of Form 8867 11
    Contemporaneously Documenting 12
    Creating Form 8867 Truthfully and Accurately 12
    Submitting Form 8867 Truthfully and Accurately 12
    Refundable Credits Due Diligence 13
    Most Common EIC Errors 13
    Consequences of Filing EIC Returns Incorrectly 13
    Questions to ask to determine if the taxpayer qualifies for Earned Income Credit 14
    Most Common Child Tax Credit (CTC), Additional Child Tax Credit (ACTC), and/or Other Dependent Credit (ODC) Errors 15
    Questions to ask to determine if the taxpayer qualifies for CTC/ACTC/ODC 15
    Consequences of Filing CTC/ACTC/ODC Returns Incorrectly 15
    Reporting Schedule C Income Common Errors 18
    Best Practice Guidelines 18
    Document Guidelines and Procedures 19
    Standards of Competence for Tax Professionals 20
    Compliance Procedures 20
    Taxpayer Information Retention 21
    Part 1 Review Questions 21
    Part 1 Review Questions Answers 22
Part 2 Office of Professional Responsibility (OPR) 24
    OPRs Mission 24
    OPR's Authority 25
    Rules Overseeing the Authority to Practice 25
    Information Provided to the IRS and OPR 25
    Practice before the IRS 26
    Individual Representation Rights 26
    Tax Return Preparer 27
    Part 2 Review Questions 28
    Part 2 Review Questions Answers 29
Part 3 Responsibilities of the Tax Preparer 30
    Due Diligence 31
    Competence 31
    Conflict of Interest 31
    Tax Return Positions 31
    Written Tax Advice 32
    Errors and Omissions 32
    Handling Matters Promptly 33
    Client Records 33
    Supervisory Responsibilities 33
    Personal Tax Compliance Responsibilities 33
    Who Prepared the Return? 34
    Part 3 Review Questions 37
    Part 3 Review Questions Answers 38
Part 4 Penalties 39
    Penalties and Interest Charges 39
    Failure-to-File Penalty 40
    Failure-to-Pay Penalty 40

Due Diligence and Penalties

Combined Penalties	40
Failure to Pay Estimated Tax	40
Dishonored Check	41
Paying or Receiving Interest	41
Information Reporting Penalties	41
Filing Late	41
Late-Filed Return with a Refund	41
Exception	41
Reduced Refund	41
Penalty for Failure to Disclose Foreign Income	42
First-Time Abate Policy	42
Failure to Supply Social Security Number	42
Failure to Furnish Correct Payee Statements	42
Interest Charges	43
Tax Evasion	43
Fraud	43
Tax Avoidance	43
Accuracy-Related Penalty	44
Negligence or Disregard	44
Civil, Criminal, and Fraud Penalties	44
Joint Return	44
Criminal Penalties	45
Adequate Disclosure	45
Substantial Understatement of Income Tax	45
Substantial Authority	45
Disclosure Statement	45
Reasonable Cause	46
Filing Erroneous Claim for Refund or Credit	46
Frivolous Tax Return Penalty	46
Failure to Furnish Tax Return Copy to Taxpayer	46
Failure to Sign Return	46
Preparers Failure to Furnish Identifying Number	47
Preparer's Failure to Retain a Copy or List of Tax Return	47
Preparer's Fraud and False Statements	47
Preparer's Fraudulent Returns, Statements, or Other Documents	47
Preparer's Disclosure or Use of Information of Client's Tax Return	47
Preparers Filing Information Returns Incorrectly	47
Preparer's Incompetence and Disreputable Conduct	48
Preparer's Understatement Due to Willful or Reckless Conduct	49
Part 4 Review Questions	49
Part 4 Review Questions Answers	50
Takeaways	52

Introduction

This course will cover tax preparer due diligence and penalties. When the taxpayer files a return with refundable credits the tax preparer needs to complete an accurate tax return and complete Form 8867, which is attached to the taxpayer's return. The following refundable credits will be discussed in this course:

1. Earned Income Credit (EIC).
2. Child Tax Credit (CTC).
3. Additional Child Tax Credit (ACTC).
4. Other Dependent Credit (ODC).
5. American Opportunity Tax Credit (AOTC).

Form 8867 has been in existence since 2006. The form was originally created for the paid preparer to report earned income credit. Originally the paid preparer penalty was $100. In 2011 the penalty was raised to $500. The penalty amount is for each failure to comply with the diligence requirements. For tax year 2021, the penalty amount was $540 for each failure. For 2022 the penalty is $545 for each failure to comply with all due diligence requirements. The 2022 Form 8867 reports all refundable credits and head of household filing status. A tax preparer could be fined a total of $2,180 per Form 8867.

The dictionary definition says due diligence means "the care that a reasonable person exercises to avoid harm to other persons or their property." In plain English, due diligence means doing homework. Before putting your business funds to work on anything, you should make yourself an expert.

Due diligence business definition refers to organizations practicing prudence by carefully assessing associated costs and risks prior to completing transactions. Due diligence should always be a part of the decision when purchasing new property or equipment, implementing new business information systems, or integrating with another firm.

Part 1 Ethics and Due Diligence

"Ethics" is defined as the discipline of dealing with what is good and bad and with moral duty and obligation. It is a set theory or system of principles or moral values. It is also the rules and standards governing the conduct of a person or the members of a profession (e.g., tax practice ethics).

The rules and standards governing the conduct of tax professionals are contained in Circular 230. These rules and standards are the ethics of tax practice. "Ethical behavior" is defined as "of ethics or relating to ethics." In addition, it is being in accordance with or conforming to the accepted principles of right and wrong that govern the conduct of a profession (i.e., professional standards of conduct).

Most people would define ethics as "doing the right thing," which leads one to believe that individuals will, as a matter of common sense and conscience, instinctively react in an ethical manner in all situations. As evidenced by financial scandals involving Bernie Madoff and Lehman Brothers, this is not always true. "Doing the right thing" was not the basis for the decisions made by leaders of those organizations. As a result, many have become generally disillusioned and untrusting of the business community.

The U.S. Treasury Department requires all attorneys, certified public accountants, enrolled agents, enrolled actuaries, and registered tax return preparers to annually complete continuing education, including two hours of ethics or professional conduct.

Purpose of Form 8867

What is due diligence? The Internal Revenue Service (IRS) requires a tax preparer who prepares a return for a client that claims certain credits or head-of-household status thoroughly interview and question the taxpayer. This includes collecting documentation to show that the taxpayer is qualified for the tax advantage.

The paid preparer is required to perform due diligence when preparing tax returns with or without refundable credit. Treasury regulations Section 6695(g) requires the paid tax preparer to meet certain requirements when interviewing the client. Questions must be asked that will give the preparer enough information to complete Form 8867. IRS provides guidelines on how to interview.

The following guidelines have been set forth by the IRS.

1. Meet the knowledge requirement by interviewing the taxpayer, asking adequate questions, contemporaneously documenting the questions and the taxpayer's responses on the return or in your notes, reviewing adequate information to determine if the taxpayer is eligible to claim the credits(s) and/or head of household (HOH) filing status, and to figure the amount(s) of the credit(s) claimed.
2. Complete Form 8867 truthfully and accurately and complete actions described on Form 8867 for any applicable credit(s) claimed and HOH filing status, if claimed.
3. Submit Form 8867 in the manner required.
4. Keep all five of the following records for 3 years from the latest of the dates specified later.
    a. A copy of Form 8867.
    b. The applicable worksheet(s) or if tax preparer created their own for any credits claimed.
    c. Copies of any documents provided by the taxpayer on which the preparer relied to determine the taxpayer's eligibility for the credit(s) and/or HOH filing status and to figure amount(s) of the credits.
    d. A record of how, when, and from whom the information used was obtained to prepare Form 8867 and the applicable worksheet(s).
    e. A record of any additional information tax preparer relied upon, including questions asked and the taxpayer's responses, to determine taxpayer's eligibility for the credit(s) and/or HOH filing status and to figure the amount(s) of the credits(s).

Contemporaneously Documenting

Contemporaneous documents are files that were created at the time of the interview with the taxpayer. Documentation is an important part of due diligence. The tax professional needs to be diligent in keeping records of how the tax return was prepared. Documents proving the taxpayer's income, expenses, credits claimed on the tax return and how the tax return was prepared should be kept. Documentation could save the preparer a due diligence penalty. Good intention of saving the taxpayers documentations and not doing keeping records of how the return was prepared, is only a good intention, and will not save the tax preparer from a due diligence penalty. There are three words that could save a preparer from penalties: DOCUMENT, DOCUMENT, & DOCUMENT.

Documentation should be completed during the interview of the client no matter how the interview takes place, such as in person, via phone, or virtually. When determining HOH filing status, make sure that the individual has paid more than half of the cost of keeping up a home with a qualifying dependent. (Discussed in more detail in the Filing Status Chapter).

Reasonable inquiries include asking pertinent questions, which should result in the needed information to complete Form 8867. Certain questions should determine age of taxpayer and/or dependents to help determine filing status and which credit(s) the taxpayer may qualify for.

The following questions are samples to determine taxpayer's filing status:

- Were you single on December 31st?
- Were you married on December 31st?
- Did you live apart the entire year from your spouse?
- Do you have qualifying children?
- Did the qualifying children live with you the entire year?
- How many months did the qualifying children live with you?
- Does anyone else live in your house?
- Do you live with another taxpayer? If so, what is that individual's relationship to you? Parent, in-laws, cousin, grandchild, etc.?

Creating Form 8867 Truthfully and Accurately

When completing Form 8867, each year is considered. Questions that were asked in the past only relate to the past, and not to the current tax year. It may seem like the same questions are being asked over and over with the same results, but this is essential. People's lives change, and the tax professional must ask the taxpayer about any changes. Asking the same questions to understand the taxpayer's situation is critical to preparing an accurate and truthful return. Even records furnished by the taxpayer must support the credits, income, and expenses claimed on the tax return.

Submitting Form 8867 Truthfully and Accurately

Tax preparer needs to complete Form 8867 by answering the questions that pertain to the taxpayer. Completing Form 8867 is not a cookie-cutter procedure. Every taxpayer is unique and so are the questions asked to determine due diligence for the taxpayer and the tax preparer.

Refundable Credits Due Diligence

Tax preparers must take additional steps to safeguard their compliance with the refundable credits' due diligence. Ignoring tax law could result in penalties and other consequences for the paid tax preparer and their clients. A paid tax preparer who prepares returns with *Earned Income Tax Credit* (EIC), *Child Tax Credit* (CTC), *Other Dependent Credit* (ODC), or the *American opportunity tax credit* (AOTC) must meet due diligence requirements. These requirements focus on accurately determining the client's eligibility and the amount of each credit. The four requirements are:

1. Complete and submit Form 8867 (Treasury Reg. §1.6695-2(b)(1))
2. Compute the credits (Treasury Reg. §1.6695-2(b)(2))
3. Knowledge of who and what is required for credits (Treasury Reg. §1.6695-2(b)(3))
4. Keep records for three years (Treasury Reg. §1.6695-2(b)(4))

Most due diligence penalties are a result of failure to comply with the knowledge requirement. To meet the knowledge requirement, one should:

- Apply common sense standards to the information provided by the client.
- Evaluate if the information given is complete and gather additional information on missing facts.
- Determine if the information is consistent; recognize contradictory statements, and statements you know are true.
- Conduct a thorough, in-depth interview with each client, every year. Don't rely on the statement "everything is the same as last year".
- Ask enough questions to know the return is correct and complete.
- Document, at the time of the interview, any questions asked and the clients' answers.

Documents must be kept for three years from the latest of:

- The due date of the return (not including extensions).
- The date the tax return was electronically filed.
- For a paper return, the date the return was presented to the client for signature.

Señor 1040 Says: The paid tax preparer cannot solely rely on software for their refundable credit due diligence. Professional software may not comply with Treasury Regulation 1.6695(b)(3). It is the paid tax preparer's due diligence responsibility to make sure that they have complied with Treasury Regulation 1.6695.

Most Common EIC Errors

1. Claiming EIC for a child who does not meet the qualifying child requirements.
2. Filing as single or head of household when married.
3. Incorrectly reporting income or expenses.

Consequences of Filing EIC Returns Incorrectly

Tax professionals should know that clients come to them to prepare an accurate tax return. The client trusts a tax professional to know and understand the guidelines to prepare correct tax returns. If a tax preparer incorrectly files EIC returns, it will affect their client, themselves, and, if an employee, their employer.

Due Diligence and Penalties

The following are some basic consequences that can occur when a paid tax preparer files an incorrect EIC tax return for his/her client.

- The client must pay back the amount in error as well as interest on the amount.
- The client may have to file Form 8862 for up to 10 years.
- The client may be banned from claiming EIC for the next 2 years if the error is because of reckless or intentional disregard of the rules.
- The client may be banned from claiming EIC for the next 10 years if the error is because of fraud.

If the IRS examines a refundable tax credit return for a preparer, and the IRS finds that the preparer did not meet the four due diligence requirements (IRC §6694), they may be given a penalty:

- A $545 penalty (per refundable credit) for tax year 2022 for each failure to comply with EIC due diligence requirements for returns filed.
- The penalty is $1,000 or 50% of the income derived by tax preparer with the respect to the return or claim for refund

Remember the four due diligence requirements are:

1. Complete and submit Form 8867 (Treasury Reg. §1.6695-2(b)(1))
2. Compute the credits (Treasury Reg. §1.6695-2(b)(2))
3. Knowledge of who and what is required for credits (Treasury Reg. §1.6695-2(b)(3))
4. Keep records for three years (Treasury Reg. §1.6695-2(b)(4))

Example: Anet prepared a tax return for Lewis. Lewis qualified for refundable credits. Anet was audited and had no documentation and was assessed a penalty for not completing her due diligence on the return. Her penalty for failure to meet the due diligence requirements containing EIC, CTC/ACTC/ODC, or AOTC filed in 2021 is $545 per credit per return. The amount Anet will be assessed for Lewis' return is $545.00 x 4 = $2,180.00.

If the tax preparer receives a return-related penalty, they can also face:

1. Loss of their tax preparer designation.
2. Suspension or expulsion from IRS e-file program.
3. Other disciplinary action by the IRS Office of Professional Responsibility (OPR).
4. Injunctions barring the preparer from preparing tax returns or imposing conditions on the tax returns they have prepared.

The IRS can also penalize the employer if an employee fails to comply with the EIC due diligence requirements.

Questions to ask to determine if the taxpayer qualifies for Earned Income Credit

Although Form 8867 is a paid preparer due diligence form, it provides answers to help tax professionals to determine appropriate questions to ask the taxpayer.

1. Did the child live with you for over half the year?
2. Have you supported the child the entire year?

3. Have you ever been disallowed to claim earned income credit?
4. Have you ever had to file Form 8862?

The tax professional should not rely on the above questions only.

To stay current on EIC changes and due diligence, go to www.irs.gov/eitc.

Most Common Child Tax Credit (CTC), Additional Child Tax Credit (ACTC), and/or Other Dependent Credit (ODC) Errors

1. Claiming the CTC/ACTC/ODC for a qualifying child or qualifying person who does not meet the age requirement.
2. Claiming the CTC/ACTC/ODC for a qualifying child or qualifying person who does not meet the dependency requirements.
3. Claiming the CTC/ACTC/ODC for a qualifying child or qualifying person who does not meet the residency requirement.
4. Not understanding that some credits are reduced based on income amounts.

Questions to ask to determine if the taxpayer qualifies for CTC/ACTC/ODC

1. Did the qualifying child live with the taxpayer for more than half the year?
2. Is the qualifying child a citizen, national, or resident of the United States?
3. Has the custodial parent released the qualifying dependent to the taxpayer?
4. Has the taxpayer supported the child? (Child support is not supporting the child).

The tax professional should not rely on the above questions only.

Consequences of Filing CTC/ACTC/ODC Returns Incorrectly

The following are some basic consequences that can occur when a paid tax preparer files an incorrect CTC/ACTC/ODC tax return for his/her client.

➢ The client must pay back the difference in income, as well as interest and penalties.
➢ The tax preparer may get bad publicity from an angry client(s).
➢ The tax preparer may have to pay a due diligence interest and penalties because of reckless or intentional disregard of the rules or other penalties that apply.
➢ The tax preparer could be disciplined by Office of Professional Responsibility (OPR).

Most Common American opportunity tax credit (AOTC) Errors

1. Claiming AOTC for a student who did not attend an eligible educational institution.
2. Claiming AOTC for a student who did not pay qualifying college expenses.
3. Claiming AOTC for a student for too many years.
4. Preparer did not ask for Form 1098-T.

Questions to ask to determine if the taxpayer qualifies for AOTC

1. Did the qualifying child attend a higher education institution?
2. Was the qualifying child at least a half-time student?
3. Did the qualifying child receive Form 1098-T? (Did box 5 have an amount larger than box 1?)

4. How many years has the taxpayer claimed this credit?
5. Is the student under age 24?
6. Was the student convicted of a felony drug possession or distribution before the end of the tax year?

Consequences of Filing AOTC Returns Incorrectly

- The client must pay back the amount in error as well as interest and penalties.
- The tax preparer may get some bad publicity from the angry client(s).
- The tax preparer could pay due diligence interest and penalties because of reckless or intentional disregard of the rules.
- The tax preparer could be disciplined by Office of Professional Responsibility (OPR).

Determining Head of Household (HOH) Filing Status

The information here is specifically what the tax preparer and taxpayer need to know about answering and completing Form 8867.

Head of household filing status was included on Form 8867 for 2021 tax returns. To be considered HOH, taxpayer must have a qualifying dependent and claim dependency exemption for the qualifying child who lived with the taxpayer more than half the year (exceptions may apply). Some documentation that the tax preparer should obtain when interviewing the taxpayer are official birth documents, marriage certificates, adoption agency letter or placement letter, or pertinent court documents to verify residence and relationship to the child.

The taxpayer must file Head of Household (HOH) if he or she meets any of the following criteria on December 31st of the tax year being filed:

- The taxpayer must be considered unmarried on the last day of the year.
- A qualifying child or relative lived in the home for more than half the year (there are exceptions for temporary absences). Children of divorced or separated parents, or of parents who lived apart, can be claimed based on the residency test in most cases.
- The taxpayer paid for more than half the cost of keeping up the home for the tax year.

Other items that could be useful to claim residency for the qualifying child are school, medical, daycare, or social services records. If the taxpayer brings in school records, then the letter should be written on school letterhead with a photo of the child on the letter. If the daycare provider is a relative, such as grandparents, siblings, or other relatives, then the tax preparer should require another letter of proof that is not from a relative.

Other items needed to determine HOH could be:

1. Qualifying person test.
2. Cost of keeping up a home test.
3. Divorce decree or separation agreement if applicable.
4. Documents that prove you and your spouse did not live together for the last 6 months of the year.
    a. Utility bills
    b. Lease agreement
    c. A letter from clergy or social services.

As a tax preparer the more information you gather, the better off you are in determining filing status.

> *Señor 1040 Says:* To qualify for HOH **all** eligibility requirements must be met.

Questions to ask to determine if the taxpayer qualifies for Head of Household

Below are sample questions to ask to determine a taxpayer's best filing status:

1. Are you single?
2. Are you married?
3. Do you have children?
4. Did the children live with you the entire year?
5. How many months did the children live with you?
6. What documentation do you have to prove the child(ren) lived with you?
7. Does anyone else live in your house?
8. Do you live with another taxpayer?

It is necessary that the tax professional determines the correct filing status by asking pertinent questions such as above.

Self-employed Taxpayer's Due Diligence

Refundable credits due diligence regarding Schedule C requires the paid preparer to take additional steps to ensure that the taxpayer filing a Schedule C with refundable credits complies with tax law. Per Internal Revenue Code (IRC) section 6695(g), paid tax preparers are required to make additional inquiries of taxpayers who appear to be making inconsistent, incorrect, or incomplete claims for the credit.

Paid tax return preparers can generally rely on the taxpayer's representations until it involves EIC due diligence requirements. The paid tax preparer must take additional steps to determine the net self-employment income used to calculate refundable credits eligibility is correct and complete. The additional inquiries made to comply with due diligence and the client's response must be documented. The statute requires the return preparer to be reasonable, well-informed, and knowledgeable in tax law.

It is very important that the information is documented, and the paid tax preparer can prove that they have asked these questions or similar ones that will arrive at the same goal. The IRS is auditing these types of returns. A good tax professional does not want to receive paid preparer penalties or sanctions.

The paid tax preparer should ask sufficient questions to taxpayers claiming self-employment income. Some questions that need to be asked include:

1. Does the client have and conduct a business?
2. Does the client have records to support the documentation of the income and expenses claimed on the return?

3. Can the client reconstruct the documentation, if necessary?
4. Has the client included all income and related expenses reported on the Schedule C?

Reporting Schedule C Income Common Errors

The most common income reporting errors are from Schedule C. Self-employed taxpayers filing a Schedule C must report the correct gross income and all related deductions on their return. The knowledge requirement must be satisfied for correct and complete information. Clients who claim income without expense on a Schedule C should be able to answer probing questions, especially if the client claims they have no records to support the numbers given. Once again, be prepared to ask probing questions with supporting documentation supplied to determine the correct facts.

Example: Esperanza has a cleaning business, and she tells her paid preparer:

- She did not receive Form 1099.
- She was self-employed.
- She earned $12,000.
- She had no related expenses to the cleaning business.

Questions to ask should include:

- Do you have records of the amount of money you received from house cleaning?
- How much did you charge to clean a house?
- How many houses did you clean?
- Who provided the cleaning supplies?
- If you provided the cleaning supplies, how much did you spend weekly?
- Did you provide your own transportation to clean the houses?

Ultimately, the goal is for the paid tax preparer to feel confident that the prepared return is correct and complete, and the paid preparer knows that they have complied with their EIC due diligence requirements.

Best Practice Guidelines

By following these best practices when providing advice and preparing tax return submissions to the IRS, tax advisors are better able to provide their clients with the highest possible representation quality concerning federal tax matters.

Tax professional best practices include the following:

- Communicate clearly with clients regarding the terms of the engagement. This means determining what the client is seeking and what he or she expects from the practitioner. In turn, make sure the client understands the scope and type of services that will be rendered.
- Establish the facts. Determine which facts are relevant to the matter at hand and evaluate the reasonableness of any assumptions or representations.
- Relate the applicable law to the relevant facts and arrive at a conclusion based on this support.

- Advise the client based on the meaning of any findings. Inform him or her of any tax repercussions as a result of any actions or lack thereof (e.g., accuracy-related penalties, interest, etc.).
- Act fairly and with integrity in practice before the IRS.

A practitioner must inform a client of any penalties that are likely to apply to the client with respect to a position taken on a tax return in the following scenarios:

- If the practitioner advised the client with respect to the position.
- If the practitioner prepared or signed the tax return or any document, affidavit, or other paper submitted to the Internal Revenue Service.
- The practitioner must also inform the client, if relevant, of the requirements for adequate disclosure and of any opportunity to avoid any such penalties by disclosure.

A practitioner, when advising a client to take a position on a tax return, document, affidavit, or other paperwork submitted to the IRS or when preparing or signing a tax return as a preparer, may generally rely in good faith, without verification, upon information furnished by the client.

The practitioner may not, however, ignore the implications of information furnished to or actually known by the practitioner and must make reasonable inquiries if the information as furnished appears to be incorrect, incomplete, or inconsistent with an important fact or other factual assumption.

Tax advisors responsible for overseeing a firm's practice of providing advice on federal tax issues and preparing or assisting in the preparation of submissions to the IRS should take reasonable steps to ensure that the firm's procedures for all members, associates, and employees are consistent with these best practices.

Document Guidelines and Procedures

A practitioner may not willfully, recklessly, or through gross incompetence sign a tax return or claim for refund that the tax practitioner knows or reasonably should know contains any of the following:

- An unreasonable basis.
- An unreasonable position as described in §6694(a)(2) of the IRC Code.
- A willful attempt by the practitioner to understate the tax liability or to intentionally disregard the rules and regulations as described in §6694(b)(2).

A paid tax preparer who guarantees a specific amount of refund is an example of the kind of action for this penalty. Others would include if the preparer intentionally disregards information given by the taxpayer to reduce the taxpayer's liability; in this case, the preparer is guilty of a willful attempt to understate tax liability. This does not mean that the preparer may not rely in good faith on the information furnished by the taxpayer. However, the tax preparer must make reasonable inquiries if the information furnished by the taxpayer appears to be incorrect or incomplete.

If the tax professional receives a request for documents, records, or information concerning one of their clients from the IRS or the OPR, he or she must comply with the request unless the tax professional reasonably believes that the information is privileged. If the requested information is not in the tax professional or the tax professional client's possession, the tax professional must promptly inform the requesting IRS or OPR personnel of that fact.

A practitioner may not advise a client to take a position on a document, affidavit, or any other paper(s) submitted to the Internal Revenue Service unless the position is not frivolous. A position is frivolous if it purposefully contains or omits information that demonstrates an intentional disregard of a rule or regulation. If challenged, it is the taxpayer's responsibility to prove to the IRS that a position is not frivolous, and it is then up to the IRS to make the final decision thereof.

A practitioner may not advise a client to submit any document, affidavit, or other paper to the IRS under the following circumstances:

- If the purpose of the submission is to delay or impede the administration of the federal tax laws.
- The information is frivolous.
- The content omits information or demonstrates an intentional disregard of a rule or regulation unless the practitioner also advises the taxpayer to submit a document that shows evidence of a good faith challenge to the rule or regulations.

A practitioner must inform the client of any penalties that are reasonably likely to apply to the client with a position that was taken on the tax return. The tax preparer also needs to inform the client on how to avoid penalties.

The tax practitioner may generally rely in good faith upon any information provided by the taxpayer without having to verify the information the client has given. However, the tax practitioner cannot ignore any potential implications of the documentation that was given to him or any actual knowledge he may have of any errors thereof. A reasonable inquiry about the information furnished is necessary if the taxpayer's provided information seems to be inconsistent or incomplete.

Standards of Competence for Tax Professionals

A practitioner must possess the appropriate level of knowledge, skill, thoroughness, and preparation necessary for competent engagement in practice before the Internal Revenue Service. A practitioner may become competent for the matter for which the practitioner has been engaged through various methods, such as consulting with experts in the relevant area or studying the relevant law.

If the tax professional is not competent in a subject matter, they may consult another individual who the tax professional knows or believes has established competence in the field of study. When the tax professional does consult with another individual, they must consider the requirements of Internal Revenue Code §7216.

Compliance Procedures

Any practitioner who has or shares principal authority and responsibility for overseeing a firm's practice of providing advice concerning federal tax issues must take reasonable steps to ensure that the firm has adequate procedures to raise awareness and to promote compliance with Circular 230 by the firm's members, associates, and employees, and that all such employees are complying with the regulations governing practice before the IRS. These compliance procedures are stated in full in Circular 230 subparts A, B, and C, which can be found on the IRS website.

Any individual or individuals who share principal authority will be subject to discipline for failing in the following ways through willfulness, recklessness, or gross incompetence:

- The individual does not take reasonable steps to ensure the procedures of the firm are adequate.
- The individual does not take reasonable steps to ensure the firm's procedures are properly followed.
- The individual fails to take prompt action to correct any noncompliance despite knowing (or being in a situation where it was the individual's duty to know) that one or more individuals who are associated with or employed by the individual are engaged in a pattern or practice that does not comply with the firm's position.

Taxpayers should receive and be advised to keep copies of the following:

- Form 8879 (PIN program).
- Any Form W-2, Form 1099, etc., and any other backup material for their return.
- A copy of the return that was electronically filed, in a form they can understand.
- A copy of Form 9325, *General Information for Taxpayers Who File Electronically*, which tells taxpayers the procedure to follow if they do not receive their refund.
- For those who request a bank product, a copy of the signed bank application and the disclosure statement.

Taxpayer Information Retention

The tax professional must provide a complete copy of the return to the taxpayer. Tax professionals may provide the copy in any media, including electronic, that is acceptable to both the taxpayer and the tax professional. The copy does not have to contain the Social Security number of the client. A complete copy of a taxpayer's return includes Form 8453 and other documents that the tax professional cannot electronically transmit, when applicable, as well as the electronic portion of the return.

The electronic portion of the return can be contained on a replica of an official form or on an unofficial form. However, on an unofficial form, the tax professional must reference data entries to the line numbers or descriptions on an official form. If the taxpayer provided a completed paper return for electronic filing and the information on the electronic portion of the return is identical to the information provided by the taxpayer, the tax professional does not have to provide a printout of the electronic portion of the return to the taxpayer.

The tax professional should advise the taxpayer to retain a complete copy of his/her return and any supporting material. The tax professional should advise their clients that, if needed, they must file an amended return as a paper return and mail it to the submission processing center that handles the taxpayer's paper return.

Part 1 Review Questions

To obtain the maximum benefit from this chapter, LTP recommends that you complete each of the following questions, and then compare them to the answers with feedback that immediately follows. Under governing self-study standards, vendors must present review questions intermittently throughout each self-study course.

These questions and explanations are not part of the final examination and will not be graded by LTP.

Due Diligence and Penalties

DDPP1.1
Which of the following procedures is not a best practice for the tax professional?

   a. Communicate clearly with the client regarding the terms and condition of the LTPA website.
   b. Act fairly and with integrity.
   c. Advise clients on whether they may avoid accuracy-related penalties if the client relies on that person's advice.
   d. Establish facts to arrive at a conclusion supported by those facts.

DDPP1.2
Which of the following is the paid tax preparer's responsibility?

   a. Being primarily responsible for the overall substantive accuracy of the taxpayer's return.
   b. Signing the return and including their PTIN on it.
   c. Practicing due diligence in questioning and examining each piece of information.
   d. All the options are correct.

DDPP1.3
Vicente prepared Esperanza's tax return but did not ask her any questions to determine if she qualified for Earned Income Tax Credit (EITC). Which of the following statements is not a paid tax preparer EITC due diligence requirement?

   a. Complete and maintain copies of all worksheets and additional questions asked.
   b. Does not have to complete the appropriate refundable credit worksheets.
   c. Know the law and use that knowledge of the law to ensure the client is being asked the right questions to get all relevant information.
   d. Complete and submit Form 8867 with each EITC return.

DDPP1.4
Deborah is a new client to Gloria. Deborah owns a cleaning business and has a part-time W-2 job. Total gross wages reported on her W-2 were $8,500. Her cleaning business earned $7,000 with no expenses. Deborah has 3 children under the age of 17. Which of the following questions does Gloria not have to ask Deborah?

   a. Does Deborah have a business license?
   b. Does Deborah have a business checking account?
   c. What proof does Deborah have of her income?
   d. Does Deborah want Gloria to do her bookkeeping?

Part 1 Review Questions Answers

DDPP1.1
Which of the following procedures is not a best practice for the tax professional?

   a. Communicate clearly with the client regarding the terms and conditions of the LTPA website.
   b. Act and with integrity.
   c. Advise clients on whether they may avoid accuracy-related penalties if the client relies on that person's advice.
   d. Establish facts to arrive at a conclusion supported by those facts.

Feedback: Please reread *Best Practice Guidelines*.

DDPP1.2
Which of the following is the paid tax preparer's responsibility?

a. Being primarily responsible for the overall substantive accuracy of the taxpayer's return.
b. Signing the return and including their PTIN on it.
c. Practicing due diligence in questioning and examining each piece of information.
d. All the options.

Feedback: Please reread *Best Practice Guidelines*.

DDPP1.3
Vicente prepared Esperanza's tax return but did not ask her any questions to determine if she qualified for Earned Income Tax Credit (EITC). Which of the following statements is not a paid tax preparer EITC due diligence requirement?

a. Complete and maintain copies of all worksheets and additional questions asked.
b. Does not have to complete the appropriate refundable credit worksheets.
c. Know the law and use that knowledge of the law to ensure the client is being asked the right questions to get all relevant information.
d. Complete and submit Form 8867 with each EITC return.

Feedback: Please reread *Purpose of Form 8867*.

DDPP1.4
Deborah is a new client to Gloria. Deborah owns a cleaning business and has a part-time W-2 job. Total gross wages reported on her W-2 were $8,500. Her cleaning business earned $7,000 with no expenses. Deborah has 3 children under the age of 17. Which of the following questions does Gloria not have to ask Deborah?

a. Does Deborah have a business license?
b. Does Deborah have a business checking account?
c. What proof does Deborah have of her income?
d. Does Deborah want Gloria to do her bookkeeping?

Feedback: Please reread *Self-employed Taxpayer's Due Diligence*.

Questions Gloria must ask:

1. Does Deborah have and conduct a business?
2. Does Deborah have records documenting the support of their income and expenses?
3. Can Deborah reconstruct that documentation if necessary?
4. Has Deborah included all income and related expenses reported on the Schedule C or C-EZ?
5. Where is the father of the children?
6. Does Deborah receive child support or any other financial assistance?

Part 2 Office of Professional Responsibility (OPR)

OPRs Mission

The Office of Professional Responsibility (OPR) follows a mission to ensure that all tax practitioners, tax preparers, and third parties in the tax system adhere to professional standards and follow the law. OPR is the governing body responsible for interpreting and applying Circular 230 to all who prepare tax returns, whether they are signing or non-signing tax practitioners. OPR has exclusive responsibility for practitioner conduct and discipline.

OPR has oversight of practitioner conduct as well as exclusive responsibility with respect to practitioner discipline, including disciplinary proceedings and sanctions. The OPR may, after notice and an opportunity for a conference, perform the following disciplinary proceedings:

- Disqualify an appraiser from further submissions in connection with tax matters.
- Propose a monetary penalty on any practitioner who engages in conduct subject to sanction. The monetary penalty may be proposed against the individual or a firm or both and can be done in addition to another form of discipline.
- Negotiate an appropriate level of discipline with a practitioner or initiate an administrative proceeding to Censure, Suspend, or Disbar the practitioner.
  - Censure: A public reprimand in which an offender is included on a quarterly list issued by the IRS that states the offender's city and state, name, professional designation, and the effective date(s) of the censure. If censured, offenders can still prepare taxes, but they are more closely monitored, and their newly-sullied names and reputations can negatively impact their businesses. This is the lightest form of punishment.
  - Suspend: If a taxpayer is suspended, it means they cannot prepare any returns for one to fifty-nine months; how long a taxpayer is suspended is determined by the OPR on a case-by-case basis.
  - Disbar: If a taxpayer is disbarred, he or she cannot prepare any returns whatsoever for at least five years.

These penalties and punishments are connected to the activities that the tax preparer has been associated with on behalf of the employer, for it is the employer's legal responsibility to know what their employees are doing as the employer may be liable for the actions of their employee.

Example: Omar Tax Service (OTS), as an entity subject to the Circular 230 guidelines, needs to have a person in charge of ensuring all OTS and IRS procedures are followed and handled correctly. If employee Travis is caught preparing returns in some way that is non-compliant with these guidelines, there are two potential scenarios:

1. If Omar Tax Service did not have someone to ensure the procedures of both the IRS and OTS were being followed correctly, then OTS is liable for their employee's actions.
2. If OTS did have somebody in place to ensure all procedures were followed properly, and did so in full compliance with Circular 230, then Travis is considered a rogue employee, and OTS may not be liable for his actions because OTS correctly followed all the required procedures.

Due Diligence and Penalties

OPR's Authority

OPR oversees the conduct of tax practice. The oversight extends to all individuals who make a presentation to the IRS relating to a taxpayer's rights, privileges, or liabilities under the laws or regulations administered by the IRS. This authority generally extends to any individual who interacts with federal tax administration in person, orally, in writing, or by the preparation and submission of documents.

OPR oversees a practitioner's conduct and discipline, including disciplinary proceedings and sanctions. After serving a practitioner a notice and granting them an opportunity for a conference, OPR could negotiate an appropriate level of discipline with the practitioner; or could in fact initiate an administrative proceeding to censure (a public reprimand), suspend (one to fifty-nine months), or disbar (five years) the practitioner.

Rules Overseeing the Authority to Practice

The Circular 230 is the written guideline that governs those who represent taxpayers before the IRS. The rules and regulations found in Circular 230 are overseen by the Office of Professional Responsibility (OPR). In this section you will find a detailed list of each section of the Circular 230 and the rules and guidelines contained within each part. It is imperative that the paid tax preparer learns these guidelines and understands his or her individual responsibility to prepare tax returns accurately based on tax law and the information provided by the taxpayer.

Information Provided to the IRS and OPR

If an authorized officer or employee of the IRS or OPR requests information or records regarding or in reference to a taxpayer, the tax preparer is required by law to comply with the request promptly unless he or she believes in good faith or on reasonable grounds that such records or information is privileged or that the request for, or effort to obtain, such record or information is of doubtful legality.

If the requested information is not in the possession of the tax professional or his or her client, the tax professional must promptly notify the requesting IRS or OPR personnel of that fact. In the case of requests from the IRS, the practitioner must make reasonable inquiries of the client regarding the identity of any person who has the records. The tax professional is not required to actually speak with anyone other than their client, but they must ask their client about the identity of any person who may have the records or information that was requested and then provide that information to the IRS.

A practitioner may not interfere, or attempt to interfere, with any proper and lawful effort by the IRS and its officers or employees or with the director of the Office of Professional Responsibility and his or her employees to obtain any record(s) or information unless the practitioner believes in good faith and on reasonable grounds that the record(s) or information is privileged.

As stated in §10.34(b) in regard to the submission of any documents that may be requested by the IRS or OPR, the tax professional cannot advise a client to submit any document to the IRS that falls under one or both of the following two categories:

➢ Frivolous.

> Contains or omits information in a manner demonstrating an intentional disregard of a rule or regulation unless the tax professional also advises the client to submit a document that evidences a good faith challenge to the rule or regulation.

Example: The IRS requests information about John Henry. Andres prepared Mr. Henry's return for the past two years; however, the year in question is prior to Mr. Henry becoming Andres' client. Andres has copies of Mr. Henry's tax return for the year in question, which contains the name, address, and identification number of the individual who prepared the return. Andres is required to provide the IRS with the information about the preparer listed on the return, but not the return itself. Andres needs to inform the client of the IRS request.
(Treasury Circular 230, §10.20, §10.34(b)).

Practice before the IRS

"Practice before the IRS" constitutes all matters connected with a presentation to the IRS, or any of its officers or employees, related to a taxpayer's rights, privileges, or liabilities under the laws or regulations administered by the IRS. Such presentations include, but are not limited to, preparing documents, filing documents, and corresponding and communicating with the IRS. It also includes rendering oral and written advice with respect to any entity, transaction, plan, arrangement, or any matter that has a potential for tax avoidance or evasion; and representing a client at conferences, hearings, and meetings.

Individual Representation Rights

The following is a summary of the individuals who can practice before the IRS and their representation rights.

a. *Attorney*: Any attorney who is not currently under suspension or disbarment from practice before the Internal Revenue Service may do so by filing a written declaration stating that the individual is currently qualified as an attorney and is authorized to represent the party or parties.
b. *Certified public accountant* (CPA): Any certified public accountant who is not currently under suspension or disbarment from practice before the Internal Revenue Service may do so by filing a written declaration that the individual is qualified as a certified public accountant and is authorized to represent the party or parties.
c. *Enrolled agents*: Any individual enrolled as an agent pursuant to this part who is not currently under suspension or disbarment from practice before the Internal Revenue Service may practice before the Internal Revenue Service. (Enrolled agents take a three-part test and must pass each part).
d. *Enrolled actuaries*: Any individual who is enrolled as an actuary by the Joint Board for the Enrollment of Actuaries pursuant to 29 U.S.C. 1242 who is not currently under suspension or disbarment from practice may do so by filing a written declaration stating that the individual is currently qualified as an enrolled actuary and is authorized to represent the party or parties on their behalf.
e. *Enrolled retirement plan agents*: An individual enrolled as a retirement plan agent pursuant to this part who is not currently under suspension or disbarment from practice before the Internal Revenue Service may practice before the IRS.

f. ***Annual Filing Season Program Participants (AFSP)***: This voluntary program recognizes the efforts of return preparers who are not attorneys, certified public accountants, or enrolled agents. The IRS issues an Annual Filing Season Program Record of Completion to return preparers who obtain a certain number of continuing education hours in preparation for a specific tax year.

Tax Return Preparer

LTP believes that taxpayers should choose a tax return preparer who will be available for them in case the IRS examines their tax return. Most tax return preparers are professional, honest, and provide excellent customer service to their clients. However, dishonest, and unscrupulous tax return preparers do exist. The taxpayer should always check their return for errors to avoid penalties, along with financial and legal problems.

First, anybody who is paid to prepare tax returns should have complete understanding of tax matters and is required to have a PTIN.

A paid tax return preparer is primarily responsible for the overall accuracy of the taxpayer's return. By law, the paid tax preparer is required to sign the return and include their PTIN. Although the tax return preparer signs the return, the taxpayer is ultimately responsible for the accuracy of every item reported on the return.

The paid tax preparer is subject to Section 6694 and is responsible for the accuracy of the return. The individual who signs the return will be primarily responsible for all the positions on the return and/or claim for refund.

LTP recommends that when the taxpayer is looking to hire a professional tax preparer, the taxpayers should keep in mind the following list.

1. Check the preparer's qualifications
2. Check the preparer's history
3. Ask about service fees
4. Ask to e-file the return
5. Make sure the preparer is available
6. Provide records and receipts
7. Never sign a blank check
8. Review your return before signing
9. Ensure the preparer signs and includes their PTIN
10. Report abusive tax preparers to the IRS
11. Visit the following link http://irs.treasury.gov/rpo/rpo.jsf to search for a tax professional in your area

Señor 1040 Says: Privilege does not apply in a criminal matter unless the practitioner is an attorney.

Due Diligence and Penalties

Part 2 Review Questions

To obtain the maximum benefit from this chapter, LTP recommends that you complete each of the following questions, and then compare them to the answers with feedback that immediately follows. Under governing self-study standards, vendors are required to present review questions intermittently throughout each self-study course.

These questions and explanations are not part of the final examination and will not be graded by LTP.

DDPP2.1
A(n) _____ is any individual who has taken and passed a special three-part test and granted enrollment to practice before the IRS.

  a. Attorney
  b. Certified public accountant
  c. Enrolled agent
  d. Notary

DDPP2.2
A(n) _____ is any person who is a member in good standing of the bar of the highest court of any State, territory, or possession of the United States, including Commonwealth or the District of Columbia.

  a. Attorney
  b. Certified public account
  c. Enrolled agent
  d. Notary

DDPP2.3
Which of the following best describes the contents of Circular 230?

  a. Written regulations that govern those who represent taxpayers before the IRS.
  b. A document containing the statute and regulations detailing a tax professional's day and night job.
  c. A document containing statements and regulations detailing how to become a tax professional.
  d. A document containing the statute and regulations detailing the duties and obligations of the IRS.

DDPP2.4
What is the Office of Professional Responsibility authority (OPR)?

  a. The OPR oversees the Commissioner.
  b. The OPR oversees the United States Treasury.
  c. The OPR oversees the conduct of tax practice.
  d. The OPR oversees the unprofessional tax preparer.

DDPP2.5
Circular 230 provides a consistent standard for the tax professional to follow. Sometimes the choices made by the paid tax professional affect themselves and the taxpayer. The first responsibility of the paid tax preparer is to the client. When making a decision as a tax preparer, which guideline below should be followed?

   a. Determine the nature of the issue in question.
   b. Get as little information and documentation from the client as possible.
   c. Examine only one possible solution.
   d. Choose a solution that the client is not able to support.

Part 2 Review Questions Answers

DDPP2.1
A(n) _____ is any individual who has taken and passed a special three-part test and granted enrollment to practice before the IRS.

   a. Attorney
   b. Certified public accountant
   c. Enrolled agent
   d. Notary

Feedback: Review section *Individual Representation Rights.*

DDPP2.2
A(n) _____ is any person who is a member in good standing of the bar of the highest court of any State, territory, or possession of the United States, including Commonwealth or the District of Columbia.

   a. Attorney
   b. Certified public account
   c. Enrolled agent
   d. Notary

Feedback: Review section *Individual Representation Rights*

DDPP2.3
Which of the following best describes the contents of Circular 230?

   a. Written regulations that govern those who represent taxpayers before the IRS.
   b. A document containing the statute and regulations detailing a tax professional's day and night job.
   c. A document containing statements and regulations detailing how to become a tax professional.
   d. A document containing the statute and regulations detailing the duties and obligations of the IRS.

Feedback: Review section *Rules Overseeing the Authority to Practice.*

DDPP2.4
What is the Office of Professional Responsibility authority (OPR)?

   a. The OPR oversees the Commissioner.
   b. The OPR oversees the United States Treasury.
   c. The OPR oversees the conduct of tax practice.
   d. The OPR oversees the unprofessional tax preparer.

Feedback: The OPR oversees the conduct of tax practices. The oversight extends to all individuals who make a presentation to the IRS relating to a taxpayer's rights, privileges, or liabilities under the laws or regulations administered by the IRS. This authority generally extends to any individual who interacts with the federal tax administration orally, in person, in writing, or by preparing and submitting documents.

DDPP2.5
Circular 230 provides a consistent standard for the tax professional to follow. Sometimes the choices made by the paid tax professional affect themselves and the taxpayer. The first responsibility of the paid tax preparer is to the client. When making a decision as a tax preparer, which guideline below should be followed?

   a. Determine the nature of the issue in question.
   b. Get as little information and documentation from the client as possible.
   c. Examine only one possible solution.
   d. Choose a solution that the client is not able to support.

Feedback: Review section *Rules Overseeing the Authority to Practice*.

Part 3 Responsibilities of the Tax Preparer

The paid tax preparer must understand the ethical responsibility to prepare accurate tax returns based on tax law and the information provided by the taxpayer.

OPR may propose censure, suspension, or disbarment of any practitioner from practice before the IRS if the individual shows to be incompetent or disreputable and/or fails to comply with any regulations found in Circular 230. OPR may impose a monetary penalty for an individual or their employer subject to Circular 230. The monetary penalty relates to activities the tax preparer associates with on behalf of the employer. The employer should have known what the employee was doing.

You can find the following explanations of tax professionals' responsibilities under Treasury Circular 230. This summary does not address all provisions of the regulations. The tax professional should read Circular 230 for a complete understanding of the duties and obligations of someone practicing before the IRS. Preparing a tax return is also considered practicing before the IRS.

Due Diligence

Tax professionals must exercise due diligence in preparing and filing tax returns and the correctness of their representation to their clients or the IRS. The tax professional can rely on another person's work if they are carefully engaged, supervised, trained, and evaluated, considering the nature of the relationship between the tax professional and that person. The tax professional generally may rely in good faith and without verification on information furnished by the client, but the tax professional cannot ignore other information furnished to them or which they know. The tax professional must make reasonable inquiries if any information furnished to them appears to be incorrect, incomplete, or inconsistent with other facts or assumptions (Treasury Circular 230, §10.22, §10.34(d)).

The tax professional could rely on the work product of another person if the individual used reasonable care in engaging, supervising, training, and evaluating that person, taking proper account of the nature of the relationship between the tax professional and the taxpayer.

The tax professional may also generally rely in good faith and without verification upon information furnished by their client, but the tax professional cannot ignore other information furnished to them or known by them. The tax professional must make reasonable inquiries if any information furnished to them appears to be incorrect, incomplete, or inconsistent with other facts or assumptions.

Competence

Tax professionals must have the necessary knowledge, skill, thoroughness, and preparation to engage in tax matters. If the tax professional is not competent in an area, they should consult a subject matter expert. When a tax professional consults with another individual, they must consider the requirements of Internal Revenue Code §7216 (Treasury Circular 230 §10.35).

Conflict of Interest

A conflict of interest exists when representing a client who is directly averse to another client of the paid tax professional. A conflict of interest also exists if there is a significant risk that representing a client will be materially limited by the tax professional responsibilities to another client, a former client, a third person, or their interests. When a conflict of interest exists, the tax professional may not represent a client in an IRS matter unless:

1. The tax professional reasonably believes that they can provide competent and diligent representation to all affected clients.
2. The law does not prohibit the tax professional's representation.
3. All affected clients give informed, written consent to the tax professional's representation. The tax professional must retain these consents for 36 months following the termination of the engagement and make them available to the IRS/OPR upon request (Treasury Circular 230, §10.29).

Tax Return Positions

Tax return positions are the strategies chosen when preparing a tax return. Tax preparers guide taxpayers in figuring out the proper positions for their return; it is the tax preparer's duty to perform due diligence and ensure the accuracy of the positions taken on the return and claim for refund. Good tax preparers will choose the positions that best help the taxpayer while complying with IRS guidelines.

The tax professional cannot sign a tax return or refund a claim or advise a client to take a position on a tax return, or refund claim that the tax professional knows (or should know) contains a position that (i) has no reasonable basis, (ii) is an unreasonable position as defined by Internal Revenue Code §6694(a)(2), or (iii) is a willful attempt to understate tax liability or a reckless or intentional disregard of rules or regulations.

On the other hand, an unreasonable position lacks substantial authority defined in IRC §6662, but it has a reasonable basis, and the taxpayer discloses the position. For Circular 230 disclosure, if the tax professional advised the client regarding a position, prepared, or signed the tax return, the tax professional must inform the client of any penalties that are reasonably likely to apply to the client with respect to the tax return position. The tax professional must then explain how to avoid the penalties through disclosure or not taking the position.

For purposes of Circular 230 disclosure, if the tax professional advises the client regarding a position or prepares or signs the tax return, the tax professional must inform the client of any penalties that will possibly apply to the client with respect to the tax return position, and how to avoid the penalties through disclosure (or, by not taking the position).

Written Tax Advice

In providing written advice concerning any federal tax matter, the tax professional must:

1. Base advice on reasonable assumptions.
2. Reasonably consider all relevant facts that a tax professional knows or should know.
3. Use reasonable efforts to identify and ascertain the relevant facts.

The tax professional cannot rely upon representations, statements, findings, or agreements that are unreasonable or known to be incorrect, inconsistent, or incomplete.

The tax professional must always consider the possibility of an IRS audit to a tax return or that a matter could raise an audit. When providing written advice, the tax professional may rely in good faith on the advice of another practitioner only if that advice is reasonable, considering all facts and circumstances. The tax professional cannot rely on the advice of a person they know, or should have known, is not competent to provide the advice, or has an unresolved conflict of interest as defined in §10.29 (Treasury Circular 230, §10.37).

Errors and Omissions

If the tax professional knows that a client has not complied with the U.S. revenue laws or has made an error in, or omission from, any return, affidavit, or other documents which the client submitted or executed under U.S. revenue laws, the tax professional must promptly inform the client of the noncompliance, error, or omission and advise the client regarding the consequences under the Code and regulations of the noncompliance, error, or omission. Depending on the facts and circumstances, the consequences of an error or omission could include (among other things) additional tax liability, civil penalties, interest, criminal penalties, and an extension of the statute of limitations (Treasury Circular 230, §10.21).

Handling Matters Promptly

The tax professional cannot unreasonably delay the prompt disposition of any matter before the Internal Revenue Service. This matter applies to responding to the tax professional's client and IRS personnel. The tax professional cannot advise a client to submit any document to the IRS for delaying or impeding the administration of the federal tax laws (Treasury Circular 230, §10.23, §10.34(b)).

Client Records

At the client's request, the tax professional must promptly return any client records necessary for the client to comply with their federal tax obligations, even if there is a dispute over fees. The tax professional may keep copies of these records. Suppose state law allows the tax professional to retain a client's records in the case of a fee dispute. In that case, the tax professional can only return the records attached to the client's return. Still, the tax professional must provide the client with reasonable access to review and copy any additional client records retained by the tax professional necessary for the client to comply with their federal tax obligations. The term "client records" includes all written or electronic materials provided by the client or a third party to the tax professional.

"Client records" also include any tax return or other document that the tax professional prepared and previously delivered to the client if that return or document is necessary for the client to comply with their current federal tax obligations. The tax professional is not required to provide a client with a copy of their work product. That is, any return, refund claim, or other documents that the tax professional prepared but has not yet delivered to the client if:

1. The tax professional is withholding the document pending the client's payment of fees related to the document.
2. The tax professional contract with the client requires the payment of those fees before delivery (Treasury Circular 230 §10.28).

Supervisory Responsibilities

If the tax professional has or shares principal authority and responsibility for overseeing the firm's tax practice, the tax professional must take reasonable steps to ensure that the tax professional firm has adequate procedures in place. These procedures should raise awareness and promote compliance with Circular 230 by the firm's members, associates, and employees. All such employees must comply with the regulations governing practice before the IRS (Treasury Circular 230, §10.36).

Personal Tax Compliance Responsibilities

The tax professional is responsible for ensuring the timely filing and payment of personal income tax returns and the tax returns for any entity over which the tax professional has, or shares, control. Failing to file 4 of the last 5 years' income tax returns, or 5 of the previous 7 quarters of employment/excise tax returns, is per se disreputable and incompetent conduct that can lead to sudden, indefinite suspension of the practitioner. The willful evasion of the assessment or payment of tax also violates Circular 230 regulations (Treasury Circular 230, §10.51(a)(6)).

Who Prepared the Return?

A tax return preparer is any person who prepares for compensation or employs one or more individuals to prepare all, or a substantial portion of the tax return or any claim for refund of tax. A signing tax return preparer is an individual tax return preparer responsible for the overall substantive accuracy of preparing such return or claim for refund.

A tax return preparer is any and all of the following:

- A preparer is any person who prepares all or a substantial portion of any tax return or claims for refund in exchange for compensation or employs one or more persons to prepare for payment.
- Any individual paid to prepare or assist with tax preparation of all or substantially all of a tax return or claim for refund must have a PTIN number and is subject to the duties and restrictions relating to practice in subpart B of Circular 230. Subpart B is §10.20 through §10.53. Anyone who prepares a return for compensation must have a PTIN.
- Any individual preparing or assisting others in preparing tax returns or claiming for refunds may appear as a witness for the taxpayer before the IRS or furnish information at the request of the IRS or any of the IRS officers or employees.
- Any individual preparing or assisting others to prepare all or a substantial portion of a document about any taxpayer's tax liability for compensation is subject to the duties and restrictions relating to practice in §10.20 through §10.53 (subpart B as well as subpart C) and §10.60 through §10.82.

A signing tax return preparer is the individual tax return preparer primarily responsible for the overall substantive accuracy of the preparation of such return or claim for refund. Even if someone else provides all the information and materials needed for the tax return, effectively "preparing" most of the return's material, the individual that inputs and arranges the material for the actual submission of the return or claim for refund is the person who must sign the return and thus claim responsibility for its accuracy. The person who needs to sign the return and claim responsibility for its accuracy is whoever decides the tax return's position.

A non-signing tax return preparer is any person who prepares all or a substantial portion of a return or claims for a refund but does not possess the primary responsibility for its accuracy. They were not individuals who input the information into the tax return or chose the tax return positions.

Whether or not an individual should be considered a non-signing or signing tax return preparer also depends on how much time the preparer spends advising the taxpayer. To be eligible to be a non-signing preparer, events that have occurred should represent less than 5% of the aggregated time incurred by the non-signing tax return preparer. You calculate the advice you give, whether written or oral, when given to the taxpayer and the signing tax preparer.

Example: An enrolled agent named Fiona hires Nick to do the literal inputting of W-2s, and other income documents, and other related materials into her preferred tax software. After Nick finishes, Fiona goes through the prepared material, ensures it is correct, and submits the return. Even though Nick spent more time on the return and was the one who put it all together, Fiona prepared the tax return because she was the one who checked its contents and performed the actual action of ensuring that the return was accurate. Therefore, Fiona must sign the return and thus claim responsibility for its accuracy. Even though Nick "prepared" the return by putting it together, Fiona checked and guaranteed its accuracy.

A person who renders tax advice on a position directly relevant to determining the existence, characterization, or amount of an entry on a return or claim for refund prepared the entry. The meaning of substantial portion is based upon whether the person knows or reasonably should know the tax characteristics of the schedule, entry, or other portion of a return or claim for refund. A single tax entry could constitute a considerable portion of the tax required to be shown on a return.

Example 1: Domingo is an attorney at ABC law firm; he provides legal advice to a large corporate taxpayer regarding a completed corporate transaction. The advice provided by Domingo is directly relevant to the determination of an entry on the taxpayer's return. Domingo, however, does not prepare any other portion of the taxpayer's return and is not signing the return. Domingo is a non-signing tax return preparer since his advice is limited to one entry on the tax return.

Example 2: The facts are the same as Example 1, except that Attorney Brittni provides supplemental advice to the corporate taxpayer on a phone call after completing the transaction. Brittni did not provide advice before the corporate transaction occurred with the primary intent to avoid being a tax return preparer. The time incurred on the supplemental advice by Brittni represents less than 5% of the aggregate amount of time spent by Brittni providing tax advice on the position. Brittni is not considered a tax return preparer.

Example 3: The facts are the same as Example 2, except that Attorney Brittni provides supplemental advice to the corporate taxpayer on a phone call after the transaction occurred with the primary intent to avoid being a tax return preparer. The time incurred on the supplemental advice by Brittni represents less than 5% of the aggregate amount of time spent by Brittni providing tax advice on the position. Brittni is not considered a tax return preparer.

Whether the schedule entry is a single-line entry or the entire schedule (A, B, K-1, etc.), or another entry on the tax return, the consideration is the substantial amount belonging to the single entry or the entire schedule. If the consideration is a significant portion of the return, then the individual responsible for the entry could be considered the signer of the tax return. The key is the amount of the entry. For example, Nick only entered Jesse's personal information and one W-2 into the tax return. Fernando completed Jesse's Schedule A, B, and C. Fernando would be the signer on the return since he entered a substantial portion of the return.

Any individual paid to prepare or assist with tax preparation of all or substantially all the tax returns or claims for refund must have a PTIN number and is subject to the duties and restrictions relating to practice in subpart B of Circular 230. Subpart B is §10.20 through §10.53.

Any individual preparing or assisting others to prepare a tax return or claims for a refund may appear as a witness for the taxpayer before the IRS. They can also furnish information at the request of the IRS or any of the IRS officers or employees.

Any individual who for compensation prepares, or assists in the preparation of, all or a substantial portion of a document pertaining to any taxpayer's tax liability is subject to the duties and restrictions relating to practice in §10.20 through §10.53 (subpart B as well as subpart C) and §10.60 through §10.82.

Example: Kristie is Maria's administrative assistant. Kristie collects information from Julie, Maria's client, to help Maria prepare the tax return. Maria signs the return. Kristie is not the paid preparer of Julie's tax return.

Factors to consider that make a substantial portion include:

1. The size and complexity of the item relative to the taxpayer's gross income
2. The size of the understatement attributable to the item compared to the taxpayer's reported tax liability

Example 1: Timothy prepares Form 8886, "*Reportable Transaction Disclosure Statement.*" He does not prepare the tax return or advise the taxpayer regarding the tax return position for the transaction to which Form 8886 relates. The preparation of Form 8886 is not directly relevant to the determination of the existence, characterization, or amount of an entry on a tax return or claim for a refund. Timothy is preparing Form 8886 to disclose a reportable transaction and not to prepare a substantial portion of the tax return and is not considered a tax return preparer under §6694.

Example 2: Vicente prepares a schedule for Jose's Form 1040, reporting $4,000 in dividend income, and gives Jose oral or written advice about his Schedule A, which results in a medical expense deduction totaling $5,000, but does not sign the return. Vicente is a non-signing tax return preparer because the aggregate total amount of the deduction is less than $10,000.

A tax refund claim includes a credit claim against any tax. A claim for refund also includes a claim for payment under sections 6420, 6421, or 6427.

Example 1: Jose received employment tax information from Maria, who prepares her recordkeeping. Jose did not render any tax advice to Maria or exercise any discretion or independent judgment on Maria's tax positions. Jose just processed the information that Maria gave to him. Jose signed the return as authorized by the client according to Form 8655, *Reporting Agent Authorization,* and filed Maria's return using the information supplied by Maria. Jose is a tax return preparer.

Example 2: Matthew rendered tax advice to Sharon on determining whether her workers are employees or independent contractors for federal tax purposes. Matthew received compensation for his advice and is the tax return preparer. The following individuals are not tax return preparers:

1. An official or employee of the Internal Revenue Service (IRS) performing official duties.
2. Any individual who provides tax assistance under the Volunteer Income Tax Assistance (VITA) program established by the IRS but the individual can only prepare returns for VITA.
3. Any organization sponsoring or administering a VITA program established by the IRS, but only concerning the sponsorship or administration.
4. An individual who provides tax counseling for the elderly under a program established under section 163 of the Revenue Act of 1978, but only concerning those returns prepared as part of that program.
5. An organization sponsoring or administering a program to provide tax counseling for the elderly established under section 163 of the Revenue Act of 1978, but only concerning that sponsorship or administration.
6. An individual who provides tax assistance as part of a qualified Low-Income Taxpayer Clinic (LITC) as defined by §7526, subject to the requirements, but only for the LITC tax returns.

7. Any organization that is a qualified LITC.
8. An individual providing just typing, reproduction, or other mechanical assistance in the preparation of a return or claim for a refund.
9. An individual preparing a return or claim for refund of a taxpayer, or an officer, a general partner, member, shareholder, or employee of a taxpayer, by whom the individual is regularly and continuously employed, compensated or in which the individual is a general partner.
10. An individual preparing a return or claim for a refund for a trust, estate, or other entity, of which the individual either is a fiduciary or is an officer, general partner, or employee of the fiduciary.
11. An individual preparing a claim for a refund for a taxpayer in response to:
    a. A notice of deficiency issued to the taxpayer.
    b. A waiver of restriction on assessment after initiating an audit of the taxpayer or another taxpayer if the audit determines the other taxpayer affects, directly or indirectly, the taxpayer's liability.
12. A person who prepares a return or claim for a refund for a taxpayer with no explicit or implicit agreement for compensation, even if the person receives an insubstantial gift, return service, or favor.

Part 3 Review Questions

To obtain the maximum benefit from this chapter, LTP recommends that you complete each of the following questions, and then compare them to the answers with feedback that immediately follows. Under governing self-study standards, vendors are required to present review questions intermittently throughout each self-study course.

These questions and explanations are not part of the final examination and will not be graded by LTP.

DDPP3.1

Fernando prepared Andres and Alberto's partnership return. Alberto sued Andres for misrepresentation of income for their partnership. Which of the partners can Fernando represent before the IRS?

a. Fernando can represent them both since he knows the truth about both.
b. Fernando cannot represent either one since it will be a conflict of interest.
c. Fernando can represent either one if both have given him consent to do so.
d. Fernando must keep the consent form when a disagreement is in place.

DDPP3.2

Tax return positions are the strategies chosen when preparing a tax return. To perform their task, what must a paid tax preparer do?

a. Guide taxpayers in figuring out the proper positions for their return.
b. Perform due diligence and ensure the accuracy of the positions taken on the return and claim for refund.
c. Choose the positions that best help the taxpayer while still complying with IRS guidelines.
d. All the options.

Due Diligence and Penalties

DDPP3.3
Which of the following due diligence should a tax preparer carry out?

1. Prepare and file accurate tax returns.
2. Rely on work of another individual.
3. Ask additional questions.
4. Understand tax positions.

a. 1 and 2
b. 1, 2, and 4
c. 2, 3, and 4
d. 1, 2, and 3

Part 3 Review Questions Answers

DDPP3.1
Fernando prepared Andres and Alberto's partnership return. Alberto sued Andres for misrepresentation of income for their partnership. Which of the partners can Fernando represent before the IRS?

a. Fernando can represent them both since he knows the truth about both.
b. Fernando cannot represent either one since it will be a conflict of interest.
c. Fernando can represent either one if both have given him consent to do so.
d. Fernando must keep the consent form when a disagreement is in place.

Feedback: Please reread *Conflict of Interest*.

DDPP3.2
Tax return positions are the strategies chosen when preparing a tax return. To perform their task, what must a paid tax preparer do?

a. Guide taxpayers in figuring out the proper positions for their return.
b. Perform due diligence and ensure the accuracy of the positions taken on the return and claim for refund.
c. Choose the positions that best help the taxpayer while still complying with IRS guidelines.
d. All the options.

Feedback: Please reread *Tax Return Positions*.

DDPP3.3
Which of the following due diligence should a tax preparer carry out?

1. Prepare and file accurate tax returns.
2. Rely on the work of another individual.
3. Ask additional questions.
4. Understand tax positions.

a. 1 and 2
b. 1, 2, and 4
c. 2, 3, and 4
d. 1, 2, and 3

Feedback: Please reread *Who Prepared the Return?*

Part 4 Penalties

If an individual owes taxes, the IRS will calculate penalties and interest on the amount owed. Penalties are calculated on the amount due. Penalties are treated as additions to taxes and are not deductible for federal income tax purposes.

Penalties and Interest Charges

In preparing the tax return with an understatement of tax liability, the tax preparer could be taking a frivolous position or one for which there is no realistic possibility of being sustained on its merits. In this case, the penalty would be the greater of $1,000 or 50% of the income derived by the tax return preparer with respect to the tax return. The tax preparer may face a penalty of $5,000 or 50% of the income derived by the tax return if the attempt to understate the tax liability is intentional (IRC, §6695(a)).

Preparer penalties that are enforced by the IRS are found in Revenue Code §6694, and in §6695 *"Understatement of taxpayer's liability by tax return preparer and,"*, "Other assessable penalties with respect to the preparation of tax returns for other persons." Several preparer penalties fall outside of §6694 and §6695.

If an individual owes taxes, the IRS will calculate penalties and interest on the amount owed. Penalties are calculated on the amount due. There are several separate types of penalties:

- Failure-to-file.
- Failure-to-pay.
- Failure to pay proper estimated tax.
- Dishonored check.

The interest accrues until the tax owed is paid in full. A late-payment penalty may be charged as well, but if the taxpayer shows a reasonable cause for not paying on time, he or she may be able to abate these penalties. The taxpayer must still make a good effort to properly estimate and pay the tax due on the due date.

The tax law imposes penalties to ensure that all taxpayers pay their taxes. Some of the penalties are discussed in this chapter. If taxpayers underpay their tax due to fraud, they may be subject to a civil fraud penalty. In some cases, the taxpayer may be subject to criminal prosecution.

Penalties are treated as additions to taxes and are not deductible for federal income tax purposes. Taxpayers can receive penalties based on their filed tax return or for not filing a return. Tax professionals can also receive penalties based on how they prepare their clients' returns. Taxpayers can pay penalties based on how the return was prepared. Due diligence is the responsibility of both the taxpayer and the tax professional. This section will discuss the penalties and interest a taxpayer could accrue for not filing a tax return, filing incorrect information on the individual tax return, and filing inflationary adjustments. Penalties and interest stop accruing when the taxpayer has paid his or her balance in full.

Failure-to-File Penalty

The penalty for failing to file a return by the due is 5% of the amount of tax due if the failure is for not more than one month, with an additional 5% for each additional month or fraction thereof, but not exceeding 25% in total of the tax. The failure-to-pay penalty reduces it for any month in which both penalties apply. However, if the return is more than 60 days late, the penalty will not be less than $435 or 100% of the tax balance, whichever is less. The taxpayer will not have to pay the penalty if they show reasonable cause for not filing on time.

If the taxpayer files an extension, the tax is still due on the filing date, normally April 15th. A tax professional needs to understand and tell their clients that they owe the tax and that penalties and interest will accrue on the unpaid tax. A taxpayer can apply for an installment agreement. See 26 U.S. Code Section 6651 and 26 Code of Federal Regulations section 301.665-1.

Failure-to-Pay Penalty

The IRS will calculate the Failure-to-Pay based on how late the tax return is from the due date and how much unpaid tax is due. This penalty cannot be more than 25% of the unpaid tax. The taxpayer will not have to pay the fine if they show a good reason for not paying the tax on time. Add the failure-to-pay penalty to interest charges on late payments. The monthly or partial month rate is half the usual rate—25% instead of 50%—if an installment agreement is in effect for the month.

When the IRS issues an intent to levy, the tax rate increases to 1% if the taxpayer does not pay the amount in 10 days of the notice. When the IRS issues a notice and demands immediate payment, the rate will increase to 1% at the start of the first month, beginning after the notice and demand are issued. See 26 U.S. Code Section 6651 and 26 Code of Federal Regulations section 301.665-1.

Combined Penalties

If both the failure-to-file penalty and the failure-to-pay penalty apply in any month, the 5% (or 15%) failure-to-file penalty is reduced by the failure-to-pay penalty. However, if the taxpayer filed the return more than 60 days after the due date or extended due date, the minimum penalty is the smaller of $135 or 100% of the unpaid tax.

Failure to Pay Estimated Tax

If the taxpayer has not paid in full the amount due on the tax return within 21 days of the notice and demand, or if the amount owed is equal to or more than $100,000, the taxpayer has 10 days to pay.

The taxpayer may owe a penalty if the total of their withholding and his or her timely filed estimated payments, sometimes called quarterlies, did not equal the smaller of:

1. 90% of the tax owed on his or her 2021 tax return.
2. 100% of the taxpayer 2020 tax. The tax return covers a 12-month period.

The penalty is figured on Form 2210 or Form 2210-F for farmers or fishermen. There are exceptions to this rule; see Instructions Form 2210 and Publication 505.

Dishonored Check

If the taxpayer writes a check to pay for the amount due and the check bounces (dishonored), the IRS may impose a penalty. The penalty is whichever is less: 2% of the amount of the check or $25 if the check is less than $1,250. See *IRC §6695(f)*.

Paying or Receiving Interest

If taxpayers have a balance due on their current year tax return or owe taxes to the IRS for prior years and fail to pay the amount due by the due date, he or she will owe interest on the unpaid balance. Taxpayers cannot deduct the interest paid to the IRS on their return. They may receive interest on a delayed refund or an amended return. If the taxpayer receives interest from the IRS, the taxpayer is required to report it as interest income on his or her current year tax return, like any other interest income.

Information Reporting Penalties

If an individual files information returns and does not file them timely, they could receive penalties. An information return is used more in business, such as filing W-2s.

Any person who does not file a complete and correct information return with the IRS by the due date is subject to a penalty for each failure. Maximum limits apply to all these penalties. The $270 is subject to an annual inflation adjustment. See *IRC §6695(e)*.

Filing Late

Taxpayers who do not file their returns by the due date (including extensions) may have to pay a failure-to-file penalty. The penalty is based on the tax not paid by the due date (without regard to extensions). The penalty is usually 5% for each month or part of a month that a return is late, but not more than 25%.

Late-Filed Return with a Refund

If the taxpayer was due a refund but did not file a return, the taxpayer generally must file within three years from the date the return was originally due to get that refund. If the taxpayer files the return late, more than 60 days after the due date or extended due date, the minimum penalty is the smaller of $135 or 100% of the unpaid tax.

Exception

The taxpayer will not have to pay the penalty if the taxpayer can show that he or she failed to file on time because of reasonable cause and not because of willful neglect.

Reduced Refund

The taxpayer's refund may be reduced by an additional tax liability that has been assessed against him/her. A refund may also be reduced by amounts owed for past-due child support, debts to another federal agency, delinquent student loans, or state tax.

Due Diligence and Penalties

Penalty for Failure to Disclose Foreign Income

Penalties for failure to disclose a foreign bank account report (FBAR) can be criminal or civil. Criminal penalties could include:

1. Willful failure to file an FBAR up to $250,000 or 5 years in jail or both.
2. Willful failure to file an FBAR while violating another law of the United States involving more than $100,000 in any 12 months. Up to $500,000 or 10 years in jail or both.

In addition to the penalty for failure to file Form 8938, the IRS assesses a new penalty under IRC §6662 for failure to report the income attributable to an undisclosed foreign financial asset. The maximum additional penalty for not filing Form 8938 is $50,000. For more information, see Instructions Form 8938.

First-Time Abate Policy

The IRS has a policy for penalty relief called First Time Abate (FTA). The FTA penalty relief option for failure-to-file, and failure-to-pay penalties, under certain conditions, does not apply if the taxpayer has not filed all returns and paid or arranged to pay all tax currently due. The taxpayer is considered current with an open installment agreement and if the current installment payments are up to date.

Penalties are imposed on taxpayers who file late and who fail to timely pay the tax in full. The late penalty is 5% of the unpaid taxes for each month or part of a month that the return is late, up to 25%. To reward past tax compliance and promote future tax compliance, the IRS waives these penalties for taxpayers who have demonstrated full compliance over the prior three years.

Failure to Supply Social Security Number

If the taxpayer does not include a Social Security number (SSN) or the SSN of another person where required on a return, statement, or other document, the taxpayer will be subject to a penalty of $50 for each failure. The taxpayer may also be subject to the penalty of $50 if he or she does not give his or her SSN to another person when it is required on a return, statement, or other document. The taxpayer will not have to pay the penalty if he or she is able to show that the failure was due to reasonable cause and not willful neglect.

Example: Lauren has a bank account that earns interest. Lauren must give her SSN to the bank. The number must be shown on Form 1099-INT or other statement the bank sends Lauren. If Lauren does not give the bank her SSN, she will be subject to the $50 penalty. Lauren could also be subject to "backup" withholding of income tax.

Failure to Furnish Correct Payee Statements

Any person who does not provide an individual with a complete and correct copy of an information return (payee statement) by the due date is subject to a penalty of $50 for each statement if filed within 30 days of the due date. If the failure is due to intentional disregard of the requirement, the penalty is $570 per information. There are civil and criminal penalties for giving false information to avoid backup withholding.

Interest Charges

April 15 is the deadline for most people to file and pay any amount due on their individual returns. Interest is generally charged on any unpaid tax from the due date until the amount is paid in full. The interest rate is determined quarterly and is the federal short-term rate plus 4% and compounded daily. If the taxpayer does not make the payment due, the IRS will charge a late-payment penalty. The taxpayer may have to pay the penalty for understating income, understating a reportable transaction, or filing an erroneous claim for a refund or credit. There are two kinds of penalties regarding understating a reportable transaction: civil and criminal.

A taxpayer who does not file a return and pay the tax by the due date may have to pay a civil penalty. The taxpayer may also have to pay the penalty if the individual substantially understates the tax, files a frivolous return, or fails to supply a Social Security number. If the taxpayer provides fraudulent information on the tax return, the individual may pay a civil fraud penalty.

Criminal penalties may be subject to criminal prosecution for actions such as the following:

- Tax evasion.
- Willful failure to file a return, supply information, or pay any tax due.
- Fraud and false statements.
- Preparing and filing a fraudulent return.

If the return is over 60 days late, there's also a minimum penalty for late filing: it's the lesser of $435 or 100% of the tax owed. See code section 7201.

Tax Evasion

Tax evasion is illegally avoiding paying taxes, failing to report, or reporting inaccurately. The government imposes strict and serious penalties for tax evasion. The following are some of the common inconsistencies that the IRS looks for to substantiate tax evasion:

- Understatement of income.
- Claiming fictitious or improper deductions.
- Accounting irregularities.
- Allocation of income.
- Acts and conduct of the taxpayer.

Fraud

If the taxpayer's failure to file is due to fraud, the penalty is 15% for each month or part of a month that the return is late, up to a maximum of 75%.

Tax Avoidance

Tax avoidance uses legal methods to modify the taxpayer's financial situation to lower the income tax owed. You accomplish this action by claiming the permissible deductions and credits. The saving of tax dollars requires specific actions to avoid the tax liability before it occurred according to the law.

Tax avoidance is different from tax evasion. What distinguishes tax avoidance from tax evasion is the intent of the taxpayer. The intent to evade tax occurs when a taxpayer knowingly misrepresents the facts. The intent is a state of mind. A taxpayer's intent is judged by others, and others judge a taxpayer's intent.

Accuracy-Related Penalty

The taxpayer may have to pay an accuracy-related penalty of 20% of the underpayment if:

- ➤ The taxpayer shows negligence or disregard of the rules or regulations.
- ➤ The taxpayer substantially understates their income tax.
- ➤ The taxpayer claims tax benefits for a transaction that lacks economic substance.
- ➤ The taxpayer fails to disclose a foreign financial asset.

Negligence or Disregard

The term "Negligence" is a failure to make a reasonable attempt to comply with the tax law or to exercise ordinary and reasonable care in preparing a return. Negligence also includes a failure to keep adequate books and records. The taxpayer will not have to pay a negligence penalty if they have a reasonable basis for the position taken. "Disregard" includes any careless, reckless, or intentional disregard of rules or regulations. Negligence or ignorance of the law does not constitute fraud.

Civil, Criminal, and Fraud Penalties

If the taxpayer does not file the tax return and pay the tax by the due date, he or she may have to pay a penalty. The law provides penalties for failure to file returns or pay taxes as required.

If any part of an underpayment is due to fraud, the penalty imposed is 75% of the underpayment (the "civil fraud" penalty). When the IRS establishes that you use fraud to claim any portion of an underpayment, the entire underpayment is assumed to be attributable to fraud unless the taxpayer proves otherwise. The 20% accuracy-related penalty does not apply to any portion of an underpayment on which the IRS imposes the fraud penalty. However, they may apply the accuracy-related penalty to any portion of the underpayment not attributable to fraud.

If IRS examiners find strong evidence of fraud, they will refer the case to the Criminal Investigation Division (CID) for prosecution. They can impose both civil sanctions and criminal prosecution.

Joint Return

The fraud penalty on a joint return does not apply to a spouse unless some part of the underpayment is due to the spouse's fraud. The spouse may want to file a separate return.

In addition to the civil fraud penalty. Section 7201 provides that "any person who willfully attempts in any manner to evade or defeat any tax imposed by this title or the payment thereof shall, in addition to other penalties provided by law, be guilty of a felony." The attempt to evade or defeat tax must be willful for criminal fraud. An individual's behavior could not be willful if their actions are through carelessness or genuine misunderstanding of what the law requires. In addition to criminal penalties, any person can be guilty of a felony and upon conviction thereof, shall be fined not more than $100,000 or imprisoned not more than 5 years, or both, and the individual will pay for the cost of prosecution.

Criminal Penalties

The taxpayer may be brought to trial for criminal prosecution for the following actions:

- Tax evasion.
- Willful failure to file a return, supply information, or pay any tax due.
- Fraud and false statements.
- Preparing and filing a fraudulent return.
- Identity theft.

A taxpayer convicted of criminal fraud is subject to a fine of up to $100,000 or imprisonment of up to 5 years, or both, together with the cost of the prosecution. For more information, see code section 7201.

Adequate Disclosure

The taxpayer can avoid the penalty for disregarding rules or regulations if the taxpayer adequately disclosed a position that has at least a reasonable basis on the return. The exception will not apply if the taxpayer did not keep adequate books or the item relates to a tax shelter.

Substantial Understatement of Income Tax

The taxpayer understates the tax if the tax shown on the tax return is less than the correct tax. The understatement is substantial if it is more than the larger of 10% of the correct tax or $5,000.

However, reduce the amount of understatement to the extent the understatement is due to:

- Substantial authority.
- Adequate disclosure and a reasonable basis.

Substantial Authority

Whether there is or was substantial authority for the tax treatment of an item depends on the facts and circumstances—consider the court opinions, Treasury regulations, revenue rulings, revenue procedures, and notices. Announcements issued by the IRS and published in the Internal Revenue Bulletin that involve the same or similar circumstances as the taxpayer will also be considered.

Disclosure Statement

The understatement may also be reduced if the taxpayer can adequately disclose the relevant facts about their tax treatment of an item. To make this disclosure, use Form 8275, *Disclosure Statement*. The taxpayer must have a reasonable basis for treating the item that way.

In cases of substantial understatement only, items that meet the requirements of Revenue Procedure 96-58 (or a later update) are considered adequately disclosed on the return without filing Form 8275. Form 8275-R, *Regulation Disclosure Statement*, is used to disclose items or positions contrary to regulations.

Due Diligence and Penalties

Reasonable Cause

The taxpayer will not have to pay the penalty if they show reasonable cause for how they treated the item. The taxpayer must also show that the act was in good faith and that the item does not apply to a transaction lacking economic substance.

Filing Erroneous Claim for Refund or Credit

The taxpayer might have to pay the penalty if they filed for an erroneous claim for refund or credit in their tax return. The penalty is 20% of the excess amount of the claim unless the taxpayer can show a rational basis for the claim. See code section 6676.

Frivolous Tax Return Penalty

The taxpayer may have to pay a penalty of $5,000 for filing a "frivolous return." A frivolous return does not include enough information to figure out the correct tax or contains information clearly showing that the tax reported is substantially incorrect.

The taxpayer would have to pay the penalty if they filed this kind of return due to a desire to delay or interfere with the administration of federal income tax laws. This action includes altering or striking out the preprinted language above the space provided for the taxpayer's signature. This penalty is added to any other penalty that is provided by law.

Failure to Furnish Tax Return Copy to Taxpayer

The penalty for the paid tax preparer is $50 for each failure to comply with IRC §6107 regarding furnishing a copy of a return or claim to a taxpayer. The maximum penalty imposed on any tax return preparer shall not exceed $27,000 (tax year 2021) in a calendar year (see IRC, §6695(a)).

Failure to Sign Return

The penalty for each failure to sign a return or claim for refund as required by regulations is $50 for the paid tax preparer. The maximum penalty imposed on any tax return preparer shall not exceed $27,000 (tax year 2021) in a calendar year.

A tax return is not considered to be valid unless the return has been signed. If the filing status is MFJ, both the taxpayer and spouse must sign the return. If the taxpayer and spouse have a representative sign the return for them, Form 2848 must be attached. If the taxpayer is filing a joint return, and he/she is the surviving spouse, the taxpayer must sign the return stating he/she is filing as the surviving spouse. The taxpayer and spouse (if filing jointly) must make sure to date the return and enter their occupation(s) and a daytime phone number. See Publication 501 and *IRC §6695(b)*.

If the taxpayer received an identity protection PIN, he/she would enter it in the boxes. The tax professional does not enter it for the taxpayer. If the taxpayer has misplaced his/her IP PIN, the taxpayer should notify the IRS by telephone at 1-800-908-4490. The IP PIN is a 6-digit number.

When filing the return electronically, the return must still be signed using a personal identification number (PIN)—this is not the same number as the identity protection PIN. There are two ways to enter the PIN: self-select or practitioner PIN. The self-select PIN method allows the taxpayer and spouse (if filing jointly) to create their own PIN and enter it as their electronic signature. The practitioner PIN method allows the taxpayer to authorize the tax practitioner to generate or enter the PIN for the taxpayer(s). A PIN is a five-digit combination that can be any number except all zeros.

Señor 1040 Says: There is a difference between the electronically-filed PIN and the IP PIN. Do not mix up these numbers.

Preparers Failure to Furnish Identifying Number

The penalty for each failure to comply with IRC §6109(a)(4) regarding furnishing an identifying number on a return or claim is $50. The maximum penalty imposed on any tax return preparer shall not exceed $27,000 (tax year 2021) in a calendar year. See *IRC §6695(c)*.

Preparer's Failure to Retain a Copy or List of Tax Return

The penalty is $50 for each failure to comply with IRC §6107(b) regarding retaining a copy or list of a return or claim. The maximum penalty imposed on any tax return preparer shall not exceed $25,000 in a return period. See *IRC §6695(d)*.

Preparer's Fraud and False Statements

Guilty of a felony and, upon conviction, a fine of not more than $100,000 ($500,000 in the case of a corporation), imprisonment of not more than three years, or both (together with the costs of prosecution) (IRC, §7206).

Preparer's Fraudulent Returns, Statements, or Other Documents

Guilty of a misdemeanor and, upon conviction, a fine of not more than $10,000 ($50,000 in the case of a corporation), imprisonment of not more than one year, or both (IRC, §7207).

Preparer's Disclosure or Use of Information of Client's Tax Return

Guilty of a misdemeanor for knowingly or recklessly disclosing information furnished about a tax return or using such information for any purpose other than preparing or assisting in the preparation of such return. Upon conviction, the tax preparer will receive a fine of not more than $1,000, imprisonment for not more than one year, or both (together with the costs of prosecution) (IRC §7216).

Preparers Filing Information Returns Incorrectly

If the tax professional is negligent or intentionally files incorrect information returns, the penalty is $50 per return or item on the return, with a maximum penalty of $27,000 (tax year 2021).

Due Diligence and Penalties

Preparer's Incompetence and Disreputable Conduct

The following is a summary of what is incompetence and disreputable conduct for which a practitioner may be sanctioned. The following was extracted from Circular 230 §10.51.

1. Conviction of any criminal offense under federal tax laws.
2. Conviction of any criminal offense involving dishonesty or breach of trust.
3. Conviction of any felony under federal or state law for which the conduct involved renders the practitioner unfit to practice before the IRS.
4. Giving false or misleading information or participating in any way in the giving of false or misleading information to the Department of the Treasury or any officer or employee.
5. Solicitation of employment as prohibited under section §10.30, the use of false or misleading representations with intent to deceive a client or prospective client to gain employment or insinuate that the practitioner can obtain special consideration with the IRS, or any officer or employee.
6. Willfully failing to make a federal tax return in violation of the federal tax laws or willfully evading or attempting to evade any assessment or payment of any federal tax.
7. Willfully assisting, counseling, encouraging a client or prospective client to violate any federal tax law, or knowingly counseling or suggesting to a client an illegal plan to evade paying federal tax.
8. Misappropriation of, or failure to remit properly or promptly, funds received from a client for the payment of taxes or other obligations due the United States.
9. Directly or indirectly attempting to influence or offer or agree to attempt to influence the official action of any officer or employee of the IRS using threats, false accusations, duress, or coercion, or any special inducement or promise of an advantage or by bestowing of any gift, favor, or item of value.
10. Disbarment or suspension from practice as an attorney, certified public accountant, public accountant, or actuary by any duly constituted authority of any state, territory, or possession of the United States, including a commonwealth or the District of Columbia, any federal court of record, or any federal agency, body, or board.
11. Knowingly aiding and abetting another person to practice before the IRS during a suspension, disbarment, or ineligibility of such other individual.
12. Contemptuous conduct in connection with practice before the IRS, including the use of abusive language, making false accusations or statements, knowing them to be false, or circulating or publishing malicious or libelous matter.
13. Giving a false opinion, knowingly recklessly or through gross incompetence including an opinion that is intentionally or recklessly misleading or engaging in a pattern of providing incompetent opinions on questions arising from federal tax laws.
14. Willfully failing to sign a tax return prepared by the practitioner when the practitioner's signature is required by federal tax laws unless the failure is due to reasonable cause and not due to neglect.
15. Willfully disclosing or otherwise using a tax return or tax return information in a manner not authorized by the IRC, contrary to the order of a court of competent jurisdiction or contrary to the order of an administrative law judge in a proceeding instituted under §10.60.
16. Willfully failing to file on magnetic or other electronic media a tax return prepared by the practitioner when the practitioner is required to do so by federal tax laws unless the failure is due to reasonable cause and not due to neglect.

17. Willfully preparing all or substantially all, or signing, a tax return or claim for refund when the practitioner does not possess a current or otherwise valid PTIN or other prescribed identifying number.
18. Willfully representing a taxpayer before an officer or employee of the IRS unless the practitioner is authorized to do so.

Preparer's Understatement Due to Willful or Reckless Conduct

The penalty is the greater of $5,000 or 50% of the income derived by the tax return preparer with respect to the return or claim for refund. See *IRC §6694(b)*.

IRC §7407—Action to enjoin tax return preparers

A federal district court may enjoin a tax return preparer from engaging in certain proscribed conduct, or in extreme cases, from continuing to act as a tax return preparer altogether.

IRC §7408—Action to enjoin a specified conduct related to tax shelters and reportable transactions

A federal district court may enjoin a person from engaging in certain proscribed conduct (including any action, or failure to take action that is in violation of Circular 230).

Part 4 Review Questions

To obtain the maximum benefit from this chapter, LTP recommends that you complete each of the following questions, and then compare them to the answers with feedback that immediately follow. Under governing self-study standards, vendors are required to present review questions intermittently throughout each self-study course.

These questions and explanations are not part of the final examination and will not be graded by LTP.

DDPP4.1
Christina prepared Frank's tax return and failed to give him a copy of his return. Upon the discovery, she also realized that she did not provide copies to any of her clients during the 2021 tax season. Christina prepared 610 tax returns for the year. What could be her maximum penalty amount?

a. $27,000
b. $30,500
c. $50 per return
d. $2,500

Due Diligence and Penalties

DDPP4.2
Maribel prepared a tax return for Sergio. The IRS returned the tax return to Maribel because she did not sign the return. Maribel failed to sign 50 tax returns. What is the maximum amount of penalty that can be imposed upon a tax preparer for not signing their returns?

a. $27,000
b. $2,500
c. $50 per return
d. $2,750

DDPP4.3
Fernando was afraid of PTIN fraud, so he intentionally left off his PTIN on all tax returns he prepared. What could be his minimum penalty for not furnishing his identifying number?

a. $27,500 per year
b. No penalty
c. $50 per return
d. $2,500

DDPP4.4
Which of the following is not an individual penalty?

a. Failure-to-file
b. Dishonored check
c. First Time Abate
d. Failure-to-pay

DDPP4.5
Which of the following penalties could a tax preparer receive for not completing the due diligence requirements?

a. $545 penalty per refundable credit for each failure to comply.
b. $1,500 penalty for unreasonable position.
c. $5,900 penalty for recklessness or intentional disregard of rules or regulations.
d. $27,000 maximum penalty per tax period.

Part 4 Review Questions Answers

DDPP4.1
Christina prepared Frank's tax return and failed to give him a copy of his return. Upon the discovery, she also realized that she did not provide copies to any of her clients during the 2021 tax season. Christina prepared 610 tax returns for the year. What could be her maximum penalty amount?

a. $27,000
b. $30,500
c. $50 per return
d. $2,500

Feedback: Review section *Failure to Furnish Tax Return Copy to Taxpayer*.

DDPP4.2
Maribel prepared a tax return for Sergio. The IRS returned the tax return to Maribel because she did not sign the return. Maribel failed to sign 50 tax returns. What is the maximum amount of penalty that can be imposed upon a tax preparer for not signing their returns?

   a. **$27,000**
   b. $2,500
   c. $50 per return
   d. $2,750

Feedback: Review section *Failure to Sign Return.*

DDPP4.3
Fernando was afraid of PTIN fraud, so he intentionally left off his PTIN on all tax returns he prepared. What could be his minimum penalty for not furnishing his identifying number?

   a. $27,000 per year
   b. No penalty
   c. **$50 per return**
   d. $2,500

Feedback: Review section *Failure to Furnish Identifying Number.*

DDPP4.4
Which of the following is not an individual penalty?

   a. Failure-to-file
   b. Dishonored check
   c. **First Time Abate**
   d. Failure-to-pay

Feedback: Review section *Penalties.*

DDPP4.5
Which of the following penalties could a tax preparer receive for not completing the due diligence requirements?

   a. **$545 penalty per refundable credit for each failure to comply.**
   b. $1,500 penalty for unreasonable position.
   c. $5,900 penalty for recklessness or intentional disregard of rules or regulations.
   d. $27,000 maximum penalty per tax period.

Feedback: Review Section *Penalties.*

Takeaways

Tax preparers must understand the ethical guidelines and practices established by the Internal Revenue Service provided in Circular 230. The Office of Professional Responsibility oversees the ethical guidelines and practices, and it also regulates practitioners' conduct and discipline. OPR also oversees the correct level of discipline to practitioners or imposes administrative proceeding to censure, suspend, or disbar practitioner from practicing before the IRS.

Tax preparers must recognize their rights, responsibilities, and representation limitations. We at LTP believe that everything a tax practitioner does—every choice one makes as a tax professional—affects not only themselves, but coworkers, the firm, and ultimately the taxpayer. We also believe that a paid tax preparer's first responsibility is to their client when making decisions and/or judgments about tax preparation.

TEST YOUR KNOWLEDGE!
Go online to take a practice quiz.

Chapter 2 Compiling Taxpayer Information

Introduction

This chapter explains the importance of interviewing the taxpayer. Each segment of the chapter will cover a section of Form 1040 with sample interview questions that are needed for the section discussed. The tax professional must understand the importance of knowledgeable questions to determine if the taxpayer is eligible to claim certain credits. Interview questions should be documented along with the answers the taxpayer provided. Knowing basic tax law is essential.

Preparing tax returns is an art; knowing which questions to ask will help determine the best tax situation for the individual. Just imputing information into software does not prepare an accurate tax return. The saying is true: "garbage in, garbage out". Entering incorrect information so that the taxpayer receives a higher refund is not the best situation for you or the client. This chapter provides you with a brief overview of current year forms and sample questions to determine the best accurate tax position for the taxpayer. Asking the taxpayer the right questions from the beginning provides the tax preparer truthful answers needed to complete the tax return.

Objectives

By the end of this chapter, the student will:

- ➢ Identify the various parts of Form 1040.
- ➢ Recognize items from each section.
- ➢ Understand the importance of asking questions to determine the best tax situation for the client.
- ➢ Memorize questions for each section to create an individual interviewing style.

Resources

Form 1040	Publication 17	Instructions Form 1040
Schedule 1	Tax Topic 301, 303, 352	Eight Facts about Filing Status
Schedule 2		
Schedule 3		

Table of Contents

Introduction	53
Part 1 Form 1040	56
The following sections are found on the 2021 Form 1040:	56
Filing Status	56
General Information: Name, Address, and Taxpayer Identification Number	57
Standard Deduction	59
Dependents	59
Income Form 1040, Lines 1 – 15	60
Income Recordkeeping	61
Form 1040, page 2, lines 16 - 33	62
Refund	62
Amount Owed	63
Third Party Designee	63
Signing Form 1040	64
Paid Preparer Use Only	65
Form 1040-SR, for seniors.	65
Part 1 Review Questions	67
Part 1 Review Questions Answers	68
Part 2 Schedule 1, 2, & 3	69
Adjustments and Deductions	69
Form 1040, Schedule 1, Part I	70
Form 1040, Schedule 1, Part II	70
Schedule 2 Additional Taxes	71
Schedule 2 Part II – Other Taxes	72
Schedule 3 Additional Credits and Payments	73
Part I Nonrefundable Credits	73
Schedule 3 Part II: Other Payments and Refundable Credits	74
Interview Pointers	74
Part 2 Review Questions	75
Part 2 Review Questions Answers	76
Part 3 Filing the Federal Tax Return	77
The Filing Process	77
How to Assemble a Federal Tax Return	77
Where to File a Paper Return	78
When to File a Return	78
Filing Deadlines	78
How to File a Return	79
Where to File a Return	79
Part 3 Review Questions	79
Part 3 Review Questions Answers	80
Part 4 What is an ITIN?	81
Who needs an ITIN?	82
Reason to Apply for an ITIN	82
Common Errors on Form W-7	84
Applying for an ITIN	85
Individual Applicants	86
Document Standards for Dependent Children	86
Documentation Needed	87
ITIN Tax Related Exceptions	88
Student and Exchange Visitor Program	88
Aliens	90

Compiling Taxpayer Information

- Resident Alien 90
- Nonresident alien 90
- Dual-status Alien 90
- Tax Return Compliance 90
- Expiration of ITINs 90
- Part 4 Review Questions 91
- Part 4 Review Questions Answers 92
- Takeaways 93

Compiling Taxpayer Information

Part 1 Form 1040

The Tax Cuts and Jobs Act changed Form 1040 and the forms changed again in 2020. Six (6) schedules were used for the 2018 tax year filing, and for 2021 tax year filing, there are 3 schedules.

The following sections are found on the 2021 Form 1040:

- Filing Status
- General Information such as:
    - Name
    - Address
    - Taxpayer Identification Number
- Standard Deduction Dependents
- Income
- Refund
- Amount You Owe
- Third Party Designee
- Sign Here
- Paid Preparer Use Only

Filing Status

There are five filing status options for the federal return:

- Single (S)
- Married filing jointly (MFJ)
- Married filing separately (MFS)
- Head of household (HOH)
- Qualifying widow(er) (QW) also referred to as surviving spouse (SS)

Filing status is determined on the last day of the tax year. A detailed explanation of filing status will be discussed in a later chapter.

Interview Pointers

Below are sample questions to determine a taxpayer's correct filing status:

- Are you single?
- Are you legally married?
- Do you have children?
- Did the children live with you the entire year? If not, how long did the children live with you?
- How many months did the children live with you?
- What documentation do you have to prove the children lived with you?
- Does anyone else live in your house?
- Do you live with another taxpayer?

It is necessary that the tax professional determines the correct filing status by asking pertinent questions such as above.

General Information: Name, Address, and Taxpayer Identification Number

Gathering information from the taxpayer is vital to prepare an accurate tax return. Information collected verifies the taxpayer's identity and the taxpayer's spouse if filing jointly. The taxpayer will be glad you asked relevant questions to complete his or her tax return correctly. Following a straightforward interview process to gather taxpayer's information makes preparing the tax return easier and prevents misunderstanding between you and your client.

The following personal information is needed from the client:

- A current government-issued form of photo identification for the taxpayer and his or her spouse, if filing jointly.
- The taxpayer or spouse's SSN, ITIN, ATIN, or TIN.
- The following information for each dependent, if applicable:
    - SSN, ITIN, ATIN, or TIN.
    - Date of birth.
    - Current address.
    - Income.
- The taxpayer's current address.
- The amount of total income earned for the year.

If the taxpayer is filing Married Filing Jointly, gather the information listed below from both the taxpayer and spouse to complete the return. Make sure to ask the following information:

- Name of taxpayer and spouse as it appears on the government-issued identification.
- Social Security numbers or taxpayer identification numbers for all individuals listed on the tax return.
- Date of birth (DOB) for everyone on the tax return.
- Date of death (DOD), if the taxpayer or spouse died during the tax year.
- Current Address (you can use a PO Box). If the client uses a bank product, a physical address could be required. The address could be in a foreign country, but not for a bank product.

Compiling Taxpayer Information

Señor 1040 Says: Remember, always ask for an official document to verify a client's DOB or DOD.

The names of the taxpayer and spouse (if applicable) must match the names on their Social Security cards, Adoption Tax Identification Numbers (ATIN), or Individual Tax Identification Numbers (ITIN). If the couple has recently married and has not filed the name change with the Social Security Administration, the current name on the Social Security card must be used. If not, the return could be rejected when filing electronically. Taxpayers who do not have a Social Security Number (SSN) should apply for an SSN or an ITIN. When filing a federal return, the Social Security Administration records are used to match all names, Social Security numbers, and dates of birth, for everyone on the tax return.

The exception to this is when a taxpayer is filing his or her tax return with an ITIN; in these cases, the SSN on the W-2 most likely will not match.

When information is gathered, the tax preparer should make sure all W-2 forms match the taxpayer and spouse's Social Security numbers displayed on their Social Security cards. If not, the taxpayer must have the employer correct the tax document(s). Tax professionals need to ensure documents are accurate before filing the return.

Interview Pointers

Here are questions to ask regarding the taxpayers' personal information, which will help in determining changes from the prior year return and the current year filing status.

- Did you bring your Social Security card(s)?
- Did any personal changes occur (divorce, marriage, new dependents, deaths, etc.)?
- Did your name change?
- Did you get married?
- Did you get divorced?
- Was there a death in the family? (Tax return related.)
- Did you have a job change?
- Did you have any births during the year? (Tax return related.)
- Do you want to contribute $3 to the Presidential Election Campaign Fund?

Presidential Election Campaign
Check here if you, or your spouse if filing jointly, want $3 to go to this fund. Checking a box below will not change your tax or refund.
☐ You   ☐ Spouse

The Presidential Election Campaign Fund is intended to reduce a candidate's dependence on large contributions from individuals and groups. This aims to place candidates on an equal financial footing for the general election. The fund also helps pay for pediatric medical research. If the taxpayer wants $3 to go to the fund, check the box. If the taxpayer is filing a joint return, both taxpayers can have $3 each go to the fund. Checking the box does not affect the refund amount or the amount owed.

Standard Deduction

Standard deduction is based on the taxpayer's filing status. Itemized deduction is generally used when the taxpayer's deduction exceeds their standard deduction. Subtracting applicable deductions from the taxpayer's total income becomes the taxpayer's adjusted gross income.

The standard deduction amount depends on the taxpayer's filing status. Other factors that determine the amount of the allowable standard deduction are as follows:

- Is the taxpayer considered age 65 or older?
- Is the taxpayer blind?
- Is the taxpayer claimed as a dependent on another individual's tax return?

Blind taxpayers and taxpayers over the age of 65 each have an additional exemption that can be marked when filing status is determined.

Deduction amounts apply to most people and are for the current year's filing status.*

Filing Status and Standard Deduction	Tax Year 2020	Tax Year 2021	Tax Year 2022
Single	$12,400	$12,550	$14,250
Married Filing Jointly and Qualifying Widow(er)	$24,800	$25,100	$26,450
Married Filing Separately	$12,550	$12,550	$13,900
Head of Household	$18,650	$18,800	$20,500

*Do not use this chart if:

- The taxpayer was born before January 2, 1957.
- The taxpayer is blind.
- Someone else can claim the taxpayer or taxpayer's spouse as a dependent if filing status is MFJ.

Dependents

Basic information to collect is:

- Dependent(s) name (as it appears on the SSN, ATIN, or ITIN).
- DOB of the dependent(s).
- Relationship.

Note: If you prepare the tax return by hand, there is no place to enter the DOB (just remember that the dependent's age is important to calculate certain credits).

Compiling Taxpayer Information

Only four lines are given for dependents. Mark the box and follow the instructions to add an additional sheet. When you prepare the tax return by hand, attach a statement with the required information for the dependents. When the return is prepared with software, the worksheet should be generated automatically. Make sure that the worksheet is attached to the tax return.

Interview Pointers

Here are questions to ask to determine if the taxpayer has qualifying dependents:

- Do you have any dependents?
- Did the dependents live with you?
- Did the dependents live with you the entire year?
- Do you have proof that the dependents live with you?
    - Lease agreement
    - School records
    - Medical records
- Do you have the dependents' SSN, ATIN, or ITIN documentation with you? If not, can you bring them in later so I can keep a copy for our records?
- What are the dependents' dates of birth?
- Can somebody else claim them as dependents?

Dependents will be studied in detail in a later chapter.

Income Form 1040, Lines 1 – 15

[Form 1040 (2021) excerpt showing lines 1–15 of the income section]

The tax information needed to complete this section includes all income for both the taxpayer and the spouse if Married Filing Jointly. Sources of income include:

- Form W-2 series
- Form 1099 series (G, DIV, INT, NEC, Misc., R, etc.)
- Social Security

Wage income is reported on Form 1040, line 1. Interest is reported on Form 1040, line 2a and 2b. Qualified dividends are reported on Form 1040, line 3a and 3b. IRAs, pensions, and annuities are reported on Form 1040, line 4a – 5b. Social Security benefits are reported on Form 1040, line 6.

Income Recordkeeping

Both taxpayer and tax professional must keep copies of all Form W-2s, 1099 series, and other income documents with the client's tax return. If parents elect to claim their children's investment income, those forms should be kept as well, with the parents' tax return.

Interest earned as a beneficiary of an estate or trust is generally taxable income. Taxpayers should receive a Schedule K-1 for their portion of the interest. A copy of the Schedule K-1 should be kept with the tax return as well.

If the taxpayer is a U.S. citizen or resident alien, he or she must report income from sources outside the United States unless the income is exempt from U.S. law. The need to report all sources of income applies to all amounts of both earned and unearned income. See Publication 54 for more information.

Interview Pointers

Here are questions to determine the type of income the taxpayer received and which tax form or schedule will be used to report the income:

- Did you receive a W-2 or W-2G?
- How many jobs did you have last year?
- Did you receive any income not reported on a W-2?
- Did you have any gambling or lottery winnings?
- Did you earn any interest or dividends?
    - Checking account
    - Savings account
- Have an investment broker?
    - Savings bonds, and CDs
- Did you receive Social Security benefits or railroad retirement benefits?
- Did you receive a pension on annuity?
- Did you take a distribution from an IRA?
    - Roth or Traditional?
- Did you receive alimony income or separate maintenance payments? (Reported on Schedule 1, line 2a)
- Did you receive disability income?
- Did you receive rental income? File the Schedule E, and net income is reported on Schedule 1, line 5.
- Do you own a business? (When a taxpayer has a business, you must perform an extensive and thorough interview to ensure the taxpayer reports all income including cash payments received for work or services performed as well as all expenses. As a preparer, you must make sure you have the necessary knowledge of Schedule C to prepare the tax return correctly. Do your due diligence!).
- Did you receive Form 1099-NEC or Form 1099-MISC?
- Did you receive Form 1099-K?
- Did you receive an education scholarship? (Reported on Schedule 1, line 8z)
- Did you receive a refund from state taxes last year? (Reported on Schedule 1, line 1)
- Did you receive income from other sources such as prizes, jury duty pay, Schedule K-1, royalties, foreign income, etc.? (Reported on Schedule 1, line 8)
- Did you receive unemployment or paid family leave? (Reported on Schedule 1, line 7)
- Did you receive any other form of income whatsoever? (Reported on Schedule 1, line 8z)

Compiling Taxpayer Information

More information on Schedule 1 will be found later in this chapter.

Form 1040, page 2, lines 16 - 33

This section reports information from other forms and schedules. Line 16 is the tax the individual will need to pay. This includes additional tax as well as the income tax. Line 33 reports the total payments made by the individual through withholding, estimated payments, or from credits.

Refund

On Form 1040, page 2, if the amount on line 33 is more than the amount on line 24, the taxpayer may receive a refund reported on line 34. If the taxpayer is receiving a refund and would like to have the refund deposited directly into a checking or savings account, enter the taxpayer's routing and account numbers on lines 35b and 35d. The account type (savings or checking) must be marked on line 35c.

Check Line 36 if the taxpayer wants the refund to be applied to their estimated payments for the following tax year.

A taxpayer must file Form 8888 if he or she would like to receive their refund by paper check or to have it deposited into up to three different accounts. Make sure to check the box at the end of line 35a to show that the form is attached. Not all software companies support this form; taxpayers wanting to file Form 8888 need to file a paper return via mail.

Interview Pointers

These questions determine how the taxpayer will receive their refund:

> ➢ Do you want the refund to be directly deposited into your checking or savings account?
> ➢ Do you want a paper check from the IRS?
>   o If so, is the address on your tax return current?
> ➢ Would you like to have your refund applied to next year's estimated payments? (Normally, you would ask this question to self-employed taxpayers who are receiving a refund; this could lower the estimated payments.)

Amount Owed

Form 1040, page 2, line 37: Amount a taxpayer owes.

Form 1040, page 2, line 38: The amount of penalty for not paying enough tax during the year.

This is reported using Form 2210, which should be attached to the return after completion.

Interview Pointers

These questions determine how the taxpayer will pay their balance due.

> ➢ Do you want to mail your balance due to the IRS?
> ➢ Do you want to pay your balance due on the EFTPS website?
> ➢ Do you want to pay your balance due with a credit card?

Third Party Designee

On Form 1040, page 2, the taxpayer would designate someone other than the preparer of the tax return.

Checking the Yes box allows a third-party to talk on behalf of the taxpayer to provide certain information to the IRS. The authorization will automatically end no later than the filing due date for the current-year tax return (without extensions). For example, if the paid preparer is filing the tax return for tax year 2021, and the return is due on April 15, 2022, the authorization automatically expires on April 15, 2023.

A PIN (personal identification number) must be entered. PINs are not given or provided by any agency but are instead created by the third-party designee. However, whatever PIN is created must be kept and documented; this is what the IRS will ask for to verify they are talking to the correct third-party designee.

Compiling Taxpayer Information

If the taxpayer chooses the tax preparer to be the designee, then box No would be checked. If the taxpayer wants another individual to be their designee, then Designee name and phone number and Personal identification number must be completed and box Yes must be checked.

The IRS may call the designee to answer any questions that arise during the processing of the return. The designee may perform the following actions:

- Give information that is missing from the return to the IRS.
- Call the IRS for information that is missing from the tax return.
- Upon request, can receive copies of notices or transcripts related to the return.
- Can respond to certain IRS notices about math errors and the preparation of the return.

When checking the box, authorization is limited to matters concerning the processing of the tax return.

The preparer would use Form 8821, *Tax Information Authorization,* if the taxpayer needed to authorize an individual or an organization to receive or inspect the taxpayer confidential tax return information, but does not want to authorize an individual to represent the taxpayer before the IRS. If the taxpayer wanted to authorize an individual to receive or inspect their transcripts or confidential return information, but does not want to authorize an individual to represent the taxpayer before the IRS, use Form 4506T, *Request for Transcript of Tax Return*.

Interview Pointers

The following questions determine if the taxpayer wants to authorize a third-party designee. Make sure you thoroughly understand what a third-party designee's responsibilities are.

- Would you like me to mark the box to be able to talk to the IRS regarding this return?
- Would you like to have another person talk to the IRS about your current year tax return?

Signing Form 1040

The taxpayer (and spouse if filing jointly) must sign the return in the section shown below from the second page of the 1040 form.

If either the taxpayer or spouse received an Identity Protection (IP) PIN from the IRS due to identity theft, the taxpayer must enter the number in the box provided. If both the taxpayer and spouse suffered from identity theft, only the taxpayer would enter the IP PIN. Make sure to enter the IP PIN on the correct line, if the spouse or taxpayer or both had identity theft.

Paid Preparer Use Only

Paid preparers must enter their PTIN, business name, business address, employer identification number (EIN), and business phone number. If the paid preparer is self-employed, he or she must check the box. The paid preparer must sign the return in the appropriate box; otherwise, the paid preparer could be charged a $50 penalty per return. This is a paid preparer penalty not a company penalty.

Form 1040-SR, for seniors.

Compiling Taxpayer Information

The added benefit of Form 1040-SR is that it automatically calculates the higher standard deduction for seniors. Form 1040-SR is 4 pages instead of 2 for the regular Form 1040.

> *Señor 1040 Says:* Remember, the additional exemption amount is only for taxpayer and spouse and is automatically added to the standard deduction.

When a taxpayer files Married filing separate and one spouse itemizes deductions, the other taxpayer must itemize their deductions even if the standard deduction gives the taxpayer a better tax break.

Interview Pointers

These questions determine if the taxpayer should use the standard or itemized deduction. For questions relating to home ownership, be aware that even though a taxpayer may own a home, it may be paid off and thus may not have enough deductions to itemize. (Itemized deductions will be covered in detail in a later chapter.)

- Do you pay rent or own a home?
    - If a home is owned:
        - Did you pay mortgage interest?
        - Did you pay real estate taxes (property taxes)?
    - If a home was recently purchased:
        - Must see the buyers final closing statement
- Did you have medical expenses?
- Did you have debt from a mortgage or credit card canceled or forgiven by a commercial lender?
- Did you live in an area that was affected by a presidentially declared natural disaster?
    - If yes, where and when?
- Did you receive the First-Time Homebuyer Credit in 2008?
- Did you make any charitable contributions last year?
    - Were they cash or noncash?
    - Do you have receipts? Can you bring them to me so I can have a copy with your tax papers?
- Do you have medical insurance? (What the taxpayer pays out of pocket may be a deduction on Schedule A.)
- Did you receive Form 1095-A? (If so, the taxpayers' insurance premiums cannot be deducted on Schedule A.)
- Do you have an exemption granted by the Marketplace? (If so, you need that number to complete the tax return.)
- Did you take any higher education classes?
- Did you pay someone to care for your children? (Only ask if there are dependents on the return).

Compiling Taxpayer Information

Part 1 Review Questions

To obtain the maximum benefit from this chapter, LTP recommends that you complete each of the following questions, and then compare them to the answers with feedback that immediately follow. Under governing self-study standards, vendors are required to present review questions intermittently throughout each self-study course.

These questions and explanations are not part of the final examination and will not be graded by LTP.

CTIP1.1
Which of the following is not a section on Form 1040?

a. Filing Status
b. Dependents
c. Income
d. Educator Expense

CTIP1.2
To confirm the taxpayer's identity, which of the following does not need to be collected?

a. Their expired government-issued photo identification.
b. Some documentation that confirms the taxpayer's current address.
c. The tax preparer should verify the Social Security number(s) for everyone on the tax return.
d. Date of birth.

CTIP1.3
When collecting information about dependents claimed on a tax return, what is the basic information that is needed to be asked?

a. What is the dependent's nickname?
b. What is the dependent's relationship to the taxpayer?
c. What is the dependent's phone number?
d. What is the dependent's school address?

CTIP1.4
Which of the following does not need to be entered in the "Paid Preparer Use Only" section?

a. Preparer Tax Identification Number
b. Business Name
c. Business Address
d. IP PIN

CTIP1.5
What is the added benefit for using the Form 1040-SR?

a. Fonts size is automatically smaller.
b. The higher standard deduction is automatically added.
c. Paid preparers do not need to sign the return.
d. There are 4 pages instead of 2 pages for Form 1040-SR.

Compiling Taxpayer Information

CTIP1.6
Esther gave permission to Susan to check the box as her Third-party Designee. When will the authorization expire?

   a. April 15, 2022
   b. April 15, 2023
   c. April 15, 2024
   d. April 15, 2025

Part 1 Review Questions Answers

CTIP1.1
Which of the following is not a section on Form 1040?

   a. Filing Status
   b. Dependents
   c. Income
   d. Educator Expense

Feedback: Review section *The following sections are found on the 2021 Form 1040.*

CTIP1.2
To confirm the taxpayer's identity, which of the following does not need to be collected?

   a. Their expired government-issued photo identification.
   b. Some documentation that confirms the taxpayer's current address.
   c. The tax preparer should verify the Social Security number(s) for everyone on the tax return.
   d. Date of birth.

Feedback: Review section *General Information: Name, Address, and Identification Number.*

CTIP1.3
When collecting information about dependents claimed on a tax return, what is the basic information that is needed to be asked?

   a. What is the dependent's nickname?
   b. What is the dependent's relationship to the taxpayer?
   c. What is the dependent's phone number?
   d. What is the dependent's school address?

Feedback: Review section *Dependents.*

CTIP1.4
Which of the following does not need to be entered in the "Paid Preparer Use Only" section?

   a. Preparer Tax Identification Number
   b. Business Name
   c. Business Address
   d. IP PIN

Feedback: Review section *Signing Form 1040.*

CTIP1.5
What is the added benefit for using the Form 1040-SR?

a. Fonts size is automatically smaller.
b. The higher standard deduction is automatically added.
c. Paid preparers do not need to sign the return.
d. There are 4 pages instead of 2 pages for Form 1040-SR.

Feedback: Review section *Form 1040-SR for seniors*.

CTIP1.6
Esther gave permission to Susan to check the box as her Third-party Designee. When will the authorization expire?

a. April 15, 2022
b. April 15, 2023
c. April 15, 2024
d. April 15, 2025

Feedback: Review section *Third Party Designee*.

Part 2 Schedule 1, 2, & 3

Schedule 1 reports additional income and adjustments to income. Each schedule's form, if used, is attached to Form 1040; however, not every schedule is used for each taxpayer. Another year and more changes to Schedule 1.

Adjustments and Deductions

Adjustments and deductions are often confused as they appear to function very similarly. The differences between the two will be explained in full throughout the course; but for now, the main difference to know is that Adjustments are used to lower one's AGI before deductions are taken into account. This is important because deduction amounts will be calculated based on that already-lowered AGI, meaning that the amount of adjustments to the income one receives can directly affect the amount of deductions received.

There are two ways to calculate deductions: "standard" and "itemized". "Standard deductions" are annually preset amounts the taxpayer will use to deduct from one's taxable income based on filing status. However, the taxpayer can also "itemize" their deductions by taking certain deductions on Schedule A and add the total categories to see if the taxpayer qualifies to itemize their deduction amount. Taxpayers are typically free to choose to either itemize their deductions or take the standard deduction amounts, and they are encouraged to calculate both and then choose which option will save them more money.

The government allows deductions, for the most part, for various types of expenses to help take the cost of maintaining your life into account when determining the amount of taxes that you owe. In other words, deductions exist to help make sure that you are being taxed on the amount of money you actually got to take home and keep after paying for all of the expenses that come with life, rather than the total amount you were paid.

Form 1040, Schedule 1, Part I

> **SCHEDULE 1 (Form 1040)** — Additional Income and Adjustments to Income — OMB No. 1545-0074 — 2021
> Department of the Treasury, Internal Revenue Service
> ▶ Attach to Form 1040, 1040-SR, or 1040-NR.
> ▶ Go to www.irs.gov/Form1040 for instructions and the latest information.
> Attachment Sequence No. 01
> Name(s) shown on Form 1040, 1040-SR, or 1040-NR | Your social security number
> **Part I** Additional Income

Additional income consists of the following items:

- Taxable refunds.
- Alimony received.
- Schedule C income or loss.
- Form 4797 other gains or losses.
- Schedule E income.
- Schedule F income or loss.
- Unemployment and paid family leave.
- Other income such as:
    - Hobby income
    - Jury duty pay
    - Alaska Permanent Fund dividends
    - Gambling winnings

Total income is the combination of all lines from Form 1040, Schedule 1, Part I. Some income reported on Schedule 1, line 3, 4, 5, and 6 could result in a negative number that is subtracted from the total income.

Form 1040, Schedule 1, Part II

> Schedule 1 (Form 1040) 2021 — Page 2
> **Part II** Adjustments to Income

Adjusting one's income is not the same as filing Schedule A to itemize deductions; it is lowering the taxpayer's gross income to pay the least amount of tax, which consists of the following:

- Educator expense.
- Alimony paid (if the agreement was signed prior to December 31, 2018).
- Deductible part of self-employment tax.
- Sale of stocks or assets (if the taxpayer had a loss and not a gain on the sale).
- Contributing to an IRA, SEP, SIMPLE, and other qualified plans.
- Student loan interest deduction.

Interview Pointers

To determine a taxpayer's adjusted gross income (AGI) on line 26, the following must be asked:

- Did you pay alimony or separate maintenance payments? (Only applicable if the agreement was signed prior to December 31, 2018).

- Were there any changes in your tax status from last year to this year?
- Do you have an IRA?
- What life changes did you have this year?
- Did you pay interest on any student loans?
- If the W-2 is from a school district: "I see that you have a W-2 from a school district. What is your job title?"
  - The answer will determine if the taxpayer(s) qualify for the educator expense.
- If the individual has more than one W-2: "I see that you have two different W-2s. Did you change jobs this year? If so, did you move? If so, how far is it from your old workplace to your new workplace?" (Due to TCJA this line is limited to certain taxpayers until 2026, more information later).
- If the W-2 is from the armed forces: "I see that you have a W-2 from the armed forces. Are you full-time or in the reserves? Were you in a combat zone?"

The taxpayer can choose to itemize deductions or use standard deductions to reduce their taxable income. Standard deductions are based on the taxpayer's filing status. Itemized deduction is generally used when the taxpayer's deduction exceeds their standard deduction. Subtracting applicable deductions from the taxpayer's total income becomes the taxpayer's adjusted gross income.

The tax to be paid is determined by the taxpayer's taxable income. Tax tables are also based on taxable income, as well. The current year's tax tables can be found in the Form 1040 Instruction on the IRS website. Schedule 2 is used to report any additional tax that needs to be declared.

Schedule 2 Additional Taxes

SCHEDULE 2 (Form 1040) Department of the Treasury Internal Revenue Service	Additional Taxes ▶ Attach to Form 1040, 1040-SR, or 1040-NR. ▶ Go to www.irs.gov/Form1040 for instructions and the latest information.	OMB No. 1545-0074 2021 Attachment Sequence No. 02
Name(s) shown on Form 1040, 1040-SR, or 1040-NR		Your social security number

Part I Tax

1	Alternative minimum tax. Attach Form 6251	1	
2	Excess advance premium tax credit repayment. Attach Form 8962	2	
3	Add lines 1 and 2. Enter here and on Form 1040, 1040-SR, or 1040-NR, line 17	3	

Other Taxes is covered in detail in a later chapter.

Schedule 2 Part II – Other Taxes

Part II	Other Taxes		
4	Self-employment tax. Attach Schedule SE		4
5	Social security and Medicare tax on unreported tip income. Attach Form 4137	5	
6	Uncollected social security and Medicare tax on wages. Attach Form 8919	6	
7	Total additional social security and Medicare tax. Add lines 5 and 6		7
8	Additional tax on IRAs or other tax-favored accounts. Attach Form 5329 if required		8
9	Household employment taxes. Attach Schedule H		9
10	Repayment of first-time homebuyer credit. Attach Form 5405 if required		10
11	Additional Medicare Tax. Attach Form 8959		11
12	Net investment income tax. Attach Form 8960		12
13	Uncollected social security and Medicare or RRTA tax on tips or group-term life insurance from Form W-2, box 12		13
14	Interest on tax due on installment income from the sale of certain residential lots and timeshares		14
15	Interest on the deferred tax on gain from certain installment sales with a sales price over $150,000		15
16	Recapture of low-income housing credit. Attach Form 8611		16

(continued on page 2)

Line 4: Self-employment tax. Schedule SE should be attached.

Line 5: Unreported tip income, attach Form 4137.

Line 6: Uncollected social security and Medicare tax on wages, attach Form 8919.

Line 7: Total additional social security and Medicare tax from lines 5 and 6.

Line 8: Additional tax on IRAs and other qualified retirement plans are reported, attach Form 5329.

Line 9: Household employment tax is reported, attach Schedule.

Line 10: First-time homebuyer credit repayment; Form 5405 is used to report this and should be attached.

Line 11: Additional Medicare Tax, attach Form 8959.

Line 12: Net investment income tax (NIIT), attach Form 8960.

Line 13: Uncollected social security and Medicare or RRTA tax on tips or group-term life insurance from box 12, Form W-2.

Line 14: Interest on tax due on installment agreement income from the sale of certain residential lots and timeshares.

Line 15: Interest on the deferred tax on gain from certain installment sales with a sales price over $150,000.

Line 16: Recapture of low-income housing credit, attach Form 8611.

Interview Pointers

These questions determine if the taxpayer will be paying other taxes:

- ➢ Did your childcare provider come to your house to babysit?
    - o May need to file Schedule H.
- ➢ Did you withdraw money from your IRA or 401(k)? (Depending upon age and what the money was used for, it could result in an additional tax.)
    - o How much did you withdraw?
    - o What did you use it for?
- ➢ Did you have healthcare coverage for the entire year?
- ➢ Did you or your spouse receive Form 1095-A? (Did you purchase health insurance through an exchange?)
- ➢ Are you self-employed? (Ask this question if you are filing a Schedule C.)
    - o Did you receive Form 1099-MISC or NEC?
    - o Did you receive Form 1099-K?
- ➢ Did you or your spouse receive a first-time home buyer loan and are paying it back?
- ➢ Did you report all your tips to your employer? (Ask this question if you know the taxpayer is a server and there is an amount in box 7 of the W-2.)
- ➢ Do you have other additional taxes?
    - o Tax on a Health Savings Account (HSA)?
    - o Additional tax on HSA distributions?
    - o Recapture of a charitable contribution?

Schedule 3 Additional Credits and Payments

Schedule 3 is used to report nonrefundable credits, other payments, and refundable credits. Refundable credits are payments toward the taxpayer's tax liability; if the result is more than the tax, the excess is a refund to the taxpayer.

Form 1040, line 25 reports the amount of federal withholding from all income sources, such as W-2, Form 1099-R, unemployment compensation, etc. Earned income credit (EIC), the additional child tax credit and the refundable portion of the American opportunity credit are reported on Form 1040, lines 27-29.

Part I Nonrefundable Credits

A nonrefundable credit is used to reduce the taxpayers tax liability to zero. If the individual has more credits, they are not able to use them to lower the tax liability. The taxpayer forfeits the remaining credit. A nonrefundable credit can reduce the taxable income dollar for dollar. Some common nonrefundable credits are:

Education credits.
Foreign tax credit.
Certain residential energy credits.
Retirement savings contributions credit.

Nonrefundable credits will be covered in a later chapter.

Compiling Taxpayer Information

[Schedule 3 (Form 1040) 2021, Part I: Nonrefundable Credits — lines 1-5 showing Foreign tax credit, Credit for child and dependent care expenses from Form 2441, Education credits from Form 8863, Retirement savings contributions credit, Residential energy credits]

Schedule 3 Part II: Other Payments and Refundable Credits

A refundable credit can generate a larger refund than the amount of tax paid through withholdings or estimated tax payments throughout the year. Which means the taxpayer could get a refund from refundable credits that he or she qualifies for. Some common refundable credits are earned income tax credits, and new for tax year 2021, being prepared in 2022, is child and dependent care expenses, which was part of the American Rescue Plan Act (ARPA).

[Schedule 3 (Form 1040) 2021, Page 2, Part II: Other Payments and Refundable Credits — lines 9-12 showing Net premium tax credit, Amount paid with request for extension to file, Excess social security and tier 1 RRTA tax withheld, Credit for federal tax on fuels]

Line 9: Net premium tax credit, reported via an attached Form 8962.

Line 10: Amount paid with extension request.

Line 11: Report excess social security and tier I railroad retirement benefits (SSA-1099).

Line 12: Used to report credit for federal tax on fuels used for a nontaxable purpose (for example, off-highway business use). Form 4136 is used to report this and must be attached.

Add lines 9-13f and put the total on line 14; this is the total amount of payments.

Other payments and refundable credits will be reviewed in a later chapter.

Interview Pointers

These questions could determine the taxpayer's total tax payments:

- Did you make any estimated payments during the tax year?
- Did you have last year's refund applied to the current tax year?

> Did you take any higher education classes?
> Did you pay any money along with the request to file an extension? (Only ask if the taxpayer filed an extension.)

Señor 1040 Says: Make sure to do your due diligence for **all** tax returns with refundable credits.

Part 2 Review Questions

To obtain the maximum benefit from this chapter, LTP recommends that you complete each of the following questions, and then compare them to the answers with feedback that immediately follow. Under governing self-study standards, vendors are required to present review questions intermittently throughout each self-study course.

These questions and explanations are not part of the final examination and will not be graded by LTP.

CTIP2.1
Which of the following is not reported on Form 1040, Schedule 1, Part II?

  a. Standard deduction
  b. Taxable refunds
  c. Educator expenses
  d. Student loan interest

CTIP2.2
Which of the following is reported on Form 1040, Schedule 1, Part II?

  a. Moving expenses for all taxpayers
  b. Lifetime Learning credit
  c. Educator expenses
  d. Social Security benefits

CTIP2.3
Which of the following reports self-employment tax?

  a. Schedule 2
  b. Schedule C
  c. Schedule 3
  d. Schedule E

CTIP2.4
Which of the following is not reported on Form 1040, Schedule 2, Part II?

  a. Additional Medicare Tax
  b. Net Investment Income Tax
  c. Early withdrawal of an IRA
  d. Unreported Social Security and Medicare tax

Compiling Taxpayer Information

CTIP2.5
Which of the following is not reported on Schedule 3?

  a. Nonrefundable credits
  b. Federal tax payments
  c. Refundable credits
  d. First time homebuyer credit

Part 2 Review Questions Answers

CTIP2.1
Which of the following is not reported on Form 1040, Schedule 1, Part II?

  a. **Standard deduction**
  b. Taxable refunds
  c. Educator expenses
  d. Student loan interest

Feedback: Review section *Form 1040, Schedule I, Part I.*

CTIP2.2
Which of the following is reported on Form 1040, Schedule 1, Part II?

  a. Moving expenses for all taxpayers
  b. Lifetime Learning credit
  c. **Educator expenses**
  d. Social Security benefits

Feedback: Review section *Form 1040, Schedule I, Part II.*

CTIP2.3
Which of the following reports self-employment tax?

  a. **Schedule 2**
  b. Schedule C
  c. Schedule 3
  d. Schedule E

Feedback: Review section *Form 1040, Schedule I, Part I.*

CTIP2.4
Which of the following is not reported on Form 1040, Schedule 2, Part II?

  a. Additional Medicare Tax
  b. Net Investment Income Tax
  c. **Early withdrawal of an IRA**
  d. Unreported Social Security and Medicare tax

Feedback: Review section *Schedule 2, Part II – Other Taxes.*

CTIP2.5

Which of the following is not reported on Schedule 3?

   a. Nonrefundable credits
   b. Federal tax payments
   c. Refundable credits
   d. First time homebuyer credit

Feedback: Review section *Schedule 3: Additional Credits and Payments.*

Part 3 Filing the Federal Tax Return

Once the tax professional has gathered the required information and ensured its accuracy, it is time to file the return.

If a United States taxpayer has worldwide income, they need to file a tax return. Immigrants who are unauthorized to be or work in the United States need to file their taxes; the IRS even makes it very clear that the information provided for returns and filing are used for tax purposes only. The IRS does not share taxpayer information with any government immigration agency.

The Filing Process

To begin, gather information and materials from the taxpayer to complete an accurate return. The tax professional will need the following:

- Income sources such as Form W-2 or 1099 Series.
- Receipts, checks, or invoices for payments and expenses.
- Other statements that show other income received by the taxpayer (such as a statement reporting gambling winnings from a casino or interest from a bank).
- Current driver's license or other form of government-issued picture identification.
- Social Security card with SSN number or some other form of taxpayer ID.
- Full name, SSN, date of birth, or other equivalent of any dependents or spouse.

This is the bare minimum needed to begin the tax preparation process. There are many other components needed to complete the return.

How to Assemble a Federal Tax Return

When assembling the return to be mailed to the IRS, make sure the attachment sequence order shown in the upper right-hand corner is in numerical order starting with Form 1040. If the taxpayer must attach supporting statements, the preparer must arrange them in the same order as the schedules and attach them at the end of the return. When mailing the return, attach a copy of income such as Form(s) W-2, W-2G, and/or 1099-R to page 1 of Form 1040.

Compiling Taxpayer Information

Where to File a Paper Return

Based on where the taxpayer lives, the type of tax return and whether there is a refund or balance due determines where the taxpayer would send a paper return. It is more beneficial to file electronically with modern technology. There are often separate mailing addresses for returns with enclosed payments and for returns without. To find the correct address to use for mailing your federal return, use the following link:

https://www.irs.gov/filing/where-to-file-addresses-for-taxpayers-and-tax-professionals-filing-form-1040

Another option is to electronically file, or e-file, the tax return. This eliminates the need to mail in a physical paper return. This option is discussed further in the e-filing chapter.

When to File a Return

The IRS states that, for tax returns and payments, the tax return must meet the "timely mailing/timely paying" rule: taxes owed must be paid by April 15th or the next business day if the 15th falls on a weekend or legal holiday, even if the taxpayer has successfully filed for an extension of time.

Filing Deadlines

Individual Tax Returns: Forms 1040 and 1040NR (Non-Resident)

- The first deadline was April 18, 2022.
- April 19, 2022, for Maine and Massachusetts.
- May 19, 2022, for Colorado.
- The extended deadline is October 17, 2022.

Partnership Returns: Form 1065

- The first deadline is March 15, 2022.
- The extended deadline is September 15, 2022.

Trust and Estate Income Tax Returns: Form 1041

- The first deadline is April 15, 2022.
- The extended deadline is October 2, 2022.

Note the change: extensions for fiduciary returns now last five-and-a-half months instead of only five months.

C-Corporation Returns: Form 1120

- The first deadline is April 15, 2022, for corporations on a calendar year; note the change of deadline.
- The extended deadline is October 17, 2022. Note the change of deadline; corporations are now permitted a six-month automatic extension.
- For corporations on a fiscal year other than the calendar year, the first deadline is the 15th day of the fourth month following the end of the corporation's fiscal year.

- EXCEPTION: for corporations with a fiscal year from July 1st to June 30th, the first deadline will remain September 15th (which is the 15th day of the third month following the end of the fiscal year) and the extended deadline will remain February 15th (five months after the first deadline) through the fiscal year ending on June 30, 2026.
- Starting with the fiscal year ending on June 30, 2017, the deadline moved to October 15th (the 15th day of the fourth month following the end of the tax year) and the extended deadline moves to March 15th (six months after the first deadline).

S-Corporation Returns: Form 1120S

- The first deadline is March 15, 2022, for corporations on a calendar year.
- The extended deadline is September 15, 2022.

Foreign Bank Account Reports: FinCen Form 114

- The first deadline is April 15, 2022; note the change of deadline.
- The extended deadline is October 17, 2022. Note: this is the first time ever that extensions are available for Foreign Bank Account Reports (FBARs).
- Note that unlike tax returns, FBARs do not have a next-business-day rule if the deadline falls on a Saturday, Sunday, or legal holiday.

See IRS section 6072.

How to File a Return

The following methods can be used to file a tax return:

- Electronic filing (e-file).
- Private delivery service: FedEx, UPS, etc.
- United States Postal Service.

If a tax professional prepares 10 or more returns, they must e-file all returns. Electronically filed returns are given a postmark that includes the date and time of the return's electronic transmission.

Where to File a Return

The Internal Revenue Service has different regional centers for the taxpayer to file their paper federal tax return based on the state they live in.

See IRS section 6091.

Part 3 Review Questions

To obtain the maximum benefit from this chapter, LTP recommends that you complete each of the following questions, and then compare them to the answers with feedback that immediately follow. Under governing self-study standards, vendors are required to present review questions intermittently throughout each self-study course.

These questions and explanations are not part of the final examination and will not be graded by LTP.

Compiling Taxpayer Information

CTIP3.1

When assembling the tax return for the client, which is the best way to put the return together?

a. Just staple everything together as it comes out of the printer.
b. Use the sequence number that is found on the top right hand of all other forms except the 1040.
c. Mail the state return with your federal return.
d. Make sure the supporting documents are added at the end in sequential order.

CTIP3.2

Which method is not used to file a tax return?

a. Electronic filing
b. Private delivery service
c. United States Post Office
d. Fax the return to the local IRS Office

CTIP3.3

Which of the following do you need from the taxpayer to prepare their return?

a. All income documents
b. Determine taxpayer filing status
c. Correct address for mailing the tax return
d. Mail the payment due on October 15th

CTIP3.4

For tax year 2021 when is the individual tax return due?

a. March 15, 2022
b. February 12, 2022
c. October 17, 2022
d. April 15, 2022

Part 3 Review Questions Answers

CTIP3.1

When assembling the tax return for the client, which is the best way to put the return together?

a. Just staple everything together as it comes out of the printer.
b. Use the sequence number that is found on the top right hand of all other forms except the 1040.
c. Mail the state return with your federal return.
d. Make sure the supporting documents are added at the end in sequential order.

Feedback: Review section *How to Assemble a Federal Tax Return*.

CTIP3.2
Which method is not used to file a tax return?

a. Electronic filing
b. Private delivery service
c. United States Post Office
d. **Fax the return to the local IRS Office**

Feedback: Review section *How to File a Return*.

CTIP3.3
Which of the following do you need from the taxpayer to prepare their return?

a. **All income documents**
b. Determine taxpayer filing status
c. Correct address for mailing the tax return
d. Mail the payment due on October 15th

Feedback: Review section *The Filing Process*.

CTIP3.4
For tax year 2021 when is the individual tax return due?

a. March 15, 2022
b. February 12, 2022
c. October 17, 2022
d. **April 15, 2022**

Feedback: Review section *Filing Deadlines*.

Part 4 What is an ITIN?

An ITIN is a tax processing number, issued by the IRS, for certain resident and nonresident aliens, their spouses, and their dependents. It is a nine-digit number beginning with the number 9. The ITIN range was expanded on April 13, 2011, to include "90" as the middle digits (70 to 88, 90-92, and 94-99) and is formatted like an SSN. The IRS started issuing ITINs in 1996 and required foreign individuals to use an ITIN as their unique identification number on federal tax returns. With ITINs, taxpayers can be effectively identified, and their tax returns processed efficiently.

ITINs play a critical role in the tax administration process and assist with the collection of taxes from foreign nationals, nonresident aliens, and others who have filing or payment obligations under U.S. tax law. Even when other institutions might use ITINs for other purposes, the IRS states that:

> ITINs are for federal tax reporting only and are not intended to serve any other purpose. IRS issues ITINs to help individuals comply with the U.S. tax laws, and to provide a means to efficiently process and account for tax returns and payments for those not eligible for social security numbers (SSNs).

Only individuals who have a valid filing requirement, a withholding requirement, or are filing a U.S. federal income tax return to claim a refund of over-withheld tax are eligible to receive an ITIN. The ITIN does not provide Social Security benefits, is not valid for identification outside of the tax system and does not change immigration status. The ITIN holder enters their ITIN in the space provided for the SSN when completing and filing their federal income tax return.

Who needs an ITIN?

All tax returns (Form 1040), statements, and other related tax documents used to file a tax report require a taxpayer identification number (TIN). If an individual does not qualify for a Social Security number, then the individual must apply for an ITIN.

Individuals who may need an ITIN include:

- A nonresident alien individual eligible to obtain the benefits of a reduced rate of withholding under an income tax treaty.
- A nonresident alien not eligible for an SSN required to file a U.S. tax return or filing a U.S. tax return only to claim a refund.
- A nonresident alien not eligible for an SSN electing to file a joint tax return with a spouse who is a U.S. citizen or resident alien.
- A U.S. resident alien who files a U.S. tax return but is not eligible for an SSN.
- An alien individual, claimed as a spouse for an exemption on a U.S. tax return, who is not eligible for an SSN.
- An alien individual, who is not eligible for an SSN, claimed as a dependent on another person's U.S. tax return.
- A nonresident alien student, professor, or researcher filing a U.S. tax return or claiming an exception to the tax return filing requirement who is not eligible for an SSN.

Reason to Apply for an ITIN

A nonresident alien must apply for an ITIN to report earned income and claim the tax treaty benefits he or she qualifies for:

Box a. This box would be checked for certain nonresident aliens who must get an ITIN to claim certain tax treaty benefits whether they file a tax return or not. If box a is checked, then check box h as well. Enter on the dotted line next to box h the exceptions that relate to the taxpayer's situation.

Box b. Nonresident alien filing a U.S. tax return.

This category includes:

1. A nonresident alien who must file a U.S. tax return to report income directly or indirectly connected with the conduct of a trade or business in the United States.
2. A nonresident alien who is filing a U.S. tax return only to get a refund.

Box c. U.S. resident alien (based on the number of days present in the United States) filing a U.S. tax return.

Box c would be checked for a foreign individual living in the United States, who does not have permission to work from the USCIS and is ineligible for an SSN, but may still have a filing requirement.

Box d. Dependent of a U.S. citizen/resident alien.

Box d would be checked for an individual who can be claimed as a dependent on a U.S. tax return and is not eligible to get an SSN. Dependents of U.S. military personnel are exempt from the requirements of submitting original documents or certified copies of identifying documents, but a standard copy is required. A copy of the U.S. military ID is required, or the applicant must be applying from an overseas APO/FPO address.

Box e. Spouse of a U.S. citizen/resident alien.

This category includes:

1. A resident or nonresident alien spouse who is not filing a U.S. tax return (including a joint return) and who is not eligible to get an SSN, but who as a spouse, is claimed as an exemption.
2. A resident or nonresident alien electing to file a U.S. tax return jointly with a spouse who is a U.S. citizen or resident alien.

A spouse or a person in the U.S. military is exempt from submitting original documents or certified copies of identifying documents, but a standard copy will be required. A copy of a U.S. military ID will be required, or the applicant must be applying from an overseas APO/FPO address

Box f. Nonresident alien student, professor, or researcher filing a U.S. tax return or *claiming an exception.*

Box f is checked if the individual applicant has not abandoned his/her residence in a foreign country and who is a bona fide student, professor, or researcher coming temporarily to the United States solely to attend classes at a recognized institution of education, to teach, or to perform research.

If this box is checked, complete lines 6c and 6g and provide a passport with a valid U.S. visa. If the applicant is present in the U.S. on a work-related visa (F-1, J-1, or M-1), but will not be employed (applicant's presence in the U.S. is study-related), attach a letter from the DSO (Designated School Official) or RO (Responsible Officer) instead of applying with the SSA for an SSN. The letter must state clearly that the applicant will not be securing employment while in the U.S. and their presence here is solely study-related. This letter can be submitted with the applicant's Form W-7 in lieu of the denial letter from the SSA.

Box g. Dependent/spouse of a nonresident alien holding a U.S. visa.

Box g is checked when the individual can be claimed as a dependent or a spouse on a U.S. tax return and is unable or not eligible to get an SSN and has entered the U.S. with a nonresident alien who holds a U.S. visa. If this box is checked, be sure to include a copy of the visa with the W-7 application.

Box h. Other.

Compiling Taxpayer Information

If box h is checked, it is because boxes a-g do not apply to the applicant. Be sure to describe in detail the reason for requesting an ITIN and attach all supporting documents.

```
Form W-7              Application for IRS Individual
(Rev. August 2019)    Taxpayer Identification Number          OMB No. 1545-0074
Department of the Treasury  ▶ For use by individuals who are not U.S. citizens or permanent residents.
Internal Revenue Service                ▶ See separate instructions.

An IRS individual taxpayer identification number (ITIN) is for U.S. federal tax purposes only.    Application type (check one box):
Before you begin:                                                                                  ☐ Apply for a new ITIN
• Don't submit this form if you have, or are eligible to get, a U.S. social security number (SSN). ☐ Renew an existing ITIN

Reason you're submitting Form W-7. Read the instructions for the box you check. Caution: If you check box b, c, d, e, f, or g, you
must file a U.S. federal tax return with Form W-7 unless you meet one of the exceptions (see instructions).
  a ☐ Nonresident alien required to get an ITIN to claim tax treaty benefit
  b ☐ Nonresident alien filing a U.S. federal tax return
  c ☐ U.S. resident alien (based on days present in the United States) filing a U.S. federal tax return
  d ☐ Dependent of U.S. citizen/resident alien       If d, enter relationship to U.S. citizen/resident alien (see instructions) ▶ ............
  e ☐ Spouse of U.S. citizen/resident alien          If d or e, enter name and SSN/ITIN of U.S. citizen/resident alien (see instructions) ▶ ............
  f ☐ Nonresident alien student, professor, or researcher filing a U.S. federal tax return or claiming an exception
  g ☐ Dependent/spouse of a nonresident alien holding a U.S. visa
  h ☐ Other (see instructions) ▶
Additional information for a and f: Enter treaty country ▶ ............          and treaty article number ▶
```

Common Errors on Form W-7

Always make sure that you input the correct information; double check each document and Form W-7 for errors.

Name Mismatch

This is the number one reason ITIN applications are rejected. Make sure the W-7 applications have the same name that is on the tax return being submitted. If an individual is helping a taxpayer complete the Form W-7 application, make sure not to abbreviate the applicant's name, use initials, or leave off the second last name on the tax return or W-7 application. The IRS employee is trained to match the names with the tax return and the W-7 application.

W-2 Issues

Many ITIN holders use a different name with a Social Security number. When the W-7 application is submitted with a tax return, the names on the W-2s should match the application. The IRS wants to make sure that the W-2 income reported is the income the person earned. Remember the purpose of the ITIN is for foreign individuals to report their income. The tricky issue is to get the W-2 to match the legal name. Taxpayers who need an ITIN do not want to ask their employer to change their records for fear of being dismissed for submitting inaccurate information.

Date of Entry

Another common mistake is the date of entry line on the passport is empty. This does not allow the IRS employee to match the taxpayer's date of entry with beginning work history. For example, submit documents that establish when they began working and the type of work they have been doing; this will help the ITIN reviewer tie in the date entered and when work began. For certain dependents, a passport without a date of entry is not accepted as a stand-alone document. For more information refer to Publication 1915.

Passport Rejection

The most common reason the IRS rejects passports is because they are not signed. The IRS will not accept an original passport that is not signed. Everyone entering the U.S. with a passport must sign it. Some countries do not allow children to sign passports, such as India; the IRS is still working on a solution to this.

Reason for Submitting W-7

There is no entry in boxes a – h. Beware that if box b, c, d, e, f, or g is checked, a current year tax return must be attached.

Not Submitting Required Documents

Make sure that the required original identification documents or certified copies (if applicable) are submitted with Form W-7.

Expired ITIN

Submitting an expired ITIN with a federal tax return without Form W-7.

Incorrect ITINs on Form W-7

Submitting ITINs that are incorrect when submitting a renewal Form W-7 and not clicking box 6e-f. When using software to complete Form W-7, be cautious when the program auto populates name and identification number. Make sure you submit the application with the correct ITIN.

Applying for an ITIN

Use Form W-7 or W-7(SP) (Español) to apply for an ITIN. After completing W-7 application, attach it to a valid federal tax return, unless the taxpayer qualifies for an exception. All ITIN applications need to be attached to a current year tax return unless one of the five exceptions exists.

1. Third Party Withholding on Passive Income.
2. Wages, Salary, Compensation, and Honoraria Payments with Tax Treaty Benefits Claimed; or Scholarships, Fellowships and Grants with or without Tax Treaty Benefits or Gambling Winnings with Tax Treaty Benefits Claimed.
3. Third Party Reporting of Mortgage Interest.
4. Third Party Withholding – Disposition by a Foreign Person of United States Real Property.
5. Reporting Obligations under Treasury Decision 9363 (T.D. 9363).

The taxpayer must file Form W-7 with the current year tax return. If the tax professional is helping the taxpayer fill out the form, make sure to use the most current form. Look at the bottom of the form and see the revision date. The ITIN application should be mailed to the following address:

Internal Revenue Service
Austin Service Center
ITIN Operation
PO Box 149342
Austin, TX 78714-9342

If a private delivery service requires a street address, use the following:

Internal Revenue Service
ITIN Operations
Mail Stop 6090-AUSC
3651 S. Interregional, Hwy 35
Austin, TX 78741-0000

When mailing the application and documentation, make sure to get confirmation that the tax return was delivered. If the W-7 application was mailed using United States Postal Service, use a certify return receipt, and a green card will come back with the date it was delivered. If you use another service, make sure to get a tracking number to check online when the package was delivered.

The ITIN number is issued by mail, and the Austin processing center is the IRS office that issues the numbers. The taxpayer can apply any time for the W-7. If the application is filed after the return's due date, the taxpayer may owe penalties and/or interest. To avoid this, file the current year tax return timely.

Individual Applicants

For individuals applying directly to the IRS for an ITIN, original documents or copies certified by the issuing agency are required. The IRS will accept only original identification documents or certified copies of these documents from the issuing agency with the Form W-7 and federal tax return attached.

Document Standards for Dependent Children

Dependent ITIN applications will continue to require original documents or copies certified by the issuing agency. This is done to adequately substantiate identity and foreign status and assist in ensuring the integrity of important child tax credits. Dependent ITIN applications submitted to the IRS by Certifying Acceptance Agents (CAA) will continue to require attachment of original documents or copies certified by the issuing agency. For children under six, one of the documents can include original medical records. For school-age children, the documentation should include original, current year school records such as a report card or a letter on the school's letterhead with a school photo of the child.

If the ITIN is for a dependent, the documentation must prove that the dependent is a U.S. national or a resident of the United States, Mexico, or Canada. However, if you are living abroad and have adopted, or have had legally placed a foreign child in your home pending an adoption, that child may be eligible for an ITIN. If the dependent is a minor, the documentation must establish the relationship between the dependent and the representative signing the application on the dependent's behalf. Documentation could include a birth certificate, adoption papers, or other court-appointed papers showing legal guardianship. In the case of dependents that are residents of the Republic of Korea (South Korea) or India, refer to Publication 519, *U.S. Tax Guide for Aliens*, for additional documentation that may be required.

Documentation Needed

The IRS requires original documentation, and one of the documents must include a recent photograph. The identity documents are needed to both verify the applicant's foreign status and the applicant's identity. The following is a list of current original documentation that can be used:

- Passport (standalone document)
- U.S. Citizenship and Immigration Services (USCIS) photo identification
- U.S. state identification card
- U.S. driver's license
- U.S. military identification card
- National identification card
- Visa issued by U.S. Department of State
- Foreign driver's license
- Foreign military identification card
- Foreign voter's registration card
- Civil birth certificate
- Medical records (for dependent applicants under age 6)
- School records (for dependent applicants under age 14, under age 18 if student)

The IRS heard from stakeholders that it was difficult, in some instances, for individuals to be without documents such as passports for extended periods of time. Thus, the IRS determined that other outlets will be available to review original documentation. As part of this effort, while original documents or copies certified by the issuing agency are still required for most applicants, there will be more options and flexibility for people applying for an ITIN.

These options provide alternatives to mailing passports and other original documents to the IRS.

Supporting Documentation	Can be used to establish	
	Foreign status	Identity
Passport (the only standalone document)	X	X
U.S. Citizenship and Immigration Services (USCIS) Photo identification	X	X
Visa issued by U.S. Department of State	X	X
U.S. driver's license		X
U.S. military identification card		X
Foreign driver's license		X
Foreign military identification card	X	X
National identification card (must be current and contain name, photograph, address, date of birth, and expiration date)	X	X
U.S. state identification card		X
Foreign voter's registration card	X	X
Civil birth certificate	X*	X
Medical records (valid only for dependents under age 6)	X*	X
School records (valid only for dependents under age 18 if a student)	X*	X

*Can be used to establish foreign status only if they are foreign documents.

Compiling Taxpayer Information

ITIN Tax Related Exceptions

Exception 1: Third Party Withholding on Passive Income

This exception may apply if the taxpayer is the recipient of partnership income, interest income, annuity income, rental income, or other passive income that is subject to third party withholding or covered by tax treaty benefits. To get an ITIN, the individual must include supporting documentation with Form W-7.

Supporting documentation is a letter or signed statement from the bank, financial institution, or withholding agent. It shows proof that the asset that generates income and belongs to the taxpayer is subject to IRS reporting requirements that take place in the current tax year.

Exception 2: Other Income

This exception may apply if:

1. Taxpayer is claiming the benefits of a U.S. income tax treaty with a foreign country and the taxpayer received any of the following:
    a. Wages, salary, compensation, and honoraria payments
    b. Scholarships, fellowships, and grants
    c. Gambling winnings
2. The taxpayer is receiving taxable scholarship, fellowship, or grant income, but not claiming the benefits of an income tax treaty.

Student and Exchange Visitor Program

The Student and Exchange Visitor Program (SEVP)-approved institutions for nonresident alien students and exchange visitors and their dependents classified under section 101(a)(15)(F), (M) or (J) of the Immigration and Nationality Act {8U.S.C. 1101(a)(15) (F), (M), or (J)}: A certification letter is required for each Form W-7 application; primary, associated secondary (spouse), and dependents.

The certification letter from a SEVP-approved institution serves as a substitute for submission of original supporting identification documents with Form W-7. The letter must:

- Be on original, official college, university, or institution letterhead with a verifiable address
- Provide the applicant's full name and Student and Exchange Visitor Information System (SEVIS) number
- Certify the applicant's registration in SEVIS
- Certify that the student presented an unexpired passport, visa, or other identification documents provided for review
- List the identification documents provided to verify identity and foreign status
- Be signed and dated by a SEVIS official
    - Principal Designated School Official (PDSO)
    - Designated School Official (DSO)
    - Responsible Officer (RO)
    - Alternative Responsible Officer (ARO)
- Attach copies of documents used to verify the applicant's identity and foreign status from the approved list of supporting documents that can be attached to Form W-7 (passports must include a copy of a valid visa issued by the U.S. Department of State)

- Attach a copy of DS-2019, *Certificate of Eligibility for Exchange Visitor Status* (J-1 status) and/or a copy of the 1-20 *Certificate for Non-Immigrant Student Status*.
- Attach a copy of Form W-8BEN submitted to the withholding agent
- Form W-7 must include the treaty country and article number that supports claiming a tax treaty benefit
- Include a letter from the DSO or RO stating that the applicant will not be securing employment in the U.S. or receiving any type of income from personal services

If the student is on an F-1, J-1, or M-1 visa and will not be working while studying in the U.S., they will not have to apply for an SSN. The student will be permitted to provide a letter from the DSO or RO stating that they will not be securing employment in the United States or receiving any type of income from personal services.

Exception 3: Third Party Reporting of Mortgage Interest

If the ITIN applicant has a home mortgage loan on real property that they own in the United States, that is subject to third party reporting of mortgage interest. Information returns applicable to exception 3 may include Form 1098, *Mortgage Interest Statement.*

If the applicant is eligible to claim exception 3, the applicant must submit documentation showing evidence of a home mortgage loan. Evidence would include a copy of the contract or sale or similar documentation.

Exception 4: Third Party Withholding Dispositions by a Foreign Person of United States Real ***Property***

This exception may apply if the individual is a party to a disposition of a U.S. real property interest by a foreign person, which is generally subject to withholding by the transferee or buyer (withholding agent). If the applicant uses this exception with their information return, one of the following may be included:

- Form 8288, *U.S. Withholding Tax Return Dispositions by Foreign Persons of U.S. Real Property Interests.*
- Form 8288-A, *Statement of Withholding on Dispositions by Foreign Persons of U.S. Real Property Interests.*
- Form 8288-B and a copy of the contract of the sale, *Application for Withholding Certificate for Dispositions by Foreign Persons of U.S. Real Property Interests.*

For the seller of the property, copies of Forms 8288 and 8288-A submitted by the buyer should be attached to Form W-7.

Exception 5: Reporting Obligations under Treasury Decision 9363(T. D. 9363)

This exception may apply if the taxpayer has an IRS reporting requirement under TD-9363 and is submitting Form W-7 with Form 13350.

If the applicant is eligible for this exception, Form 13350 should be submitted with the W-7 application, along with a letter from their employer on corporate letterhead stating they have been designated as the person responsible for ensuring compliance with IRS information reporting requirements.

Aliens

Determining if a taxpayer is a resident, nonresident, or dual-status alien dictates whether and how the taxpayer must file a return.

Resident Alien

The taxpayer is a resident alien of the United States for tax purposes if he/she meets either the "green card test" or the "substantial presence test" for the current calendar tax year. If the taxpayer has been a resident for the entire year, he/she must file a tax return following the same rules that apply to a U.S. citizen. See Publication 519.

Nonresident alien

A nonresident alien is one who has not passed the green card test or the substantial presence test. Tax forms are different for the nonresident alien. For example, there are only 3 options for filing status on Form 1040NR: Single, Married Filing Separately, and Qualifying Widow(er).

Dual-status Alien

Aliens who make a change from nonresident alien to resident alien or from resident alien to nonresident alien are considered a dual-status alien. Different rules apply for each part of the year the taxpayer is a nonresident or a resident alien.

Publication 519 will help in determining the taxpayer's alien status. This topic is not covered in depth in this textbook.

Tax Return Compliance

The IRS is enhancing compliance activities relating to certain credits, including the child tax credit. The changes will improve the ability of the IRS to review returns claiming this credit, including those returns utilizing ITINs for dependents. For example, additional residency information will be required on Schedule 8812, Child Tax Credit, to ensure eligibility criteria for the credit is met.

Information derived from the ITIN process will be better utilized in the refund verification process. New pre-refund screening filters were put in place to flag returns for audits that claim questionable refundable credits. Increased compliance resources will also be deployed to address questionable returns in this area. As part of these overall efforts, ITIN holders may be asked to revalidate their ITIN status as part of certain audits to help ensure the numbers are used appropriately.

Expiration of ITINs

An ITIN only needs to be renewed if it has expired and is needed on a U.S. federal tax return. If an ITIN has not been used on a tax return for 2018, 2019, and 2020, then the ITIN expired December 31, 2021. The following middle digits (the fourth and fifth positions) have expired if they were assigned prior to 2013:

- 90, 91, 92, 94, 95, 96, 97, 98, or 99.

If these digits have not been renewed, they have expired as well:

- 70, 71, 72, 73, 74, 75, 76, 77, 78, 79, 80, 81, 82, 83, 84, 85, 86, 87, or 88

The uniform policy applies to any ITIN, regardless of when it was issued. Only about a quarter of the 21 million ITINs issued since the program began in 1996 are being used on tax returns. The new policy will ensure that anyone who legitimately uses an ITIN for tax purposes can continue to do so, while at the same time resulting in the likely eventual expiration of millions of unused ITINs.

Part 4 Review Questions

To obtain the maximum benefit from this chapter, LTP recommends that you complete each of the following questions, and then compare them to the answers with feedback that immediately follow. Under governing self-study standards, vendors are required to present review questions intermittently throughout each self-study course.

These questions and explanations are not part of the final examination and will not be graded by LTP.

CTIP4.1
Which of the required supporting documents for ITIN applications is generally a standalone document?

   a. Passport
   b. U.S. Citizenship and Immigration Services (USCIS) photo identification
   c. National identification card
   d. Foreign driver's license
   e. Foreign voter's registration card

CTIP4.2
Which of the following is not a common error found when processing an application for an ITIN?

   a. Name does not match the name on the tax return
   b. Date of entry is not entered
   c. Passport is not signed
   d. W-2s match the name on the application

CTIP4.3
Which of the following is not a common error on Form W-7?

   a. Name mismatch
   b. No date of entry
   c. Unsigned passports
   d. Incomplete acceptance agent information

CTIP4.4
Preparers must determine how a taxpayer must file his/her file a tax return based on which of the following?

   a. If taxpayer is a resident alien
   b. If taxpayer is a nonresident alien
   c. If taxpayer is a dual-status alien
   d. All the options are correct

CTIP4.5
The taxpayer is a resident alien of the United States for tax purposes if he/she meets which of the following tests?

   1. The "green card" test
   2. The "Quarterly Test"
   3. The "substantial presence test"

   a. 1 Only
   b. 2 & 3 Only
   c. 3 Only
   d. 1 & 3

Part 4 Review Questions Answers

CTIP4.1
Which of the required supporting documents for ITIN applications is a standalone document?

   a. **Passport**
   b. U.S. Citizenship and Immigration Services (USCIS) photo identification
   c. National identification card
   d. Foreign driver's license
   e. Foreign voter's registration card

Feedback: Review section *Documentation needed*.

CTIP4.2
Which of the following is not a common error found when processing an application for an ITIN?

   a. Name does not match the name on the tax return
   b. Date of entry is not entered
   c. Passport is not signed
   d. **W-2s match the name on the application**

Feedback: Review section *Common Errors on Form W-7*.

CTIP4.3
Which of the following is not a common error on Form W-7?

   a. Name mismatch
   b. No date of entry
   c. Unsigned passports
   d. **Incomplete acceptance agent information**

Feedback: Review section *Common Errors on Form W-7*.

CTIP4.4

Preparers must determine how a taxpayer must file his/her tax return based on which of the following?

   a. If taxpayer is a resident alien
   b. If taxpayer is a nonresident alien
   c. If taxpayer is a dual-status alien
   d. All the options are correct

Feedback: Review section *Aliens*.

CTIP4.5

The taxpayer is a resident alien of the United States for tax purposes if he/she meets which of the following tests?

   1. The "green card" test
   2. The "Quarterly Test"
   3. The "substantial presence test"

   a. 1 Only
   b. 2 & 3 Only
   c. 3 Only
   d. 1 & 3

Feedback: Review section *Aliens*.

Takeaways

Knowing tax law and gathering the necessary information to satisfy the due diligence knowledge requirement is just the beginning of becoming a great tax preparer. What truly marks a successful career is applying this knowledge correctly to a tax return; this is the paramount responsibility of a tax professional.

Knowing the tax law and how to apply each law to each individual situation is the puzzle that the tax professional must solve for the rest of their career. Every situation is different, and the tax professional must learn how to put the pieces of the puzzle together to prepare an accurate tax return.

TEST YOUR KNOWLEDGE!
Go online to take a practice quiz.

Chapter 3 Filing Status, Dependents, and Deductions

Introduction

The Tax Cuts and Jobs Act (TCJA) of 2017 impact several areas of the tax law until 2025. This chapter describes how TCJA and recent changes have impacted the federal filing statuses, qualifying dependents, and the standard deduction. Filing status is determined on the last day of the year. This chapter will discuss the requirements to determine when a dependent is considered a qualifying dependent, who can claim the qualifying dependent, and how the IRS uses tie breaker rules for individuals who qualify as a dependent for multiple taxpayers. The IRS has created an interactive tax assistant (ITA) to answer questions that can help you select the best course of action. Make sure to answer all the questions correctly. A tax professional must be aware of the consequences of determining dependents incorrectly—practice due diligence in all tax matters. Verifying the correct filing status and the qualifying dependents will determine the taxpayer's standard deduction.

Objectives

At the end of this chapter, the student will:

- Recognize how to determine the standard deduction.
- Understand who qualifies for the higher standard deduction.
- Explain the qualifying child test requirements.
- Identify the difference between a qualifying child and a qualifying relative.
- Describe the difference between custodial and noncustodial parents.
- List the five filing statuses.
- Recall the requirements for each filing status.
- Identify types of income to determine support.
- Recognize the requirements to claim a qualifying dependent.

Resources

Form 1040	Publication 17	Instructions Form 1040
Form 2120	Publication 501	Instructions Form 2120
Form 8332	Publication 555	Instructions Form 8332
	Tax Topic 352, 851, 857, 858	

Table of Contents

Introduction	94
Part 1 Filing Status	96
Single (S)	96
Married Filing Jointly (MFJ)	97
Community Property and Income	97
Married Filing Separately (MFS)	99
Head of Household (HOH)	100
Qualifying Widow(er) (QW) with Dependent Child	101
Determining the Correct Federal Filing Status	102
Exemptions and Suspensions	106
Rules for Dependent Exemptions	106
Part 1 Review Questions	107
Part 1 Review Questions Answers	107
Part 2 Member of Household or Relationship Test	108
Relatives Who Do Not Have to Live with the Taxpayer to be Considered a Member of Household or Relationship Test	108
Adopted Child	108
Joint Return	108
Temporary Absence	108
Death or Birth	109
Local Law Violated	109
Cousin	109
Gross Income Test	109
Qualifying Relative Support Test	110
Armed Forces Dependency Allotments	110
Tax-Exempt Income	110
Social Security Benefits for Determining Support	111
Support Provided by the State (Welfare, Food Stamps, Housing, and others)	111
Total Support	114
Multiple Support Agreement (Form 2120)	114
Deceased Taxpayers	115
Allowances for a Surviving Spouse	115
Inherited Property	115
Income in Respect of the Decedent	115
Deductions in Respect of the Decedent	115
Part 2 Review Questions	115
Part 2 Review Question Answers	117
Part 3 Dependent Filing Requirements	118
Dependent Exemptions	118
Dependency Rules	118
Qualifying Child	121
Residency Test	122
Part 3 Review Questions	126
Part 3 Review Questions Answers	127
Part 4 Deductions	129
Standard Deductions	129
Standard Deduction for Most People	130
Standard Deduction for Age 65 and Older or Blind	130
Standard Deduction for Dependents	132
Part 4 Review Questions	133
Part 4 Review Questions Answers	134
Takeaways	135

Filing Status, Dependents, and Deductions

Part 1 Filing Status

At first glance filing status appears to be simple to determine; however, tax professionals must know, understand, and apply the requirements for each filing status. By choosing the correct filing status, this determines the filing requirements, deductions, correct tax, and taxpayer eligibility for certain credits and deductions. See Publication 17 and Publication 501.

The five federal filing statuses are:

1. Single (S)
2. Married filing jointly (MFJ)
3. Married filing separately (MFS)
4. Head of household (HOH)
5. Qualifying widow(er) (QW) with a dependent child

State law governs whether a taxpayer is married or legally separated under a divorce or separate maintenance decree when it comes to filing status. A taxpayer is generally considered unmarried for the whole year if, on the last day of the current tax year, the taxpayer is unmarried or legally separated from his/her spouse under a divorce or separate maintenance decree.

Revenue Ruling 2013-17 applies to same-sex couples who live in a state that recognize same-sex marriage. The revenue ruling does not apply for couples who are registered domestic partners (RDPs) and have not been married in a state recognizing same-sex marriage.

Under the ruling, same-sex couples will be treated as married for all federal tax purposes, including income, gifts, and estate taxes. The ruling applies to all federal tax provisions where marriage is a factor, including filing status, claiming a person and dependency exemptions, taking the standard deduction, employee benefits, contributing to an IRA, and claiming the earned income tax credit or child tax credit.

Single (S)

File as Single (S) if by December 31st, the taxpayer:

- is unmarried on the last day of the year,
- is legally separated by divorce or separate maintenance decree, or
- does not qualify for another filing status.

A taxpayer files as Single if, on the last day of the current tax year, the taxpayer is unmarried or legally separated from their spouse under a divorce or separate maintenance decree. Divorced taxpayers are unmarried the entire year if the divorce was finalized on, by, or before the last day of the year they are filing. If the divorce was strictly for tax purposes and the taxpayers remarry the following year, the couple will need to file a joint return for both tax years. State law governs whether a taxpayer is married or legally separated under a divorce or separate maintenance decree. The tax professional needs to know the individual state laws in which one works and prepares taxes.

The taxpayer and the spouse are unmarried, even if they file a joint tax return; when they annulled their marriage (a legal action that means the marriage never existed in the eyes of the law). In that case, the taxpayers would need to file an amended return as Single or Head of Household for all years affected.

A widow(er) may file Single if they were widowed before January 1st of the current tax year and did not remarry before the end of the same tax year. However, the taxpayer may qualify for a different filing status that might lower the tax liability further.

Married Filing Jointly (MFJ)

The taxpayer must file Married Filing Jointly (MFJ) if he or she meets any of the following criteria on December 31st of the tax year being filed:

- Taxpayers are married and filing a joint return even if one had no income or deductions.
- Taxpayers are living together in a common-law marriage that is recognized in the state where the taxpayers now live, or in the state where the common-law marriage began.
- Taxpayers are married and living apart but are not legally separated under a decree of divorce or separate maintenance.
- A spouse died during the tax year, and the taxpayer did not remarry before the end of the tax year.
- If a spouse died during the current tax year, and the taxpayer remarried before the end of the tax year, the taxpayer and his or her new spouse may file MFJ. A tax return must still be filed for the deceased spouse, and, in this instance, the decedents' filing status would be MFS for the tax year.

Revenue Ruling 2013-17 states that same-sex couples will be treated as married for all federal purposes, including income, gift, and estate taxes. The ruling applies to all federal tax provisions where marriage is a factor, including filing status, claiming a person as a dependent, dependency exemptions, taking the standard deduction, employee benefits, contributing to an IRA, and claiming the earned income tax credit (EITC) or child tax credit (CTC).

Community Property and Income

Community property states treat property acquired by a husband and wife after marriage as owned by them "in community." In other words, if a wife purchases property under her name before she is married, it is hers alone. If she purchases it after her marriage, then it is regarded as the property of both herself and her spouse, even if the property is only under her name.

The community property states (Arizona, California, Idaho, Louisiana, Nevada, New Mexico, Texas, Washington, and Wisconsin) handle community property tax liability differently. When preparing state taxes for a community property state the tax professional should research before preparing the tax return to ensure a complete understanding of the differences. Alaska is an equitable property state, and it allows couples to choose community property rules, a community property agreement, or community trust. Wisconsin divorce laws contain a presumption that all marital property must be equally divided between the divorcing spouses.

There are also exceptions to community property rules that the tax preparer must know. For example, property acquired before marriage or inherited by one spouse during the marriage is considered a separate property of that spouse. In Arizona, California, Nevada, New Mexico, Washington, and Wisconsin, any income from these separate properties is also considered separate income for that spouse. Therefore, if the spouses are filing separately, the income is not shared and reported on the owner's return. This is known as the "California Rule." Conversely, in Idaho, Louisiana, and Texas, income from separate properties is still considered community income; thus, if the spouses file separately, the income would be shared income on their tax returns. This is known as the "Texas Rule."

According to §66 of the Internal Revenue Code (IRC), when spouses are living apart, the spouse who earned the income will keep it. Living apart entails the following:

> They are married to each other.
> They lived apart for an entire tax year.
> They did not file a joint return.
> One or both have earned income, none of which is transferred between them.

Individuals who meet all the above requirements must follow the rules below to cover the reporting of income on their separate returns:

> Earned income (other than trade, business, or partnership income) is treated as income of the spouse who rendered the personal services.
> Trade or business income is treated as the taxpayer's income unless the spouse substantially exercises control and management of the entire business.
> Community income derived from the separate property owned by one spouse is treated as the income of the owner.

All other community income is taxed in accordance with the applicable community property laws. See Code §897(a).

Innocent Spouse

Married taxpayers often choose to file a joint tax return due to the filing status's benefits. However, both taxpayers are jointly and individually responsible for any tax, interest, or penalty due on a joint tax return. Even after a couple is separated or divorces, a former spouse could be held responsible for amounts due on previously filed joint returns.

In this instance, the taxpayer might be able to claim that they are an "innocent spouse": an individual who was not aware of a position claimed on a tax return by their other half that resulted in liability for understatement of income filed on the joint return. In this situation, the innocent spouse can file for relief using Form 8857 to try to prove that they were not aware of the position on the return. The IRS will review the request for relief, come to a decision, and respond with their ruling. The taxpayer may appeal the decision if they find the ruling unacceptable.

To be eligible for the relief, the taxpayer must meet the following criteria:

> Must have filed a joint return with an erroneous understatement of tax responsibility relating directly to their spouse.
> Must have no knowledge of the error.
> The IRS identified the error and must agree that it is fair to relieve the taxpayer of the tax penalties.
> The taxpayer must apply for relief within two years of the IRS initial collections notice.

Example: Robert and Debbie were married and filed joint tax returns for 2019 and 2020. Debbie, who didn't know much about taxes, usually let her husband handle the finances. She simply signed the tax return when Robert told her to, never questioning the man she thought she could implicitly trust. However, after finalizing their divorce on May 15, 2022, Debbie received a letter demanding penalties and interest from the IRS. Alarmed, Debbie found a tax preparer who helped her discover that her ex-husband Robert had illegally claimed business expenses on their personal 2018 and 2019 tax returns, causing significant penalties and interest to accrue for filing a fraudulent return. Based on her lack of knowledge, the tax preparer correctly advised her to file Form 8857 to apply for relief on the 2019 and 2020 tax returns.

Spousal Abandonment

"Spousal abandonment" and "innocent spouse" are two different tax implications. Spousal abandonment occurs when the abandoning spouse has left their family with no intention of returning or having responsibility for their family. In a legal context, failing to provide for a dependent, ailing spouse, or a minor child could be considered criminal spousal abandonment. Separation with no intent of reconciling is not spousal abandonment. Spousal abandonment often requires the abandoned spouse to file a separate return and receive all the unfavorable tax consequences that come with it. For example, the taxpayer must use the Tax Rate Schedule for married taxpayers filing separately. To mitigate such harsh treatment, Congress enacted provisions commonly referred to as the "abandoned spouse rules" which allow married taxpayers to file as Head of Household to bypass the tax consequences of married filing separate.

Señor 1040 Says: Remember, assistance given by TANF to pay for rent must be included in the total cost of keeping up a home.

Married Filing Separately (MFS)

Married taxpayers, whether living together or apart, may choose to file Married Filing Separately (MFS) if any of the following apply if:

- They want to be responsible for their own tax liability.
- It results in less tax than they would owe on a joint return. Advise taxpayers who consider MFS that this filing status has limitations in deductions, adjustments, and credits.

Taxpayers who elect to file MFS must enter their spouse's full name and Social Security number or ITIN in the spaces provided and are also generally subject to the following special rules:

- Tax rates are generally higher.
- Must have lived apart the entire year to claim credit for the elderly or disabled.
- Unable to take certain credits.
- Capital loss deduction limited to $1,500.
- Must itemize deductions if spouse itemizes deductions.
- Individual retirement account (IRA) contributions are limited due to income amount.

Filing Status, Dependents, and Deductions

> ➤ The interest can't be excluded from qualified U.S. savings bonds for higher education expenses.
> ➤ Child tax credit and retirement savings account may be reduced at income levels.
> ➤ May be required to include more Social Security or railroad retirement benefits in taxable income (unless the couple lived apart the entire year).
> ➤ Generally, they cannot take credit for childcare or dependent care expenses.

If the taxpayers live in a community property state and files a separate return, the laws of the state in which the taxpayer reside governs whether they have community property income or separate property income for federal tax purposes. See Publication 555 for more information.

Head of Household (HOH)

The taxpayer must file Head of Household (HOH) if they meet any of the following criteria on December 31st of the tax year being filed:

> ➤ The taxpayer must be considered unmarried on the last day of the year.
> ➤ A qualifying child or relative lived in the home for more than half the year (there are exceptions for temporary absences). Children of divorced or separated parents, or parents who lived apart, can be claimed based on the residency test in most cases.
> ➤ The taxpayer paid for more than half the cost of keeping up the home for the tax year.

Keeping Up a Home

To qualify for the HOH filing status, a taxpayer must pay more than half of the cost for maintaining a household. Expenses can include rent, mortgage interest payments, repairs, real estate taxes, insurance, utilities, and food eaten in the house. Costs do not include clothing, education, medical treatment, vacations, life insurance, and the rental value of the home the taxpayer owns. (Keeping up a house and monetary support will be discussed later in this chapter).

Suppose the taxpayer receives payments from Temporary Assistance for Needy Families (TANF) or other public assistance programs to pay rent or upkeep on the home. In that case, those payments cannot be included as money the taxpayer paid. However, they must be included in the total cost of keeping up the home to figure whether the taxpayer paid over half of the cost.

Differences Between Filing Head of Household and Single

The difference between filing S and filing HOH is whether the unmarried taxpayer keeps up a home for a Qualifying Person. To qualify to register as Head of Household, there must first be a household to be the head of, and for there to be a household, there must first be a group of individuals that live together and are of qualifying relation to be considered a family unit. If these specifications do not apply to the taxpayer's living situation, the taxpayer must file Single.

A taxpayer would file Single rather than Head of Household in the following situations:

> ➤ The taxpayer lives alone. Although he is technically the head person in his home because he is the only person who lives there, there is no household to be the head of, and he thus must file Single.

- ➤ The taxpayer lives within a household but does not qualify to be its head. Whether it's because he doesn't provide a sufficient percentage of support or for another reason, although he is in a household, he is not its head and thus would file Single.
- ➤ If a taxpayer has a qualifying dependent but lives within a household without qualifying as Head of Household, they will file Single with a Dependent instead of Head of Household.

Example 1: Tyler lives alone in a suburban house, and no one else lives with him. He files Single because even though he is the "head" of his house, no household or group of individuals that live together of qualifying relation to be considered a family unit.

Example 2: Joseph and four of his friends live in a house they rent together and split all the living costs evenly amongst themselves. Assuming none of them are married or in a registered domestic partnership, they will all file Single since none provide more than 50% of support for the house to qualify as a Head of Household. The group does not possess sufficient qualifying relationships to be considered a family unit and cannot be considered a household; therefore, there is neither a head of household nor a household. All taxpayers must file Single.

Example 3: Barry and his son Don live with Barry's parents, Henry and Nora, who make $350,000 annually. Barry makes $27,840 a year as a part-time educational aide; he does not provide more than 50% percent of support for the household; yet does provide more than 50% of support for his son Don. Barry must file Single with a Dependent for the following reasons:

- ➤ He is a household member but is not its head because he provides too little support; thus, he would not file as Head of Household.
- ➤ He is unmarried and not in a registered domestic partnership; thus, he would file Single even with a dependent.
- ➤ Don is Barry's qualifying dependent because Don is Barry's child, and Barry provides more than 50% of Don's support; thus, he would file Single with a dependent.

Qualifying Widow(er) (QW) with Dependent Child

The taxpayer can file as a Qualifying Widow(er) (QW) with Dependent Child if they meet any of the following criteria on December 31st of the tax year being filed:

- ➤ The taxpayer was entitled to file a joint return with their spouse for the tax year in which the spouse died (whether the taxpayer filed a joint return or not).
- ➤ The taxpayer did not remarry before the end of the tax year.
- ➤ The taxpayer has a dependent child who qualifies as their dependent for the tax year.
- ➤ The taxpayer paid more than half the cost of keeping up a home that was the main home for the taxpayer and the dependent child for the entire year.

For the tax year in which the spouse died, the taxpayer can file MFJ or QW. If the taxpayer still meets the requirements, the taxpayer can choose to file as QW with a dependent child for the next two years. If the taxpayer has not remarried and still has a qualifying dependent child living with them after two years, the taxpayer's filing status would change to HOH.

Filing Status, Dependents, and Deductions

Example: John's wife died in 2020, and John has not remarried and has continued to keep up a home with his qualifying children, Riley and Galvan. For tax year 2020, John filed MFJ. In 2021 and 2022, he would qualify to file as QW if Riley and Galvan are still qualifying dependents. Starting in tax year 2023, however, if John still has qualifying children and has not remarried, he would not be able to file as a QW with dependent children and would instead qualify to file as HOH.

Determining the Correct Federal Filing Status

The following scenarios are based on the information you have been studying so far. Determine the best answer for each question.

1. James, age 19, works full time, and his W-2 shows $17,000 in box 1. He claims that his 14-year-old sister lived with him all year long. He tells you that his mother and brother have lived in the same household all year long. His mother's income is $32,000. James wants to claim his sister as his dependent. Which scenario best describes James' filing status based on the information provided?

    a. James will file Single and claim his sister as a dependent.
    b. James will file Single with no dependents.
    c. James will file Head of Household and claim his sister as a dependent.
    d. James does not have to file a tax return because his mother will claim him as a dependent.

Feedback: James cannot claim his sister since his mother lives in the same home, and she has the higher income. James is not a dependent on his mother's return since his income is $17,000. James will file Single with no dependents.

2. Linda, age 56, works full time and her W-2 shows $27,000 in box 1. She tells you that her 22-year-old daughter, Julie, was a full-time student until she graduated in June. Julie lived with her until November when she got married to Todd. Linda wants to claim Julie as her dependent. Linda tells you that Julie and Todd filed a joint return to receive their federal withholding, and their total income was less than $6,000. Which scenario best describes Linda's filing status based on the information provided?

    a. Linda will file Head of Household without Julie as her dependent.
    b. Linda will file Head of Household and claim Julie as her dependent.
    c. Linda will file Single with no dependents.
    d. Linda will file Single with Julie as her dependent.

Feedback: Linda can claim Julie as her dependent since Julie meets the residency requirements, the relationship requirements, and the joint return test. Therefore, Linda's filing status would be Head of Household, and Linda will file Head of Household and claim Julie as her dependent.

3. Javier, age 45, and Janice, age 42, support Javier's uncle, Chris, who does not live with them. Javier gives Chris $500 per month for support. Which of the following questions must you ask Javier to determine if Chris is their dependent?

    1. How much and what kind of income did Chris receive?
    2. Can any other taxpayer claim Chris as a dependent?

3. Do you have documentation that shows your support?
4. Does Chris have any dependents?

   a. All the questions must be asked
   b. 3 and 4
   c. 1 and 2
   d. 1, 2, and 3

Feedback: To make sure the taxpayer can claim a relative as a dependent, the tax professional must ask specific questions to determine if the relative is a Qualifying Relative. All the questions need to be asked. The following Qualifying Relative Checklist who does not live with the taxpayer will help determine additional questions to ask and determine a member of the household test:

➤ Your child, stepchild, foster child, or a descendant of any of them (for example, your grandchild). (A legally adopted child is considered your child.)
➤ Your brother, sister, half-brother, half-sister, stepbrother, or stepsister.
➤ Your father, mother, grandparent, or other direct ancestors, but not foster parent.
➤ Your stepfather or stepmother.
➤ A son or daughter of your brother or sister.
➤ A son or daughter of your half-brother or half-sister.
➤ A brother or sister of your father or mother.
➤ Your son-in-law, daughter-in-law, father-in-law, mother-in-law, brother-in-law, or sister-in-law.
➤ Any of these relationships that were established by marriage aren't ended by death or divorce.

4. Jonathan, age 37, wants to claim his mother as a dependent on his tax return. His mother receives Social Security benefits of $22,000. Jonathan's W-2 box 1 shows $22,000. Based on the information provided, which scenario best describes Jonathan's filing status?

   a. Jonathan will file Single and claim his mother as a dependent.
   b. Jonathan will file Single with no dependents.
   c. Jonathan will file Head of Household and claim his mother as a dependent.
   d. Jonathan does not have to file a tax return because his mother will claim him as a dependent.

Feedback: Jonathan cannot claim his mother since he did not provide more than 50% of her support due to his mother's Social Security benefits. Jonathan will file Single with no dependents.

5. Mia, age 28, has a son Bobby, age 6. They have lived all year with Mia's mother. Mia has a full-time job and is a full-time student. Box 1 of her W-2 shows $19,000. Mia's mother, Billie, wants to claim Bobby as her dependent. Billie's W-2 has $12,000 in box 1. Mia provides all the support for Bobby. Which scenario best describes Mia's filing status based on the information provided?

   a. Mia will file Single with no dependent.
   b. Billie will file Head of Household and claim Bobby.
   c. Mia will file Head of Household and claim Bobby as her dependent.
   d. Billie will file Head of Household and claim Mia and Bobby as her dependents, since they live with her.

Filing Status, Dependents, and Deductions

Feedback: Billie is unable to claim either Mia or Bobby since Mia makes more than Billie does. Mia can file Head of Household since she provides 100% of Bobby's support. Billie is not able to claim Mia or Bobby since she made less income than Mia. Mia will file Head of Household and claim Bobby as her dependent.

6. Esperanza, age 19, is a full-time student and has a part-time job. Esperanza and her daughter Elissa, age 3, live with Esperanza's parents. Her W-2 box 1 shows $4,000 in income. Esperanza's parents' combined income is $75,000. Both Esperanza and Elissa are on her parents' medical insurance. Which scenario best describes Esperanza's filing status based on the information provided?

   a. Esperanza will file Single with no dependent.
   b. Esperanza will file Single, as a dependent, on another return, with no dependent.
   c. Esperanza will file Head of Household and claim Elissa as a dependent.
   d. Esperanza will file Single and claim Elissa as a dependent.

Feedback: Esperanza and Elissa are both dependents on Esperanza's parents' tax return because her parents provided the majority of support for both Esperanza and her daughter. Because Esperanza only earned $4,000 on her W-2, which is below what is required, she will only file a tax return to receive her federal tax withholding back (if applicable). Esperanza will file Single, as a dependent, on another return with no dependent.

7. Colton and Brittney are legally married. They have a separation agreement and have been living apart since November 2020. They filed a joint return for 2020. Brittney's earned income is $46,000 and her daughter Mika lives 100% of the time with her. Colton's earned income is $31,000. Colton wants to claim Mika as his dependent for the tax year 2022. Based on the information provided, which scenario best describes what must happen for Colton to be able to claim Mika?

   a. Colton can file Head of Household and claim Mika since she is his daughter.
   b. Colton must have Brittney sign Form 8332 to be able to claim Mika.
   c. Mika can choose which parent she wants to claim her.
   d. Brittney will file Head of Household and claim Mika since her income is higher than Colton's, and Mika has lived with her 100% of the time.

Feedback: Colton will not be able to claim Mika unless Brittney signs Form 8332. Mika has lived with Brittney 100% of the time, and Brittney's earned income is more than Colton's. Tie-breaker rules could also help determine filing status and who can claim Mika. Colton must have Brittney sign Form 8332 to be able to claim Mika. Apply the following rules to determine which person can claim the child as a qualifying child:

> - If the parents file jointly, both will claim the child as a qualifying child.
> - If only one taxpayer is the child's parent, the child is the qualifying child of the parent.
> - If the parents do not file a joint return, the IRS will treat the child as a qualifying child of the parent whom the child lived with for the longest time during the year. Children who live with each parent an equal amount of time are qualifying children for both parents. The IRS then treats them as qualifying children of the parent with the highest AGI for the year.
> - If no parent can claim the child as a qualifying child, the child is the qualifying child of the person with the highest AGI for the year.

> If a parent can claim the child as a qualifying child and no parent claims the child, the child is the qualifying child of the person with the highest AGI for the year.

8. Pedro and Celeste are legally married and have two children. Celeste does not want to pay Pedro's back taxes and self-employment tax. Pedro has his own business. Celeste owned the house before their marriage (they do not live in a community property state). Celeste's W-2 box 1 shows $150,000. Pedro's gross income from his Schedule C is $15,000. Which scenario best describes Pedro and Celeste's filing status based on the information provided?

   a. Pedro should file as Head of Household with the two children, and Celeste should file Single.
   b. Celeste should file as Head of Household with the two children, and Pedro should file Single.
   c. Pedro and Celeste should file Married Filing Separately and then decide who claims the children and the deductions.
   d. Pedro and Celeste don't have to file a tax return since they can't decide how to file.

Feedback: A married taxpayer may choose MFS if any of the following applies:

> If they are married, living together, or apart.
> If they want to be responsible for their tax liability.
> If it results in less tax than they would owe on a joint return; however, let taxpayers know that MFS filing status has severe limitations in deductions, adjustments, and credits.

Pedro and Celeste should file Married Filing Separately and then decide who claims the children and the deductions.

9. Peter, age 21, and his son Paul lived with his parents the entire year. His W-2 box 1 shows $4,050. Peter is a full-time student. Peter would like to file on his own and claim his son, Paul. Peter and his son are both on his parents' medical insurance. His parents, Roberto and Melissa, have a combined income of $175,000. Which scenario best describes Peter's filing status based on the information provided?

   a. Peter will file Single and be a dependent on his parents' return.
   b. Peter will file Single and be a dependent on another return and claim Paul as a dependent.
   c. Roberto and Melissa will file Married Filing Joint and claim Peter and Paul as dependents.
   d. Peter will file Single on his return and declare he is a dependent on another return, and Roberto and Melissa will file Married Filing Joint and claim Peter and Paul as their dependents.

Feedback: The taxpayer should pay more than half of the cost of keeping up a home for the year, but Peter has not provided more than 50% for his and his son's support, which means he cannot claim Paul as his dependent. Peter will file Single on his return and declare he is a dependent on another return, and Roberto and Melissa will file Married Filing Joint and claim Peter and Paul as their dependents.

Filing Status, Dependents, and Deductions

10. Fernando and Tabitha are legally married (Tabitha has an ITIN) with three children with SSNs. Tabitha is a stay-at-home mom, and Fernando's W-2 box 1 shows $29,000. Fernando and his family live with his brother Charles. Which scenario best describes Fernando and Tabitha's filing status based on the information provided?

    a. Fernando and Tabitha will file Married Filing Jointly and claim all three children as dependents.
    b. Fernando will file as Head of Household and claim Tabitha and his three children as dependents.
    c. Fernando will file single and let Charles claim the others as dependent.
    d. Charles will claim Fernando and his family as dependents since they all live with him.

Feedback: Even though Tabitha has an ITIN, this does not eliminate her from the tax return. Fernando and Tabitha are legally married, and Fernando and Tabitha are not dependents on Charles' tax return just because the family lives there. Similarly, since neither Fernando and Tabitha nor Charles provide more than 50% of support for each other, neither would claim the other as a dependent. Fernando and Tabitha will file Married Filing Jointly and claim all their children as dependents.

Exemptions and Suspensions

The Tax Cuts and Jobs Act in 2017 suspended the personal exemption for tax years **2018 to 2025**. Though there may not be a filing requirement for the federal portion of a return currently, a taxpayer might still have a filing requirement for the state and, in the future, potentially for the federal return as well.

Similar to a deduction, a personal exemption reduces the amount of income used to compute tax liability. Unlike tax deductions, an exemption is simply a set amount of reduction given on the return. The taxpayer can generally claim an exemption for himself, his or her spouse, and any qualifying dependents. The total amount of reduction provided from any personal exemptions before the tax year 2017 goes on Form 1040, line 42, and Form 1040A, line 26. Form 1040EZ, line 5, is the sum of the total standard deduction amount added to the personal exemption amount.

Rules for Dependent Exemptions

- The taxpayer cannot claim any dependents if they file a joint return or if they could be claimed as a dependent by another taxpayer.
- The taxpayer cannot claim a married person who files a joint return as a dependent unless the joint return is only a claim for a refund, and there would be no tax liability for either spouse on separate returns.
- The taxpayer cannot claim a person as a dependent unless the individual is a U.S. citizen, a U.S. resident, a U.S. national, or a resident of Canada or Mexico for some part of the year; there are exceptions to this rule, but they are beyond the scope of this course.
- A taxpayer cannot claim a person as a dependent unless that person is their qualifying child or qualifying relative.

The taxpayer is allowed one exemption for each person claimed on the tax return. The taxpayer can claim an exemption for a dependent even if they file a tax return.

Part 1 Review Questions

To obtain the maximum benefit from this chapter, LTP recommends that you complete all questions and then compare them to the answers with feedback that immediately follow. Under governing self-study standards, vendors are required to present review questions intermittently throughout each self-study course.

These questions and explanations are not part of the final examination and will not be graded by LTP.

FSDDP1.1
On what date is the taxpayer's filing status determined?

   a. October 31
   b. December 31
   c. January 1
   d. April 15

FSDDP1.2
Which of the following is not a federal filing status?

   a. Single
   b. Married filing separately
   c. Head of household
   d. Married filing single

Part 1 Review Questions Answers

FSDDP1.1
On what date is the taxpayer's filing status determined?

   a. October 31
   b. December 31
   c. January 1
   d. April 15

Feedback: Review section *Filing Status*.

FSDDP1.2
Which of the following is not a federal filing status?

   a. Single
   b. Married filing separately
   c. Head of household
   d. Married filing single

Feedback: Review section *Filing Status*.

Part 2 Member of Household or Relationship Test

To meet this test, either of the following must be true:

- The person lived with the taxpayer all year as a member of the taxpayer's household.
- If the person did not live with the taxpayer all year, then they must be related to the taxpayer in one of the ways listed in the next section of the chapter.

If the person was the taxpayer's spouse at any time during the year, that person cannot be the taxpayer's qualifying relative.

Relatives Who Do Not Have to Live with the Taxpayer to be Considered a Member of Household or Relationship Test

A person related to the taxpayer in any of the following ways does not have to live with the taxpayer all year as a member of the taxpayer's household to meet this test:

- The taxpayer's child, stepchild, eligible foster child, or any descendant thereof (e.g., a grandchild).
- The taxpayer's brother, sister, half-brother, half-sister, stepbrother, or stepsister.
- The taxpayer's father, mother, grandparent, any other direct ancestor, or stepfather or stepmother, but **not** a foster parent.
- A son or daughter of the taxpayer's brother, sister, half-brother, or half-sister.
- A brother or sister of the taxpayer's father or mother.
- The taxpayer's son-in-law, daughter-in-law, father-in-law, mother-in-law, brother-in-law, or sister-in-law.

Any of these relationships that were established by marriage do not end by death or divorce.

Adopted Child

An adopted child is always treated as the taxpayer's own child. The term "adopted child" includes a child who was lawfully placed with the taxpayer for legal adoption.

Joint Return

If the taxpayer files a joint return, the qualifying relative does not have to be related to the spouse who provides support. For example, Sal and Julie are married, and Julie's uncle received more than half of his support from Sal. Julie's uncle could be Sal's qualifying relative, even though he does not live with Sal. However, if Sal and Julie file separate tax returns, Julie's uncle is a qualifying relative only if he lives with Sal all year as a member of Sal and Julie's household.

Temporary Absence

A qualifying relative is considered to have lived with the taxpayer as a member of the taxpayer's household during periods of time when either the taxpayer or spouse is absent due to specific circumstances such as:

- Illness
- Education

- Business
- Vacation
- Military service

Even if the person has been placed in a nursing home to receive medical care for an indefinite period, the absence can be considered temporary.

Death or Birth

A person who died during the year would meet the test if they lived with the taxpayer as a household member until their death. The same is true if a child was born and lived with the taxpayer during the year.

Local Law Violated

A person does not meet this test if the relationship between the taxpayer and that person violates local law at any time during the year.

Example: David's girlfriend Alicia lived with him as a member of his household all year. However, David's relationship with Alicia violated the state's laws where he lives because she was married to someone else. Therefore, Alicia does not meet the household member or the relationship test, and David cannot claim her as a dependent.

Cousin

A cousin is a descendant of a brother or a sister of the taxpayer's mother or father. If the cousin lives with the taxpayer all year as a member of the taxpayer's household, the cousin can meet the member of household relationship test.

Gross Income Test

To meet this test, a person's gross income must be less than $4,300. "Gross income" is any and all non-tax-exempt revenue that comes in the form of money, property, or services, including gross receipts (sales) from rental property, specific scholarships and fellowship grants, all taxable unemployment compensation, and a partner's share of the gross (not net) income from a partnership. Certain social security benefits that are tax-exempt income are not considered gross income (See Publication 501).

Disabled Dependent Working at a Sheltered Workshop

For the purposes of the gross income test, gross income does not include income received for services provided at a sheltered workshop by an individual who is permanently and totally disabled at any time during the year. Some conditions apply; the availability of medical care at the workshop must be the main reason for the individual's presence there, and the income must come solely from activities at the workshop that are incidental to medical care. A "sheltered workshop" is a school that does the following:

- Provides special instruction or training designated to alleviate the individual's disability.
- It is operated by specific tax-exempt organizations or by a state, U.S. possession, political subdivision of a state or possession of the U.S., or the District of Columbia.

Filing Status, Dependents, and Deductions

Qualifying Relative Support Test

The taxpayer determines whether they have provided more than half of a relative's total support by using the taxpayer's contribution to their support with the entire amount of support the person received from all sources. These amounts include any support the relative provided from their funds. A taxpayer's funds are not a means of support unless used exclusively for this purpose. See Worksheet 1 in Publication 501.

Example: Robin is retired and lives with her adult son, Ryan. She has received $2,400 in Social Security benefits and $300 in interest. Robin paid $2,000 for lodging and $400 for recreation, and has $300 in her savings account. Even though Robin received a total of $2,700, she only spent $2,400 for her support, and Ryan spent more than $2,400 for his mother's support and received no other help, so Ryan has provided more than half of Robin's support.

The individual total support includes tax-exempt income, savings, and borrowed amounts. These are examples of tax-exempt income: Certain social security benefits, welfare benefits, nontaxable life insurance proceeds, armed forces family allotments, nontaxable pensions, and tax-exempt interest.

Calculated yearly support when paid. The taxpayer cannot use support paid in 2020 for 2021, and a taxpayer's support is still calculated on a calendar year even if they use a fiscal-year accounting method.

Armed Forces Dependency Allotments

If the government contributes a certain amount of support and the taxpayer has a portion of their income taken out of their wages, the total amount is half of their support. If the taxpayer uses part of the income to support individuals other than the ones the taxpayer has previously claimed, those individuals could also qualify as dependents.

Example: Doug is in the Armed Forces. He authorizes an allotment to his widowed mother, Debbie, and she uses it to support herself and her brother, Doug's uncle. If the portion that Doug gives her is more than half of their support, Doug can claim Debbie and his uncle as dependents.

Military housing allowances that are tax-exempt are treated as dependency allotments when figuring the support test.

Tax-Exempt Income

Calculating a person's total support includes tax-exempt income, savings, and borrowed amounts used to support the qualifying relative. Though tax-exempt income consists of all the following, we are only emphasizing the first two, which are the most common:

- ➢ Certain social security benefits.
- ➢ Welfare benefits.
- ➢ Nontaxable life insurance proceeds.
- ➢ Armed forces family allotments.
- ➢ Nontaxable pensions.
- ➢ Tax-exempt interest.

Example: Danelle is Jose's brother's daughter (Jose's niece), and she lives with Jose. Danelle has taken out a student loan of $2,500 to pay her college tuition, and Jose has provided $2,000 for Danelle's support. Jose cannot claim an exemption for Danelle because, due to her loan, he has not provided more than half of her support.

Social Security Benefits for Determining Support

If a husband and wife each received benefits paid by one check made out to both, the total amount is divided equally between each spouse and counted as having provided support for each of them, unless they can show otherwise. If a child receives Social Security benefits and uses them toward his or her support, it is support provided by the child.

Support Provided by the State (Welfare, Food Stamps, Housing, and others)

Benefits provided by the state to a needy person are amounts provided by the state. However, payments based on the recipients' needs will not be used entirely for their support if they do not use part of the support payments.

Payments received for the support of a foster child from a child placement agency are considered support provided by the agency, not the foster parents. In the same way, payments received for the support of a foster child from a state or county agency are considered support provided by the state or county, not the foster parents.

The taxpayer must pay more than half of the cost of an individual's support to claim them as a qualifying relative. Expenses can include rent, mortgage interest payments, repairs, real estate taxes, utilities, insurance, and food eaten in the home. Costs do not include clothing, education, medical treatment, vacations, life insurance, or the rental value of the house the taxpayer owns.

Suppose the taxpayer receives payments from Temporary Assistance for Needy Families (TANF) or any other public assistance programs to help him or her pay rent or pay for upkeep on the home. In that case, those payments are not money the taxpayer paid. However, taxpayer must include the payments in the total cost of keeping up the home to figure who paid over half of the cost-of-living expenses.

Example: Tammy spent $700 of her own money and $300 of her TANF support to pay for the upkeep of the home she and her dependents live in the entire year. The $300 she received from TANF does not count as support from Tammy to any of her dependents, but it does count toward the total upkeep amount ($1,000) used to determine the head of household filing status and claimant strength.

Use the following blank worksheet to determine if the dependent is a qualifying relative of the taxpayer's household for the two upcoming examples. When interviewing clients and asking support questions, LTP sees that most clients give a monthly amount, so the tax preparer would need to clarify if the numbers given were monthly or annually. In the scenarios below, the calculated numbers are annual amounts.

Filing Status, Dependents, and Deductions

Example 1: Scenario

Mary Vega (age 37) and her daughter, Sierra (age 9), lived with Mary's aunt all year. Using the following information, determine if Mary paid more than half of her support. If the total amount paid by Mary is less than the amount paid by her aunt, Mary and her daughter are qualifying relatives of her aunt.

Expenses paid by Mary:		Expenses paid by Mary's aunt:	
Electric	$2,149	Mortgage interest	$3,202
Water	$480	Property taxes	$798
Repairs	$1,500	Food eaten in the house	$600
Food eaten in the house	$2,600	Property insurance	$280
Telephone	$576		

Cost of Keeping a Household

	Amount Paid by Taxpayer	Total Costs
Property taxes	$_____	$_____
Mortgage interest expense	$_____	$_____
Rent	$_____	$_____
Utility charges	$_____	$_____
Repairs/maintenance	$_____	$_____
Property insurance	$_____	$_____
Food consumed on the premises	$_____	$_____
Other household expenses	$_____	$_____
TOTALS	$_____	$_____
Subtract total amount taxpayer paid		(_____)
Amount others paid		$_____

Example 1: Answers

Cost of Keeping a Household

	Amount Paid by Taxpayer (Mary)	Total Costs
Property taxes	$_____	$798
Mortgage interest expense	$_____	$3,202
Rent	$_____	$_____
Utility charges	$3,205	$3,205
Repairs/maintenance	$1,500	$1,500
Property insurance	$_____	$280
Food consumed on the premises	$2,600	$3,200
Other household expenses	$_____	$_____
TOTALS	**$7,305**	**$12,185**
Minus total amount taxpayer paid		**($7,305)**
Amount others paid		**$4,880**

If the total amount paid by Mary is more than the amount paid by her aunt, Mary meets the requirement of paying more than half the cost of keeping up the home.

Mary paid more than 50% of her support; therefore, she would not be claimed as a qualifying relative on her aunt's tax return.

Filing Status, Dependents, and Deductions

Example 2: Scenario

Steven Renwick (age 27) and his cousin, Sasha Sweet (age 21), lived together all year. Use the following information to determine if Steven can claim Sasha as a dependent. Sasha receives $550 per month from TANF to help pay rent.

Expenses paid by Steven (taxpayer)		Expenses paid by Sasha	
Electric	$1,200	Rent	$6,600
Food eaten in the home	$6,100	Repairs	$661
Telephone	$800	Food eaten in the home	$965
Water	$325		
Renters insurance	$1,200		

Cost of Keeping a Household

	Amount Paid by Taxpayer	Total Costs
Property taxes	$_____	$_____
Mortgage interest expense	$_____	$_____
Rent	$_____	$_____
Utility charges	$_____	$_____
Repairs/maintenance	$_____	$_____
Property insurance	$_____	$_____
Food consumed on the premises	$_____	$_____
Other household expenses	$_____	$_____
TOTALS	$_____	$_____
Minus total amount taxpayer paid		(_____)
Amount others paid		$_____

Example 2: Answers

Cost of Keeping a Household

	Amount Paid by Taxpayer (Steven)	Total Costs
Property taxes	$_____	$_____
Mortgage interest expense	$_____	$_____
Rent	$_____	$6,600
Utility charges	$2,325	$2,325
Repairs/maintenance	$_____	$661
Property insurance	$_____	$_____
Food consumed on the premises	$6,100	$965
Other household expenses	$1,200	$_____
TOTALS	**$9,625**	**$10,551**
Minus total amount taxpayer paid		**($9,625)**
Amount others paid		**$926**

Steven paid more than 50% of Sasha's support; he can claim Sasha as a qualifying relative.

Filing Status, Dependents, and Deductions

Total Support

When calculating to determine total support for a qualifying relative, the following items are not included in the calculation:

> ➤ Federal, state, and local income taxes paid by the individual out of their personal income.
> ➤ Social Security and Medicare tax paid individually.
> ➤ Life insurance premiums.
> ➤ Funeral expenses.
> ➤ Scholarships received by the student's relative or child.
> ➤ Survivors' and Dependents' Educational Assistance payments are used for the support of the child.

Total support does include food, lodging, clothing, education, medical and dental care, recreation, transportation, and other daily provisions.

Multiple Support Agreement (Form 2120)

Generally, the taxpayer must provide more than half of a qualifying relative's total support during the calendar year. However, if two or more people provided support but any person provided more than half of the individual's full support, the taxpayers may be able to file Form 2120, *Multiple Support Agreement.* A multiple support agreement is a document signed by the various taxpayers providing support that states which of the individuals will claim the qualifying relative as a dependent. The agreement identifies the taxpayers who agreed not to claim the exemption and must be attached to the return of the taxpayer claiming the exemption.

Each member of such a group, including whichever individual claiming the exemption, must provide more than 10% of the support. To qualify for claiming the dependency exemption, the individual must also obtain the consent of the other members of the support group. The group does not have to file signed consents with the IRS; however, they must be kept with the taxpayer's records and be available as proof of eligibility to claim the person as a dependent.

Members of the group may decide who is entitled to the dependency exemption on a year-by-year basis. They do not have to allocate the exemption to the taxpayer providing the most support; however, the person claiming the exemption must provide a total of more than 10%. The members of the group must collectively contribute with more than 50%. Again, the group cannot claim someone as a collective; only one individual can claim the qualifying child or relative.

Example: Carlos, Lydia, Ernest, and Caroline provided full support for their mother, Emma. Carlos provided 45%, Lydia provided 35%, and Ernest and Caroline provided 10% each. Since Caroline and Ernest give only 10% of the support (not more than 10% as required), neither can claim an exemption for Emma, nor do they have to sign the statement. Only Lydia and Carlos qualify to claim an exemption for Emma. Whoever does not claim the exemption must sign Form 2120 or a similar statement agreeing not to take Emma as a qualifying relative.

Deceased Taxpayers

The general filing requirements that apply to other taxpayers also apply to a decedent (someone who has died). Write the word "Deceased," the decedent's name, and the date of death across the top of the return. Only report the items of income that the decedent actually or constructively received before he died. Likewise, only deduct the expenses the decedent paid before his death. Claim the total exemption amount if the decedent was the taxpayer's dependent prior to death.

Should a personal representative be appointed (an executor, administrator, or anyone who oversees the decedent's property), that person should sign the return. If the spouse acts as the personal representative, write "filed as surviving spouse" in the signature location. If someone other than the spouse claims a refund for a decedent, the representative should file Form 1310, *Statement of Person Claiming Refund Due to a Deceased Taxpayer*, with the return. Either way, a final return for the decedent must be filed.

Allowances for a Surviving Spouse

If the taxpayer's spouse died during the current tax year and the taxpayer does not remarry in the year of death, the surviving spouse may file a joint return.

Inherited Property

The property the taxpayer received as a gift, bequest, or inheritance is not included as income and is not taxable. However, if the inherited property produces income such as interest or rent, that income is taxable.

Income in Respect of the Decedent

Income in respect of the decedent includes all gross income that the decedent had a right to receive and was not includable in the decedent's final return. If the estate acquires the right to receive revenue from the decedent, the income is reported in the decedent's estate's return (Form 1041) by tax year received rather than in the decedent's final return. Should payment not be reported on Form 1041, the person to whom the estate properly distributes the income will have to do so. However, if someone acquires the direct right to the income without going through the estate, then that person will have to report the income.

Deductions in Respect of the Decedent

Decedent deductions can include items such as business expenses, interest, taxes, or income-producing expenses for which the decedent was liable but that were not deductible on the decedent's final tax return. The decedent's estate can pay and deduct these items in the same year. If the estate is not liable for the expenses, the individual who acquired the decedent's property due to death is subject to tax liability.

Part 2 Review Questions

To obtain the maximum benefit from this chapter, LTP recommends that you complete each of the following questions, and then compare them to the answers with feedback that immediately follow. Under governing self-study standards, vendors are required to present review questions intermittently throughout each self-study course.

Filing Status, Dependents, and Deductions

These questions and explanations are not part of the final examination and will not be graded by LTP.

FSDDP2.1
James is filing head of household for the current tax year. Which person related to James must live with him the entire tax year for the head of household filing status?

   a. Peyton, his daughter, is away at college as a full-time student.
   b. Fernando, his cousin, lives with him and is a full-time student at the local junior college.
   c. Taylor, his mother who lives in her home and James supports 100%.
   d. Ezra, who is his grandson by marriage and is a full-time student he supports.

FSDDP2.2
Which scenario best describes the treatment of an adopted child?

   a. Manny and Victoria adopted her niece's son at birth, and Victoria passed away and Manny is still considered the father of the adopted child.
   b. Joel and Susan are godparents for Joel's cousin Joshua. Joshua has lived with them the entire year.
   c. Andres and Stephanie are filing married filing joint and still live with Stephanie's parents.
   d. Josue and Sandra support his daughter, Sydney, who lives with her mother, and Josue would like to claim Sydney as their dependent.

FSDDP2.3
Mercedes is a disabled individual and a qualifying relative of her sister Mary. Which of the following is not included in Mercedes' gross income test to determine if Mercedes is Mary's qualifying dependent?

   a. Child away at school, working part time.
   b. Disabled dependent working at a sheltered workshop.
   c. Mary's Social Security benefits.
   d. Taxpayer who babysits.

FSDDP2.4
Lisa and Larry were married with two qualifying dependents, and Larry died in August of 2021. What would be Lisa's best filing status for 2021?

   a. Head of household
   b. Single
   c. Married filing jointly
   d. Qualifying widow(er) with dependent child

FSDDP2.5
Ted is single, 18-years-old, and a full-time student. He works part-time and lives at home with his parents year-round. His W-2 shows $4,000 in box 1. Can Ted's parents claim him as a dependent on their tax return?

   a. Yes
   b. No

Part 2 Review Question Answers

FSDDP2.1
James is filing head of household for the current tax year. Which person related to James must live with him the entire tax year for the head of household filing status?

   a. Peyton, his daughter, is away at college as a full-time student.
   b. Fernando, his cousin, lives with him and is a full-time student at the local junior college.
   c. Taylor, his mother who lives in her home and James supports 100%.
   d. Ezra, who is his grandson by marriage and is a full-time student he supports.

Feedback: Review section *Cousin*.

FSDDP2.2
Which scenario best describes the treatment of an adopted child?

   a. Manny and Victoria adopted her niece's son at birth, and Victoria passed away and Manny is still considered the father of the adopted child.
   b. Joel and Susan are godparents for Joel's cousin Joshua. Joshua has lived with them the entire year.
   c. Andres and Stephanie are filing married filing joint and still live with Stephanie's parents.
   d. Josue and Sandra support his daughter, Sydney, who lives with her mother, and Josue would like to claim Sydney as their dependent.

Feedback: Review section *Adopted Child*.

FSDDP2.3
Mercedes is a disabled individual and a qualifying relative of her sister Mary. Which of the following is not included in Mercedes' gross income test to determine if Mercedes is Mary's qualifying dependent?

   a. Child away at school, working part time.
   b. Disabled dependent working at a sheltered workshop.
   c. Mary's Social Security benefits.
   d. Taxpayer who babysits.

Feedback: Review section *Disabled Dependent Working at a Sheltered Workshop*.

FSDDP2.4
Lisa and Larry were married with two qualifying dependents, and Larry died in August of 2021. What would be Lisa's best filing status for 2021?

   a. Head of household
   b. Single
   c. Married filing jointly
   d. Qualifying widow(er) with dependent child

Feedback: Review section *Allowance for a Surviving Spouse*.

FSDDP2.5
Ted is single, 18-years-old, and a full-time student. He works part-time and lives at home with his parents year-round. His W-2 shows $4,000 in box 1. Can Ted's parents claim him as a dependent on their tax return?

   a. Yes
   b. No

Feedback: Review section *Gross Income Test.*

Part 3 Dependent Filing Requirements

If a parent (or someone else) can claim a person as a dependent, and if any of the situations listed below apply, the dependent must file a return. Income that qualifies as "unearned income" includes taxable interest, dividends, capital gains, unemployment compensation, taxable Social Security, pensions, annuities, and distributions of unearned income from a trust. Income that qualifies as "earned income" includes wages, tips, taxable scholarships, and fellowship grants.

The term "dependent" is defined as a qualifying child or relative, which will be explained below.

Caution: If gross income is $4,300 or more, generally, the taxpayer cannot be claimed as a dependent unless the taxpayer is under age 19 or a full-time student under the age of 24.

For lodging, it is the fair rental value of the lodging. Expenses that are not directly related to any one member of a household, such as food, must be divided between the total members of the family. For example, the food bill for the year was $17,200. There are four household members, so $17,200 must be divided by four to become $4,300 per member of the household.

Dependent Exemptions

A taxpayer can claim a qualifying child or a qualifying relative as a dependent if the following three tests are met:

- Dependent taxpayer test.
- Joint return test.
- Citizen or resident test.

Dependent Taxpayer Test

Should the taxpayer be claimed as a dependent by another person, the taxpayer cannot claim anyone else as a dependent on their own. Even if the taxpayer has a qualifying child or a relative, the taxpayer still cannot claim that individual as a dependent.

If the taxpayer is filing a joint return and the spouse and somebody claim her as a dependent by someone else, they cannot claim any dependents on their joint return.

Dependency Rules

Children of Parents Who Live Apart, Divorce, or Separate

In most cases, a child will be treated as the dependent of the custodial parent. A child will be treated as the qualifying child of his or her noncustodial parent if all the following apply:

1. The parents were any of the following:
    a. Divorced or legally separated under a decree of divorce or separate maintenance,
    b. Separated under a written separation agreement,
    c. Living apart for the last six months of the year, whether married or not;
2. The child received over half of the support for the year from the parents;
3. The child is in the custody of one or both parents for more than half of the year;
4. If either of the following is true:
    a. The custodial parent signed a written declaration stating that the custodial parent will not claim the child as a dependent for the current year, and the noncustodial parent attaches the written declaration to his or her return.
    b. A pre-1985 decree of divorce, separate maintenance, or written separation agreement, which applies to 2021, states that the noncustodial parent can claim the child as a dependent and will provide at least $600 for the support of the child during the year.

If all four of the above statements are true, the noncustodial parent can only do the following:

➤ Claim the child as a dependent.
➤ Claim the child as a qualifying child for the child tax credit or the credit for other dependents.

Custodial vs. Noncustodial Parent

If the parents divorced or separated during the year and if the child lived with both parents before the separation, the "custodial parent" is the parent with whom the child lived for the greater part of the year.

A child is treated as living with a parent for a night if the child sleeps as follows:

➤ At the parent's home, whether the parent is present or not.
➤ In the company of the parent when the child does not sleep at a parent's house (for example, going on vacation).

The rule for divorced or separated parents also applies to parents who never married and lived apart for the last six months of the year.

If the child lived with each parent for an equal number of nights, the parent with the higher adjusted gross income (AGI) is the custodial parent. If the child is emancipated under state law, the child is treated as having not lived with either parent.

Written Declaration Form 8332

The custodial parent should use Form 8332 to make the written declaration to release the exemption to the noncustodial parent. If the custodial parent has more than one dependent, a separate form should be used for each child. The exemption can have the following conditions:

➤ Be released for one year.
➤ Have specified years (for example, alternate years).
➤ Be designated for all future years, as specified in the declaration.
➤ Can revoke the release from the noncustodial parent.

Filing Status, Dependents, and Deductions

If the custodial parent released his or her claim to the exemption for the child for any future year, Form 8332 must be attached to each year that the taxpayer can claim the exemption. If the return is filed electronically, Form 8332 should be filed with the tax return. Tax professionals should keep copies of Form 8332 for their records.

> *Señor 1040 Says*: The household of the divorced or separated parent, whom a court order has given legal and physical custody, is the child's principal place of residency. Ask the taxpayer questions about adding a qualifying dependent who is not a newborn baby.

Tie-Breaker Rules

The following rules apply to determine which parent will claim the qualifying child:

> - If both claimants are the parents and file a joint return, they can claim the child as a qualifying child. Even if there are other qualified claimants, the child cannot be the qualifying child of another person.
> - If only one claimant is the child's parent, the child will be the parent's qualifying child.
> - If both claimants are parents and do not file a joint return, the IRS will treat the child as a qualifying child of the parent with whom the child lived the longest during the year.
> - If one of the above does not resolve the dispute, then the IRS will treat the child as the qualifying child of the claimant with the highest AGI for the year. Also, use this rule as a tiebreaker in the following instances:
>   - If the child lived with each of his two parents for the same amount of time.
>   - If no parent can claim the child as a qualifying child.
>   - If a parent can claim the child as a qualifying child, but no parent claims the child.

Qualifying Relative

There are four tests that must be met for a person to be a qualifying relative:

1. Not a qualifying child test.
2. Member of household or relationship test.
3. Gross income test.
4. Support test.

Unlike a qualifying child, a qualifying relative can be any age, and there is no age test for a qualifying relative. A child is not the taxpayer's qualifying relative if the child is the taxpayer's qualifying child or the qualifying child of anyone else.

Not a Qualifying Child Test

A child who is not the qualifying child of another taxpayer could qualify as the taxpayer's qualifying relative if:

1. The child's parent is not required to file an income tax return or
2. The child's parent only files a return to get a refund.

Child in Canada or Mexico

A child living in a foreign country cannot be claimed as a dependent unless the child is a U.S. citizen, U.S. resident alien, or U.S. national. By not living in the household, the taxpayer could claim their child for a qualifying dependent credit if the child fails the residency test. However, a taxpayer may claim their child as a dependent if the child lives in Canada or Mexico, even if the child is not a U.S. citizen, resident alien, or national.

Qualifying Child

There are five tests that must be met for a child to be considered a qualifying dependent of the taxpayer. Do not confuse these tests with the Dependent Exemptions qualifications. The five tests are:

1. Relationship
2. Age
3. Residency
4. Support
5. Joint Return

Relationship Test

To meet this test, a child must be the taxpayer's:

- son or daughter,
- stepchild,
- eligible foster child,
- brother or sister,
- half-brother or half-sister,
- stepbrother or stepsister,
- or a descendant of any of these (for example, the taxpayer's grandchild).

An adopted child is always the taxpayer's child. The term "adopted child" includes one lawfully placed with the taxpayer for legal adoption.

A foster child is an individual who is placed with the taxpayer by an authorized placement agency or by judgment, decree, or other order of any court of competent jurisdiction.

The Adopted Child Exception

Taxpayer is a U.S. citizen and legally adopted a child who is not a U.S. citizen or U.S. national. The child lived with the taxpayer all year as a member of the household will meet the citizen test. Children lawfully placed with the taxpayer for legal adoption also meet the requirement.

Exceptions for Stillborn Children and Children Born Alive

A child born or who died during the year is considered to have lived with the taxpayer the entire year while alive. The same is true if the child lived with the taxpayer all year except for any required hospital stay following birth.

Filing Status, Dependents, and Deductions

The taxpayer cannot claim a stillborn child as a dependent but may claim an exemption for a child born alive during the year but died shortly after, even if the child only lived for a moment. State or local law must treat the child as having been born alive.

There must be proof of a live birth shown by an official document, such as a birth certificate. To be a dependent, the child must be a qualifying child or relative and meet all the other tests.

Kidnapped Children

A kidnapped child can meet the residency test if the following statements are factual:

> - Law enforcement authorities presumed someone kidnapped the child, not a member of the taxpayer's family or the child's family.
> - The child lived with the taxpayer more than half of the time before the date of the kidnapping.
> - On the child's return, the child lived with the taxpayer more than half of the portion of the year following the date of the child's return to home.

This treatment applies until the child returns; however, the last year you can treat the child as such is the earlier of the two following situations:

> - The year there is a determination that the child is dead.
> - The year the child would have reached age 18.

Age Test

To meet this test, a child must be one of the following:

> - A student.
> - Under the age of 19 at the end of the year.
> - A student under the age of 24 at the end of the year.
> - Younger than the taxpayer or spouse if filing a joint return.
> - Permanently and totally disabled at any time during the year, regardless of age.

Example 1: Mr. and Mrs. Swift have Jonathon, Mr. Swift's brother, living with them. Jonathon, age 23, is a full-time student. Mr. and Mrs. Swift are both 21-years-old. Even though he is a student, Jonathon cannot be their dependent since he is older than both.

Example 2: Mr. and Mrs. Swift have Jonathon, Mr. Swift's brother, living with them. Jonathon, age 23, is a full-time student. Mr. and Mrs. Swift are both 25-years-old. If Jonathon meets all the other tests, he can be their dependent since he is younger than both.

Residency Test

Additional Qualifying Child Rules

Dependents must also meet the following conditions to qualify as a child of a taxpayer:

> - The child must have lived with the taxpayer for more than half of the year, though some exceptions may apply.
> - The child must not have provided more than half of their support for the year.

> If the child meets the rules to be a qualifying child of more than one person, the taxpayer must be the person most entitled to claim the child as a qualifying child. This information is explained in full in "Special Rules for a Qualifying Child of More Than One Person" below.

Special Rules for a Qualifying Child of More Than One Person

Sometimes, a child meets the relationship, age, residency, and support tests to be a qualifying child for more than one person. Even if an individual is a qualifying child of several people, only one claimant (a person attempting to claim something) can claim the child as their qualifying child.

If a taxpayer and one or more others have the same qualifying child, it is up to everyone involved to decide who will claim the child as a qualifying child. The individual can claim the following tax benefits based on the qualifying child (provided the taxpayer is eligible for each one):

> Child tax credit.
> HOH filing status (if applicable).
> Child and dependent care expenses.
> Earned income credit.

When one parent claims the child, other taxpayers do not share the tax benefits. Since you cannot divide the benefits between taxpayers, it is not uncommon for the parents to decide who will claim the qualifying child. If two or more taxpayers attempt to claim the child, the IRS will determine who will be able to claim the child based on the Tie-breaker Rules.

Qualifying Relative

Meet the following conditions to be considered a qualifying relative:

> The person cannot be the taxpayer's qualifying child or anyone else's qualifying child.
> The person must be only one of these things:
>   o Be related to the taxpayer in one of the ways listed under "Relatives Who Do Not Have to Live with the Taxpayer."
>   o Live with the taxpayer all year as a member of their household. This relationship must not violate local law.
> The person's gross income for the year must be less than $4,300. Exceptions apply.
> The taxpayer must provide more than half of the person's total support for the year. Exceptions apply.

Citizen and Residency Tests

The taxpayer's child must have lived with the taxpayer for more than half of the year to meet these tests. Additionally, the taxpayer cannot claim a person as a dependent unless that person is a U.S. citizen, U.S. resident, U.S. national, or a resident of Canada or Mexico. However, there are exceptions to these requirements for a group of adopted children, temporary absences, children born or died during the year, kidnapped children, and children of divorced or separated parents.

A Child's Citizenship and Place of Residence

Generally, you determine a child's citizenship and residency by the citizenship and residence of their parents. If the taxpayer was a U.S. citizen when their child was born, the child might be a U.S. citizen even if the other parent was a nonresident alien and the child was born in a foreign country. If so, the child meets the citizen test.

Students brought to this country under a qualified international education exchange program and placed in American homes temporarily are generally not U.S. residents and will not meet the test. The taxpayer cannot claim them as a dependent. However, if the taxpayer provided a home for a foreign exchange student, the taxpayer could take a charitable contribution deduction. Go to the official IRS website and see "Expenses Paid for Student Living with You" in Publication 526, *Charitable Contributions*, for more information. A U.S. national is an individual who owes their allegiance to the United States. U.S. nationals include American Samoans and Northern Mariana Islanders who became U.S. nationals instead of U.S. citizens.

The taxpayer's home can be any location where they regularly live, and the taxpayer does not need a traditional home. For example, if a child lived with the taxpayer for more than half of the year in one or more homeless shelters, the child meets the residency test.

Full-Time Student

Taxpayers may receive additional deductions for qualifying costs to dependents who are full-time students. A full-time student is a student who enrolls for the number of hours or courses the school considers to be full-time attendance.

To qualify as a student, the taxpayer's dependent must be one of the following during some part of each of any five calendar months of the year (the five calendar months do not need to be consecutive):

> - A full-time student at a school with regular teaching staff, course of study, and regularly enrolled student body at the school.
> - A student taking a full-time, on-farm training course given by a school as described above or by a state, county, or local government agency.

A "school" can be an elementary school, junior or senior high school, college, university, or a technical, trade, or mechanical school for the full-time student deduction. However, on-the-job training courses, correspondence schools, or online schools are not qualifying schools.

Vocational high school students who work on "co-op" jobs in the private industry as part of a school's classroom study course and practical training are considered full-time students for the deduction.

Temporary Absence Exceptions

The taxpayer's child lived with them during periods of time when one or both are temporarily absent due to any of the following:

> - Illness
> - Education
> - Business

- Vacation
- Military service
- Detention in a juvenile facility

One must assume that the child will return home after the temporary absence.

Joint Return Test

Generally, the taxpayer cannot claim a married person as a dependent when filing a joint return. The joint return test does not apply if the dependent and the spouse file a joint return to claim a refund.

Example 1: April, age 17, is married to Joe, age 18, and they live with April's parents. Both April and Joe have some earned income but are not required to file a return, and the only reason they file a joint return is to get a refund on the taxes withheld. If they meet all the other tests, April's parents may be able to claim them both.

Example 2: Aaron, age 18, lived with his parents while his wife was in the military. His parents supported him. His wife Mackenzie earned $25,000 for the year. Aaron and Mackenzie will file a joint return. Aaron cannot be dependent on his parents' return because he and his wife filed jointly, and Mackenzie's income is too high.

Permanently and Totally Disabled

The taxpayer's child is permanently and totally disabled if both apply:

- The child cannot engage in any substantial gainful activity because of a physical or mental condition.
- A doctor determines the condition has lasted or can be expected to last continuously for at least a year or can lead to death.

Support Tests to be a Qualifying Child

Determine the total amount of support that a taxpayer provides for a proposed dependent before the taxpayer can claim a qualifying child or qualifying relative. Full support includes amounts spent to provide food, lodging, clothing, education, medical and dental care, recreation, transportation, and similar necessities. Generally, the amount of an item of support is the amount of the expense incurred by providing the item.

To meet the support test successfully, the child cannot have provided more than half of his or her support for the year. This test is different from the support test to be a qualifying relative. To determine whether they meet the test, the taxpayer should complete the "Keeping Up a Home" section found in Publication 501 (Worksheet 1). If a child receives a scholarship, but is a full-time student, this does not count toward determining whether the child provided more than half of his or her support.

Foster Care Payments and Expenses

Payments received as a foster parent from a placement agency for the child's support are considered support provided by the agency. If the agency is state- or county-based, provided payments are considered support from the state or county for the child.

Filing Status, Dependents, and Deductions

Joint Return Test to be a Qualifying Child

The child cannot file a joint return for the year to meet this test. The exception to this rule is if the taxpayer's child and the child's spouse are not required to file a tax return but choose to file a return jointly anyway solely to claim a refund.

Part 3 Review Questions

To obtain the maximum benefit from this chapter, LTP recommends that you complete each of the following questions, and then compare them to the answers with feedback that immediately follow. Under governing self-study standards, vendors are required to present review questions intermittently throughout each self-study course.

These questions and explanations are not part of the final examination and will not be graded by LTP.

FSDDP3.1
Perla is 65-years-old, and her income is $12,600. She claims she has a qualifying dependent living with her. Which of the following questions is best to ask to determine her filing status?

1. How is the qualifying dependent related to you?
2. How old is the qualifying child?
3. How much income did the qualifying dependent earn?
4. Can the child be a qualifying child of another taxpayer?

   a. 1 and 4
   b. 2 and 3
   c. 1, 2, and 4
   d. 1, 2, 3, and 4

FSDDP3.2
Which of the following temporary absences will not allow the taxpayer to claim the qualifying child or qualifying relative as a dependent?

   a. Illness
   b. Education
   c. Military service
   d. Dependent of another taxpayer

FSDDP3.3
Tyler, age 27, is single and lives with his parents Sharon and Rory. Tyler was unable to work due to a temporary medical condition. He received $4,250 for a speaking engagement. Can Sharon and Rory claim Tyler as a dependent?

   a. Yes
   b. No

FSDDP3.4

Trini is single, 18-years-old, and a full-time student. She works part-time and lives at home with her parents. Her W-2 shows $4,000 in box 1. Can Trini's parents claim her as a dependent on their tax return?

   a. Yes
   b. No

FSDDP3.5

Alma must meet five tests to claim Freddy as a dependent. Which of the following is not one of the tests?

   a. Residency
   b. Relationship
   c. Disability Test
   d. Joint Return Test

FSDDP3.6

Which scenario describes custodial parent?

   a. Ezra lives with his dad 300 days a year, and only sees his mother on school holidays.
   b. David and Maria have joint custody of their children.
   c. Cara and her daughter Joyce live with her parents, and Joyce is on her grandparent's insurance.
   d. Eli is 18-years-old and has a full-time job and still lives with his parents.

FSDDP3.7

Danelle is the noncustodial parent and would like to claim her children on her current year tax return. What does Jake need to do so Danelle can claim the children?

   a. Jake would need to file first by filing Form 1040 and claim the children.
   b. Jake would need to sign Form 8332 and give the form to Danelle to file with her tax return.
   c. Jake would need to revoke Form 8332 and give the form to his tax preparer.
   d. Jake would still be able to claim his children even if Danelle does.

Part 3 Review Questions Answers

FSDDP3.1

Perla is 65-years-old, and her income is $12,600. She claims she has a qualifying dependent living with her. Which of the following questions is best to ask to determine her filing status?

   1. How is the qualifying dependent related to you?
   2. How old is the qualifying child?
   3. How much income did the qualifying dependent earn?
   4. Can the child be a qualifying child of another taxpayer?

   a. 1 and 4
   b. 2 and 3
   c. 1, 2, and 4
   d. 1, 2, 3, and 4

Feedback: Review section *Qualifying Child*.

Filing Status, Dependents, and Deductions

FSDDP3.2
Which of the following temporary absences will not allow the taxpayer to claim the qualifying child or qualifying relative as a dependent?

a. Illness
b. Education
c. Military service
d. Dependent of another taxpayer

Feedback: Review section *Temporary Absence Exceptions.*

FSDDP3.3
Tyler, age 27, is single and lives with his parents Sharon and Rory. Tyler was unable to work due to a temporary medical condition. He received $4,250 for a speaking engagement. Can Sharon and Rory claim Tyler as a dependent?

a. Yes
b. No

Feedback: Review section *Qualifying Child.*

FSDDP3.4
Trini is single, 18-years-old, and a full-time student. She works part-time and lives at home with her parents. Her W-2 shows $4,000 in box 1. Can Trini's parents claim her as a dependent on their tax return?

a. Yes
b. No

Feedback: Review section *Qualifying Child.*

FSDDP3.5
Alma must meet five tests to claim Freddy as a dependent. Which of the following is not one of the tests?

a. Residency
b. Relationship
c. Disability Test
d. Joint Return Test

Feedback: Review section *Qualifying Child.*

FSDDP3.6
Which scenario describes custodial parent?

a. Ezra lives with his dad 300 days a year, and only sees his mother on school holidays.
b. David and Maria have joint custody of their children.
c. Cara and her daughter Joyce live with her parents, and Joyce is on her grandparent's insurance.
d. Eli is 18 years old and has a full-time job and still lives with his parents.

Feedback: Review section *Custodial vs. Noncustodial Parent.*

FSDDP3.7

Danelle is the noncustodial parent and would like to claim her children on her current year tax return. What does Jake need to do so Danelle can claim the children?

    a. Jake would need to file first by filing Form 1040 and claim the children.
    b. Jake would need to sign Form 8332 and give the form to Danelle to file with her tax return.
    c. Jake would need to revoke Form 8332 and give to his tax preparer.
    d. Jake would still be able to claim his children even if Danelle does.

Feedback: Review section *Written Declaration Form 8332*.

Part 4 Deductions

There are two types of deductions available to taxpayers: standard and itemized deductions. The total amount is subtracted from the taxpayer's adjusted gross income to reduce the taxpayer's tax liability. However, taxpayers cannot use both types and must choose only one. As such, a tax professional should use the process that reduces a taxpayer's tax liability the most.

Itemized deductions are certain personal expenses that have been designated explicitly as itemized deductions to help taxpayers by claiming those expenses. The standard deduction is a pre-determined dollar amount based on the taxpayer's filing status. Standard deductions do not require taxpayers to save receipts for actual personal expenses such as medical bills, charitable contributions, and certain deductible taxes.

Generally, taxpayers can choose the method that gives them the lowest tax liability, but this is not always the case. The standard deduction is not always an option for every taxpayer. In cases like these (for example, if the taxpayer's standard deduction amount is zero), it is best to check if itemizing deductions would benefit the taxpayer. Taxpayers are required to itemize deductions in the following:

- A taxpayer is married, filing a separate return, and their spouse itemizes deductions.
- The taxpayer is filing a tax return for a short tax year because of a change in his or her annual accounting period.
- The taxpayer is a nonresident or dual-status alien during the year. The taxpayer is a dual-status alien if both a nonresident and a resident alien during the year. Suppose the nonresident alien is married to a U.S. citizen or resident alien at the end of the year. In that case, the nonresident alien or the resident alien can choose to be treated as a U.S. resident.

Itemized deductions are discussed further in another chapter. See Publication 519 for more information.

Standard Deductions

The Standard deduction amount varies depending on the taxpayer's filing status. Other factors that determine the amount of the allowable standard deduction are as follows:

- Is the taxpayer considered age 65 or older?
- Is the taxpayer blind?
- Is the taxpayer claimed as a dependent on another individual's tax return?

Filing Status, Dependents, and Deductions

Standard Deduction for Most People

These deduction amounts apply to most people and are for the current year's filing status. *

Filing Status and Standard Deduction	Tax Year 2020	Tax Year 2021	Tax Year 2022
Single	$12,400	$12,550	$12,950
Married Filing Jointly and Qualifying Widow(er)	$24,800	$25,100	$25,900
Married Filing Separately	$12,550	$12,550	$12,950
Head of Household	$18,650	$18,800	$19,400

*Do not use this chart if:

- ➤ The taxpayer was born before January 2, 1957.
- ➤ The taxpayer is blind.
- ➤ Someone else can claim the taxpayer or taxpayer's spouse as a dependent if filing status is MFJ.

Example 1: It is tax year 2021, and Lilly is 26-years-old, has never been married and does not have children or other dependents. Lilly will file a tax return using the Single filing status. Look at the above chart. Her standard deduction will be $12,550.

Example 2: Using example 1 with one change: Lilly is now married. She and her husband plan to file a joint return, and Lilly and her husband will use the standard deduction. As shown on the chart, $25,100 will be their standard deduction.

Example 3: Using example 2 with additional changes: Lilly and her husband have a son born during the tax year. Lilly and her husband have decided to file separate tax returns. Since they are still married and living together, they must use the MFS filing status. As per the chart, Lilly's standard deduction will be $12,550.

Example 4: Using example 2 with additional changes: Lilly and her husband divorced during the tax year. According to the chart, Lilly now has sole custody of her son and is eligible to file using the Head of Household filing status, making her standard deduction $18,800.

Standard Deduction for Age 65 and Older or Blind

A higher standard deduction is allowed for taxpayers aged 65 or older by the end of the tax year. A taxpayer is age 65 on their 65th birthday and the date immediately beforehand.

Example: Frank turned 65 on January 1, 2022, and thus, he is also 65 on the day before his birthday, December 31, 2021. Because the information used to file a return is whatever information you have on the last day of the tax year filed, Frank is considered 65 for all of 2021. The tax return can take the higher standard deduction amount granted to a person aged 65 or older.

A higher standard deduction is also allowed for taxpayers who are considered blind on the last day of the year. If the taxpayer is partially blind, they must get an official statement from a licensed eye physician (either an optometrist or an ophthalmologist). The note should state that the taxpayer's field of vision is not more than twenty degrees or that the taxpayer cannot see better than 20/200 in their best eye, even with glasses or contact lenses.

Filing Status, Dependents, and Deductions

If the examining physician determines that the eye condition will never improve beyond its limits, the physician must include this fact in their statement. Suppose you correct the vision beyond these limits solely using contact lenses that can only be worn briefly due to pain, infection, or ulcers. In that case, the taxpayer can take the higher standard deduction for which they otherwise qualify. Keep the doctor's statement with the rest of the taxpayer's records.

The higher standard deduction is also allowed for the spouse of a taxpayer who is age 65 or older or blind under the following circumstances:

> The taxpayer and their spouse file a joint tax return.
> The taxpayer filed a separate return, the spouse had no gross income, and another taxpayer could not claim an exemption for the spouse.

If the taxpayer is a dependent on another tax return and was born before January 2, 1957, or is blind, multiply the amount of the additional standard deduction by $1,700 if that taxpayer is Single. If taxpayers are married, multiply the amount of the other standard deduction by $1,350.

2021 Standard Deduction Worksheet for People Born Before January 2, 1957, or Blind

Check the correct number of boxes below, then proceed to the chart.

1. Taxpayer   Born before January 2, 1957 ☐ Blind ☐
2. Spouse, if claiming exemption   Born before January 2, 1957 ☐ Blind ☐

Total number of boxes checked ____

If filing status is:	And the number in the blank above is:	Standard Deduction is:
Single	1. 2. 1. 2.	$12,550 under 65 $14,250 under 65 and blind $14,250 over 65 $15,950 over 65 and blind
Married Filing Jointly or Qualifying Widow(er) with Dependent Child (Use 1 & 2)	1. 2. 3. 1. 2. 3.	$25,100 both under 65 $26,450 under 65, one blind $27,800 under 65, both blind $27,800 both over 65 $29,150 both over 65, one blind $30,500 both over 65, both blind
Married Filing Separately	1. 2. 1. 2.	$12,550 under 65 $14,250 under 65 and blind $14,250 over 65 $15,950 over 65 and blind
Head of Household	1. 2. 1. 2.	$18,800 under 65 $20,500 under 65 and blind $20,500 over 65 $22,200 over 65 and blind

Filing Status, Dependents, and Deductions

> *Señor 1040 Says*: If the taxpayer is MFS and their spouse itemizes or is a dual-status alien, the taxpayer **cannot** take the standard deduction. The taxpayer *must* itemize their deductions.

Example 1: For the tax year 2021, David and his wife Nancy are both over age 65. They are required to file a tax return and will file MFJ. Neither is blind, so they will use the standard deduction.

Standard deduction for MFJ taxpayers:	$25,100
Additional standard deduction for MFJ, 65+	$ 2,700 ($1,350 × 2)
Total standard deduction:	$27,800

Example 2: The scenario is the same as example 1 but with one change: Nancy is legally blind. The couple will file MFJ and use the standard deduction.

Standard deduction for MFJ taxpayers:	$25,100
Additional standard deduction for MFJ, blind	$ 1,350
Additional standard deduction for MFJ, 65+	$ 2,700 ($1,350 × 2)
Total standard deduction:	$29,150

Example 3: Tax year 2021, and David, Nancy's husband, died two years ago. Nancy is over age 65, legally blind, and must file a return. In this situation, she files using the Single filing status and uses the standard deduction with the additional standard deductions for being blind and over 65. As she is not a dependent or married, multipliers do not modify the additional standard deductions.

Standard deduction for single taxpayers:	$ 12,550
Additional standard deduction for single, blind	$ 1,700
Additional standard deduction for single, 65+	$ 1,700
Total standard deduction:	$ 15,950

Standard Deduction for Dependents

The standard deduction amount is generally limited if someone else claims the taxpayer as dependent on their return. Suppose a taxpayer has been claimed as a dependent. In that case, the claimed taxpayer's standard deduction amount is limited. It will either be $1,100 or the taxpayer's earned income amount for the year plus $350 if it does not exceed the regular standard deduction, whichever is greater. If the taxpayer is age 65 or older or blind, they may still be eligible for a higher standard deduction even if claimed as a dependent.

For the standard deduction, earned income consists of salaries, wages, tips, professional fees, and all other monetary amounts received for any work the taxpayer performed. Include scholarships or fellowship grants in the gross income to calculate the standard deduction correctly. See Publication 970 for more information on what qualifies as a scholarship or fellowship grant.

2021 Standard Deduction Worksheet for Dependents

Use this worksheet only if someone can claim an exemption for the taxpayer or for his or her spouse if MFJ.*

Filing Status, Dependents, and Deductions

1. Enter the taxpayer's earned income (defined below). If none, enter a zero.	1. $
2. Additional amount	2. $350
3. Add lines 1 and 2	3. $
4. Minimum standard deduction	4. $1,100
5. Enter the larger of line 3 or line 4	5. $

6. Enter the amount shown below for taxpayer's filing status.
    Single or MFS: $12,550
    MFJ or QW(er): $25,100
    Head of Household: $18,800
	6. $

7. Standard deduction a. Enter the smaller of line 5 or line 6. If born after January 1, 1957, and not blind, stop here. This is the standard deduction. Otherwise, go to line 7b.	7a. $
b. If born before January 2, 1957, or blind, multiply the number of checked boxes on Form 1040, by $1,350 ($1,700 if Single or Head of household).	7b. $
c. Add lines 7a and 7b. Enter the total here and on Form 1040 or Form 1040-SR, line 12a.	7c. $

*The earned income includes wages, salaries, tips, professional fees, and other compensation received for personal services performed. It also includes any amount received as a taxable scholarship or fellowship grant.

Part 4 Review Questions

To obtain the maximum benefit from this chapter, LTP recommends that you complete each of the following questions, and then compare them to the answers with feedback that immediately follow. Under governing self-study standards, vendors are required to present review questions intermittently throughout each self-study course.

These questions and explanations are not part of the final examination and will not be graded by LTP.

FSDDP4.1
Which of the following best describes standard deduction?

a. Standard deduction is a yearly pre-determined dollar amount.
b. Standard deduction includes certain expenses that require the taxpayer to save receipts to determine the amount he or she can deduct.
c. Standard deduction is the amount of the taxpayer's charitable contribution.
d. Standard deduction is only for taxpayers who are married.

Filing Status, Dependents, and Deductions

FSDDP4.2

Samuel, filing single, is 64-years-old and is legally blind. What would be his standard deduction for tax year 2021 (prepared in 2022)?

a. $12,550
b. $15,950
c. $18,800
d. $14,250

FSDDP4.3

For tax year 2021 (prepared in 2022) what is the federal standard deduction for Maria who is filing head of household?

a. $12,550
b. $25,100
c. $18,650
d. $18,800

Part 4 Review Questions Answers

FSDDP4.1

Which of the following best describes standard deduction?

a. **Standard deduction is a yearly pre-determined dollar amount.**
b. Standard deduction includes certain expenses that require the taxpayer to save receipts to determine the amount he or she can deduct.
c. Standard deduction is the amount of the taxpayer's charitable contribution.
d. Standard deduction is only for taxpayers who are married.

Feedback: Review section *Part I: Deductions*.

FSDDP4.2

Samuel, filing single, is 64-years-old and is legally blind. What would be his standard deduction for tax year 2021(prepared in 2022)?

a. $12,550
b. $15,950
c. $18,800
d. **$14,250**

Feedback: Review section *Standard Deduction for Age 65 and Older or Blind*.

FSDDP4.3

For tax year 2021 (prepared in 2022) what is the federal standard deduction for Maria who is filing head of household?

a. $12,550
b. $25,100
c. $18,650
d. **$18,800**

Takeaways

The tax professional must understand filing statuses and ask questions that will determine the correct filing status for their client. Some clients might tell you their filing status is Head of Household because a friend told them so. However, the tax preparer's responsibility is to perform a thorough interview and complete the paid tax preparer's Due Diligence Form 8867. A taxpayer's filing status determines the taxpayer's tax liability and many tax credits, so make sure to claim the correct filing status.

Tax Topic 303 has a checklist of the most common errors on a tax return. "What is My Filing Status?" is on the list. The IRS has created an interactive tax assistant to answer questions relating to determining filing status. "What was your marital status on the last day of the year?" is the first question in the interactive tax assistant (ITA). Be aware of the consequences of doing this wrong, and make sure you do your due diligence to get it right.

It is important to understand how to determine a qualifying child or a qualifying relative to prepare an accurate tax return. Knowledge of tax law is imperative; the tax professional cannot rely on software to prepare an accurate tax return. Ensure the individual qualifies to be the taxpayer's dependent by understanding the rules for a qualifying child and a qualifying relative. Knowledge of the taxpayer's situation is key to preparing an accurate tax return. If the IRS audits a tax return, the IRS will not accept the excuse that you did not ask enough questions.

TEST YOUR KNOWLEDGE!
Go online to take a practice quiz.

Chapter 4 Income

Introduction

This chapter will cover Lines 1 – 7 on Form 1040 and Schedule 1, *Additional Income and Adjustments to Income.*

The IRS has the authority to tax all income from whatever source it is derived. This includes compensation for services, gains from dispositions of property, interest and dividends, rent and royalties, pensions and annuities, gambling winnings, and even illegal activities. All such income a person receives is collectively referred to as "worldwide income." However, not all money or property is taxable or subject to tax. This chapter will cover the different types of taxable and nontaxable income and show where and how to report income. A tax professional must identify the different types of taxable income, tax-exempt income, and other income included in Schedule 1, line 10, and must know how to figure out the taxable percentage on Social Security benefits.

Any interest or dividends can be taxable income if they are credited to the taxpayer's account and can be withdrawn. This chapter will cover the exceptions to this rule and show which interest and dividends are not taxable income and which expenses can be deducted on the taxpayer's Schedule A if the taxpayer itemizes.

Almost everything a taxpayer owns and uses for personal or investment purposes is a capital asset. When a capital asset is sold, the difference between the basis in the asset and the amount the item is sold for is either a capital gain or a capital loss. A capital gain is the profit that results from selling an investment (stocks, bonds, or real estate) for a higher price than it was purchased. Capital gains may refer to investment income that arises in relation to real assets (such as property), financial assets (such as shares of stocks or bonds), and intangible assets (such as goodwill). A capital loss arises if the proceeds from the sale of a capital asset are less than the purchase price. The taxpayer can deduct up to a $3,000 loss ($1,500 if filing MFS). The capital loss that exceeds the limit amount may be taken in future years.

Objectives

At the end of this chapter, the student will:

- ➢ Explain "worldwide income".
- ➢ Understand where to report wages and other compensation.
- ➢ Differentiate earned vs. unearned income.
- ➢ Identify where income is reported.
- ➢ Identify the different types of interest income.
- ➢ Recognize which tax forms report interest income.
- ➢ Recite which dividends are reported as interest.
- ➢ Understand the different types of savings bonds.
- ➢ Explain where to report dividend income.
- ➢ Understand when Schedule B is required to be filed with the tax return.
- ➢ Indicate how to report interest and dividend income on the tax return.
- ➢ Explain the holding periods for different types of property.

- ➢ Understand the difference between short-term and long-term capital gains.
- ➢ Identify capital assets.
- ➢ Determine the basis before selling an asset.
- ➢ Know when the primary residence is excluded from capital gain.

Resources

Form W-2	Schedule B	Instructions Schedule B
Form W-2G	Schedule D	Instructions for Schedule D
Form 1040	Publication 15-B	Instructions Form W-2
Form 1099-B	Publication 17	Instructions Form W-2G
Form 1099-DIV	Publication 514	Instructions Form 1040
Form 1099-G	Publication 505	Instructions Form 1099-B
Form 1099-INT	Publication 523	Instructions Form 1099-DIV
Form 1099-OID	Publication 525	Instructions Form 1099-INT
Form 1099-Q	Publication 531	Instructions Form 1099-OID
Form 1099-R	Publication 544	Instructions Form 1099-Q
Form RRB-1099	Publication 550	Instructions Form 1099-R
Form SSA-1099	Publication 551	Instructions RRB-1099
Form 4070	Publication 554	Instructions Form SSA-1099
Form 4070A	Publication 575	Instructions Form 4070
Form 4797	Publication 590 A & B	Instructions Form 4797
Form 5329	Publication 915	Instructions Form 5329
Form 6252	Publication 929	Instructions Form 6252
Form 8606	Publication 939	Instructions Form 8606
Form 8615	Publication 1244	Instructions Form 8615
Form 8814	Publication 4078	Instructions Form 8814
Form 8815	Tax Topics 403, 404, 409, 411, 412, 413, 417, 418, 419, 420, 421, 451, 553, 557, 558, 703	Instructions Form 8815
Form 8818		Instructions Form 8818
Form 8949		Instructions Form 8949
Form 8960		Instructions Form 8960

Table of Contents

Introduction	136
Part 1 Form W-4 and Form W-2	141
Tax Withholding	141
Form W-4, Prior to TCJA	142
2021 Form W-4	143
Exemption from Withholding	144
Household Workers Withholding	145
How to Read the W-2	145
The Lettered Boxes of Form W-2	146
The Numbered Boxes of Form W-2	147
Box 1: Wages, Tips, and Other Compensation	147
Box 2 through Box 11	148
Box 12: Codes	150
Box 14 through Box 20	154
Boxes 15 through 20	154
Part 1 Review Questions	154
Part 1 Review Questions Answers	155
Part 2 Income	156
Form 1040, Page 1, lines 1 - 7	156
Line 2: Interest	157
When to Report Interest Income	157
Constructively Received	157
Form 1099-INT	158
Backup Withholding	160
Accounts and Payee-Identifying Numbers	160
Truncating	160
Certification	160
Number and Certification	161
Line 2a Tax-Exempt Interest	161
Government Bonds	161
Series EE and Series E Bonds	162
Series H and HH Bonds	162
Series I Bonds	162
Municipal Bonds	163
State or Local Government Obligations	163
Line 2b Taxable Interest	163
Taxable Interest	164
U.S. Obligations	164
Interest and Community Property States	164
Foreign Accounts and Trust Requirements	164
Reporting Requirements	165
How to Report	165
How to Calculate the Greatest Account Value of Foreign Financial Accounts	166
Personal Loans	166
Part 2 Review Questions	166
Part 2 Review Questions Answers	168
Part 3 Dividends	171
Form 1099-DIV: Reporting Dividend Income	171
Form 1040, line 3a, Qualified Dividends	173
Form 1040, line 3b, Ordinary Dividends	173
Dividends That Are Really Interest	173

Dividends Used to Buy More Stock 174
Money Market Funds 174
Capital Gains Distributions 174
Nontaxable Dividends 175
Return of Capital 175
Liquidating Distributions 175
Exempt-Interest Dividends 175
Dividends on Insurance Policies 175
Dividends on Veterans' Insurance Policies 176
Patronage Dividends 176
Form 1040, line 4: IRA Distributions 176
Form 1040, line 5a and Line 5b, Pensions and Annuities 176
Form 1040, line 6a: Social Security Benefits 177
Form 1040, line 6b: Taxable Amount 177
Social Security and Equivalent Railroad Retirement Benefits (Tier 1) 178
Railroad Retirement Benefits 178
Part 3 Review Questions 179
Part 3 Review Questions Answers 179

Part 4 Schedule 1: Additional Income 180
Schedule 1, line 1: Taxable Refunds 180
Recovery of Items Previously Deducted 181
Schedule 1, line 2: Alimony Received 181
Alimony Recapture Rule 182
Schedule 1, line 3: Business Income or Loss 182
Schedule 1, line 4: Other Gains or Losses 182
Schedule 1, line 5: Rental Income Form 1040 183
Schedule 1, line 6: Farm Income or Loss 183
Schedule 1, line 7: Unemployment Compensation 183
Paid Medical Family Leave 183
Schedule 1, line 8: Other Income 183
Form 1099-C 187
Who Must File Form 1099-C? 188
Distributions from HSA line 8e 189
Alaska Permanent Fund Dividends line 8f 189
Line 8i Activity Not for Profit 189
Hobby Income 190
Line 8j Employee Stock Options 190
Part 4 Review Questions 190
Part 4 Review Questions Answers 192

Part 5 Other Taxable Income 193
Advance Commission and Other Earnings 193
Back Pay 193
Bartering 194
Employee Achievement Awards 194
Government Cost-of-Living Allowances 194
Relocation for Temporary Work Assignment 194
Scholarship prizes 194
Severance Pay 194
Sick Pay 195
Tips and Gratuities 195
Disability Income 197
Clergy 198
Part 5 Review Questions 198

Income

Part 5 Review Questions Answers	199
Part 6 Fringe Benefits	199
Cafeteria Plans	200
Adoption Assistance	201
Dependent Care Assistance	202
Group-Term Life Insurance	202
Health Savings Accounts (HSAs)	203
Employee Stock Options	203
Holiday Gifts	204
Retirement Plan Contributions	204
Transportation	204
Other Fringe Benefits	204
Nontaxable Income	207
Part 6 Review Questions	209
Part 6 Review Questions Answers	210
Takeaways	210

Part 1 Form W-4 and Form W-2

A tax professional needs to understand the importance of Form W-4, *Employee's Withholding Certificate*. Form W-4 is the IRS document that an employee completes for their employer to determine how much should be withheld from the employee's paycheck for federal income taxes and sent to the IRS. Accurately completing the W-4 will avoid overpaying taxes or having a balance due come tax time. Many taxpayers do not understand the form and want to have as much income on their paycheck. Not calculating accurately is the issue whether it is having too much withheld or not enough. Not having enough withheld is when the taxpayer has a balance due.

Since 2020, the IRS has changed the W-4 *Employee's Withholding Certificate*. The IRS has created an online tax withholding estimator to help taxpayers determine their withholding is enough. The IRS has the viewpoint to "pay as you go". This is to make sure that the taxpayer pays enough withholding, whether by having enough money withheld from the employees withholding or paying estimated payments quarterly. To use the estimator online, make sure that you gather the following needed documents.

1. Most recent paycheck(s), if filing jointly; need both taxpayer and spouse.
2. Income from other sources, if applicable.
3. Have the most recent tax return handy.

The estimator is only as accurate as the information that is entered. Below is the link to the estimator. https://www.irs.gov/individuals/tax-withholding-estimator.

Tax Withholding

Income tax is withheld from employee compensation; the amount of income tax the employer withholds is based on two factors:

- The amount one earns in each payroll period.
- The information provided to the employer when the employee completes Form W-4.

The withholding counts toward paying the annual income calculated tax bill when the taxpayer files their current year tax return. Prior to the new 2020 version, taxpayers were allowed to claim personal allowances. The more allowances claimed, the less an employer would withhold from the taxpayer's paycheck. Allowances were tied to personal and dependent exemptions claimed on the tax form. Due to Tax Cuts and Jobs Act (TCJA), personal exemptions have been suspended until 2025. TCJA is federal law, and some states did not conform to TCJA.

To declare a filing status, the employee would determine that in Step 1(c) by marking one of the boxes. If steps 2-4 apply to the taxpayer, then the individual would complete the steps; otherwise, continue to step 5.

Step 2 is used if the taxpayer has multiple jobs simultaneously or the taxpayer and spouse have jobs.

Income

Step 3 is used if the taxpayer and spouse are claiming child tax credit and have a qualifying other dependent. To qualify for child tax credit, the taxpayer must have a qualifying dependent child under the age of 17 as of December 31 and has lived with the taxpayer for over half of the year. Other tax credits can be used in this step as well to reach a more accurate credit allowance.

Step 4 is used when the taxpayer has other income that would affect their W-2 withholding, such as interest earned and dividend distributions. If the taxpayer claims itemized deductions, and/or extra withholding deducted from each pay period, this action could influence the withholding amount.

Form W-4, Prior to TCJA

The *Employee's Withholding Allowance Certificate* included four types of information that an employer would use to figure the taxpayer's withholding. Some payroll companies (private or commercial) are still using the old system to calculate tax withholding. The following would apply to the prior Form W-4:

1. Whether to withhold at the single rate or at the lower married rate.
2. How many withholding allowances the taxpayer claims; each allowance reduces the amount withheld.
3. Whether the taxpayer wants an additional amount withheld.
4. Whether the taxpayer is claiming an exemption from withholding in 2021.

The taxpayer must complete Form W-4 to determine the amount of withholding to claim. It is the taxpayer's responsibility to determine the correct withholding.

The taxpayer should evaluate his or her Form W-4 annually and provide employer(s) with a new Form W-4 as needed. If the taxpayer wants to withhold from pensions or annuities, use a W-4P.

In most situations, the tax withheld from the taxpayer's pay will be close to the tax figured on the return if one of the following applies:

> The taxpayer accurately completes Form W-4.
> The taxpayer changes Form W-4 when their tax situation changes.

The worksheets provided with the W-4 do not account for all possible situations, and thus the taxpayer may not have the correct amount withheld. This is most likely to happen in the following situations:

1. The taxpayer is married, and both the taxpayer and spouse work.
2. The taxpayer has more than one job at a time.
3. The taxpayer has nonwage income such as interest, dividends, alimony, unemployment compensation, or self-employment income, rental income, or capital gains.
4. The taxpayer will owe additional amounts with the tax return such as self-employment tax or household employment tax.
5. The taxpayer had tax withholdings from an obsolete Form W-4 for a substantial part of the year.
6. The taxpayer works only part of the year.
7. The taxpayer has changed the number of withholding allowances during the year.

If the taxpayer has income from two or more jobs at the same time, put all allowances on one W-4 but split allowances between the jobs. Withholding will usually be more accurate when all allowances are claimed on Form W-4 for the highest-paying job and zero allowances are claimed on the others.

The taxpayer can claim all allowances with one employer and none with the other, or he or she can divide them between the two. Review Publication 505.

If both the taxpayer and the spouse are employed and expected to file a joint return, they should figure their withholding allowance using their combined income, adjustments, deductions, exemptions, and credits. They can divide their total allowances any way they want, but they cannot claim an allowance that the other spouse has also claimed.

2021 Form W-4

Income

Exemption from Withholding

If a taxpayer had no tax liability in the previous year and fully expects to have no tax liability in the coming year, he or she can write "Exempt" on Form W-4 in the space below Step 4(c). Then complete Steps 1(a), 1(b), and 5. Do not complete any other steps. If the taxpayer claims exemption from withholding, the exemption applies only to income tax and not to Social Security or Medicare tax.

The taxpayer may claim an exemption for the current tax year if the following apply:

> ➤ The taxpayer had a right to a refund of all federal income tax withheld because the taxpayer had no tax liability the previous year.
> ➤ The taxpayer expects a refund of all federal income tax withheld because he or she expects to have no tax liability for the current year.

The employer must send the IRS a copy of the taxpayer's Form W-4 if the taxpayer claims to be exempt from withholding and if the taxpayer's pay is expected to usually be more than $200 a week. If the taxpayer does not qualify for the exemption, the IRS will send both the taxpayer and the taxpayer's employer a written notice.

If the taxpayer claims to be exempt on Form W-4 but the situation changes so that he or she must pay income tax after all, the taxpayer must file a new Form W-4 within 10 days of the change. If the taxpayer claims to be exempt in 2021 but expects to owe income tax for 2022, the taxpayer should file a new Form W-4 as soon as possible. An exemption is valid for one year. The taxpayer must provide the employer with a new Form W-4 yearly by February 15th of each year to continue the exemption.

The taxpayer is also required to complete and file a new Form W-4 with the employer within 10 days in the following cases:

> ➤ The taxpayer was claiming to be married and becomes divorced.
> ➤ Any event occurs that decreases the number of withholding allowances the taxpayer can claim.

Señor 1040 Says: Students are not automatically exempt from tax withholding.

If the taxpayer wishes to change his or her W-4 during the year, the employer must put the new Form W-4 into effect no later than the start of the first payroll period ending on or after the 30th day after the taxpayer turned in a new Form W-4. If the taxpayer's change is for the next year, the new form will not take place until the next year.

Household Workers Withholding

If a taxpayer paid an employee $2,300 or more in cash wages for 2021, the taxpayer must report and pay Social Security and Medicare taxes on all the wages. A household worker is an employee who performs household work in a private home, local college club, or local fraternity or sorority chapter. Tax is withheld only if the taxpayer has asked the employer to do so. If the taxpayer does not have enough tax withheld, the individual must make estimated payments. To be able to file the appropriate forms to have the taxes withheld, the employer of the household worker must obtain an employer identification number by submitting a SS-4 EIN Application to the IRS. The taxpayer needs to employ an individual that can legally work in the United States. The employee needs to complete Form I-9, and the employer needs to verify the information and give the employee a W-2.

A taxpayer who is an employee should receive a Form W-2 from their employer(s) that shows the wages the taxpayer earned in exchange for services performed. A W-2 is the tax form generated by employers that details the employees' earnings and government withholdings for a given tax year. A tax year's W-2 should be distributed to the employees by the end of the first month after the tax year ends; for example, W-2s for tax year 2021 should have been delivered before the end of January 31, 2022. A taxpayer will receive a W-2 from each employer he or she is employed by and should give each W-2 they have received to the individual preparing the tax return. Most taxpayers will only receive one W-2; it is possible to receive more than one if a taxpayer has worked multiple jobs during a given tax year. If employees notice an error on their Form W-2, they should notify their employer and request a corrected Form W-2 before filing their taxes.

Tax professionals use the information provided on a W-2 to determine the client's earned income for the year. The total amount of wages is reported on Form 1040, line 1. Wages include salaries, vacation allowances, bonuses, commissions, and fringe benefits. Compensation includes everything received in payment for personal services.

How to Read the W-2

Below is a W-2 that an employee receives from his employer. It is important for the tax professional to know what is reported on each line of the W-2 so that he or she will know how to use the information provided in the form when preparing the employee's tax return.

Income

[Form W-2 Wage and Tax Statement 2021]

The Lettered Boxes of Form W-2

Box a: Employee's Social Security Number

The Social Security number should match the number shown on the employee's Social Security card. If the Social Security number is incorrect, the employee should notify the employer and request a corrected Form W-2.

> Note: ITINs are not replacements for Social Security numbers. ITINs are only available to resident and nonresident aliens ineligible for U.S. employment that need identification for tax purposes. Under normal circumstances, ITIN holders cannot receive a W-2 because they lack an SSN, but it is possible for an ITIN holder to receive a W-2 using an unlawful SSN. When entering the W-2 information into software for these clients, make sure that the SSN does not auto-populate into box a, because this is where the ITIN number needs to go.

Box b: Employer Identification Number (EIN)

This box shows the employer identification number (EIN) assigned to the employer by the IRS. EINs consist of two digits and a dash followed by seven more digits, as seen in this example: 00-0000000.

Box c: Employer's Name, Address, and ZIP Code

This entry should be the same as the information shown on the employer's Form 941, 941-SS, 943, 944, CT-1 or Form 1040, Schedule H.

Box d: Control Number

Though it is often left blank, this box can be used by employers to distinguish between individual W-2s whenever needed. For example, if an employer has multiple employees with the same first and last names, they can distinguish between them by using control numbers.

Boxes e and f: Employee's Name and Address

The taxpayer's name should match the name as shown on the Social Security card (first, middle initial, and last). The taxpayer's name may be different if the taxpayer has recently married, divorced, or had a name change of any kind. The taxpayer's address should include the number, street, apartment and suite number, or a P.O. Box number if mail is not delivered to a street address.

The Numbered Boxes of Form W-2

Box 1: Wages, Tips, and Other Compensation

Shows the total taxable wages, tips, and other compensation paid to the employee during the year before any payroll deductions or tax withholdings were subtracted.

The following items are included in the total amount provided in box 1:

- Total wages and bonuses (including signing bonuses, prizes, and awards) paid to employee during the year.
- Total noncash payments, including certain fringe benefits.
- Total tips reported by the employee to the employer; allocated tips are not reported in this box.
- Certain employee business expense reimbursements.
- An S corporation's cost of accident and health insurance premiums for a shareholder with 2% or more of the company.
- Employee chooses cash for certain taxable benefits from a section 125 cafeteria plan.
- Employee contributions to an Archer MSA.
- Contributions to an Archer MSA from an employer if included in the employee's income.
- Employer contributions for qualified long-term care services to the extent that such coverage is provided through flexible spending plans or similar arrangements.
- Taxable portion of the cost of group-term insurance of more than $50,000.
- Unless excludable under an education assistance program, payments for non-job-related education expenses or for payments under a nonaccountable plan.
- The amount included as wages because the employer paid the employee's share of Social Security and Medicare taxes.
- Designated Roth contributions made under a section 401(k) plan, a section 403(b) salary reduction agreement, or a governmental section 457(b) plan.
- Distributions to an employee or former employee from a nonqualified deferred compensation plan (NQDC) or a nongovernmental section 457(b) plan.
- Amounts included as income under an NQDC (nonqualified deferred compensation) plan because of section 409A.
- Amounts includable in income under section 457(f) because the amounts are no longer subject to a substantial risk of forfeiture.

- ➢ Payments to statutory employees who are subject to Social Security and Medicare taxes but are not subject to federal income tax withholding must be shown in box 1 as "other compensation".
- ➢ Cost of current insurance protection under a compensatory split-dollar life insurance arrangement.
- ➢ Employee contributions to a health savings account (HSA).
- ➢ Employer's contributions to an HSA if included in the employee's income.
- ➢ Nonqualified moving expenses and expense reimbursement.
- ➢ Payments made to former employees while on active duty in the armed forces or other uniformed services.
- ➢ All other compensation, including certain scholarships and fellowship grants; other compensation includes taxable amounts paid to the employee from which federal income tax was not withheld. An employer may use another Form W-2 to show an employee's compensation apart from their earned wages based on their bookkeeping practices.

Box 2 through Box 11

Box 2: Federal Income Tax Withheld

Shows the total federal income tax withheld from the employee's wages for the year. Parachute payments include compensation for certain covered employees and are taxed at 20%, including the 20% excise tax withheld on excess parachute payments.

If the taxpayer claims itemized deductions, and/or extra withholding deducted from each pay period, this action could influence the withholding amount.

Box 3: Social Security Wages

Shows the total amount of non-tip wages used to figure out the taxpayer's Social Security pay-in and pay-out amounts. The total of boxes 3 and 7 cannot exceed the Social Security yearly pay-in limit of $142,800.00.

Box 4: Social Security Tax Withheld

Shows the total employee Social Security tax withholding, which is determined by multiplying the taxing percentage (6.2%) against the Social Security wage limit of $142,800.00 for 2021. The Social Security Administration sets the Social Security wage limit every year and can also change the taxed percentage, though they rarely do. The amount in this box should not exceed $8,853.60 for 2021.

Box 5: Medicare Wages and Tips

The wages and tips subject to Medicare tax are determined using the same method as the Social Security tax in boxes 3 and 7 except that there is no wage base limit for Medicare tax.

Box 6: Medicare Tax Withheld

This box shows the total employee Medicare tax withheld. The tax withholding percentage is 1.45%. Medicare tax withholdings are determined from the employee's total income amount in box 1.

Income

Example: Ryan's total wages for 2021 was $150,000.00; thus, this is the amount reported in box 1. Because $150,000.00 exceeds the 2021 Social Security yearly pay-in limit, $142,800.00 will be the amount shown in box 3. Box 4 is determined by multiplying the amount in box 3 by the taxing percentage of 6.2%, meaning the amount shown in box 4 is $8,853.60. Since the wages and tips subject to Medicare tax have no wage base limit, the amount reported in box 5 will simply be Ryan's total wages for 2021 ($150,000.00), the same as in box 1. Determine box 6 by multiplying the amount in box 5 by the Medicare tax withholding percentage of 1.45%, meaning the amount shown in box 6 will be $2,175. Thus, the amounts reported in the boxes will appear as follows:

Box 1: $150,000.00
Box 3: $142,800.00
Box 4: $8,853.60
Box 5: $150,000.00
Box 6: $2,175.00

Federal Insurance Contributions Act (FICA) is the money taken out of workers' paychecks to pay the Social Security retirement income and Medicare. The employer and employee portion of the Social Security and Medicare tax is also referred to as FICA. The amount of FICA payments depends on the taxpayer's income. Consider the following scenarios:

Alberto earns $50,000 for tax year 2021, so his FICA contributions would be $3,825. In this case, $3,100 is his Social Security portion and $725 for Medicare.

$50,000 X 6.2% = $3,100 $50,000 X 1.45% = $725 $3,100 + $725 = $3,825

Ezra earns $250,000 for tax year 2021; he would pay $12,612.40. He would pay 6.2% on the first $142,800 for Social Security ($8,853.60), then 1.45% on the first $200,000 earned for Medicare ($2,900) and the additional 2.35% for earning $250,000, which is $1,175.

$142,800 × 6.2% = $8,853.60
$200,000 × 1.45% = $2,900
$50,000 × 2.35% = $1,175
$8,854 + $2,900 + $1,175 = $12,929

Box 7: Social Security Tips

This box shows the tips the employee reported to the employer, which is not included in box 3. The combined amount of boxes 3 and 7 is used to figure Social Security tax and should exceed the maximum yearly Social Security wage base limit.

Box 8: Allocated Tips

Shows tips allocated to the employee. Allocated tips will be discussed later in this chapter. The amount in box 8 is not included in the amounts in boxes 1, 3, 5, or 7.

Box 9: Verification Code

If the employer participates in the W-2 Verification Code, the code numbers are in this box. Apart from this, box 9 will be left blank.

Income

Box 10: Dependent Care Benefits

Shows the total dependent-care benefits under a dependent-care assistance program (section 129) paid for or incurred by the employer for the employee. This amount will also include the fair market value (FMV) of employer-provided or employer-sponsored day-care facilities and the amounts paid or incurred in a section 125 cafeteria plan. All amounts paid or incurred are reported in this box, regardless of employee forfeitures, including those exceeding the $10,500 exclusion.

Box 11: Nonqualified Plans

The purpose of box 11 is for the SSA to determine if any part of the amount reported in boxes 1, 3, or 5 was earned in a prior year. The SSA uses this information to verify that it has properly applied the Social Security earnings test and paid the correct amount of benefits. Box 11 shows a distribution to an employee from a nonqualified plan or a nongovernmental section 457 plan, and this amount is also reported in box 1.

Box 12: Codes

Box 12 consists of "sub-boxes" 12a, 12b, 12c, and 12d

Though sometimes left completely blank, these boxes are used as needed when specific, uncommon items must be reported to the taxpayer by their employer for tax purposes. Each "sub-box" consists of a small space followed by a line and a larger space. If used, the employer will place a letter in the small place that designates one of the codes explained below, with the code's corresponding amount placed in the larger space. Which "sub-box" a code is placed in and what order they are shown is arbitrary. No more than four codes can be entered in box 12. Box 12 has 4 sub-boxes that are used to report the following income. If the employer only needs to report one item, enter it in box a. Only four items are reported on one W-2; if more than four items are reported, then an additional W-2 must be used. The following are the codes that must be reported in box 12.

> *Code A*: Uncollected Social Security or RRTA tax on tips. The employee's Social Security or Railroad Retirement Tax Act (RRTA) tax on all the employee's tips that the employer could not collect because the employee did not have enough funds to deduct the tax. This amount is not included in box 4.
>
> *Code B*: Uncollected Medicare tax on tips (but not Additional Medicare Tax). Shows the employee's Medicare tax or RRTA Medicare tax on tips that the employer could not collect because the employee did not have enough funds from which to deduct the tax. This amount is not included in the total shown in box 6.
>
> *Code C*: Taxable cost of group-term life insurance over $50,000. Shows the taxable cost of group-term life insurance coverage over $50,000 provided to the employee (including a former employee). This amount is included in boxes 1 and 3 up to the Social Security wage limit.
>
> *Code D*: Elective deferrals to a section 401(k) cash or deferred arrangement. Shows deferrals under a SIMPLE retirement account part of section 401(k) arrangement. This amount is included in box 3 but not box 1.

Code E: Elective deferrals under a section 403(b) salary reduction agreement. This amount is included in box 3 but not box 1.

Code F: Elective deferrals under a section 408(k)(6) salary reduction SEP. This amount is included in box 3 but not box 1.

Code G: Elective deferrals and employer contributions (including non-elective deferrals) to any governmental or nongovernmental section 457(b) deferred compensation plan. This amount is included in box 3 but not box 1.

Code H: Elective deferrals to a section 501(c)(18)(D) tax-exempt organization plan. This amount is included in box 1 as wages.

Code J: Nontaxable sick pay. Shows any sick pay not included in income (not shown in boxes 1, 3, and 5) because the employee contributed to the sick-pay plan. Not included are nontaxable disability payments made directly to the state.

Code K: 20% excise tax on excess golden parachute payments.

Code L: Business expense reimbursements under an accountable plan are excluded from the employee's gross income. An employer will use this code to report the excess portion of paid reimbursements for employee business expenses, but only if the expense was calculated using a per diem or mileage allowance.

Code M: If the taxpayer is a former employee of the business that provided the W-2, uncollected Social Security or RRTA tax on the cost of group-term life insurance over $50,000 will be shown here.

Code N: If the taxpayer is a former employee of the business that provided the W-2, uncollected Medicare tax on the taxable cost of group-term life insurance over $50,000 (but not Additional Medicare Tax) will be shown here.

Code P: Excludable moving expense reimbursements paid directly to an employee. Shows the total moving expense reimbursements paid directly to the employee for qualified (deductible) moving expenses. The total for moving expense reimbursement is not included in boxes 1, 3, or 5. Effective for tax years 2018 through 2025, these reimbursements only apply to members of the U.S. Armed Forces on active duty.

Code Q: Nontaxable combat pay. Shows nontaxable combat pay.

Code R: Employer contributions to an Archer MSA. The tax professional must use Form 8853 to report the amount and attach the form to the return.

Code S: Employee salary reduction contributions under a section 408(p) SIMPLE (not included in box 1). This amount is included in box 3 but not box 1.

Income

Code T: Adoption benefits (not included in box 1). If Code T is used, the tax professional must complete Form 8839 to determine which benefits are taxable and nontaxable.

Code V: Income from the exercise of nonstatutory stock options(s). This amount shows the fair market value of the exercise price of stock options that were granted to the employee. Include the amount up to the Social Security wage base on this box in boxes 1, 3, and 5.

Code W: Employer contributions to a health savings account (HSA) including amounts contributed using a section 125 cafeteria plan. Tax professionals will use Form 8889 to report the amount and then attach the form to the client's return.

Code Y: Deferrals under a section 409A nonqualified deferred compensation plan.

Code Z: Income under section 409A on a nonqualified deferred compensation plan that fails to satisfy section 409A is shown here. This amount is also included in box 1 of the W-2, but the amount shown here will be subject to an additional tax when reported on Form 1040.

Code AA: Designated Roth contributions under a section 401(k) plan. The amount shown here is separate from the elective deferrals shown using code D. This amount is included in box 3 but not box 1.

Code BB: Designated Roth contributions under a section 403(b) plan. The amount shown here is separate from the elective deferrals shown using code E. This amount is included in box 3 but not box 1.

Code DD: Cost of employer-sponsored health coverage. The amount reported with this code is nontaxable.

Code EE: Roth contribution under a governmental section 457(b) plan. The amount shown here is separate from the elective deferrals shown using code G. This amount is included in box 3 but not box 1.

Code FF: Permitted benefits under a Qualified Small Employer Health Reimbursement Arrangement (QSEHRA). This code is used to report the total amount of permitted benefits under a QSEHRA. For 2021 the maximum amount of an eligible employee is $5,300 or $10,700 for family members.

Code GG: Income from qualified equity grants under section 83(i). The amount included here is a part of the total gross wages reported in box 1.

Code HH: Aggregate deferrals under section 83(i) elections as of the close of the calendar year. Report the total amount of income deferred under section 83(i).

Box 13: Statutory Employee, Retirement Plan, and Third-Party Sick Pay

Box 13 shows three options to select: Statutory Employee, Retirement Plan, and Third-Party Sick Pay. If the "Retirement plan" box is checked, special limits may apply to the amount of traditional IRA contributions that can be deducted. Review Publication 590.

Statutory Employee

This box is checked for statutory employees whose earnings are subject to Social Security and Medicare taxes but are not subject to federal income tax withholding. Do not check this box for common-law employees. There are workers who are independent contractors under the common-law rules but are treated as employees by statute. The following are considered statutory employees:

- A driver who is an agent or is paid on commission and distributes beverages (other than milk), meat, vegetables, fruit, bakery products, or who picks up and delivers laundry or dry cleaning.
- A full-time life insurance sales agent whose principal business activity (primarily for one life insurance company) sells life insurance, annuity contracts, or both.
- An individual working from home on materials or goods that his/her employer supplied must be returned to the employer or to an employer's representative if the employer furnished specifications on how to do the work.
- A full-time traveling or city salesperson who works on the employer's behalf and turns in orders to the employer from wholesalers, retailers, contractors, and operators of hotels, restaurants, or other similar establishments. The goods sold must be merchandise for resale or supplies for use in the buyers' business operations. The work performed for the employer must be the salesperson's principal business activity.

Review Publication 15-A, section 1.

Retirement Plan

This box is checked if the employee was an "active participant" (for any part of the year) in any of the following:

- A qualified pension, profit-sharing, or stock bonus plan described in section 401(a), including a 401(k) plan.
- An annuity plan described in section 403(a).
- An annuity contract or custodial account described in section 403(b).
- A simplified employee pension (SEP) plan described in section 408(k).
- A SIMPLE retirement account described in section 408(p).
- A trust described in section 501(c)(18).
- A plan for federal, state, or local government employees or by an agency or instrumentality thereof, other than a section 457(b) plan.

Generally, an employee is an active participant if covered by:

- A defined benefit plan for any tax year in which he or she is eligible to participate.
- A defined contribution plan for any tax year that employer or employee contributions (or forfeitures) are added to his or her account.

Income

Third-Party Sick Pay

This box will be checked only if a third-party sick-pay provider's program covers the individual. Sick pay can include both short- and long-term benefits—review Publication 15-A.

Box 14 through Box 20

Box 14: Other.

The amount in box 14 is included in box 1 and includes miscellaneous items (like the lease value of a vehicle provided to an employee), which must be reported here or in a separate statement to the employee. The employer may also use this box for any other information he or she may want to give to the employee. Examples include withheld state disability insurance taxes, union dues, uniform payments, deducted health insurance premiums, nontaxable income, educational assistance payments, parsonage allowance, and utilities for a clergy member.

In addition, the employer may enter the following contributions to a pension plan:

- Non-elective employer contributions made on behalf of an employee.
- Voluntary after-tax contributions (but not designated Roth contributions) are deducted from an employee's pay.
- Required employee contributions.
- Employer matching contributions.

Boxes 15 through 20

State and local income tax information. Use these boxes to report state and local income tax information, which will vary from state to state. Tax professionals will need to do research to know what they will need to prepare their individual state (if applicable).

Again, if the employee notices an error on Form W-2, he or she should notify the employer and request a corrected Form W-2.

Part 1 Review Questions

To obtain the maximum benefit from this chapter, LTP recommends that you complete each of the following questions, and then compare them to the answers with feedback that immediately follows. Under governing self-study standards, vendors are required to present review questions intermittently throughout each self-study course.

These questions and explanations are not part of the final examination and will not be graded by LTP.

IP1.1
When should the taxpayer receive their W-2's?

a. W-2's should be postmarked by January 31 of the following year.
b. W-2's should be in the taxpayer's possession by January 31 of the current tax year.
c. W-2's should be in the taxpayer's possession by February 1 of the current tax year.
d. W-2's need to be emailed to all employees by January 31 of the current tax year.

IP1.2

Which of the following best describes what is not reported in box 1 of the W-2?

   a. Box 1 reports total wages.
   b. Box 1 reports allocated tips.
   c. Box 1 reports all compensation.
   d. Box 1 reports noncash payments.

IP1.3

Which of the following circumstance does not require a taxpayer to change their W-4 within 10 days?

   a. Daniel divorced his wife in March and has been filing separate tax returns for the past 2 years.
   b. Jake and Danelle had a new baby in February.
   c. Karina began supporting her mother in January.
   d. Gigi and David got married in May.

Part 1 Review Questions Answers

IP1.1

When should the taxpayer receive their W-2's?

   a. W-2's should be postmarked by January 31 of the following year.
   b. W-2's should be in the taxpayer's possession by January 31 of the current tax year.
   c. W-2's should be in the taxpayer's possession by February 1 of the current tax year.
   d. W-2's need to be emailed to all employees by January 31 of the current tax year.

Feedback: Review section *Form W2.*

IP1.2

Which of the following best describes what is not reported in box 1 of the W-2?

   a. Box 1 reports total wages.
   b. Box 1 reports allocated tips.
   c. Box 1 reports all compensation.
   d. Box 1 reports noncash payments.

Feedback: Review section *Box 1 of the W2.*

IP1.3

Which of the following circumstance does not require a taxpayer to change their W-4 within 10 days?

   a. Daniel divorced his wife in March and has been filing separate tax returns for the past 2 years.
   b. Jake and Danelle had a new baby in February.
   c. Karina began supporting her mother in January.
   d. Gigi and David got married in May.

Feedback: Review section *Exemption from Withholding,* under Schedule 1.

Income

Part 2 Income

Although most clients will probably only have employer-provided income to report via a W-2, this is only one type of income and one way to report it. The IRS has the authority to tax all income from whatever source it is derived. This provision includes compensation for services, gains from dispositions of property, interest and dividends, rent and royalties, pensions and annuities, gambling winnings, and even illegal activities. All such income a person receives is collectively referred to as "worldwide income." However, not all money or property is taxable or subject to tax.

There are two major types of income: *earned income* and *unearned income*. Earned income is income the taxpayer received for working and includes the following types of income:

- Wages, salaries, tips, and other types of taxable employee pay.
- Net earnings from self-employment.
- Gross income received as a statutory employee.
- Union strike benefits.
- Long-term disability benefits received prior to reaching the minimum retirement age.

Unearned income is any amount received indirectly and not as a direct repayment of any services rendered or work provided. Unearned income includes:

- Interest and dividends.
- Pensions and annuities.
- Social Security and railroad retirement benefits (including disability benefits).
- Alimony and child support.
- Welfare benefits.
- Workers' compensation benefits.
- Unemployment compensation.
- Income while an inmate.
- Workfare payments (review Publication 596 for a definition).

Form 1040, Page 1, lines 1 - 7

The following picture shows which income form is used to report income. All income is reported based on the tax form the taxpayer receives and the form used to report it.

	1	Wages, salaries, tips, etc. Attach Form(s) W-2				1	W-2
Attach Sch. B if required.	2a	Tax-exempt interest	2a Form 1099-INT	b Taxable interest		2b	Form 1099-INT
	3a	Qualified dividends	3a Form 1099-DIV	b Ordinary dividends		3b	Form 1099-DIV
	4a	IRA distributions	4a Form 1099-R	b Taxable amount		4b	Form 1099-R
	5a	Pensions and annuities	5a Form 1099-R	b Taxable amount		5b	Form 1099-R
Standard Deduction for—	6a	Social security benefits	6a SSA 1099	b Taxable amount		6b	SSA 1099
	7	Capital gain or (loss). Attach Schedule D if required. If not required, check here			▶ ☐	7	

Line 1: Wages and Other Compensation

If the taxpayer is an employee, the taxpayer should receive Form W-2 showing the wages he or she earned in exchange for services performed. A W-2 is a tax form created by employers to detail earnings and government withholdings for a given tax year. The W-2 should be distributed to the employees by the end of January for the prior tax year. The tax professional uses the W-2 to determine his or her client's earned income for the year. A taxpayer will receive a W-2 from each employer the individual is employed by; usually, this means a taxpayer will only receive one W-2, but taxpayers could have multiple W-2s to report for the current tax year if they worked more than one job at any point during the year.

Line 1 of Form 1040 reports the total amount of wages earned. Wages include salaries, vacation allowances, bonuses, commissions, and fringe benefits, and compensation includes everything received in payment for personal services.

Line 2: Interest

When to Report Interest Income

Interest income is reported based on the accounting method the taxpayer is using to report his or her income. If taxpayers use the cash method, they generally report their interest income in the year in which it was actually or constructively received. Use the special rules to report the discount on certain debt instruments such as U.S. savings bonds and original issue discount (OID).

Taxpayers should always keep a list showing their sources of income. For example, all Forms 1099-INT and Forms 1099-DIV should be kept with their yearly tax return. If parents elect to claim the investment income of their child, those forms should be kept with their tax returns as well. Interest earned as a beneficiary of an estate or trust is generally taxable income. Taxpayers should receive a Schedule K-1 for their portion of the interest. A copy of the Schedule K-1 should be kept with the tax return as well.

Constructively Received

Interest is constructively received when it is credited to the taxpayer's account or made available to the taxpayer; the taxpayer does not need to have physical possession of the money. The taxpayer is considered to have received interest, dividends, or other earnings from any deposit, bank accounts, savings, loans, similar financial institution, or life insurance policy when the income has been credited to the taxpayer's account and becomes subject to withdrawal.

Income is constructively received on the deposit or account even if the taxpayer must do any of the following:

➢ Make withdrawals in multiples of even amounts.
➢ Give notice of a withdrawal before making the withdrawal.
➢ Withdraw all or part of the account to be able to withdraw the earnings.
➢ Pay a penalty on early withdrawals unless the interest received on an early withdrawal or redemption is substantially less than the interest payable at maturity of the account.

Income

Under the *accrual method*, interest income is reported when the income is earned, whether it was received or not. Interest is earned over the life of the debt. With *coupon bonds*, interest is taxable the year the coupon becomes due and payable; it does not matter when the coupon payment is mailed.

Form 1099-INT

This form is provided to taxpayers by companies such as banks or investment companies (in much the same way as W-2s are issued by employers) for informational purposes to be entered on the taxpayer's current year tax return.

Interest is generally reported on Form 1099-INT or a substitute statement. Form 1099-INT shows the interest earned for the year but is not attached to the tax return. Some interest is not reported on Form 1099-INT, yet it must still be reported on the tax return. For example, if Samantha received interest from the partnership that she is a member of, her interest would be reported to her on the Schedule K-1 that she received. A substitute statement can come from an individual payer and not a large institution and must contain all the information found on Form 1099-INT.

As with any form reported with the taxpayer's name, address, and taxpayer identification number (TIN), make sure the information is correct.

Box 1: Reports interest income paid to the recipient not included in box 3. Form 1099-INT is issued for earned interest of $10 or more.

Box 2: Reports interest or principal that was forfeited because of an early withdrawal penalty. Do not reduce the amount in box 1 by the forfeited amount. Form 1040, Schedule 1, line 17 reports Box 2 since this action will adjust the taxpayer's tax liability.

Box 3: Reports interest from U.S. Savings Bonds and Treasury obligations (another word used for bonds). For taxable covered securities and acquired at a premium, see Box 12. The amount in this box may or may not be taxable. Review Publication 550.

Box 4: Reports federal income tax withheld. If the taxpayer does not receive a TIN (taxpayer identification number), the payer is required to withhold at a 24% rate on the amount in box 1.

Box 5: Investment expenses for a single-class real estate mortgage investment conduit (REMIC) only. Also, include the amount in box 1.

Box 6: Reports foreign taxes paid.

Box 7: Shows the foreign country or U.S. possession taxes paid.
Box 8: Shows tax-exempt interest paid to the person's account during the calendar year. This amount may be subject to backup withholding.

Box 9: This box shows the Specified Private Activity bond interest. Specified Private Activity Bonds are defined in section 141 and issued after Aug 7, 1986.

Box 10: This box shows the value of a taxable or tax-exempt covered security acquired with a market discount, but only if the taxpayer made an election under section 1278(b) to include the market discount in income as it accrues. The taxpayer must notify the payer of the election in writing [certain restrictions apply, see Regulations section 1.6045-1(n)(5)].

Box 11: Bond premium. A taxable covered security other than a U.S. Treasury obligation acquired at a premium.

Box 12: For a U.S. Treasury obligation that is a covered security. This box shows the amount of premium amortization allocable to the interest payment(s).

Box 13: Bond Premiums on Tax-Exempt Bonds. If you report a tax-exempt covered security acquired at a premium, the amount entered is the bond premium amortization that is allocable to the interest paid during the year.

Box 14: Tax-Exempt and Tax Credit Bond CUSIP Number. The CUSIP is entered for single bonds or accounts containing a single bond.

Box 15-17: State's information. These boxes designate where the taxpayer lives as well as any state in which the taxpayer may have earned the income.

Señor 1040 Says: Make sure that the year on Form 1099-INT is the year that you are preparing the tax return for. It is important to verify the year on all documents that report income to the taxpayer to ensure that the income being reported is for the correct tax year.

Income

Backup Withholding

Interest income is generally not subject to regular withholding, but it may be subject to the backup withholding rate of 28% in the following situations:

- ➢ The taxpayer did not give the income provider his or her TIN (taxpayer identification number) in the required manner.
- ➢ The IRS notifies the income provider that the TIN is incorrect.
- ➢ The taxpayer is required to certify that he or she is not subject to backup withholding but fails to do so.
- ➢ The IRS notifies the income provider to start withholding on interest and dividends because the taxpayer has underreported interest or dividends on the taxpayer's tax return.

There are civil and criminal penalties for giving false information to avoid backup withholding. The civil penalty is $500. If the taxpayer willfully falsified information, he or she may be subject to criminal penalties including fines and/or imprisonment. If backup withholding is deducted from the interest income, the income provider, (or payer), must give the taxpayer Form 1099-INT to indicate the amount that was withheld.

Accounts and Payee-Identifying Numbers

Banks and other financial institutions pay certain kinds of income when an account or an investment has been opened. When opening the account, the individual is required by federal law to provide his or her SSN to any financial institution or individual who needs the information to make a return, statement, or any other form of document. For instance, when opening a joint account, the primary SSN must be provided.

Example: Gina and her son, Trenton, opened a joint account with Trenton's birthday money. Trenton's SSN would be given to the bank, and his name would appear on the account first. If the primary SSN is not given to the payer, the account holder (Trenton) would have to pay a $50 penalty for each incident.

Truncating

A payer identification number is any number issued by a government agency for the purpose of identification, including Social Security numbers (SSN), individual tax identification numbers (ITIN), employer identification numbers (EIN), taxpayer identification numbers (TIN), and adoption identification numbers (ATIN). Anyone issuing documents containing taxpayer identification information may truncate payee-identifying numbers by replacing the first 5 numbers of payer identification numbers with an X or * (XXX-XX-0000 or ***-**-1111, for example). This can be done on payee statements such as Forms 1097, 1098, 1099, 3921, 9322, and 5498, but it may not be done on Form W-2G.

Certification

For new accounts paying interest or dividends, the taxpayer must certify under penalty of perjury that his or her SSN is correct and that he or she is not subject to backup withholding. The payer will give the taxpayer Form W-9: *Request for Taxpayer Identification*.

Number and Certification

If the taxpayer fails to make this certification, backup withholding will begin immediately on the taxpayer's new account or investment.

If the taxpayer has been notified by a payer that backup withholding will be deducted from the taxpayer's interest or dividend income because the taxpayer did not provide a correct SSN or EIN, the taxpayer can stop the withholding by following the instructions given to him or her by the payer. A payer is the one who administers the account, such as the bank.

Line 2a Tax-Exempt Interest

Certain types of interest income are tax-exempt and are reported on Form 1040, line 2a. Interest paid by state and local governments are exempt from federal taxation but may be taxable at the state level. The fact that this interest is tax-exempt does not mean that it is not reported; tax-exempt interest must be reported. Tax-exempt interest is included when determining how much Social Security could be taxable to the taxpayer and spouse.

Taxpayers are required to use Schedule B if any of the following are true:

- The taxpayer received over $1,500 of taxable interest or ordinary dividends.
- The taxpayer received interest from a seller-financed mortgage and the buyer used the property as a personal residence.
- The taxpayer received interest or ordinary dividends.
- The taxpayer had a financial interest in, or signature authority over, a financial account in a foreign trust.
- The taxpayer accrued interest from a bond.
- The taxpayer is reducing the interest income on a bond by the amortizable bond premium.
- The taxpayer is reporting original issue discount (OID) in an amount less than the amount on Form 1099-OID.
- The taxpayer is claiming the exclusion of interest from U.S. savings bonds series EE or I issued after 1989.

Government Bonds

A government bond is a debt security issued by the government to support government spending. This section will give an overview of the most common federal government bonds. If the taxpayer purchases a government bond for a discount when interest has been defaulted or when interest has accrued and has not been paid, the transaction is considered as "trading a bond flat." The defaulted or unpaid interest is not income and is not taxable to the taxpayer. When an interest payment is received, it reduces the capital of the remaining cost of the bond. Interest that accrues after the date of purchase is taxable interest for the year received or accrued.

Interest for a bond can be reported in one of two ways. First, the taxpayer can elect to pay the interest as it is accrued. In this case, the taxpayer would pay taxes on the interest each year. Taxpayers who use the accrual basis must report interest as it accrues. They cannot postpone reporting interest until they receive it or until the bonds mature. The second option is the cash method in which taxes on the savings bonds are paid when they are redeemed or when the bond has matured. If this option is selected, the taxpayer would report all the interest in the year the bond is redeemed.

Series EE and Series E Bonds

Series EE and series E bonds are issued at a discount and sold for less than the face value of the bond. The buyer makes money by holding them to the bond's maturity date, at which point the face value is paid to the taxpayer. Series EE bonds were first offered in January 1980 and have a 30-year maturity period. Before July 1980, series E bonds were issued. The original 10-year maturity period of series E has been extended to 40 years for bonds issued before December 1965 and to 30 years for bonds issued after November 1965. Both paper series EE and E bonds were issued at a discount. Electronic bonds are issued at face value. Paper savings bonds are no longer sold at financial institutions. Owners of paper series EE bonds can convert them to electronic bonds. These converted electronic bonds do not retain the denomination listed on the paper certificate but are posted at their purchase price with accrued interest.

Series H and HH Bonds

Series H and HH bonds are issued at face value. Interest is paid twice a year and must be reported when received. Series H bonds have a maturity period of 30 years. Series HH bonds were first offered in 1980 and were last offered in August 2004. Series H bonds are treated the same way as series HH. Series HH bonds mature at 20 years. The last series H bonds matured in 2009, and the last series HH bonds will mature in 2024.

Series I Bonds

Series I bonds were first offered in 1998. These are inflation-indexed bonds issued at their face amount with a maturity period of 30 years. The face value plus all accrued interest is payable at maturity.

If the taxpayer uses the cash method of reporting income, he or she can report the interest on his or her series EE, series E, and series I bonds using one of the following two methods:

- Method 1: Postpone reporting the interest earned until either the year in which the bonds were cashed or disposed of, or the year the bonds mature, whichever is earliest.
- Method 2: Choose to report the increase in redemption value as interest earned each year.

The taxpayer must use the same method for all series EE, series E, and series I bonds they own. If method 2 is not used, method 1 must be used. If the taxpayer wants to change from method 1 to method 2, the taxpayer does not need the permission of the IRS. However, if the taxpayer wants to change from method 2 to method 1, permission must be requested by attaching a statement with the following information to the tax return for the year of the change:

- "131" printed or typed at the top of the statement.
- The taxpayer's name and Social Security number written beneath "131."
- The year the change was requested (beginning and ending dates).
- Identification and information from the savings bonds for which the change is being requested.
- The statement includes the following:
  - All interest received on any bonds acquired during or after the year of change when it is realized upon disposition, redemption, or final maturity, whichever is earliest.

- o All interest on the bonds acquired before the year of the change when the interest is realized upon disposition, redemption, or final maturity; whichever is earliest, with the exception of interest already reported in prior years.

Taxpayers may file an automatic extension on their tax returns to give them more time to file the paperwork. On the statement, the following should be typed: "Filed pursuant to section 301.9100-2(b)." To qualify for the extension, the original tax return should have been filed by the required due date (normally April 15th) based on the type of tax return being filed. Review Publication 550.

Señor 1040 Says: Interest on U.S. savings bonds is exempt from state and local taxes. Form 1099-INT will indicate the amount of interest that is earned for U.S. savings bonds in box 3.

Municipal Bonds

State and local governments issue municipal bonds to provide funding for capital improvement projects. Municipal bonds are not taxable by the federal government. Not all states or localities tax municipal bond interest income. Some states and localities tax all municipal bond interest, while others tax municipal bond interest income from other states or localities only.

A mortgage revenue bond (MRB) is issued by a local housing authority to finance mortgages for qualifying taxpayers. Those who qualify are normally first-time homebuyers with low income. Investors often prefer these bonds since they are tax-free and are secured by the monthly mortgage payments. Every state has MRBs and are limited by the state minimum issuance. The purchase price of the home cannot exceed a certain percentage of the area's average purchase price.

State or Local Government Obligations

Interest received on a state or local government obligation is generally not taxable. The issuer should tell the receiver if the interest is taxable or not and then give the receiver a periodic statement showing the tax treatment of the obligation. If the obligation was invested through a trust, a fund, or other organization, that issuer should provide that information.

Even if the interest may not be subject to income tax, the receiver may have to report capital gains or losses when the obligation is sold.

Line 2b Taxable Interest

Interest is a cost created by those who lend money (lenders) that is charged to the people they lent money to (borrowers). A taxpayer will pay interest whenever he or she borrows money and will earn money whenever he or she lends or deposits money, such as into a bank account.

Income

Certain interest is taxable income if it is credited to the taxpayer's account and can be withdrawn. Interest is typically not calculated based on the original amount of borrowed money (called the principal) but is instead usually determined by multiplying a predetermined percentage point by the total amount of money currently owed to the lender by the borrower. For example, John borrowed $5,000 at a 5% interest rate. Although his principal was $5,000, after making several payments, he now owes $4,365, making his interest payment for the month 5% of $4,365, or $218.25.

Taxable Interest

Taxable interest is reported using Schedule B and includes interest received from bank accounts, loans made to others, and interest from other sources. The taxpayer could be the payer or the recipient of the interest. Examples of sources of interest are as follows:

- Banks.
- Credit unions.
- Government entities (federal and state).
- Certificates of deposit (CDs).
- Life insurance.
- Installment sales.

U.S. Obligations

Interest on U.S. obligations (U.S. Treasury bills, notes, or bonds) is taxable at the federal level, but exempt from taxation in most states. Make sure to know if your state taxes the interest.

Interest and Community Property States

If a taxpayer lives in a community property state and receives an interest or dividend distribution, one-half of the distribution is considered to be received by each spouse. If the taxpayer and spouse file MFS, each must report one-half of the distribution on their separate returns. If the distribution is not considered community property under state law, each taxpayer must report his or her separate distributions.

Example: Johanna and Jacob are filing MFS, and they have a joint money market account. Under state law, half the income belongs to Johanna and the other half belongs to Jacob. Each would report half of the income.

Foreign Accounts and Trust Requirements

In a global economy, many people in the United States have foreign financial accounts. The law requires owners of foreign financial accounts to report their accounts to the U.S. Treasury Department, even if the accounts don't generate any taxable income. Account owners need to report accounts by the April due date following the calendar year that they own a foreign financial account.
The U.S. government requires individuals to report foreign financial accounts because foreign financial institutions may not be subject to the same reporting requirements as domestic ones.

Reporting Requirements

The Bank Secrecy Act requires a U.S. taxpayer who owns a foreign bank account, brokerage account, mutual fund, unit trust, or other financial account to file a *Report of Foreign Bank and Financial Accounts (FBAR)* if the taxpayer has any of the following:

1. Financial interest in, signature authority, or other authority over one or more accounts in a foreign country, and
2. The aggregate value of all foreign financial accounts exceeds $1,500 at any time during the calendar year.

A U.S. person is a citizen or resident of the United States or any domestic legal entity such as a partnership, corporation, limited liability company, estate, or trust. A foreign country includes any area outside the United States or outside the following U.S. territories and possessions:

- Northern Mariana Islands
- District of Columbia
- American Samoa
- Guam
- Puerto Rico
- United States Virgin Islands
- Trust Territories of the Pacific Islands
- Indian lands, as defined in the **Indian Gaming Regulatory Act**

How to Report

Taxpayers required to report their foreign accounts should file the FBAR electronically using the **BSA E-Filing System**. The FBAR is due April 15. If April 15 falls on a Saturday, Sunday, or legal holiday, the FBAR is due the next business day. Taxpayers don't file the FBAR with individual, business, trust, or estate tax returns.

If two people jointly own a foreign financial account or if several people each own a partial interest in an account, then each person has a financial interest in that account. Each person must report the entire value of the account on an FBAR.

Spouses do not need to file a separate FBAR if they complete and sign **Form 114a, Record of Authorization to Electronically File FBARs**, and:

1. All reportable financial accounts are jointly owned with the filing spouse, and
2. The filing spouse reports the jointly-owned accounts on a timely-filed FBAR.

Otherwise, both spouses must file separate FBARs, and each spouse must report the entire value of the jointly-owned accounts. The e-filing system will not allow both spouses' signatures on the same electronic form. Spouses need to complete Form 114a to designate which one will file the FBAR. The Form 114a is not submitted with the FBAR; it should be kept with other financial and tax records.

Generally, a child is responsible for filing their own FBAR. If a child can't file their own FBAR for any reason, such as age, the child's parent or guardian must file it for them. If the child can't sign their FBAR, a parent or guardian must sign it.

Income

How to Calculate the Greatest Account Value of Foreign Financial Accounts

Those filing the FBAR need to reasonably figure and report the greatest value of currency or non-monetary assets in their accounts during the calendar year. The taxpayer may rely on their periodic account statements if the statements fairly show the greatest account value during the year.

Taxpayers figure the greatest value in the currency of the account, then convert that value into U.S. dollars using the **exchange rate on the last day of the calendar year**. The taxpayer may use another valid exchange rate and give the source of the rate, if there's no Treasury Financial Management Service rate available. For example, someone would typically value an account located in Mexico in pesos. The taxpayer would figure the greatest value of the account in pesos and then convert it into U.S. dollars. See IRS FBAR Reference Guide for more information.

Personal Loans

A personal loan that a taxpayer is collecting interest on is a taxable event. For example, Samuel purchased a house for his cousin Samantha and is charging her 2.5% interest on the price of the house. Samuel will need to create an amortization schedule in order to track that he is getting paid and reporting the interest earned from Samantha. Samantha is able to report the interest paid to Samuel on her Form 1040, Schedule A, if she is able to itemize. Itemized deductions will be discussed in a later chapter.

Part 2 Review Questions

To obtain the maximum benefit from this chapter, LTP recommends that you complete each of the following questions, and then compare them to the answers with feedback that immediately follows. Under governing self-study standards, vendors are required to present review questions intermittently throughout each self-study course.

These questions and explanations are not part of the final examination and will not be graded by LTP.

IP2.1
Which of the following is not the best description of constructively received income?

a. Amanda received an interest payment on December 31 but did not put it into the bank until Jan 2.
b. Andres earned money from his employer for the prior year. He did not pick the money up until the following year.
c. Karina received an early penalty withdrawal that was substantially less than what she would have earned if she left the money in the account until maturity.
d. Kevin had some bond payments credited to his account on January 1. He did not withhold the payment until April 15.

IP2.2

Where would interest earned be reported on Form 1099INT?

a. Box 1
b. Box 2
c. Box 4
d. Box 8

IP2.3

Where would exempt interest earned be reported on Form 1099INT?

a. Box 1
b. Box 2
c. Box 6
d. Box 8

IP2.4

Which of the following best describes how U.S. obligations are taxed?

a. U.S. obligations are taxed on the federal and state.
b. U.S. obligations are not taxed on the federal and state.
c. U.S. obligations are taxed on the federal return and may not be taxable on the state return.
d. U.S. obligations are not taxed on the federal but are taxed by the state.

IP2.5

Josie has an annuity contract that was sold prior to the maturity rate. Which of the following best describes her situation?

a. Josie will have no tax consequence.
b. Josie will have to pay tax on the accumulated interest.
c. Josie will receive a new annuity contract.
d. Josie will need to purchase an insurance contract for her protection.

IP2.6

Kay and Mark are married and live in a community property state. They want to file their returns separately. How would they report their $1,000 earned interest?

a. Kay would report 100% of the interest since her name is first.
b. Mark would report 100% of the interest since his name is first.
c. Since Mark's name is first, he would report 60%, and Kay would report 40%.
d. Each would report 50% on their tax return.

IP2.7

Which of the following does the individual taxpayer need to do regarding federal tax-exempt interest?

a. Report the interest and pay tax.
b. Report the interest and pay no tax.
c. Does not need to report the interest.
d. Report the interest only on the state return.

Income

IP2.8
Original issue discount (OID) is a form of which of the following?

a. Interest
b. Dividend
c. Non-dividend distribution
d. Nontaxable interest

IP2.10
Which of the following is not a government debt security?

a. Series EE and E bonds
b. Series I bonds
c. Series H bonds
d. Series A bonds

IP2.11
Which of the following is the way to report the interest earned on a bond?

a. Pay quarterly as interest accrues.
b. Pay monthly as interest accrues.
c. Pay yearly as interest accrues.
d. Pay yearly on July 1 as interest accrues.

IP2.12
Which of the following is the way to report the interest earned on a bond?

a. Pay quarterly as interest accrues.
b. Pay monthly as interest accrues.
c. Pay when the bonds have been redeemed.
d. Pay yearly on July 1 as interest accrues.

Part 2 Review Questions Answers

IP2.1
Which of the following is not the best description of constructively received income?

a. Amanda received an interest payment on December 31 but did not put it into the bank until Jan 2.
b. Andres earned money from his employer for the prior year. He did not pick the money up until the following year.
c. Karina received an early penalty withdrawal that was substantially less than what she would have earned if she left the money in the account until maturity.
d. Kevin had some bond payments credited to his account on January 1. He did not withhold the payment until April 15.

Feedback: Review section *Constructively Received.*

Income

IP2.2
Where would interest earned be reported on Form 1099INT?

  a. Box 1
  b. Box 2
  c. Box 4
  d. Box 8

Feedback: Review section *Form 1099-INT*.

IP2.3
Where would exempt interest earned be reported on Form 1099INT?

  a. Box 1
  b. Box 2
  c. Box 6
  d. Box 8

Feedback: Review section *Form 1099-INT*.

IP2.4
Which of the following best describes how U.S. obligations are taxed?

  a. U.S. obligations are taxed on the federal and state.
  b. U.S. obligations are not taxed on the federal and state.
  c. U.S. obligations are taxed on the federal return and may not be taxable on the state return.
  d. U.S. obligations are not taxed on the federal but are taxed by the state.

Feedback: Review section *U.S. Obligations*.

IP2.5
Josie has an annuity contract that was sold prior to the maturity rate. Which of the following best describes her situation?

  a. Josie will have no tax consequence.
  b. Josie will have to pay tax on the accumulated interest.
  c. Josie will receive a new annuity contract.
  d. Josie will need to purchase an insurance contract for her protection.

Feedback: Review section *Miscellaneous Types of Interest*.

IP2.6
Kay and Mark are married and live in a community property state. They want to file their returns separately. How would they report their $1,000 earned interest?

  a. Kay would report 100% of the interest since her name is first.
  b. Mark would report 100% of the interest since his name is first.
  c. Since Mark's name is first, he would report 60%, and Kay would report 40%.
  d. Each would report 50% on their tax return.

Feedback: Review section *Interest and Community Property States*.

Income

IP2.7
Which of the following does the individual taxpayer need to do regarding federal tax-exempt interest?

   a. Report the interest and pay tax.
   b. Report the interest and pay no tax.
   c. Does not need to report the interest.
   d. Report the interest only on the state return.

Feedback: Review section *Tax-Exempt Interest.*

IP2.8
Original issue discount (OID) is a form of which of the following?

   a. Interest
   b. Dividend
   c. Non-dividend distribution
   d. Nontaxable interest

Feedback: Review section *When to Report Interest Income.*

IP2.10
Which of the following is not a government debt security?

   a. Series EE and E bonds
   b. Series I bonds
   c. Series H bonds
   d. Series A bonds

Feedback: Review section *Government Bonds.*

IP2.11
Which of the following is the way to report the interest earned on a bond?

   a. Pay quarterly as interest accrues.
   b. Pay monthly as interest accrues.
   c. Pay yearly as interest accrues.
   d. Pay yearly on July 1 as interest accrues.

Feedback: Review section *Government Bonds.*

IP2.12
Which of the following is the way to report the interest earned on a bond?

   a. Pay quarterly as interest accrues.
   b. Pay monthly as interest accrues.
   c. Pay when the bonds have been redeemed.
   d. Pay yearly on July 1 as interest accrues.

Feedback: Review section *Government Bonds*

Part 3 Dividends

Dividends are a share of the profits generated by a company that can be paid in money, stock, stock rights, other property, or services; they can also be paid by a corporation, mutual fund, partnership, estate, trust, or association that is taxed as a corporation. Distributions are benefits from a closely held entity such as the S-corporation, Partnership, Limited Liability Company, and Trusts.

Dividends can be paid in the form of additional stock, which is sometimes referred to as a reinvested dividend. These are fully taxable to the recipient and must be reported, although some amounts reported as dividends may be taxed at different rates.

Form 1099-DIV: Reporting Dividend Income

As with all forms, make sure the taxpayer's name, address, and TIN are correct. The following is just for informational purposes about what each box on the Form 1099-DIV reports. The most common entries on Form 1099-DIV are: Box 1a, 1b, 2a, 3, 5, 7, and 11.

Box 1a, Total ordinary dividends: Included are money market funds, net short-term capital gains from mutual funds, and other distributions on stock. Reinvested dividends and section 404(k) dividends paid directly from the corporation are taxable. Report this amount on Form 1040, page 2, line 3b.

Box 1b, Qualified dividends: Shows the portion in box 1a that might be eligible for reduced capital gains rate.

Income

Box 2a, Total (long-term) capital gain distributions: Shows total capital gain distributions from a regulated investment company or real estate investment trust. Amount shown in box 2a is reported on Schedule D, line 13.

Box 2b, Unrecaptured section 1250 gain: From certain depreciable real property. This box shows the amount in box 2a that is unrecaptured section 1250 gain from depreciable property.

Box 2c, Section 1202 gain: Shows any amount in box 2a that is a section 1202 gain from certain small business stocks.

Box 2d, Collectibles (28%) gain: Shows any amount included in box 2a that has a 28% rate gain from sales or exchanges of collectibles. Apart from this fact, this concept is beyond the scope of this course.

Box 3, Non-dividend distributions: non-dividend distributions are shown here, if determinable.

Box 4, Federal income tax withheld: This box shows the amount of federal income tax withheld. Federal taxes are usually withheld when backup withholding is required.

Box 5, Section 199A Dividends: Shows the section 199A dividends paid to the taxpayer. This amount is included in box 1a.

Box 6, Investment Expenses: Shows the taxpayer's reported pro rata share of certain amounts deductible by a non-public offering from a regulated investment company (RIC) in computing the taxable income. Do not include any investment expense in box 1b.

Box 7, Foreign tax paid: Shows foreign tax paid on dividends and other distributions on stock. Report this amount in U.S. dollars.

Box 8, Foreign country or U.S. possession: Lists the foreign country or U.S. possession to which the foreign taxes were paid. There should be no entry if the investment company paid the tax for the funds.

Box 9, Cash liquidation distributions: Shows cash distributed as part of a liquidation.

Box 10, Noncash liquidation distributions: Shows noncash distributions made as part of a liquidation. Place the fair market value as of the date of distribution.

Box 11, Exempt-interest dividends: Shows exempt-interest dividends paid during the calendar year from a mutual fund or other regulated investment company. Include specified private activity bond interest in box 11.

Box 12, Specified private activity bond interest dividends: This box shows exempt-interest dividends paid by a RIC on specified private activity bonds to the extent that the dividends are attributable to interest on bonds received by the RIC.

Box 13-15, State Boxes: Shows state information depending upon the state the taxpayer lives in.

Income

Dividends and other distributions that earn $10 or more are reported to the taxpayer on Form 1099-DIV by the payee. If the taxpayer's ordinary dividends are more than $1,500, the taxpayer would complete Schedule B, Part III, in addition to receiving Form 1099-DIV. Ordinary dividends stated in box 1a are reported on Form 1040, line 3b. Qualified dividends are reported on line 3a of Form 1040. The amount reported on 1b is a portion of the amount shown in box 1a.

Form 1040, line 3a, Qualified Dividends

Qualified dividends are taxed at the capital gains rate for the taxpayer. Qualified dividends are included with ordinary dividends on Form 1040, page 2, line 3b. Qualified dividends are shown in box 1b of Form 1099-DIV. The rates are 0, 15 or 20% based on taxpayer's income.

0% Qualifying Dividends Tax Rate

$0 to $40,400	Single or married filing separately
$0 to $80,800	Married filing jointly or qualifying widow(er)
$0 to $54,100	Head of household

15% Qualifying Dividends Tax Rate

$40,401 to $445,850	Single
$40,401 to $250,800	Married filing separately
$80,801 to $501,600	Married filing jointly or qualifying widow(er)
$54,101 to $473,750	Head of household

20% Qualifying Dividends Tax Rate

$445,851 or more	Single
$250,801 or more	Married filing separately
$501,601 or more	Married filing jointly or qualifying widow(er)
$473,751 or more	Head of household

Form 1040, line 3b, Ordinary Dividends

Ordinary dividends are the most common type of dividend distributions and are taxed as ordinary income (as are mutual fund dividends) at the same tax rate as wages and other ordinary income of the taxpayer. All dividends are considered ordinary unless they are specifically classified as qualified dividends. Dividends received from common or preferred stock are considered ordinary dividends and are reported in box 1a of Form 1099-DIV. Ordinary dividends received on common or preferred stock can be reinvested and taxed as ordinary income.

Dividends That Are Really Interest

Certain distributions that are often reported as "dividends" are actually interest income. The taxpayer will report as interest any received dividends from deposits, or shared accounts, from the following sources:

- ➢ Credit unions.
- ➢ Cooperative banks.

- Domestic building and loan associations.
- Federal savings and loan associations.
- Mutual savings banks.

These dividends will be reported as interest in box 1 of Form 1099-INT. Generally, amounts received from money market funds are dividends and should not be reported as interest.

Dividends Used to Buy More Stock

The corporation in which the taxpayer owns stock may have a dividend reinvestment plan. This plan allows the taxpayer to choose whether to use the dividends to purchase more shares of stock or to simply receive the dividends in cash. If the reinvestment plan is chosen, the taxpayer still reports the dividends as income.

The taxpayer may choose to use dividends to purchase additional shares of stock if the corporation has such a plan. The plan is called a "dividend reinvestment plan." If the taxpayer chooses to have the dividends reinvested, the taxpayer is still required to report the dividends as income in the year they are received. The amount of the dividend is then considered part of the purchase price of the stock. Taxpayers should be reminded to keep records of reinvested dividends to help establish an accurate cost basis for their stocks at the time of purchase. "Reinvested dividend" is not a tax term; it is a phrase that is used by investors to refer to dividends earned by reinvesting dividend distributions to purchase more stock instead of receiving money.

Money Market Funds

Income received from money market funds is considered dividend income. Money market funds are a kind of mutual fund and should not be confused with money market accounts that one may get at the local bank, which report the income earned as interest, not dividends. A mutual fund is a regulated investment company generally created by "pooling" funds of investors to allow them to take advantage of a diversity of investments and professional management.

A distribution received from a mutual fund may be an ordinary dividend, a capital gain distribution, an exempt-interest dividend, a nontaxable return of capital, or a combination of two or more of these types of distributions. The fund company reports the distributions on Form 1099-DIV or a similar statement that indicates the type of distributions received.

If a mutual fund or another regulated investment company declares a dividend, including any exempt-interest dividend or capital gain distribution in the last quarter of the tax year, the dividend is considered paid in the year that the dividend was declared.

Capital Gains Distributions

Capital gains distributions (CGD) received as part of dividends from a mutual fund or real estate investment trusts (REIT) are taxed on Schedule D. These distributions are found in box 2a of Form 1099-DIV. These dividends should be considered long-term regardless of the length of time the taxpayer owned the share in the regulated investment companies more commonly known as real estate investment trusts.

Capital gains distributions are paid to the taxpayer by brokerage firms, mutual funds, and investment trusts. The capital gains distributions from mutual funds are long-term capital gains regardless of how long the taxpayer owned the stock. Distributions of net-realized short-term capital gains are reported on Form 1099-DIV as ordinary dividends.

Nontaxable Dividends

Nontaxable dividends are a return of a shareholder's original investment. These distributions are not treated the same as ordinary dividends or capital gain distributions. Non-dividend distributions reduce the taxpayer's basis in the stock. Return of capital distributions are not taxable until the taxpayer's remaining basis (investment) is reduced to zero. The basis of the stock has been reduced to zero when the taxpayer receives a distribution, and then it is reported as a capital gain. The holding period determines the reporting of short-term or long-term capital gain.

Return of Capital

A return of capital is a distribution that is not paid out of the earnings and profits of a corporation. It is a return of the taxpayer's investment in the stock of the company. The taxpayer will receive Form 1099-DIV or another statement from the corporation showing what part of the distribution is a return of capital. If the taxpayer does not receive such a statement, he will report the distribution as an ordinary dividend.

Liquidating Distributions

Liquidating distributions, also known as liquidating dividends, are distributions received during a partial or complete liquidation of a corporation. These distributions are, at least in part, one form of a "return of capital" and may be paid in two or more installments.

Any liquidating dividend received is not taxable until the basis of the stock has been recovered. However, the basis of the stock, which earned the right to the dividends, must be reduced by the amount of the dividends. After the basis of the stock is reduced to zero, the liquidating dividend must be reported as a capital gain.

Exempt-Interest Dividends

Exempt-interest dividends received from a regulated investment company or mutual fund are not included in taxable income. Exempt-interest dividends are reported on Form 1099-DIV, box 10. The taxpayer should receive a notice from the mutual fund giving information concerning the dividends the taxpayer received. The exempt-interest dividends should be shown on the return (if the taxpayer is required to file) as tax-exempt interest on line 2a of Form 1040.

Specified private activity bonds that have paid tax-exempt interest may be subject to alternative minimum tax. The exempt-interest dividends subject to alternative minimum tax should be shown on Form 1099-DIV, box 12.

Dividends on Insurance Policies

Insurance policy dividends that the insurer keeps and uses to pay premiums are not taxable. However, the taxpayer must report the interest that is paid or credited on dividends left with the insurance company as taxable income.

Dividends on Veterans' Insurance Policies

Dividends received on veterans' insurance policies and ones that were left with the Department of Veterans Affairs are not taxable.

Patronage Dividends

Patronage dividends received as money from a cooperative organization are included as income. Do not include the following patronage dividends as income:

- ➤ Property bought for personal use.
- ➤ Capital assets or depreciable property bought for use in business. If the dividend is more than the adjusted basis of the asset, it is reported as excess income.

Form 1040, line 4: IRA Distributions

Any money received from a traditional IRA is a distribution and must be reported as income in the year it was received. On Form 1040, report the nontaxable distribution on line 4 and report the taxable distributions on line 4b. Distributions from a traditional IRA are taxed as ordinary income. Not all distributions will be taxable if the taxpayer made nondeductible contributions. Complete Form 8606 to report the taxable and nontaxable portions of the IRA distribution.

The following distributions are not subject to the early withdrawal penalty:

- ➤ A rollover from one IRA to another.
- ➤ Tax-free withdrawals of contributions.
- ➤ The return of nondeductible contributions.

These funds will be reported as received, but the taxable portion will be reduced or eliminated.

Normal IRA distributions are usually fully taxable because contributions to the IRA account were fully tax-deferred when they were originally contributed. Form 5329, *Additional Taxes on Qualified Plans*, is not required if the early withdrawal penalty is the only reason for using the form. This penalty is in addition to any tax due on the distributions, though some exceptions to it exist.

Form 1040, line 5a and Line 5b, Pensions and Annuities

A distribution is a payment received by taxpayers from their pension or annuity. If taxpayers contributed "after-tax" dollars to their pension or annuity plan, they could exclude part of each annuity payment from income as a recovery of their cost. This tax-free part of the payment is figured when their annuity starts and remains the same each year, even if the amount of the payment changes. Pension is a contract for a fixed sum to be paid regularly following retirement from service. The rest of each payment is taxable. The tax-free portion of the payment is calculated using one of the following methods:

General Rule

This method is generally used to determine the tax-free treatment of pension and annuity income from nonqualified plans.

The taxpayer must use the general rule if:

1. The taxpayer receives pension and annuity payments from a nonqualified plan (such as a private annuity, a purchased commercial annuity, or a nonqualified employee plan).
2. The taxpayer is age 75 or older on the annuity starting date, and the annuity payments are guaranteed for at least five years.

Simplified Method

Using the simplified method, the taxpayer will figure the tax-free part of each monthly annuity payment by dividing the cost by the total number of expected monthly payments. For an annuity that is payable for the life of the annuitant, this number is based on the annuitant's age on the annuity starting date and is determined from a table. For any other annuity, this is the number of monthly annuity payments under the contract. If the taxpayer received a pension or annuity payment from a qualified plan, and he/she is not able to use the general rule, the taxpayer must use the simplified method.

Guaranteed Payments

The annuity contract provides guaranteed payments based on the investment amount and may be payable even if the taxpayer and the survivor annuitants do not live to receive the minimum payment.

Form 1040, line 6a: Social Security Benefits

The Social Security system was designed to provide supplemental monthly benefits to taxpayers who contributed to the system. It is indexed for inflation, provides Medicare benefits, disability, and certain death insurance, and is reported on Form SSA-1099 based on the amount listed in Box 5 of W-2. Taxpayers also have the option to have federal taxes withheld from Social Security.

Social Security benefits are not taxable if income does not exceed these base amounts:

- $25,000: If Single, Head of Household, or Qualifying widow(er).
- $25,000: If Married Filing Separately and he or she lived apart from spouse the entire year.
- $32,000: If Married Filing Jointly.
- $0: If Married Filing Separately and lived with spouse at some time during the year.

Form 1040, line 6b: Taxable Amount

50% taxable: If the income plus half of the Social Security benefits is more than the above stated base amounts, up to half of the benefits must be included as taxable income. The following are base amounts for the applicable filing statuses:

- $25,000–$34,000: Single, Head of Household, Qualifying widow(er), and Married Filing Separately and lived apart from spouse
- $32,000–$44,000: Married Filing Jointly
- $0: Married Filing Separately and lived with spouse

85% taxable: For taxpayers who file MFS and live with their spouse, 85% of their benefits will always be taxable. If the income plus half the benefits is more than the following adjusted base amounts, up to 85% of the benefits must be included as taxable income.

> - $34,000: Single, Head of Household, or Qualifying widow(er)
> - $34,000: Married Filing Separately and lived apart from spouse for entire year
> - $44,000: Married Filing Jointly
> - $0: Married Filing Separately and lived with spouse at any time during the tax year

Most taxpayers assume they will not be taxed if their income falls below the base amount, but they fail to include tax-exempt interest or half of their Social Security income when determining the amount.

Example: Napoleon and Ilene file a joint return. Both are over the age of 65 and have received Social Security benefits during the current tax year. In January, Napoleon's Form SSA-1099 showed benefits of $7,500 in box 5. Ilene's Form SSA-1099 showed a net benefit of $3,500 in box 5. Napoleon received a taxable pension of $20,800 and interest income of $500, which was tax exempt. Their benefits are not taxable for the current year because their income is not more than the base amount of $32,000.

Any benefit repayments made during the current year would be subtracted from the gross benefits received. It does not matter whether the repayment was for a benefit received in the current year or in an earlier year; it only matters what year the repayment was received.

Social Security and Equivalent Railroad Retirement Benefits (Tier 1)

The taxpayer should receive Form SSA-1099 from the SSA, which reports the total amount of Social Security benefits paid in box 3. Box 4 of the form shows the amount of any benefits that were repaid from a prior year. Railroad retirement benefits that should be treated as Social Security benefits are reported on Form RRB-1099.

Railroad Retirement Benefits

Railroad Retirement Benefits (RRB) is a benefits program that began before Social Security; its recipients are not covered under Social Security because they receive more money than they would have under the SSA. Tier 1 benefits are reported to the taxpayer on Form RRB 1099, are equivalent to Social Security benefits, and they are treated as such. Tier 1 benefits are reported to the IRS on Form 1040, Line 6b.

Tier 2 benefits are above the Social Security equivalent and are treated like pensions, allowing retirees to receive both tier 1 and tier 2 benefits. As with other pensions, the "cost" they invested is recovered tax-free. It is usually necessary to use the simplified method to figure the taxable portion of tier 2 benefits. To use the *Simplified Method Worksheet*, the tax preparer must know the age of the taxpayer, how many payments were received in the tax year, and how much has been recovered tax-free since 1986. When the taxpayer has recovered his or her cost, the entire tier 2 benefit becomes taxable.

The difference between Form RRB 1099 for tier 1 and tier 2 is that the form for tier 1 is known simply as Form RRB 1099. Tier 2 is a retirement; therefore, it has the letter "R" following the 1099 (Form RRB 1099-R).

Part 3 Review Questions

To obtain the maximum benefit from this chapter, LTP recommends that you complete each of the following questions, and then compare them to the answers with feedback that immediately follows. Under governing self-study standards, vendors are required to present review questions intermittently throughout each self-study course.

These questions and explanations are not part of the final examination and will not be graded by LTP.

IP3.1
Which of the following is a form of dividend income?

a. Qualified dividends
b. Dividends from a credit union
c. Dividends from mutual funds
d. Dividends from a partnership

IP3.2
Which of the following is a form of dividend income?

a. Ordinary dividends
b. Dividends from a credit union
c. Reinvested dividends
d. Dividends from a partnership

IP3.3

Jacob's daughter Peyton inherited some money from her great grandma. Peyton's interest earned this year was $2,210. Which of the following is the best answer for the scenario?

a. Peyton will file her own tax return since the amount earned is more than $2,200.
b. Jacob can file Form 8814 and report Peyton's earned interest.
c. Jacob and Peyton need to decide which is the lowest tax consequence for the two of them and that is who files the interest earned.
d. Peyton does not need to file a return since it is lower than her filing requirements.

Part 3 Review Questions Answers

IP3.1
Which of the following is a form of dividend income?

a. Qualified dividends
b. Dividends from a credit union
c. Dividends from mutual funds
d. Dividends from a partnership

Feedback: Review section *Dividend Income.*

Income

IP3.2

Which of the following is a form of dividend income?

   a. **Ordinary dividends**
   b. Dividends from a credit union
   c. Reinvested dividends
   d. Dividends from a partnership

Feedback: Review section *Dividend Income.*

IP3.3

Jacob's daughter Peyton inherited some money from her great grandma. Peyton's interest earned this year was $2,210. Which of the following is the best answer for the scenario?

   a. **Peyton will file her own tax return since the amount earned is more than $2,200.**
   b. Jacob can file Form 8814 and report Peyton's earned interest.
   c. Jacob and Peyton need to decide which is the lowest tax consequence for the two of them and that is who files the interest earned.
   d. Peyton does not need to file a return since it is lower than her filing requirements.

Feedback: Review section *Child's Interest and Dividend Income.*

Part 4 Schedule 1: Additional Income

Schedule 1, line 1: Taxable Refunds

If a taxpayer claims state income taxes were paid as an itemized deduction in the prior tax year, he or she must report the state income tax refund (part of the state taxes claimed in the previous year) as income in the year it was received. If the state income tax refund is taxable, report it on Form 1040, Schedule 1, line 1. Tax refunds are reported to the taxpayer on Form 1099-G, not to be confused with unemployment, which is also reported on the same form number. The state sends Form 1099-G to all refund recipients by January 31st of the current year.

To understand how a state income tax refund may be taxable, the tax professional must understand the "tax benefit rule," which states the following:

If a taxpayer recovers an amount that was deducted or credited against tax in a previous year, the recovery must be included in income to the extent that the deduction or credit reduced the tax liability in the earlier year. However, if no tax benefit was derived from a prior year deduction or credit, the recovery does not have to be included as income.

Recovery of Items Previously Deducted

A recovery is a return of an amount the taxpayer deducted or took a credit for in a prior year. The most common recoveries are state tax refunds, reimbursements, and rebates of deductions itemized on Form 1040, Schedule A. The taxpayer may also have recoveries of nonitemized deductions (such as payments on previously deducted bad debts) and recoveries of items for which the taxpayer previously claimed a tax credit. Taxpayers who used a deduction or credit to reduce their tax liability in the previous year must include those reductions as income on their current tax return.

Schedule 1, line 2: Alimony Received

Alimony is a payment or series of payments to a spouse or former spouse required under a divorce or separation instrument that must meet certain requirements. Alimony payments are deductible by the payer and are includable as income by the recipient. Alimony received should be reported on Form 1040, Schedule 1, line 2. Alimony paid should be deducted as an adjustment on Form 1040, Schedule 1, line 19. The Tax Cuts and Jobs Act changed the alimony rule; alimony will no longer be an adjustment to income or a source of income if the divorce or separation agreement was completed after December 31, 2018.

Payments are alimony if *all* the following are true:

- Payments are required by a divorce or separation agreement.
- The taxpayer and the recipient spouse do not file a joint return.
- Payments are in cash (including checks or money orders).
- Payments are not designated in the instrument as "not alimony."
- Spouses are legally separated under a decree of divorce or separate maintenance agreement and are not members of the same household.
- Payments are not required after the death of the recipient spouse.
- Payments are not designated as child support.

Payments are not alimony if *any* of the following are true:

- Payments are designated as child support.
- A noncash property settlement, such as giving the spouse the house.
- Payments that are the spouse's part of community property income.
- Used for property upkeep of the alimony payer's house.

These payments are neither deductible by the payer nor includable in income by the recipient.

For additional information regarding rules for payments under a pre-1985 instrument, review Publication 504: *Divorced or Separated Individuals*.

Payments made by cash, check, or money order for the taxpayer's spouse's medical expenses, rent, utilities, mortgage, taxes, tuition, etc., are considered third-party payments. If the payments are made on behalf of the taxpayer's spouse under the terms of the divorce or separation agreement, they may be considered alimony.

If the payer must pay all mortgage payments (both principal and interest) on a jointly-owned home and if the payments otherwise qualify, he or she may deduct one-half of the payments as alimony payments. The spouse will report one-half as alimony received.

The deductibility of real estate taxes and insurance depend on how the title is held. Additional research may be needed to determine how to handle the taxpayer's situation.

Example: In November 1984, Kael and Braxton executed a written separation agreement. In February 1985, a decree of divorce was substituted for the written separation agreement. The decree of divorce did not change the terms for the alimony that Kael had to pay Braxton because it is treated as having executed before 1985 because the terms of the alimony are still the same as the original agreement made in 1984. Alimony payments under this decree are not subject to the rules for payments under instruments after 1984.

Alimony Recapture Rule

If the amount of alimony paid by the taxpayer decreases or terminates within the first three calendar years, the payments may be subject to the recapture rule. If the taxpayer is subject to the rule, he will include a portion of the previously deducted alimony payments as income in the third year. The spouse would then be entitled to deduct previously included alimony that was received as income in the same year. The three-year period begins with the first calendar year in which the payer makes a qualifying alimony payment under a decree of divorce or separate maintenance or a written separation agreement. No further discussion of alimony recapture will be covered in this course.

Schedule 1, line 3: Business Income or Loss

Use Schedule C for business income if you operated a business, or if you practice your profession as a sole proprietor. An activity will qualify as a business if the primary purpose for engaging in such activity is for income or profit and if the proprietor is continually and regularly involved in such activity. You will get in-depth information on how to prepare Schedule C in the Business Income chapter.

Schedule 1, line 4: Other Gains or Losses

Use Schedule D to report capital gains and losses. Use Form 4797 to report other capital gains and losses not reported on Schedule D, line 13. Use Schedule D to figure out the overall gain and loss from transactions reported on Form 8949 and to report gain from Form 2439 or 622 or Part I of Form 4797.

Income

Schedule 1, line 5: Rental Income Form 1040

To report income or loss from rental real estate, royalties, partnerships, S corporations, estates, trusts, and residual interests in Real Estate Mortgage Investment Conduits (REMICs), use Schedule E. Rental income is any payment received for the use or occupation of real estate or personal property. Payment received by the taxpayer is reportable. More information about Schedule E will be found in the Business Income chapter.

Schedule 1, line 6: Farm Income or Loss

Schedule F would be used to report farm income or loss. A brief overview of Schedule F is in the Business Income chapter.

Schedule 1, line 7: Unemployment Compensation

Unemployment compensation is taxable, and the taxpayer may elect to have those taxes withheld for income tax purposes. To make this choice, the taxpayer must complete Form W-4V, *Voluntary Withholding Request.* The recipient of unemployment compensation will receive Form 1099-G to report the income.

If the taxpayer had to repay unemployment compensation for a prior year because they received unemployment while employed, he or she would subtract the total amount repaid for the year from the total amount received and enter the difference on Form 1040, Schedule 1, line 7. On the dotted line, next to the entry on the tax return, write "Repaid" and enter the amount repaid.

Paid Medical Family Leave

Paid family leave is an element of a state disability insurance program, and workers covered by State Disability Insurance (SDI) are also covered for this benefit. The maximum claim is six weeks; this is reported as unemployment on the individual's tax return. In some states, paid family leave and unemployment are reported on separate forms. Be aware of how individual states report the two. Both are considered a form of unemployment compensation that must be reported on Form 1040, Schedule 1, line 7.

> *Señor 1040 Says*: A good tax professional may have to add the totals of paid family leave with unemployment to report the correct amount of unemployment.

Schedule 1, line 8: Other Income

Use Form 1040, Schedule 1, line 8, to report any income not reported on the previous lines of the tax return or schedules. If necessary, attach a statement to give the required details concerning the income. The type of income should be identified on the dotted line.

Income

Income that is not reported on line 8 are:

1. Self-employment
2. Notary public income
3. Income reported on Form 1099-MISC
4. Income reported on Form 1099-NEC, unless it is NOT self-employment income, such as a hobby
5. Form 1099-K

Examples of Other Income reported on line 8 are:

- Net operating loss (8a).
- Gambling winnings, including the lottery and raffles (8b).
- Form 1099-C, *Cancellation of Debt* (8c).
- Foreign income exclusion from Form 2555 (8d).
- Taxable Health Savings Account distributions (8e).
- Alaska Permanent Fund dividend (8f).
- Jury duty pay (8g).
- Prizes and awards (8h).
- Activity not for profit income (8i).
- Stock options (8j).
- Income from the rental of personal property if taxpayer engaged in the rental for profit but was not in the business of renting such property (8k).
- Olympic and Paralympic medal and USOC prize money (8l).
- Section 951(a) inclusion (8m).
- Section 951A(a) inclusion (8n). Attach Form 8992.
- Section 461(l) excess business loss adjustments (8o).
- Taxable distributions from an ABLE account (8p).
- Other income, such as bartering.

Not all the above will be discussed in this chapter. Review Publication 525.

Señor 1040 Says: Form 1099-NEC, *Nonemployee Compensation,* is reported on line 8 unless it is not self-employment income.

Line 8a, Net Operating Loss

When a taxpayer made an election under section 965(n) and results in a net operating loss (NOL), the taxpayer may be able to claim the reduction on Schedule 1, line 8(a). More research is needed.

Line 8b, Gambling Winnings

There are two types of withholding on gambling winnings: regular gambling withholding and backup withholding. Regular gambling is withheld at a flat 24% rate from certain kinds of gambling. Gambling winnings of more than $5,000 (not including the wager) from the following sources are subject to income tax withholding:

1. Any sweepstakes, wagering pools (including payments made to winners of poker tournaments), or lotteries.
2. Any other winnings if the proceeds are at least 300 times the amount of the bet.

Regular gambling withholdings are calculated on the total amount of gross proceeds (winnings minus the amount wagered). Generally, the 24% withholding is not withheld from bingo, keno, or slot machines. It does not matter how the taxpayer is paid for the winnings; payments could be in cash, in property, or as an annuity. Winnings not paid in cash are considered at their fair market value. The taxpayer may have to provide the payer his or her Social Security number to avoid withholding.

Gambling winnings are reported to the taxpayer by the gambling organization (such as a casino) on Form W-2G, which shows both the amount won and withheld. The tax withheld (box 4) is reported with all other federal income tax withholding on Form 1040, page 2, line 25. "Backup" withholding on gambling winnings occurs when the payee does not give the payer his or her Social Security number. The withholding rate will be 30% and applies to winnings more than $600.

Line 8c, Cancellation of Debt

A debt is any amount owed to the lender; this includes, but is not limited to, stated principal, stated interest, fees, penalties, administrative costs, and fines. If a taxpayer's debt is canceled or forgiven, the canceled amount would generally be included as income. The amount of canceled debt can be all or part of the total amount owed. For a lending transaction, the taxpayer is required to report only the stated principal. If the cancellation of a debt is a gift, it would not be included as income. If a federal government agency, financial institution, or credit union forgives or cancels a debt of $600 or more, the taxpayer should receive a Form 1099-C, *Cancellation of Debt*. The amount to be included as income is listed in box 2 of Form 1099-C.

If the forgiven or canceled debt includes interest, the amount considered interest would be listed in box 3 and can only be included as income if it would have been deductible on the taxpayer's tax return.

The taxpayer should not include a canceled debt as income in the following situations:

- The debt is canceled in a bankruptcy case under Title 11 of the U.S. Code (review Publication 908, Bankruptcy Tax Guide).
- The debt is canceled when the taxpayer is insolvent. However, this does not apply to the extent the debt exceeds the amount by which the taxpayer is insolvent.
- The debt is qualified farm debt and is canceled by a qualified person (see chapter 4 of Publication 225, Farmer's Tax Guide, in illustration 7-C for more information).
- The debt is qualified real property business debt (review Publication 4681).
- The debt is qualified principal residence indebtedness.

If the taxpayer has included a canceled debt amount in their income and later pays the debt off, the taxpayer may be able to file an amended return for a refund. The statute of limitations for filing would apply.

There may be terms in the following section that you are not familiar with; you will need to conduct outside research to become familiar with them.

Depending upon the actual date of the discharge, a debt is deemed canceled on the date one of the following identifiable events occur:

- A discharge in bankruptcy under Title 11 of the U.S. Code. There are certain discharges in bankruptcy that are not required to be reported.
- A cancellation or extinguishment making the debt unenforceable in a receivership, foreclosure, or similar federal non-bankruptcy or state court proceeding.
- A cancellation or extinguishment when the statute of limitations for collecting the debt expires, or when the statutory period for filing a claim or beginning a deficiency judgment proceeding expires. Expiration of the statute of limitations is an identifiable event only when the debtor's affirmative statute of limitations defense is upheld in a final judgment or decision of a court and the appeal period has expired.
- A cancellation or extinguishment when the creditor elects the foreclosure remedies, which by law extinguishes or bars the creditor's right to collect the debt. This event applies to a mortgage lender or holder who is barred by local law from pursuing debt collection after a "power of sale" in the mortgage or deed of trust is exercised.

- A cancellation or extinguishment making the debt unenforceable under a probate or similar proceeding.
- A discharge of indebtedness under an agreement between the creditor and the debtor to cancel the debt at less than full consideration; for example, short sales.
- A discharge of indebtedness because of a decision or a defined policy of the creditor to discontinue collection activity and cancel the debt. A creditor's defined policy can be in writing or an established business practice of the creditor. A creditor's established practice to stop collection activity and abandon a debt when a particular nonpayment period expires is a defined policy.
- The expiration of nonpayment testing period. This event occurs when the creditor has not received a payment on the debt during the testing period. The testing period is a 36-month period ending on December 31, plus any time when the creditor was precluded from collection activity by a stay in bankruptcy or similar bar under state or local law. The creditor can rebut the occurrence of this identifiable event if:
    - The creditor (or a third-party collection agency on behalf of the creditor) has engaged in significant bona fide collection activity during the 12-month period ending on December 31.
    - Facts and circumstances that exist on January 31 following the end of the 36-month period indicate that the debt was canceled. Significant bona fide collection activity does not include nominal or ministerial collection action, such as an automated mailing. Facts and circumstances indicating that a debt was not canceled include the existence of a lien relating to the debt (up to the value of the security) or the sale of the debt by the creditor.
- Other actual discharge before identifiable event.

Form 1099-C

Canceled debt is income to the taxpayer, since the recipient received a benefit without paying for it. The taxpayer would receive Form 1099-C to report the taxable event. There are some exceptions that apply.

Box 1, Date of identifiable event: The date shown is the date the debt was canceled.

Box 2, Amount of debt discharged: Shows the amount of the canceled debt. The amount of the canceled debt cannot be greater than the total debt or less than any amount the lender receives in satisfaction of the debt by means of agreement, foreclosure sale, and a short sale that partially satisfied the debt.

Box 3, Interest, if included in box 2: The lender would show any interest that is included in the canceled debt in box 2.

Box 4, Debt description: Shows a description of the origin of the debt (such as if it's from a student loan, mortgage, or credit card expenditure). Be as specific as possible. The lender must include a property description when filing Form 1099-C and 1099-A.

Box 5, Check here if the debtor was personally liable for repayment of the debt: If the taxpayer (debtor) was personally liable for repayment of the debt at the time it was canceled, then an X will be in the box.

Box 6, Identifiable event code: This code shows the nature of the identifiable event.

Box 7, Fair market value (FMV) of property: Generally, the gross foreclosure bid price is the FMV. If an abandonment or voluntary conveyance to the lender in lieu of foreclosure occurred, enter the appraised value of the property.

Who Must File Form 1099-C?

- ➢ A financial institution such as a domestic bank, trust company, building and loan, or savings and loan association.
- ➢ A credit union.
- ➢ Any of the following or successors or subunits thereof:
    - o Federal Deposit Insurance Corporation.
    - o Resolution Trust Corporation.
    - o National Credit Union Administration.
    - o Any other federal executive agency, including government corporations.
    - o Any military department.
    - o U.S. Postal Service.
    - o Postal Rate Commission.
- ➢ Any corporation that is a subsidiary, financial institution, or credit union are subject to supervision and examination by a federal or state regulatory agency.
- ➢ A federal government agency including:
    - o A department.
    - o An agency.
    - o A court administrative office.
    - o An instrumentality in the judicial or legislative branch of the government.
- ➢ Any organization whose significant trade or business is the lending of money, such as a finance company or credit card company (whether affiliated with a financial institution or not). The action of lending money is a significant trade or business if money is lent on a regular and continuing basis.

If the debt is owned by more than one creditor, each creditor that is defined under "Who must file" above must issue a Form 1099-C if the debt is more than $600. A creditor will be deemed to have met its filing requirements if a lead bank, fund administrator, or other designee of the creditor complies on its behalf. Debt owned by a partnership is treated as being owned by all the partners and must follow the rules for multiple creditors.

Distributions from HSA line 8e

Generally, medical expenses that have been paid during the year are not reimbursed by the plan until the taxpayer has met the deductible. The taxpayer may receive a tax-free distribution from the HSA to pay or reimburse for qualified medical expenses after the taxpayer has established an HSA. Distributions received for any other reason are subject to an additional 20% tax.

Alaska Permanent Fund Dividends line 8f

The Alaska Permanent Fund is a dividend that is paid to all qualifying residents of Alaska. The dividend is based upon a five-year average of the Permanent Fund's performance, which depends on the stock market and other factors. The dividend is taxable on the recipients' federal tax returns.

Line 8i Activity Not for Profit

Income received through activities from which the taxpayer does not expect to make a profit (such as money made from a hobby) must be reported on Form 1040, Schedule 1, line 8. Deductions for the business or investment activity cannot offset other income. To determine if the taxpayer is carrying on an activity for profit, you must consider the following factors:

- The taxpayer carries on the activity in a businesslike manner.
- The time and effort put into the activity indicate the taxpayer intended to make a profit.
- Losses are due to circumstances beyond the taxpayer's control.
- Methods of operation were changed to improve profitability.
- The taxpayer or the taxpayer's advisor(s) have the knowledge needed to carry on the activity as a successful business.
- The taxpayer was successful in making a profit in similar activities in the past.
- The activity makes a profit in some years.
- The taxpayer can expect to make a future profit from the appreciation of the assets used in the activity.
- The taxpayer depends on the income for his or her livelihood.

An activity is presumed to be carried on for profit if it produced a profit in at least three of the last five years, including the current year. Activities that consist of breeding, training, showing, or racing horses are presumed to be carried on for profit if they produced a profit in at least two of the last seven years. The activity must be substantially the same for each year within the period, and the taxpayer has a profit when the gross income from the activity exceeds the deductions.

Hobby Income

Hobby income is one example of an activity not for profit; however, a hobby can become a business. The ability to claim losses on a hobby have been suspended until 2026 due to the Tax Cuts and Jobs Act (TCJA). To show the IRS that an activity is a business, the taxpayer should maintain the following:

- Comprehensive recordkeeping.
- A separate business checking account for the income.
- Separate credit cards for business and personal purchases.
- Logbook(s) to keep records of business and personal use of such items as computers, charter boats, camcorders, etc.
- Required licenses, insurance, certifications, etc.
- If operated from home, keeping a separate phone line for business use.
- An attempt to make a profit.
- Research on market trends or technology related to the taxpayer's business.
- If the taxpayer has employees, the taxpayer must file forms to report employment taxes (Review Publication 15, Circular E, *Employer's Tax Guide* for more info). Employment taxes include the following items:
  - Social Security and Medicare.
  - Federal income tax withholding.
  - Federal unemployment (FUTA) tax.

Not for profit income could include income from a hobby or rental income from tangible property; both are reported on Form 1040, Schedule 1, line 8. (Review Publication 527).

Line 8j Employee Stock Options

There are three kinds of stock options:

- Incentive stock options.
- Employee stock purchase plan options.
- Non-statutory (non-qualified) stock options.

The employer must report excess of the fair market value (FMV) of the stock received, and will be reported in box 12 with the code *V*. For more information about employee stock options, see Internal Revenue Code (IRC) section 1.83-7, §421, §422, and §423 and related regulations.

Part 4 Review Questions

To obtain the maximum benefit from this chapter, LTP recommends that you complete each of the following questions, and then compare them to the answers with feedback that immediately follows. Under governing self-study standards, vendors are required to present review questions intermittently throughout each self-study course.

These questions and explanations are not part of the final examination and will not be graded by LTP.

IP4.1

What is the maximum taxable amount of Social Security?

a. 85%
b. 35%
c. 10%
d. 25%

IP4.2

Which of the following could be a taxable event, if a credit was taken in the prior tax year?

a. Repayment of a personal loan
b. State income tax paid
c. Real estate tax payments
d. Bad debt

IP4.3

Which of the following income is taxable?

a. Workers' compensation
b. Welfare and other public assistance benefits
c. Veterans' benefits
d. Alimony (prior to December 31, 2018)

IP4.4

Which of the following is taxable on the federal return?

a. Unemployment
b. Paid family leave
c. Child support
d. Unemployment and paid family leave

IP4.5

Marlene paid $4,000 for real estate taxes on her rental property at 1850 Happy Street, Jersey City, New Jersey. She paid $6,850 of real estate taxes on her primary residence. Marlene has household employees for whom she paid Social Security taxes of $1,300 and state income taxes of $2,500. What amount of real estate tax will Marlene deduct on her Schedule E?

a. $14,650
b. $6,850
c. $4,000
d. $1,300

IP4.6

Sophia won a $21,000 jackpot from Wild Bill's in Atlantic City. She did not provide her SSN to the casino. What would the casino do before it pays Sophia her money?

a. Withhold 21%
b. Withhold 25%
c. Withhold 30%
d. Withhold 28%

Income

Part 4 Review Questions Answers

IP4.1
What is the maximum taxable amount of Social Security?

    a. **85%**
    b. 35%
    c. 10%
    d. 25%

Feedback: Review section *Line 5b: How Much Is Taxable?* Under Schedule 1.

IP4.2
Which of the following could be a taxable event, if a credit was taken in the prior tax year?

    a. Repayment of a personal loan
    b. **State income tax paid**
    c. Real estate tax payments
    d. Bad debt

Feedback: Review section *Line 1: State Tax Refunds,* under Schedule 1.

IP4.3
Which of the following income is taxable?

    a. Workers' compensation
    b. Welfare and other public assistance benefits
    c. Veterans' benefits
    d. **Alimony (prior to December 31, 2018)**

Feedback: Review section *Line 2: Alimony*, under Schedule 1.

IP4.4
Which of the following is taxable on the federal return?

    a. Unemployment
    b. Paid family leave
    c. Child support
    d. **Unemployment and paid family leave**

Feedback: Review section *Line 7: Unemployment Compensation,* under Schedule 1.

IP4.5

Marlene paid $4,000 for real estate taxes on her rental property at 1850 Happy Street, Jersey City, New Jersey. She paid $6,850 of real estate taxes on her primary residence. Marlene has household employees for whom she paid Social Security taxes of $1,300 and state income taxes of $2,500. What amount of real estate tax will Marlene deduct on her Schedule E?

   a. $14,650
   b. $6,850
   c. $4,000
   d. $1,300

Feedback: Review section *Line 5: Rental Income Form 1040,* under Schedule 1.

IP4.6

Sophia won a $21,000 jackpot from Wild Bill's in Atlantic City. She did not provide her SSN to the casino. What would the casino do before it pays Sophia her money?

   a. Withhold 21%
   b. Withhold 25%
   c. Withhold 30%
   d. Withhold 28%

Feedback: Review section *Gambling Winnings,* under Schedule 1.

Part 5 Other Taxable Income

Taxable income is more than just earned wages; it can include several sources that may be overlooked. Some of these taxable income types will be reported on a W-2, but others may be reported to the taxpayer on a 1099MISC.

Advance Commission and Other Earnings

If the taxpayer received an advance commission or some other amount for services to be performed in the future, that amount is included as income in the year received. If the taxpayer repays unearned commission in the same year as was received, then the amount included in income is reduced by the repayment. If the repayment will be in a later year, then the taxpayer would deduct the repayment on Schedule A as an itemized deduction. This cannot be done if the taxpayer does not, or cannot, itemize their deductions.

Back Pay

If a taxpayer receives a settlement or judgment for back pay, it is included in their income. Back pay is treated as wages in the year paid, not the year it was supposed to have been paid. If a settlement was reached in 2018 for pay that should have been given in 2015, and the back pay is given in 2020, then the back pay is reported as income for tax year 2020, not 2015 or 2018.

Payments made to the taxpayer for damages, unpaid life insurance premiums, and unpaid health insurance premiums are reported to the taxpayer on Form W-2. There are special rules on how to report these wages to the Social Security Administration, and those guidelines are not covered in this course. See ssa.gov for more information.

Bartering

Bartering is an exchange of property or services. Goods and services acquired through bartering must be included as income at the value they held when they were received.

Employee Achievement Awards

Employee achievement awards received for outstanding work are included in the employee's income and should be reported on the W-2. These include prizes such as vacation trips for meeting sales goals. If the prize or reward received is a good or service, include the fair market value of the goods and services in the income. If the employee receives tangible personal property as an award for length of service or a safety achievement, then the value of the award is generally excluded from income unless the compensation is cash, a gift certificate, or some equivalent item. The amount that can be excluded is limited to no more than $1,600 ($400 for awards that are non-qualified plans) or the employer's cost of the award if less than the maximum.

Other items such as the value of a turkey, ham, or other nominally valued items given to an employee must be included as income. The amount of compensation required to be reported is the gross amount prior to any deductions for taxes withheld.

Prepaid income, in most cases, is included as compensation in the year the taxpayer received the income. If the taxpayer is on the accrual method of accounting, the income is reported when it is earned in the performance of the services.

Government Cost-of-Living Allowances

Cost-of-living allowances are generally included in income if the employee was a federal civilian or a federal court employee. Allowances and differentials that increase basic pay as an incentive for taking a less desirable position is included as compensation and must be included in income. Review Publication 516.

Relocation for Temporary Work Assignment

If an employee is away from his regular place of work on a temporary work assignment, certain travel expenses that are reimbursed or paid directly by the employer with an accountable plan may be excluded from wages. Generally, a temporary work assignment is in one location and lasts for one year or less.

Scholarship prizes

Scholarships won in a contest are not considered scholarships or fellowships if the taxpayer is not required to use them for educational purposes. The prize amounts are reported as income on Form 1040, Schedule 1, line 8 (other income) whether or not they are used for educational purposes.

Severance Pay

When an employee receives a severance package, any payment for the cancellation of his or her employment contract is included in the employee's income. A severance package is considered wages and is subject to Social Security and Medicare taxes.

Sick Pay

Pay received from an employer while the employee is sick or injured is part of the employee's salary or wages. Taxpayers must include sick pay benefits in their income that are received from any of the following sources:

- A welfare fund.
- A state sickness or disability fund.
- An association of employers or employees.
- An insurance company if the employer paid for the plan.

If the employee paid the premiums on an accident or health insurance policy, the benefits received under the policy are not taxable.

Sick pay is intended to replace regular wages while an employee is unable to work due to injury or illness. Payments received from the employer or an agent of the employer that qualify as sick pay must have federal withholding, just as any other wage compensation. Payments under a plan in which the employer does not participate (i.e., the taxpayer paid all the premiums) are not considered sick pay and are not taxable.

Sick pay does not include any of the following payments:

- Disability retirement payments.
- Workers' compensation.
- Payments to public employees as workers' compensation.
- Medical expense payments.
- Payments unrelated to absences from work.

Señor 1040 Says: Do not report any amounts as income that were reimbursed for medical expenses that were incurred after the plan was established.

Tips and Gratuities

All tips (also called gratuities) received are income, subject to federal income tax, and must be reported to employers regardless of whether they were received directly or indirectly via a tip-splitting pool, a tip-pooling arrangement, or some other method. Noncash tips, such as tickets, passes, or other items of value must also be reported to employers. The market value of the item is counted as income and subject to tax, although the taxpayer does not pay Social Security or Medicare taxes on them. The IRS states that all tips received from customers must be included as income regardless of what an employer considers to be a tip; an employer's characterization of a payment as a "tip" is not determinative for withholding purposes.

Employees who receive tips should keep daily records of the tips received. A daily report will help the employee when it comes to filing his or her tax return. Employees should do the following:

Income

- Report tips accurately to their employer.
- Report all tips accurately on their tax return.
- Provide their tip income report if their tax return is ever audited.

There are two ways to keep a daily tip log. Employees can:

- Write information about their tips in a tip diary.
- Keep copies of documents that show their tips.

Señor 1040 Says: The taxpayer can use Publication 1244 to track their daily tips totals and amount reported to their employer.

This daily record should be kept with tax and other personal records. The daily tip report should include:

- The date and time of work.
- Cash tips received directly from customers or other employees.
- Credit and debit card charges that customers paid directly to the employer.
- Total tips paid out to other employees through tip pools or tip splitting.
- The value of noncash tips received, such as tickets, passes, etc.

If $20 worth of tips or more are received per month from one employer, they must be reported to the taxpayer's employer on Form 4070: *Employee's Report of Tips to Employer.* Just like with normal earned wages, the employer will withhold Social Security, Medicare, federal taxes, and state taxes from the employee's reported tips based on the total amount of the employee's regular wages and reported tips. Form 4070 should be filed with the employer no later than the 10th of each month. If the 10th of the month falls on a Saturday, Sunday, or legal holiday, the due date to report tips becomes the next business day. Tips not reported to the employer are still required to be reported as income on Form 1040. If the taxpayer fails to report tips, the taxpayer may be subject to a penalty equal to 50% of the Social Security and Medicare taxes or railroad retirement tax owed on unreported tips. This penalty amount is in addition to the taxes owed; although the taxpayer can try to avoid this penalty by attaching a statement to the return showing he or she had a reasonable cause for not reporting tips to the employer. The taxpayer must use Form 4137: *Social Security Tax on Unreported Tip Income*, to report unreported tips to the IRS. Service charges that are added to the customer's bill and paid to the employee are treated as wages, not tips. Taxpayers should not include service charges in their tip diary. The absence of any of the following factors creates doubt as to whether a payment is a tip and indicates that the payment may be a service charge:

- The payment must be made free from obligation.
- The customer must have an unrestricted right to determine the amount.
- The payment should not be subject to negotiation or dictated by employer policy.
- The customer has the right to determine who receives the payment.

Example: Fish 'n' Chips for You specifies that an 18% service charge will be added to bills with parties of six or more. Julio's bill included the service charge for food and beverages for the party of eight he served. Under these circumstances, Julio did not have the unrestricted right to determine the amount of payment because it was dictated by Fish 'n' Chips for You. The 18% charge is not a tip; it is distributed to the employees as wages. Julio would not include that amount in his tip diary.

Employees who work in an establishment that must allocate tips to its employees or who fail to earn or report an amount of tips that is equal to at least 8% of the total amount of their gross receipts are subject to "allocated tips". In this case, the employer will assign them (or "allocate") additional tips to ensure they reach the 8% minimum. Allocated tips are calculated by adding the tips reported by all employees from food and drink sales (this does not include carryout sales or sales with a service charge of 10% or more). The employee's share is then determined using his or her sales or his or her hours worked.

Allocated tips are shown separately in box 8 of Form W-2 and are reported as wages on Form 1040, line 7. Social Security and Medicare taxes have not been taken out of allocated tips, but since they are still subject to them, they must be reported on Form 4137: *Social Security Tax on Unreported Tip Income*. Employers must also report them by filing Form 8027: *Employer's Annual Information Return of Tip Income and Allocated Tips*. The purpose of Form 4137 is to calculate the Social Security and Medicare tax on tips that were not reported to the taxpayer's employer. Once calculated, report the amount of unreported Social Security and Medicare tax on Form 1040, Schedule 2, line 5.

Disability Income

Disability income is the amount paid to an employee under the employee or employer's insurance or pension plan (under some plans, employees can also contribute) while the employee is absent from work due to a disability. Disability income reported as wages on Form W-2 is taxable, but income attributable to employee contributions would not be taxable. If the employee pays for the entire cost of the accident or health plan, he or she should not include any amount received as income. If the premiums of a health or accident plan were paid through a cafeteria plan, and the amount of the premium was not included as taxable income, then it is assumed that the employer paid the premiums, and the disability benefits are taxable.

If a taxpayer retires using disability payments before reaching the minimum retirement age of 59½, the payments will be treated as wages until the taxpayer reaches the minimum retirement age. Once a taxpayer is over the age of 59½, their disability payments will be taxed as a pension and not as regular income. Tax professionals should not confuse disability income (which may be taxable) with workers' compensation (which may not be taxable) for those who are injured at work.

> *Señor 1040 Says*: The minimum retirement age is 59½ or the age at which the taxpayer could first receive an annuity or pension if he or she was not disabled. The taxpayer must report all his or her taxable disability payments until the taxpayer reaches the minimum retirement age.

Income

Clergy

Clergy are the formal leaders within certain religious groups. The roles and functions of clergy members vary amongst different religious traditions, but these usually involve presiding over specific rituals and teaching religious doctrines and practices.

If the taxpayer is a member of the clergy, offerings and fees received for marriages, baptisms, funerals, masses, etc., are included as income in addition to his salary. If the offering is made to the religious institution, it is not taxable to the member of the clergy. If he is a member of a religious organization, and if he gives his outside earnings to the organization, he must still include the earnings in his income. However, he may be entitled to a charitable contribution deduction for the amount he paid to the organization.

Special rules for housing allowances apply to members of the clergy. Under these rules, the taxpayer does not include in his income the rental value of a home (including utilities) or a housing allowance provided to him as a part of his pay. However, the exclusion cannot be more than the least of the following amounts:

- The exact amount used to provide or rent a home.
- The fair market rental value of the home (including furnishings, utilities, etc.).
- The amount officially designated (in advance of payment) as a rental or housing allowance.
- An amount that represents reasonable pay for services.

The home or allowance must be provided as compensation for the taxpayer's duties as an ordained, licensed, or commissioned minister. However, the rental value of the home or the housing allowance as earnings from self-employment is included on Schedule SE (Form 1040), *Self-Employment Tax.* Taxation of clergy income is beyond the scope of this course. For more information, review Publication 517.

If parents make the election to report their child's income, they will report the income on Form 8814. The tax rate may be higher with this election. For more information, see Instructions Form 8814 and Publication 929.

Part 5 Review Questions

To obtain the maximum benefit from this chapter, LTP recommends that you complete each of the following questions, and then compare them to the answers with feedback that immediately follows. Under governing self-study standards, vendors are required to present review questions intermittently throughout each self-study course.

These questions and explanations are not part of the final examination and will not be graded by LTP.

IP5.1

Reverend Alex performs marriages and is paid from the offering for the performance. Are the offerings taxable to Alex?

a. Yes, they are because all offerings are taxable.
b. No, they are not, because it was given from the church members and not the offerings.
c. Yes, they are because he performed the marriage and was given the offering.
d. No, they are not, because he is a clergyman.

IP5.2

Which of the following is taxable income?

a. Workers' compensation
b. Welfare benefits
c. Veterans' benefits
d. Disability reported on Form W-2

Part 5 Review Questions Answers

IP5.1

Reverend Alex performs marriages and is paid from the offering for the performance. Are the offerings taxable to Alex?

a. **Yes, they are because all offerings are taxable.**
b. No, they are not, because it was given from the church members and not the offerings.
c. Yes, they are because he performed the marriage and was given the offering.
d. No, they are not, because he is a clergyman.

Feedback: Review section *Clergy*.

IP5.2

Which of the following is taxable income?

a. Workers' compensation
b. Welfare benefits
c. Veterans' benefits
d. **Disability reported on Form W-2**

Feedback: Review section *Disability Income*.

Part 6 Fringe Benefits

A fringe benefit is any benefit provided by an employer to individuals in addition to their normal compensation. A person who performs services for the employer does not have to be an employee; he or she can be an independent contractor, partner, or director. The employer is the provider of the fringe benefit if it is provided for services performed for the employer, and the person who performs services for the employer is the recipient of the fringe benefit.

Income

Fringe benefits received from an employer are considered compensation and are taxable and must be included in income unless tax law specifically excludes the benefits, or the taxpayer paid fair market value for the benefit (in which it would no longer be a provision from the employer or a fringe benefit). The employer usually determines the amount of the fringe benefits and includes this amount in the employee's W-2. The total value of the fringe benefits should be shown in box 12. The employer is the provider of the benefit even if a customer of the employer provided the services. The employee who is the recipient of the benefit must report the fringe benefit as income.

Employers can report noncash fringe benefits in box 1 of the W-2 (with a notation in box 14) using one of the two following accounting periods:

- The general rule, under which benefits are reported for a full calendar year (January 1st through December 31st).
- The special accounting period rule, under which benefits provided during the last two months of the calendar year (or any shorter period) are treated as being paid during the following calendar year.

Example 1: Smith's Enterprises has provided Frank Jones and Courtney Keys noncash fringe benefits since 2015 and reports some of them to the IRS using the special accounting period rule. To report the value of those provided benefits on their W-2s, Smith's Enterprises will count November and December of 2020 and January through October of 2021 as one calendar year.

Employers do not have to use the same accounting period for each fringe benefit they provide, but they must use whichever accounting period they choose for every person who receives the benefit. The employee must use the same accounting period as his or her employer to report taxable noncash fringe benefits.

Example 2: Smith's Enterprises provided employee discounts and athletic facilities as fringe benefits to both Frank Jones and Courtney Keys. The company can report each fringe benefit using a different accounting rule, but no matter what rule they use for each benefit, the fringe benefit must be reported the same way for both Frank and Courtney. In other words, the company can report the employee discounts using the general rule and the athletic facilities using the special accounting period rule, but they cannot report athletic facilities under the general rule for Courtney and then report them under the special accounting period rule for Frank.

Cafeteria Plans

Cafeteria plans are a type of benefit package consisting entirely of fringe benefits; most are written flexible spending arrangement plans that allow employees to choose between receiving cash or taxable benefits instead of certain qualified benefits that are excluded from wages. Generally, a cafeteria plan does not include any plan that offers a benefit that defers pay, but a cafeteria plan can include a qualified 401(k) plan as a benefit. Qualified benefits under a cafeteria plan can include the following:

- Accident and health benefits (but not Archer medical savings accounts or long-term care insurance).
- Adoption assistance.

- Dependent care assistance.
- Group-term life insurance coverage.
- Health savings accounts (HSAs). Distributions from an HSA may be used to pay eligible long-term care insurance premiums or qualified long-term care services in addition to unreimbursed medical expenses.

Excluded fringe benefits are not subject to federal income tax withholding; in most cases, they are not subject to Social Security, Medicare, or federal unemployment tax (FUTA) and aren't reported on Form W-2. A cafeteria plan cannot include the following benefits:

- Archer medical savings accounts (MSAs).
- Athletic facilities.
- *De minimis* (minimal) benefits.
- Educational assistance (including scholarships or fellowships; review Publication 970, *Tax Benefits for Education*).
- Employee discounts.
- Employer-provided cell phones.
- Lodging on the business premises.
- Meals.
- No-additional-cost services.
- Retirement planning services.
- Transportation (commuting) benefits.
- Tuition reduction.
- Working condition benefits.

The following are some of the possible fringe benefits that can be included under the cafeteria plan.

Adoption Assistance

Adoption assistance is considered a benefit when it meets the following requirements:

- The plan must benefit the employees who qualify under the rules set up by the employer, and the rules cannot give special treatment or perks to highly compensated employees or their dependents.
- The plan does not pay more than 5% of its payments during the year to shareholders, owners, their spouses, or their dependents.
- The employer gives reasonable notice of the adoption plan to all eligible employees.
- Employees provide substantiation that the payments or the reimbursements are used for qualifying expenses.

A highly compensated employee is an employee who meets either of the following tests:

- The employee was a 5% owner at any time during the year or the preceding year.
- The employee received more than $120,000 in pay for the preceding year.

The second test listed above can be ignored if the employee was not in the top 20% of the employees' pay ranking for the preceding year. All payments or reimbursements made under the adoption assistance program must be excluded from wages subject to federal income tax withholding.

Income

All qualifying adoption assistance expenses paid or reimbursed by the employer must be reported in box 12 of the employee's Form W-2. Code *T* is used to identify the amount. This credit is nonrefundable. Nonrefundable credits lower the taxpayer's tax liability. Review Publication 15-B.

Dependent Care Assistance

If the employer provides dependent care assistance under a qualified plan, the taxpayer may be able to exclude the amount from income. Dependent care benefits include the following:

- Amounts the employer paid directly to the care provider.
- The fair market value of the care in a day-care facility provided or sponsored by the employer.

The amount that can be excluded is limited to the least of these:

- The total amount of dependent care benefits received for the year.
- The total amount of the qualified expenses incurred during the year.
- The taxpayer's earned income.
- The spouse's earned income (if filing MFJ).
- $5,000 ($2,500 if MFS).

The amounts paid are reported on Form W-2, box 10. To claim the exclusion, the taxpayer would complete Part III of Form 2441: *Child and Dependent Care Expenses*.

Señor 1040 Says: Individuals who provide childcare in their own home are considered self-employed and should report their income on Schedule C. If the childcare is provided in the child's home, they are considered employees and should receive a W-2 from the child's parent or guardian, who should report the caretaker's income on Schedule H.

Group-Term Life Insurance

Generally, group-term insurance coverage provided by an employer (current or former) to his or her employees is not included as income up to the cost of $50,000 after being reduced by any amount the employee paid toward the purchase of the insurance.

If the coverage is worth more than $50,000, the employee must include the amount of money that the employer-provided insurance is costing his or her employer as the employee's personal income. If the employer provided more than $50,000 of coverage, the amount to be included as income is reported as part of the employee's wages in boxes 1, 3, and 5 of Form W-2. It is also shown separately in box 12 with code C on the W-2.

Some exceptions apply for life insurance coverage that meets the following conditions:

- The employer provided a general death benefit that is not included in income.
- The employer provided it to a group of employees (generally 10 or more employees).
- The employer provided an amount of insurance to each employee based on a formula that prevents individual selection.

➢ The employer provided the insurance under a policy that was directly or indirectly carried. Even if the employer did not pay any of the cost, the employer is considered to carry it since the employer arranged for payment of its cost by the employees and charged at least one employee less than, and one employee more than, the cost of their insurance.

Group-term insurance that is payable on the death of the employee, employee's spouse, or dependent, and with a payment amount of less than $2,000, is considered a *de minimis* benefit.

The following types of insurance plans are not group-term insurance:

➢ Insurance that does not provide general death benefits such as travel insurance or only provides accidental death benefits.
➢ Life insurance on the life of the employee's spouse or dependent.
➢ Insurance provided under a policy that provides a permanent benefit (an economic value that extends more than 1 year unless certain requirements are met). See Internal Revenue Code (IRC) section 1.79-1 for more information.

Health Savings Accounts (HSAs)

A Health Savings Account (HSA) is a form of pretax savings account set up to help you set aside and save up money to pay for medical costs. If the taxpayer is an eligible individual, HSA contributions can be made by the employer, the taxpayer, or any of the taxpayer's family members.

Contributions made by the employer are not included in income. Distributions from the HSA that are used to pay for qualified medical expenses are included in income. Contributions to the account are used to pay current or future medical expenses of the account owner, spouse, and any qualified dependent.

Contributions by a partnership to a bona fide partner's HSA are not considered to be contributions by an employer. The contributions are treated as a distribution of money and thus are not included in the partner's gross income.

If the contributions by the partnership are for the partner's services rendered, they are treated as guaranteed payments that are included in the partner's gross income.

Contributions by an S corporation to a 2% shareholder-employee's HSA for services rendered are treated as guaranteed payments and are included in the shareholder-employee's gross income. The shareholder-employee may deduct the contribution made to the shareholder-employee's HSA. Review Publication 969.

Employee Stock Options

There are three kinds of stock options:

➢ Incentive stock options.
➢ Employee stock purchase plan options.
➢ Non-statutory (non-qualified) stock options.

Income

The employer must report excess of the fair market value (FMV) of the stock received, and will be reported in box 12 with the code *V*. For more information about employee stock options, see Internal Revenue Code (IRC) section 1.83-7, §421, §422, and §423 and related regulations.

Holiday Gifts

If the employer provides nominal-value holiday gifts such as a turkey or ham, they do not have to be included in the employees' income. If the employer gives the employee cash, a gift certificate, or a similar item that can be exchanged for cash, the gift is compensation and must be included in the employee's income.

Retirement Plan Contributions

The employer's contributions to a qualified retirement plan for an employee are not included as income at the time contributed. If the employer pays into a nonqualified plan for the employee, those contributions are included in income. If a client is unsure if their retirement plan qualifies, they should ask their employer.

Transportation

If an employer provides a qualified transportation fringe benefit, a certain amount may be excluded from income. Providing any of the below can be a qualified transportation fringe benefit:

- A transit pass.
- Qualified parking.
- Transportation in a commuter highway vehicle (must seat at least 6 adults) between the taxpayer's home and workplace.

Cash reimbursements by an employer for these expenses under a bona fide reimbursement arrangement are also excludable. However, cash reimbursement for a transit pass is excludable only if a voucher or similar item that can be exchanged only for a transit pass is not readily available for direct distribution to the taxpayer.

The exclusion for commuter highway vehicle transportation and transit pass fringe benefits cannot be more than a total of $270 a month, regardless of the total value of both benefits.

The exclusion for the qualified parking fringe benefit cannot be more than $270 a month, regardless of its value. For benefits with a value higher than the limit, the excess must be included as income.

If the benefits have a value that is more than these limits, the excess is included as income.

Other Fringe Benefits

The following fringe benefits are not included under the cafeteria plan.

Athletic Facilities

The value of an employee's on-site use of a gym or another athletic facility operated by the employer can be excluded from the employee's income. The gym must be primarily used by employees, their spouses, and their dependent children. However, if the employer pays for a fitness program provided to the employee that is off-site at a hotel or athletic club, the value of the program is included as income.

De Minimis Fringe Benefits

If an employer provides its employees with a product or service, and the cost of it is so small that it would be unreasonable for the employer to account for it, the value is not included in the employee's income. These are *de minimis* fringe benefits. Generally, the value of these benefits, such as discounts at company cafeterias, cab fares when working overtime, and company picnics, are not included in the employee's income.

While many of the *de minimis* fringe benefits are typically not included in an employee's gross income, in most circumstances, the employer is allowed a deduction for costs incurred. Any cash benefit or its equivalent (such as the use of a company credit card) cannot be excluded as a *de minimis* benefit under any circumstance.

Educational Assistance

If the taxpayer received educational assistance benefits from his or her employer under a qualified educational assistance program, up to $5,250 of eligible assistance can be excluded yearly, in which case it would not be included on the W-2 or be a part of a return. However, if the education was not work-related or if the taxpayer is a highly compensated employee, the assistance from the employer may be taxable (Publication 970).

An employee who meets either of the following tests is a highly compensated employee:

> - The employee was a 5% owner at any time during the year or the preceding year.
> - The employee received more than $120,000 in pay for the preceding year.

The second test listed above can be ignored if the employee was not in the top 20% of the employees' pay ranking for the preceding year. All payments or reimbursements made under the adoption assistance program must be excluded from wages subject to federal income tax withholding.

A student in a degree-program can exclude amounts received from a qualified scholarship or fellowship. Excludable income from a qualified scholarship or fellowship is any amount received that is used for the following:

> - Tuition and fees to enroll at or attend an eligible educational institution.
> - Fees, books, and equipment required for courses at the eligible educational institution.

Payments received for services required as a condition of receiving a scholarship or fellowship grant must be included in the taxpayer's income, even if the services are required of all students for the degree. Amounts used for room and board do not qualify for the exclusion. This includes amounts received for teaching and research. Include these payments on Form 1040, line 1.

Employee Discounts

The exclusion applies to a price reduction given to the employee for property or services offered to the customer in the ordinary course of the line of business. The discount does not apply to discounts given on real property or discounts on personal property of a kind commonly held for investment, such as stocks and bonds.

Employer-Provided Cell Phones

The value of an employer-provided cell phone that is provided primarily for non-compensatory business reasons is excludable from an employee's income as a working condition. Personal use of an employer-provided cell phone is excludable from an employee's income as a *de minimis* fringe benefit.

Employer-Provided Lodging and Meals

Do not include the value of meals and lodging the employer provided at no charge to the taxpayer and the taxpayer's family as income, if the following conditions are met:

The meals are:

- Furnished on the business premises of the employer.
- Furnished for the convenience of the employer.

The lodging is:

- Furnished on the business premises of the employer.
- Furnished for the convenience of the employer.
- A condition of employment (the taxpayer must accept the lodging to properly perform his or her duties).

No-Additional-Cost Services

The value of services received from one's employer for free, at no cost, or for a reduced price is not included in the taxpayer's income if the employer does the following:

- Offers the same service for sale to customers in the ordinary course of the line of business in which the employee works.
- Does not have a substantial additional cost (including any sales income given up) to provide the employee with the service (regardless of what the employee paid for the service).

No-additional-cost services are excess capacity services, such as tickets for airlines, buses, or trains, hotel rooms, or telephone services provided for free or at a reduced price to employees working in that line of service.

Example: Amanda is employed as a flight attendant for a company that owns both an airline and a hotel chain. The employer allows Amanda to take free personal flights if there is an unoccupied seat and to stay in any of the company's hotels for free if there is an unoccupied room. What would and wouldn't be included as income?

Explanation: The value of the personal flight isn't included in her income because there is no cost involved in letting her take a seat that would have remained unoccupied anyway. However, if the company allowed Amanda to reserve her seat, then the value of the ticket would be included as income because the company can no longer sell that seat and has lost the potential revenue that they could have gained from it. However, this potential loss or gain isn't a factor with the hotel room; since Amanda does not work in the hotel side of the business, the value of the hotel room would be included as income either way.

Nontaxable Income

Although it may seem like taxes are collected on all income, there are several types of income that are exempt from taxation because of the nature of the reason behind the payment.

Child Support

Taxpayers who receive child support payments do not report the payments as income. Payments designed to be child support should be defined in legal documents such as divorce or separation agreements or the child custody paperwork.

Workers' Compensation

Amounts received as workers' compensation for an occupational sickness or injury are fully exempt from tax if they are paid under a workers' compensation act or some similar statute. The exemption also applies to the taxpayer's survivors. This exception does not apply to retirement plan benefits received based on age, length of service, or prior contributions to the plan, even if the taxpayer retired because of an occupational sickness or injury.

If the taxpayer returns to work after qualifying for workers' compensation, payments received while assigned to light duties are taxable. Report these payments as wages on line 1 of Form 1040.

Income paid under a statute that provides benefits only to employees with service-connected disabilities could be considered workers' compensation or disability for pension. The rest is taxable as annuity or pension income. If a taxpayer dies and his or her survivor benefits from the pension, the workers' compensation remains exempt from tax.

Welfare and Other Public Assistance Benefits

Benefit payments made by a public welfare fund to individuals with disabilities (such as blindness) should not be included as income. Welfare or public assistance payments from a state fund for the victims of a crime should not be included in the victims' income. Do not deduct medical expenses that are reimbursed by such a fund. Any welfare payments obtained fraudulently are not tax-exempt and must be included as income.

Veterans' Benefits

Veterans' benefits paid under any law, regulation, or administrative practice administered by the Department of Veterans Affairs (VA) should not be included as income.

Income

For veterans and their families, the following benefits are not taxable:

- Education, training, and subsistence allowances.
- Disability compensation and pension payments for disabilities paid either to veterans or their families.
- Grants for homes designed for wheelchair living.
- Grants for motor vehicles for veterans who lost their sight or the use of their limbs.
- Veterans' insurance proceeds and dividends paid either to veterans or to their beneficiaries, including the proceeds of a veteran's endowment policy paid before death.
- Interest on insurance dividends left on deposit with Veterans Affairs.
- Benefits under a dependent-care assistance program.
- The death gratuity paid to a survivor of a member of the armed forces who died after September 10, 2001.
- Payments made under the compensated work therapy program.
- Any bonus payment by a state or political subdivision because of services in a combat zone.

Volunteers

Living allowances provided to Peace Corps volunteers for housing, utilities, household supplies, food, and clothing are exempt from tax.

However, the following items do not fulfill basic living requirements and thus must be included as income and reported as wages:

- Allowances paid to the spouse and minor children while the taxpayer was a volunteer leader training in the United States.
- Living allowances designated by the director of the Peace Corps as basic compensation; these allowances are for personal items such as domestic help, laundry and clothing maintenance, entertainment and recreation, transportation, and other miscellaneous expenses.
- Leave allowances.
- Readjustment allowances or termination payments.

How to Read the Tax Tables

Tax tables are charts that show how much tax is charged per income amount for each of the federal filing statuses. Tax tables apply to income that is less than $100,000 and each filing status has a separate table. If the taxpayer's income is over $100,000, then the tax is calculated differently.

To read the tax table, you must find the income range your client's income amount falls between and then look along the line until you come to your client's filing status. If a client's income is the exact amount of one of the ranges, always round up and use the higher tax amount. Tax tables are found in the Form 1040 Instructions. Tax tables can also be accessed through the IRS website.

At least	But less than	Single	Married filing jointly *	Married filing sepa- rately	Head of a house- hold
			Your tax is—		
12,000					
12,000	12,050	1,253	1,203	1,253	1,203
12,050	12,100	1,259	1,208	1,259	1,208
12,100	12,150	1,265	1,213	1,265	1,213
12,150	12,200	1,271	1,218	1,271	1,218
12,200	12,250	1,277	1,223	1,277	1,223

The tax tables are not used by the following:

> Estates or trusts.
> Individuals claiming the exclusion for foreign tax credits.
> Taxpayers who file a short-period return.
> Taxpayers whose income exceeds $100,000.

Part 6 Review Questions

To obtain the maximum benefit from this chapter, LTP recommends that you complete each of the following questions, and then compare them to the answers with feedback that immediately follows. Under governing self-study standards, vendors are required to present review questions intermittently throughout each self-study course.

These questions and explanations are not part of the final examination and will not be graded by LTP.

IP6.1
Which of the following best describes fringe benefits?

　　a. Employer provided an employee birthday lunch.
　　b. Employer provided a plaque for continuous service to their faithful employees.
　　c. Employer provided airfare for their employees to work at a different location for 3 days.
　　d. Employer provided benefits to their employees in addition to their normal compensation.

IP6.2
Which of the following is not included in a Cafeteria plan?

　　a. Archer medical savings account
　　b. Adoption assistance
　　c. Group-term life insurance
　　d. Dependent care assistance

IP6.3

Which of the following is nontaxable income?

   a. Child support
   b. Social Security benefits
   c. Fringe benefits
   d. Earned income

Part 6 Review Questions Answers

IP6.1

Which of the following best describes fringe benefits?

   a. Employer provided an employee birthday lunch.
   b. Employer provided a plaque for continuous service to their faithful employees.
   c. Employer provided airfare for their employees to work at a different location for 3 days.
   d. Employer provided benefits to their employees in addition to their normal compensation.

Feedback: Review section *Fringe Benefits.*

IP6.2

Which of the following is not included in a Cafeteria plan?

   a. Archer medical savings account
   b. Adoption assistance
   c. Group-term life insurance
   d. Dependent care assistance

Feedback: Review section *Cafeteria Plan.*

IP6.3

Which of the following is nontaxable income?

   a. Child support
   b. Social Security benefits
   c. Fringe benefits
   d. Earned income

Feedback: Review section *Nontaxable Income.*

Takeaways

Gross income, or "worldwide income," includes all income received from any source not specifically excluded. In this chapter, we discussed basic examples of gross income including compensation for services, rents, and annuities.

If the taxpayer repays an amount that was included in an earlier year as income, the taxpayer may be able to deduct the amount repaid from income for the year in which it was repaid. If the amount repaid is more than $3,000, the taxpayer may be able to take a credit against his or her tax for the year in which it was repaid. This credit is taken on Schedule A, so the taxpayer must have enough deductions to itemize. Being able to deduct the credit has been suspended by the TCJA from after December 31, 2017 to December 25, 2025. Generally, the taxpayer can claim a deduction or credit only if the repayment qualifies as an expense or loss incurred in the taxpayer's business or in a for-profit transaction.

Any individual with taxable compensation may be eligible to contribute to a traditional IRA. In the taxable year in which an individual turns 70½, he or she cannot make future contributions to a traditional IRA. The individual may be able to contribute to a Roth IRA, establish a new traditional IRA, or fund the new IRA with funds transferred from either another traditional IRA or an employer-sponsored qualified retirement plan.

TEST YOUR KNOWLEDGE!
Go online to take a practice quiz.

Chapter 5 Adjustments to Income

Introduction

In this chapter, students will learn how various expenses "adjust" or lower the taxpayer's income to arrive at their adjusted gross income (AGI). They will also learn how the Tax Cuts and Jobs Act (TCJA) has impacted adjustments at the federal level and how to handle any previous-year returns that preceded those TCJA-mandated changes.

Objectives

At the end of this lesson, the student will:

> ➤ Understand how an adjustment to income can decrease the taxpayer's AGI.
> ➤ Explain the differences between tuition and fees deduction and education credits.
> ➤ Define who qualifies for a student loan deduction.

Resources

Form 1040	Publication 17	Instructions Form 1040
Form 1098-E	Publication 504	Instructions Form 1098-E
Form 2106	Publication 521	Instructions Form 2106
Form 3903	Publication 560	Instructions Form 3903
Form 8889	Publication 969	Instructions Form 8889
Form 8917	Publication 4334	Instructions Form 8917
Schedule SE	Tax Topics 450, 451, 452, 455, 456, 458	Instructions Schedule SE
Schedule 1		

Table of Contents

Introduction 212
Part 1 Adjustments to Income 214
    Changes Made by the Tax Cuts and Jobs Act 214
    Form 2106: Unreimbursed Employee Business Expense 215
    Educator Expense 215
    Armed Forces Reservists 216
    Fee-Based Government Officials 216
    impairment-related Work Expenses of Disabled Employees 217
    Health Savings Accounts 217
    Last-Month Rule 218
    Contributions to an HSA 218
    Distributions from an HSA 219
    The Three Primary Types of HSAs 219
    Part 1 Review Questions 220
    Part 1 Review Questions Answers 220
Part 2 Other Adjustments to Income 221
    Form 3903: Moving Expenses 221
    Moving Expenses Before the TCJA 221
    Moving Expenses After the TCJA 223
    Penalty on Early Withdrawal of Savings 223
    Alimony Paid 223
    Divorce Agreement Post 2018 224
    Individual Retirement Account (IRA) Deduction 224
    Part 2 Review Questions 225
    Part 2 Review Questions Answers 226
Part 3 Self-Employment Adjustments 227
    Self-Employment Tax 227
    Self-Employment Retirement Plans 227
    SEP (Simplified Employee Pension) 227
    SIMPLE Retirement Plan 228
    Part 3 Review Questions 230
    Part 3 Review Questions Answers 230
Part 4 Education Credits and Qualifying Expenses 231
    Form 1098-E: Qualified Student Loans 231
    Student Loan Interest Deduction 231
    Reading Form 1098-E 232
    Qualified Tuition and Fees 232
    Which Expenses Qualify for Tuition and Fee Deductions? 233
    Form 8917: Tuition and Fee Deduction 233
    Who Can Claim the Deduction? 233
    Who Cannot Claim the Deduction? 233
    Academic Period 234
    Part 4 Review Questions 234
    Part 4 Review Questions Answers 235
Takeaways 236

Adjustments to Income

Part 1 Adjustments to Income

Adjustments are certain expenses that directly reduce the taxpayer's total income and are known as "above the line" tax deductions in the industry. Adjustments reduce total income to arrive at the adjusted gross income (AGI), the total income from all sources minus any adjustments to income. Adjustments are calculated and reported using Form 1040, Schedule 1, lines 11 – 24z.

	Schedule 1 (Form 1040) 2021		Page 2
Part II	**Adjustments to Income**		
11	Educator expenses	11	
12	Certain business expenses of reservists, performing artists, and fee-basis government officials. Attach Form 2106	12	
13	Health savings account deduction. Attach Form 8889	13	
14	Moving expenses for members of the Armed Forces. Attach Form 3903	14	
15	Deductible part of self-employment tax. Attach Schedule SE	15	
16	Self-employed SEP, SIMPLE, and qualified plans	16	
17	Self-employed health insurance deduction	17	
18	Penalty on early withdrawal of savings	18	
19a	Alimony paid	19a	
b	Recipient's SSN ▶		
c	Date of original divorce or separation agreement (see instructions) ▶		
20	IRA deduction	20	
21	Student loan interest deduction	21	
22	Reserved for future use	22	
23	Archer MSA deduction	23	
24	Other adjustments:		

Claim certain expenses, contributions, and payments as adjustments to income to reduce taxpayers' total income and calculate their AGI. When taxpayers claim qualifying expense, contribution, or payment as an adjustment, report the amount of the qualifying expense, contribution, or payment on the appropriate line on Schedule 1. Subtract this amount from the taxpayer's income.

Example: Andrew, a captain in the Navy, was ordered to move to Norfolk, VA, from San Diego, CA, and was not reimbursed for his moving expenses; for reasons explained in full later in the chapter, his unreimbursed moving expenses qualify as adjustments to income. Report his total expenses on line 14, and that amount would be subtracted from his total income to calculate his AGI.

Changes Made by the Tax Cuts and Jobs Act

Due to the Tax Cuts and Jobs Act (TCJA), adjustments have been suspended from December 31, 2017, to December 31, 2026. Not all states conformed to the TCJA.

The TCJA eliminated Form 1040A and 1040EZ from 2018 to 2026. Here are some adjustments to be looked at:

> ➢ Educator expenses.
> ➢ IRA deductions.

> Student loan interest deductions.
> Tuition and fees.

All other adjustments must be reported on a prior year Form 1040, lines 23-35. When preparing a 2018-2026 tax return, adjustments are made on Form 1040, Schedule 1, lines 11-24z (assuming Congress does not make any tax law changes during those years).

Form 2106: Unreimbursed Employee Business Expense

Due to the suspension of Form 2106 for tax years 2018 through 2025, most employees cannot use the form. Individuals who can still file Form 2106 include Armed Forces reservists, qualified performing artists, fee-basis state or local government officials, or individuals with a disability claiming impairment-related work expenses. These individuals may qualify to deduct unreimbursed employee business expenses as an adjustment to gross income. This happens by calculating the adjustment using Form 2106 and then flowing the calculated amount to Form 1040, Schedule 1, line 14. To qualify, the taxpayer must meet the following requirements:

1. During the tax year, performing artists performed for at least two employers.
2. The taxpayer received at least $200 from each of at least two of these employers.
3. The taxpayer's related performing arts business expenses are more than 10% of the gross income from the performance of those services.
4. The taxpayer's adjusted gross income is not more than $16,000 before deducting these business expenses.

If the taxpayer meets all the above requirements, the taxpayer should complete Form 2106. If Form 2106 is for performing arts-related expenses, write "QPA" and the amount of expenses in the space to the left of line 12 of Form 1040, Schedule 1, line 12. See section 67(a) by PL 115-97, section 11045.

If the taxpayer is married, they must file a joint return to claim the adjustment unless they lived apart during the tax year. When filing jointly, the couple must figure out requirements 1, 2, and 3 separately for each of them. However, requirement 4 applies to their combined AGI. If all the requirements are met, the amount on Form 2106, line 10, is entered on Form 1040, Schedule 1, line 12.

Educator Expense

If the taxpayer was an eligible educator, they might deduct up to $250 of qualified expenses paid in 2021. An eligible educator is a teacher for kindergarten through 12th grade or an instructor, counselor, principal, or aide who works in a school for at least 900 hours during a school year. If the taxpayer and spouse are filing jointly and eligible educators, the maximum deduction is $500. Neither spouse may deduct more than $250 of qualified expenses on line 11 of Form 1040, Schedule 1. The PATH act made this adjustment permanent.

Qualified expenses include ordinary and necessary expenses paid in connection with books, supplies, equipment (including computer equipment, software, and services), and other materials used in their classroom. An ordinary expense is common and accepted in the taxpayer's education field, and a necessary expense is helpful and appropriate for the taxpayer's profession as an educator. An expense does not have to be required to be considered necessary.

Qualified expenses do not include homeschooling expenses or nonathletic supplies for health or physical education courses. The income adjustment amount must be reduced if the educator has any of the following:

- Excludable interest on qualified US savings bonds series EE and I, and Form 8815 is filed on the same tax return.
- Any distribution from a qualified tuition program that was excluded from income.
- Any tax-free withdrawals from Coverdell education savings account(s).
- Any reimbursements received for expenses not reported in box 1 of the W-2.

Armed Forces Reservists

If the taxpayer is a member of the US military's reserve, National Guard, or a member of the Public Health Service Reserve Corps, the expense for traveling more than 100 miles from their main home is deductible. The deductible expenses are limited to the federal per diem rates for the city the taxpayer is traveling to.

Armed Forces reservists are members of a reserve component of the following organizations:

- The United States Army, Navy, Marine Corps, or Air Force.
- The Coast Guard Reserve.
- The Army National Guard of the United States.
- The Air National Guard of the United States.
- The Reserve Corps of the Public Health Service.

Fee-Based Government Officials

If the taxpayer is a government official who is compensated entirely or partly on a fee basis, their job-related expenses are deductible.

If the taxpayer does not meet the unreimbursed employee business expense requirements, the taxpayer does not qualify to deduct expenses as an adjustment to gross income. Instead, the taxpayer must complete Form 2106 and deduct their employee business expenses as an itemized deduction on Schedule A.

Fee-basis state or local government officials qualify if they are employed by a state or a political subdivision of a state and are compensated in whole or in part on a fee basis. Under the Fair Labor Standards Act (FLSA), a "fee basis" is defined as follows:

> Administrative and professional employees may be paid on a fee basis. An employee will be considered to be paid on a "fee basis" within the meaning of these regulations if the employee is paid an agreed upon sum for a single job regardless of the time required for its completion. These payments resemble piecework payments with the important distinction that generally a "fee" is paid for the kind of job that is unique rather than for a series of jobs repeated an indefinite number of times and for which payment on an identical basis is made over and over again. Payments based on the number of hours or days worked and not on the accomplishment of a given task are not considered payments on a fee basis (Section 541.605).

impairment-related Work Expenses of Disabled Employees

Disabled employees with impairment-related work expenses are individuals with physical or mental disabilities requiring attendant care at their employment. Adjustable expenses could include items needed to perform the job satisfactorily, provided they are not deductible or adjustable under some other statute.

Example 1: John is blind; for John to do his work satisfactorily, he needs to have an individual read his documents. John uses the reader both inside and outside of regular work hours; however, John can only use the expense business-related reading as an adjustment and not any reading outside work hours.

Example 2: Yesenia is deaf and must use a sign language interpreter during meetings while at work. The interpreter's services are used only for work so that Yesenia can claim all the interpreter's expenses as adjustments to income.

Health Savings Accounts

Health savings accounts contributions from both the employer and the employee are reported on Form 8889 and can be claimed as an adjustment to income on Form 1040, Schedule 1, line 12. Distributions made from the HSA that were paid for qualifying medical expenses are excludable from income. If the maximum possible amount of the HSA were contributed, then that amount would become taxable on the tax return.

A health savings account (HSA) is a tax-exempt trust or custodial account that is set up with a qualified HSA trustee to pay or reimburse certain incurred medical expenses. While this account is always paired with a medical insurance plan, an HSA is not health insurance. What separates this type of account from a regular savings account is the tax advantages that come with it. The taxpayer will receive a tax form stating the exact amount deposited into the account at the end of the year, and that amount is tax-deductible.

To qualify to contribute to an HSA as an eligible individual, the taxpayer must meet the following requirements:

- ➢ As explained further in the chapter, have a high-deductible health plan (HDHP).
- ➢ Have no other health coverage except permitted coverage.
- ➢ Not be enrolled in Medicare.
- ➢ Not be claimed as a dependent on another return.

Anyone can contribute to the plan for the taxpayer, and no permission or authorization from the IRS is necessary to establish an HSA. When an HSA is set up, the taxpayer will have to work with a qualified HSA trustee, which can be a bank, an insurance company, or anyone already approved by the IRS to be a trustee of individual retirement accounts (IRAs) or Archer medical savings accounts (MSA). The HSA can be established through a trustee that is not a health plan provider.

Last-Month Rule

If the taxpayer is an eligible individual on the first day of the last month of the taxpayer's tax year, they are considered an eligible individual for the entire year. The taxpayer must remain an eligible individual during the tax year. For most taxpayers, this would be January 1st through December 31st, meaning the last-month rule would go into effect as of December 1st. If the taxpayer fails to be eligible other than becoming disabled or deceased, the taxpayer's contributions made during the tax year will become taxable. This amount is also subject to a 10% additional tax.

2021 HSA Contribution Limits with an HDHP:

Type of Coverage	Contribution Limit
Self-only	$3,600
Family	$7,200

2022 HSA Contribution Limits with an HDHP:

Type of Coverage	Contribution Limit
Self-only	$3,650
Family	$7,300

2021 Annual Deductible Limits:

Type of Coverage	Minimum Annual Deduction	Maximum Annual Deduction
Self-only	$1,400	$7,000
Family	$2,800	$14,000

2022 Annual Deductible Limits:

Type of Coverage	Minimum Annual Deduction	Maximum Annual Deduction
Self-only	$1,400	$7,000
Family	$2,800	$14,000

The maximum annual out-of-pocket limit does not apply to deductibles and expenses for out-of-network services if the plan uses a network of providers. Only deductibles and out-of-pocket expenses for services within the network should be used to figure out whether the limit is reached.

Contributions to an HSA

Contributions made to the HSA on behalf of the employee by the employer are not included in the taxpayer's income. An employer's contributions to an employee's account using a salary reduction through a cafeteria plan are treated as an employer contribution. All contributions are reported on Form 8889 and must be filed with Form 1040.

Distributions from an HSA

Generally, medical expenses that have been paid for during the year are not reimbursed by the plan until the taxpayer has met the deductible. The taxpayer may receive a tax-free distribution from the HSA to pay for or reimburse qualified medical expenses after the taxpayer has established an HSA. Distributions received for any other reason are subject to an additional tax.

The Three Primary Types of HSAs

1. High-Deductible Health Plan (HDHP)

An HDHP has:

- A higher annual deductible than typical health plans.
- There is a maximum limit on the total yearly deductible amount and out-of-pocket medical expenses.

An HDHP can provide preventive care and other benefits with no deductible or deductible below the annual minimum. Preventive care can include the following:

- Routine exams and periodic health evaluations
- Routine prenatal and well-childcare
- Child and adult immunizations
- Stop-smoking programs
- Weight-loss programs
- Screening services, which can include the following:
    - Cancer
    - Heart and vascular diseases
    - Infectious diseases
    - Mental health conditions
    - Substance abuse
    - Metabolic, nutritional, and endocrine conditions
    - Musculoskeletal disorders
    - Obstetric and gynecological conditions
    - Pediatric conditions
    - Vision and hearing conditions

2. Archer Medical Savings Accounts (MSAs)

Archer MSAs are an IRA-type savings account for use when the taxpayer has medical expenses. They were created to help self-employed individuals and employees of certain small employers meet the medical costs of the account holder, the account holder's spouse, or the account holder's dependent(s). MSAs can be used when the taxpayer has low-cost health insurance with a high-deductible health plan (HDHP). MSA contributions are tax-deductible.

The portion of the medical expense not covered by insurance can be withdrawn tax-free from the MSA. The participant cannot pay their insurance premiums using funds in the MSA. Taxpayers who use Medicare, which counts as health insurance, cannot use any MSA they may have unless it is a Medicare MSA. If the taxpayer has no medical expenses in one year, the contributions remain in the account to be used in the future. The maximum the taxpayer can contribute is 65% of the health-plan deductible for individuals (self-only plan) and 75% for families.

Adjustments to Income

3. Health Flexible Spending Arrangements (FSAs)

A health FSA is usually funded through voluntary salary reduction and reimbursing employees for medical expenses. An FSA is not reported on the tax return, and the salary-reduction contribution limit is $2,750. Regardless of the amount contributed, the taxpayer can receive tax-free is the contribution amount used to pay for qualified medical expenses. Self-employed individuals do not qualify for this reduction.

Part 1 Review Questions

To obtain the maximum benefit from this chapter, LTP recommends that you complete each of the following questions and then compare them to the answers with feedback immediately following. Under governing self-study standards, vendors must present review questions intermittently throughout each self-study course.

These questions and explanations are not part of the final examination and will not be graded by LTP.

ATIP1.1
Which of the following is not an adjustment to income?

a. Educator expense
b. Early penalty withdrawal
c. Alimony
d. Itemized deductions

ATIP1.2
Julie is a junior high school teacher, and she spent $1,200 for her classroom. What would be the total of her qualified educator expense?

a. $1,200
b. $1,450
c. $250
d. $500

ATIP1.3
What is the 2021 HSA Family Contribution limit with a High-Deductible Health Plan?

a. $3,600
b. $7,200
c. $7,300
d. $7,000

Part 1 Review Questions Answers

ATIP1.1
Which of the following is not an adjustment to income?

a. Educator expense
b. Early penalty withdrawal
c. Alimony
d. Itemized deductions

Feedback: Review section *Adjustments to Income.*

ATIP1.2
Julie is a junior high school teacher, and she spent $1,200 for her classroom. What would be the total of her qualified educator expense?

   a. $1,200
   b. $1,450
   c. $250
   d. $500

Feedback: Review section *Educator Expenses.*

ATIP1.3
What is the 2021 HSA Family Contribution limit with a High-Deductible Health Plan?

   a. $3,600
   b. $7,200
   c. $7,300
   d. $7,000

Feedback: Please reread "*Contributions to an HSA.*"

Part 2 Other Adjustments to Income

This part covers other adjustments that may have been changed due to the Tax Cuts and Jobs Act. The two with the most changes are moving expenses and alimony.

Form 3903: Moving Expenses

Under some circumstances, moving expenses can be claimed as adjustments to income. Moving expenses are reported on Form 1040, Schedule 1, line 14. Complete and attach Form 3903, *Moving Expenses*, to the tax return to claim this adjustment. The taxpayer does not have to itemize deductions to claim the adjustment. Although the Tax Cuts and Jobs Act has made several changes to moving expenses, it is still important for the tax professional to know how moving expense adjustments worked before and after the TCJA.

Moving Expenses Before the TCJA

To claim moving expenses as adjustments to income, the taxpayer must meet the following requirements:

   ➢ The move is closely related to the start of work.
   ➢ The taxpayer meets the distance test.
   ➢ The taxpayer meets the time test.

> *Señor 1040 Says:* Recordkeeping is vital to maintaining an accurate record of expenses for a move. The taxpayer should save receipts, bills, canceled checks, credit card statements, and mileage logs to correctly report the amount of moving expense.

Adjustments to Income

Before the Tax Cuts and Jobs Act was enacted, moving expenses were claimed based on whether the move was made in conjunction with the taxpayer's job or business. The distance between the old home and the new workplace must be at least 50 miles more than the old home to the old workplace. Also, if the taxpayer did not have any reimbursed moving expenses, they could report the expenses in the year they were incurred or when they were paid in full. The following moving expenses could be claimed as adjustments to income before the TCJA:

> The cost of packing and moving household goods and personal effects.
> The cost of storing and insuring household goods once 30 days have passed.
> The cost of connecting and disconnecting utilities.
> The cost of one trip, including lodging but not meals, to the new home.
> The cost of tolls and parking fees.

The taxpayer would first report the moving expenses on Form 3903 and then on line 13 of Form 1040, Schedule 1. If the taxpayer had reimbursed moving expenses under an *accountable plan*, the expenses would be reported on the taxpayer's Form W-2 in box 12 and designated with code *P*. Reimbursed expenses reported with code *P* do not have to be reported on the tax return. If taxpayers were reimbursed for the moving expenses, they cannot double-dip and claim moving expenses as adjustments to income on their tax return.

To be considered an accountable plan, the employer's reimbursement or allowance arrangement must include the following rules:

> The expenses must have a business connection, which means the taxpayer must have paid or incurred deductible expenses while performing services as an employee.
> The taxpayer must adequately account to the employer for these expenses within a reasonable time.
> The taxpayer must return any excess reimbursement or allowance within a reasonable time.

Example: Donald lives in Seattle, WA, and accepted a job in Portland, ME. Donald's new employer reimbursed him using their accountable plan for his travel expenses from Seattle to Portland. Donald's employer would report the reimbursement with code *P* on his W-2, box 12.

Distance Test

The distance between a job's location and the taxpayer's main home is the shortest of the most commonly traveled routes between them. The distance test considers only the location of the former home, and it does not account for the location of any new home. If the taxpayer had more than one job during the year, only use the "main job" location to calculate the distance for this test. To determine which job was the "main job," examine the following factors:

> The total time spent at each job.
> The amount of work completed at each job.
> The amount of money earned at each job.

Whichever job had the highest or the majority of the above is the main job.

Time Test

The taxpayer must also meet a time test to qualify for moving expenses. According to the time test, if a taxpayer moves to another location and claims it was job-related, they must work in the new location for at least 39 weeks during the first 12 months of their stay to claim the moving expenses as adjustments to income.

The taxpayer would need to work 39 weeks out of 52 weeks after the move to calculate full-time work as an employee.

Moving Expenses After the TCJA

One of the many changes made by the TCJA was to suspend adjustments for moving expenses with one exception: Active Armed Forces who have a military order to move or permanently change their station can claim moving expenses if they meet the normal qualifications. The standard mileage rate for moving reimbursements is 18 cents per mile. If the taxpayer has made multiple moves in one tax year, then a different Form 3903 will be used for each move.

A permanent station change can be any of the following:

> - A move from the taxpayer's current home to their first post of duty.
> - A move from one permanent post to another.
> - A move from the taxpayer's last permanent post to a new home in the United States. The move must occur within one year of the end of active duty or within the allowable period designated by the Joint Travel Regulations, which is beyond the scope of this course.

Penalty on Early Withdrawal of Savings

If a taxpayer withdraws money from a savings program and incurs a penalty, the penalty is an allowable adjustment to gross income. This penalty is reported to the taxpayer on Form 1099-INT or Form 1099-OID. The bank or other private institution imposes the early withdrawal penalty. Report the early withdrawal penalty on Form 1040, Schedule 1, line 17, as an adjustment to income.

Alimony Paid

Alimony is a payment or a series of payments to a spouse or former spouse required under a divorce or under a separation agreement that meets certain requirements. Any alimony a taxpayer receives should be reported on Form 1040, Schedule 1, line 2a. The amount of alimony paid should be reported on Form 1040, Schedule 1, line 19a, as an adjustment to income. The paying spouse must report the recipient's Social Security number on line 19b. Not all payments received from a spouse are considered alimony. For a description of what is considered alimony, see Publication 17.

The term "divorce or separation instrument" refers to the following:

> - A decree of divorce or separate maintenance or a "written instrument incident" (see IRS Publication 504) to that decree.
> - A written separation agreement.
> - A decree or a type of court order requiring a spouse to make payments for the support or maintenance of the other spouse.

Payments that are not alimony include:

- Child support
- Noncash property settlements
- Payments that are the taxpayer's spouse's part of community income
- Payments to keep up the payer's property
- Use of the payer's property
- Noncash property settlements, whether in lump sum or installments
- Voluntary payments

Divorce Agreement Post 2018

Alimony will no longer be an adjustment to income or a source of income if the divorce or separation agreement is completed after December 31, 2018. The new law applies if an agreement was executed on or before December 31, 2018, and then modified after that date. The new law applies if the modification does these two things:

- It changes the terms of the alimony or separate maintenance payments.
- It says explicitly that alimony or separate maintenance payments are not deductible by the payer spouse or includable in the income of the receiving spouse.

Agreements executed on or before December 31, 2018, follow the previous rules. If an agreement was modified after January 1, 2019, the new agreement should state that they are following the 2018 laws if the modifications didn't change what's described above.

Community property laws may not apply to an item of community property income, and special rules may apply to community property states. More research may be needed if the taxpayer lives in a community property state.

Example: Kathy and Lloyd live in Arizona and are a married couple. Kathy's father passed away in 1995. Her mother sold her country residence and moved to a town close to friends and church. Her mother had a trust and passed away in 2019. Kathy was a beneficiary of the trust and received $75,000 as an inheritance. Since Kathy and Lloyd live in a community property state, she would need to put her inherited money in a separate bank account to preserve her inheritance. If the money was deposited into a joint account, then the inheritance becomes both of theirs. For more information, see Publication 504. Inheritance is beyond the scope of this course.

Individual Retirement Account (IRA) Deduction

Taxpayers may participate in a personal savings plan that offers tax advantages to set aside money for retirement or education expenses. This personal savings plan is known as an individual retirement account or IRA. There are different types of IRAs: traditional, Roth, SIMPLE, or education.

It is necessary to understand the difference between a contribution and a deduction. Contributions are amounts paid to a taxpayer's plan, whereas deductions are the actual amount the taxpayer may reduce their taxable income.

Adjustments to Income

Individuals who have not reached the age of 72 with taxable compensation may contribute to an IRA (with certain other conditions). Compensation for IRA purposes includes wages, salaries, commissions, tips, professional fees, bonuses, and other amounts received for personal services. Also included are taxable alimony and separate maintenance payments.

The deductible amount of the IRA contributions may be limited depending on the following two factors:

> ➤ If the taxpayer or spouse had an employer-provided pension plan.
> ➤ The amount of the modified adjusted gross income.

The maximum a single taxpayer can contribute either $6,000 or the taxpayer's taxable compensation, whichever is lowest. If the taxpayers are married and only one spouse has taxable compensation, the maximum contribution the couple can make is $12,000. The maximum that can be contributed to one account is $6,000. If the married spouses have compensation in excess of $6,000 each, they both may contribute $6,000.

If the taxpayer is 50-years-old or older, they may make a "catch-up" contribution to their IRA account in the amount of $1,000. Taxpayers may not contribute more than $7,000 to their IRA account during the tax year. Contributions must be in the form of money, and property cannot be contributed to an IRA.

Suppose a taxpayer contributes more than $6,000 ($7,000 if age 50 or older) in one year to an IRA. In that case, the taxpayer will be penalized with a tax on the excess contribution and earnings each year until the taxpayer withdraws the excess contribution. This penalty is not limited to the year the excess contribution is made. The excess contributions must be reported on Form 5329, *Additional Taxes Attributable to IRAs, Other Qualified Retirement Plans, Annuities, Modified Endowment Contracts, and MSAs*, Part II.

In addition to adjusting the taxpayer's gross income, interest earned on a traditional IRA account is accumulated tax-deferred until it is withdrawn, thus benefiting the taxpayer.

Part 2 Review Questions

To obtain the maximum benefit from this chapter, LTP recommends that you complete each of the following questions and then compare them to the answers with feedback that immediately follows. Under governing self-study standards, vendors must present review questions intermittently throughout each self-study course.

These questions and explanations are not part of the final examination and will not be graded by LTP.

ATIP2.1
Before TCJA was written into law, which taxpayer could claim moving expenses before TCJA?

 a. Daniel, an electrician, moved to Idaho for a new job.
 b. Dennis, who retired and moved to Florida.
 c. Danelle moved to attend the state university.
 d. Debbie has lived in the same town and recently got married and moved in with her spouse.

Adjustments to Income

ATIP2.2
Which individual can claim moving expenses after TCJA?

   a. David is an active military electrician moving to Idaho for a new job.
   b. Damon retired and moved to Florida.
   c. Diana, who moved to attend the university.
   d. Domingo recently got married and moved in with his spouse.

ATIP2.3
Sergio and Faith got divorced on January 2, 2020. Sergio needs to pay Faith alimony of $1,500 per month. Which scenario best describes how to claim their alimony?

   a. Sergio will claim the adjustment, and Faith will claim the alimony as income.
   b. Sergio will not claim the adjustment, and Faith does not claim the alimony as income.
   c. Faith will claim the adjustment, and Sergio will claim the alimony as income.
   d. Faith will not claim the adjustment, and Sergio can claim the adjustment to income.

Part 2 Review Questions Answers

ATIP2.1
Before TCJA was written into law, which taxpayer could claim moving expenses before TCJA?

   a. Daniel, an electrician, moved to Idaho for a new job.
   b. Dennis, who retired and moved to Florida.
   c. Danelle moved to attend the state university.
   d. Debbie has lived in the same town and recently got married and moved in with her spouse.

Feedback: Review section *Form 2106: Unreimbursed Employee Expense.*

ATIP2.2
Which individual can claim moving expenses after TCJA?

   a. David is an active military electrician moving to Idaho for a new job.
   b. Damon retired and moved to Florida.
   c. Diana, who moved to attend the university.
   d. Domingo, who recently got married and moved in with his spouse

Feedback: Review section *Armed Forces Reservist.*

ATIP2.3
Sergio and Faith got divorced on January 2, 2020. Sergio needs to pay Faith alimony of $1,500 per month. Which scenario best describes how to claim their alimony?

   a. Sergio will claim the adjustment, and Faith will claim the alimony as income.
   b. Sergio will not claim the adjustment, and Faith does not claim the alimony as income.
   c. Faith will claim the adjustment, and Sergio will claim the alimony as income.
   d. Faith will not be able to claim the adjustment, and Sergio cannot claim the alimony payment as an adjustment to income.

Feedback: Review section *Alimony Paid*.

Part 3 Self-Employment Adjustments

Self-employed taxpayers must pay both the employer and employee portions of the Medicare and Social Security taxes. Since the self-employed person pays the entire amount, they can claim an adjustment to income equal to one-half of the total self-employment tax. This tax is figured on Schedule SE, and the adjustment is then carried to Form 1040, Schedule 1, line 15. If the taxpayer has W-2 wages, the taxpayer's net self-employment earnings are combined with their wages when determining the earning limit for the self-employment tax.

Self-Employment Tax

Self-employment tax does not apply to income earned as a shareholder of an S corporation or as a limited partner of a partnership (except for guaranteed payments). Self-employment tax is calculated on Schedule SE and must be paid if the following apply:

> Net earnings for the year from self-employment (excluding income as a church employee) were $400 or more.
> Church-employee income for the year is more than $108.28.

The self-employment tax rules apply even if the taxpayer receives Social Security and Medicare benefits. Special rules apply to workers who perform in-home services for elderly or disabled individuals. Caregivers are typically classified as employees of the individuals they provide care for. Self-employed individuals may have to make estimated quarterly payments to the IRS. See Publication 505, Tax Withholding, and Estimated Tax for more information.

Self-Employment Retirement Plans

This line item for adjustments is for self-employed taxpayers who provide retirement plans for themselves and their employees.

The plans that can be deducted on this line are as follows:

> Simplified Employee Pension (SEP) plans.
> Savings Incentive Match Plan for Employees (SIMPLE).
> Qualified plans, including HR (10) or Keogh plans, are beyond this course's scope.

SEP (Simplified Employee Pension)

A business of any size may establish a specific type of traditional IRA for their employees called a Simplified Employee Pension (SEP), also referred to as a SEP-IRA. A self-employed individual is also eligible to participate in this plan. There are three basic steps in starting a SEP:

> Must have a formal written agreement to provide benefits to all eligible employees.
> Must give each eligible employee certain information.
> A SEP-IRA must be set up for each employee.

Adjustments to Income

The formal written agreement must state that the employer will benefit all eligible employees under the SEP. The employer may adopt an IRS-provided model by filing Form 5305-SEP. Professional advice should be sought when setting up the SEP. Form 5305-SEP cannot be filed if any of the following apply:

- The company already has a qualified retirement plan other than a SEP.
- The company has eligible employees whose IRAs have not been set up.
- The company uses the service of leased employees who are not common-law employees.
- The company is a member of one of the following trades or businesses:
    - An affiliated service group is described in section 414(m).
    - A controlled group of corporations is described in section 414(b).
    - A trade or business under common control is described in section 414(c).
- The company does not pay the cost of the SEP contributions.

The contributions are made to IRAs (SEP-IRAs) of the eligible participants in that plan. Interest accumulates tax-free until the participant begins to make withdrawals. Contribution limits are based on net profits.

A taxpayer is eligible for a SEP if they meet the following requirements:

- Has reached age 21.
- Has worked for the employer for at least 3 of the past five years.
- Has received at least $600 in compensation from the employer during each of the last three tax years.

The least of the following amounts is the maximum amount that an employer may annually contribute to an employee's IRA:

- $58,000 (for 2021).
- $61,000 (for 2022).
- 25% of the employee's compensation, or 20% for the self-employed taxpayer.

Contributions made by the employer are not reported as income by the employee, nor can they be deducted as an IRA contribution. Excess contributions are included in the employee's income for the year and are treated as contributions. Do not include SEP contributions on the employee's Form W-2 unless the contributions are pre-tax contributions.

Example: Susan Plant earned $21,000 in 2021. Because the maximum employer contribution for 2021 is 25% of the employee's compensation, the employer can contribute only $5,250 to her SEP-IRA (25% x $21,000).

SIMPLE Retirement Plan

A SIMPLE retirement plan is a tax-favored retirement plan that certain small employers (including self-employed individuals) can set up to benefit their employees.

A SIMPLE plan can be established for any employee who received at least $5,000 in compensation during the two years before the current calendar year and is reasonably expected to receive at least $5,000 during the current calendar year. Self-employed individuals are also eligible. The plan may also use less restrictive guidelines, but it may not use more stringent ones.

The employee's elective deferrals from salary reduction are limited to $13,500; or $16,500 (an additional $3,000) if age 50 or older (for 2021). Salary-reduction contributions are not treated as catch-up contributions. The employer can match employee deferrals dollar-for-dollar up to 3% of the employee's compensation.

SIMPLE IRA

A SIMPLE IRA is a plan that uses separate IRA accounts for each eligible employee. A SIMPLE plan is a written agreement (salary-reduction agreement) between the taxpayer and their employer that allows the taxpayer to choose to do either of the following:

> ➢ Reduce the taxpayer's compensation by a certain percentage each pay period.
> ➢ Have the employer contribute the salary reductions to a SIMPLE IRA on the taxpayer's behalf. These contributions are called "salary-reduction contributions."

All contributions under a SIMPLE IRA plan must be made to SIMPLE IRAs and not to any other type of IRA. The SIMPLE IRA can be an individual retirement account or an individual retirement annuity. In addition to salary reduction contributions, the employer must make either matching contributions or non-elective contributions. The taxpayer is eligible to participate in their employer's SIMPLE plan if the taxpayer meets the following requirements:

> ➢ They received compensation from their employer two years before the current year.
> ➢ They are reasonably expected to receive at least $5,000 in compensation during the calendar year in which contributions were made.

The difference between the SIMPLE retirement plan and the SIMPLE IRA is that the retirement plan is part of a 401(k) plan, and the IRA plan uses individual IRAs for each employee. For more information, see Publication 560.

Self-Employed Health Insurance Deductions

Self-employed taxpayers can claim (as adjustments to income on Form 1040, Schedule 1, line 17) 100% of the amount paid in 2021 for medical insurance and qualified long-term care insurance for the taxpayer and the taxpayer's family if any of the following apply:

> ➢ The taxpayer is a self-employed individual.
> ➢ The taxpayer is a general partner (or limited partner receiving guaranteed payments) in a partnership.
> ➢ The shareholder owns more than 2% of the outstanding stock of an S corporation.

Premiums are not deductible any month that the taxpayer or spouse was eligible to participate in an employer-subsidized health plan. The earned income also limits the deduction. Schedule C would be the net profit minus the SE tax deduction (Schedule 2, line 4) and SEP deductions (Schedule 1, line 16). Self-employed individuals must have a net profit for the year to deduct their paid premiums as adjustments to income.

The self-employed health insurance deduction should be calculated using the *Worksheet for the Health Insurance Deduction* found in Publication 535.

If any of the following exceptions apply, the above worksheet cannot be used:

Adjustments to Income

> ➢ The taxpayer had more than one source of income subject to self-employment.
> ➢ The taxpayer filed Form 2555 or Form 2555-EZ.
> ➢ The taxpayer uses amounts paid for qualified long-term care insurance to figure the deduction.

If the above worksheet cannot be used, use Worksheet 6-A, *Self-Employed Health Insurance Deduction Worksheet*, instead.

Part 3 Review Questions

To obtain the maximum benefit from this chapter, LTP recommends that you complete each of the following questions and then compare them to the answers with feedback that immediately follows. Under governing self-study standards, vendors must present review questions intermittently throughout each self-study course.

These questions and explanations are not part of the final examination and will not be graded by LTP.

ATIP3.1
Which of the following is not a self-employment retirement plan?

a. Simplified Employee Pension (SEP) plan
b. Savings Incentive Match Plan for Employers (SIMPLE)
c. HR 10 or Keogh plan
d. 401(k) plan

ATIP3.2
Which of the following is an adjustment to income?

a. Moving expense for everyone except active military
b. Qualified tuition expense
c. Employee health insurance
d. Deductible part of self-employment

ATIP3.3
Which of the following reports self-employed health insurance?

a. Schedule A
b. Schedule SE
c. Schedule 1, Part II
d. Schedule C

Part 3 Review Questions Answers

ATIP3.1
Which of the following is not a self-employment retirement plan?

a. Simplified Employee Pension (SEP) plan
b. Savings Incentive Match Plan for Employers (SIMPLE)
c. HR 10 or Keogh plan
d. 401(k) plan

Feedback: Review section *Self-Employment Retirement Plans*.

ATIP3.2
Which of the following is an adjustment to income?

a. Moving expense for everyone except active military
b. Qualified tuition expense
c. Employee health insurance
d. Deductible part of self-employment

Feedback: Review section *Self-Employment Tax.*

ATIP3.3
Which of the following reports self-employed health insurance?

a. Schedule A
b. Schedule SE
c. Schedule 1, Part II
d. Schedule C

Feedback: Review section *Self-Employment Health Insurance Deductions.*

Part 4 Education Credits and Qualifying Expenses

Form 1098-E: Qualified Student Loans

Student loan providers will give Form 1098-E to their borrowers to report the interest gained on their student loans. A student will not receive Form 1098-E unless the student loan interest is $600 or more, regardless of the number or amount of student loans the student has. To be reportable for the current tax year, the student loan must be either of the following:

> Subsidized, guaranteed, financed, or otherwise treated as a student loan under a federal, state, or local government program or a postsecondary education institution.
> He is certified by the borrower as a student loan incurred solely to pay qualified higher education expenses.

Student Loan Interest Deduction

Taxpayers with education loans can claim up to $2,500 of education loan interest paid in 2020 as adjustments to income. Although prior-year student loan interest was reported on line 33 of Form 1040 or line 18 of Form 1040A, the deduction is now taken as an adjustment to income on Form 1040, Schedule 1, line 20. The adjustment is allowed on qualifying loans for the taxpayer's benefit or the taxpayer's spouse or dependent when the debt was incurred. The adjustment begins to phase out at incomes of $80,000 ($165,000 for MFJ). MFS individuals are unable to adjust student loan interest. If more than $600 were paid in interest on the student loan, Form 1098-E would be received.

The person for whom the expenses were paid must have been an eligible student; however, a loan is not a qualified student loan if both of the following are true:

> Any of the proceeds were used for other purposes.
> The loan was from either a related person, a person who borrowed the proceeds under a qualified employer plan, or a contract purchased under such a plan.

Adjustments to Income

- An eligible student is a person who meets the following conditions:
- Was enrolled in a degree, certificate, or another program (including a studying abroad program approved for credit by the institution the student is registered with), leading to a recognized education credential at an eligible education institution.
- They carried at least half of the normal full-time workload for the course of study the student is pursuing.

Use Publication 970, *Tax Benefits for Education*, if the taxpayer filed Form 2555, Form 2555-EZ, or Form 4563 excludes income from Puerto Rico sources.

Reading Form 1098-E

Box 1: The interest received by the taxpayer for their student loan is shown here, including capitalized interest, as well as loan origination fees.

Box 2: This box is checked if box 1 has loan origination fees and or capitalized interest that, for some reason, were not included in box 1.

Qualified Tuition and Fees

The TCJA has suspended the contents of this section from 2018 to 2026. Despite this, beginning tax professionals need to understand this section for when they might be required to prepare or amend a prior year's return. Please note, although the official term used by the IRS includes the word "deduction," the following concept is, in fact, an adjustment to income.

Qualified tuition and fee deductions are for amounts paid in 2021 for tuition and fees required for the student's enrollment or attendance at an eligible educational institution during 2021. Amounts paid include those paid by credit card or with borrowed funds. An eligible educational institution includes most colleges, universities, and vocational schools. Qualified tuition and fees do not have any of the following:

- Amounts paid for room and board, insurance, medical expenses (including student health fees), transportation, or other similar personal, living, or family expenses.
- Amounts paid for course-related books, supplies, equipment, and nonacademic activities, except for fees charged by the institution as a condition of enrollment or attendance.

- Amounts paid for any course involving sports, games, or hobbies unless such course is part of the student's degree program.
- Qualified tuition and fees must be reduced by the following benefits:
- Excludable US series EE and I savings bond interest from Form 8815.
- Nontaxable qualified state tuition program earnings.
- Nontaxable earnings from Coverdell education savings accounts.
- Any scholarships, education assistance allowances, or other payments (but not gifts or inheritances) are excluded from income.

Which Expenses Qualify for Tuition and Fee Deductions?

As of now, this deduction has been suspended. The tuition and fees deduction is based on qualified education expenses the taxpayer pays for themselves, their spouse, or a dependent that the taxpayer claimed as an exemption on their tax return. Generally, the deduction is allowed for qualified education expenses paid in 2020 in connection with enrollment at an institution of higher education during 2020 or for an academic period beginning in 2021 that carries through to at least the first three months of 2021. An eligible educational institution is one that participates in the US Department of Education's Federal Student Aid (FSA) programs. For example, suppose the taxpayer paid $1,500 for qualified tuition in December 2020 for the spring 2021 semester beginning in January 2021. In that case, they may be able to use that $1,500 when figuring the 2020 deduction.

Form 8917: Tuition and Fee Deduction

This deduction is based on the qualified education expenses paid to an eligible postsecondary educational institution. The taxpayer may be able to take the deduction if the taxpayer, their spouse, or a dependent claimed on their tax return was a student who was enrolled in or attended an eligible education institution. Form 8917 must be attached to the tax return when claiming this credit.

Who Can Claim the Deduction?

Generally, the taxpayer can claim the tuition and fees deduction if all three of the following requirements are met:

- The taxpayer paid qualified education expenses for higher education.
- The taxpayer paid the education expenses for an eligible student.
- The eligible student is the taxpayer, spouse, or dependent that the taxpayer claimed as an exemption on their tax return.

Who Cannot Claim the Deduction?

The taxpayer cannot claim the tuition and fees deduction if any of the following apply:

- The taxpayer's filing status is married filing separately.
- Another person can claim an exemption for the taxpayer as a dependent on their tax return, and the taxpayer cannot take the deduction even if the other person does not claim that exemption.
- The taxpayer's modified adjusted gross income (MAGI) is more than $80,000 ($160,000 if filing a joint return).

Adjustments to Income

> For tax purposes, the taxpayer was a nonresident alien for any part of the year and did not elect to be treated as a resident alien. More information on nonresident aliens can be found in Publication 519, *US Tax Guide for Aliens.*

Modified adjusted gross income (MAGI) is adjusted gross income, plus all of the following:

> The amount excluded under IRC §911, *Foreign-Earned Income Exclusion.*
> Tax-exempt interest income.
> The excluded portion of social security benefits.

Academic Period

An academic period includes a semester, trimester, quarter, or other study period (such as a summer school session) as reasonably determined by an educational institution. In the case of an educational institution that uses credit hours or clock hours and does not have academic terms, each payment period can be treated as an academic period.

Part 4 Review Questions

To obtain the maximum benefit from this chapter, LTP recommends that you complete each of the following questions and then compare them to the answers with feedback immediately following. Under governing self-study standards, vendors are required to present review questions intermittently throughout each self-study course.

These questions and explanations are not part of the final examination and will not be graded by LTP.

ATIP4.1
Rita graduated from the local university five years ago. Which form would she receive so she can claim her student loan interest?

   a. Form 1098-T
   b. Form 1098
   c. Form 1098-E
   d. Form 1099-A

ATIP4.2
Gabriel's son Junior is going to the local 4-year college. Junior has received Form 1098-T with $4,123 in box 1. Which of the following would give Gabriel the Qualified Tuition and Fees credit?

   a. Junior used the entire amount on room and board
   b. Gabriel and his wife's MAGI was $210,000
   c. Gabriel and his wife's MAGI was $150,000
   d. Junior's income was $65,000

ATIP4.3

Which of the following scenarios best describes when Gilbert can claim his student loan?

a. A non-guaranteed student loan program subsidizes gilbert's student loan.
b. Gilbert's student loan is guaranteed as a student loan solely to pay higher education expenses.
c. Gilbert does not attend a qualifying higher education school.
d. Gilbert attends a private high school, and his parents took out a loan on their house.

Part 4 Review Questions Answers

ATIP4.1

Rita graduated from the local university five years ago. Which form would she receive so she can claim her student loan interest?

a. Form 1098-T
b. Form 1098
c. Form 1098-E
d. Form 1099-A

Feedback: Review section *Reading Form 1098-E.*

ATIP4.2

Gabriel's son Junior is going to the local 4-year college. Junior has received Form 1098-T with $4,123 in box 1. Which of the following would give Gabriel the Qualified Tuition and Fees credit?

a. Junior used the entire amount on room and board
b. Gabriel and his wife's MAGI was $210,000
c. Gabriel and his wife's MAGI was $150,000
d. Junior's income was $65,000

Feedback: Review section *Qualified Tuition and Fees.*

ATIP4.3

Which of the following scenarios best describes when Gilbert can claim his student loan?

a. A non-guaranteed student loan program subsidizes gilbert's student loan.
b. Gilbert's student loan is guaranteed as a student loan solely to pay higher education expenses.
c. Gilbert does not attend a qualifying higher education school.
d. Gilbert attends a private high school, and his parents took out a loan on their house.

Feedback: Review section *Which Expenses Qualify for Tuition and Fee Deductions?*

Takeaways

Taxpayers can take various "deductions" directly on the tax return. These "deductions," however, are not itemized or standardized deductions (discussed later) but are instead called adjustments to income since they "adjust" the taxpayer's gross income. The adjustments are also referred to as "above the line," which appears above the tax form for adjusted gross income.

An HSA is a health savings account set up exclusively for paying the qualified medical expenses of the account beneficiary or the account beneficiary's spouse or dependents. Other adjustments to income that can be claimed are deductible parts of self-employment tax, IRA deductions, self-employed health insurance, and student loan interest of more than $600 and less than $2,500.

TEST YOUR KNOWLEDGE!
Go online to take a practice quiz.

Chapter 6 Other Taxes

Introduction

This chapter provides an overview of taxes reported on Schedule 2. Some common other taxes that a tax preparer will see are:

- Alternative Minimum Tax (AMT)
- Additional taxes on IRAs
- Additional Medicare Tax
- Additional tax on IRAs
- Excess Social Security tax
- Household employment taxes
- Net investment income tax (NIIT)
- Self-employment tax (will be covered in a later chapter)
- Unreported tip income

Objectives

At the end of this lesson the student will:

- Complete Form 1040, Schedule 2.
- Explain when a taxpayer must repay the Premium Tax Credit.
- Understand the taxability of excess Social Security.
- Identify when a taxpayer must pay an additional tax on IRAs.
- Clarify when to use Schedule H.

Resources

Form 1040	Publication 17	Instructions Form 1040
Form 4137	Publication 334	Instructions Form 4137
Form 5329	Publication 560	Instructions Form 5329
Form 5405	Publication 575	Instructions Form 5405
Form 6251	Publication 590-B	Instructions Form 6251
Form 8919	Publication 594	Instructions Form 8919
Form 8959	Publication 721	Instructions Form 8959
Form 8962	Publication 939	Instructions Form 8962
Form 8965	Publication 974	Instructions Form 8965
Schedule 2	Tax Topic 410, 554, 556,	Instructions for Schedule H
Schedule H	557, 558, 560, 561, 611,	Instructions for Schedule SE
Schedule SE	612, 653	Instructions for Schedule SE-EZ
Schedule SE-EZ		

Table of Contents

Introduction	237
Part 1 Additional Taxes from Schedule 2	239
Line 1 Alternative Minimum Tax (Form 6251)	239
Line 2 Excess Advanced Premium Tax Credit (Form 8962)	240
Terms to know for PTC purposes:	240
Minimum Essential Coverage (MEC)	241
Marketplace Plan Levels	243
Employer-sponsored Coverage	243
Advance Payments of the Premium Tax Credit	244
Excess Advanced Premium Tax Credit Repayment	246
Shared Policy Allocation	246
Part 1 Review Questions	246
Part 1 Review Questions Answers	248
Part 2 Taxes for Self-Employment	249
Line 4 Self-Employment tax. Attach Schedule SE	249
Line 5 Social Security and Medicare Tax on Unreported Tip Income (Form 4137)	249
Line 6 Uncollected Social Security and Medicare Tax (Form 8919)	249
Line 8 Additional Tax on IRAs and Other Similar Plans and Accounts	250
Line 9 Household Employment Taxes	252
Line 10 First-Time Homebuyer Credit Repayment (Form 5405)	253
Line 11 Additional Medicare Tax (Form 8959)	253
Line 12 Net Investment Income Tax (NIIT)	255
Additional Taxes	256
Line 18 Total Additional Taxes	256
Line 20 Net Tax Liability Installment	256
Kiddie Tax (Form 8615)	256
Part 2 Review Questions	257
Part 2 Review Question Answers	258
Takeaways	260

Part 1 Additional Taxes from Schedule 2

Line 1 Alternative Minimum Tax (Form 6251)

SCHEDULE 2 (Form 1040) Department of the Treasury Internal Revenue Service	Additional Taxes ▶ Attach to Form 1040, 1040-SR, or 1040-NR. ▶ Go to www.irs.gov/Form1040 for instructions and the latest information.	OMB No. 1545-0074 2021 Attachment Sequence No. 02
Name(s) shown on Form 1040, 1040-SR, or 1040-NR		Your social security number

Part I Tax

1	Alternative minimum tax. Attach Form 6251	1	
2	Excess advance premium tax credit repayment. Attach Form 8962	2	
3	Add lines 1 and 2. Enter here and on Form 1040, 1040-SR, or 1040-NR, line 17 . .	3	

The alternative minimum tax (AMT) applies to taxpayers who qualify for certain deductions under tax law. It is calculated using Form 6251 and reported on Schedule 2, line 1. The additional tax is on preference items, which is normally tax-free income or a high amount of itemized deductions. If the taxpayer has deducted preference items and their income exceeds a certain amount, AMT recalculates income tax after adding tax preference items back into the adjusted gross income. As the name suggests, the AMT is the minimum tax possible so that taxpayers cannot go without paying taxes, despite whatever exclusions, credits, or deductions may have been taken. If an adequate amount of a taxpayer's income is from the preference items, and that income exceeds the preset amounts discussed below, they will have to pay AMT even if they had otherwise lowered their tax liability below zero.

Whether or not a taxpayer is subject to AMT is determined based on income. If a taxpayer with an excess amount of deductions received an amount of income that exceeds $73,600 (2021) (for Single and Head of Household), and $114,600 (2021) (for Qualifying Widow(er) or Married Filing Jointly), and $57,300 (for taxpayers filing separately), then the AMT tax will be triggered and applied. The 2021 AMT tax rate was 26% on the first $199,900 worth of income. If the taxpayer's income exceeds $199,900, the tax rate is 28%. Married Filing Separate taxpayers' AMT threshold is $99,950.

AMT is calculated using Alternative Minimum Tax Income (AMTI) instead of their adjusted gross income (AGI). If the AMTI amount is zero, then the taxpayer would use his or her AGI to calculate the AMT after reducing the AGI amount by his or her itemized or standard deduction and qualified business income deduction. AMTI cannot be reduced by the standard deduction or the net qualified disaster loss that increased the standard deduction. This amount will be added back into the AMT calculation later.

The following are taxpayers who must file Form 6251:

1. If line 7 on Form 6251 is greater than line 10.
2. Taxpayer claimed a general business credit, and either line 6 or 25 in Part I of Form 3800 is more than zero.
3. Taxpayer claimed the qualified electric vehicle credit on Form 8834, using the personal part of the alternative fuel vehicle refueling property credit on Form 8911 or the prior year minimum tax on Form 8801.
4. The total of lines 2c through 3 on Form 6251 is negative and line 7 is greater than line 10, if lines 2c through 3 were not taken into account.

Other Taxes

The exemption begins to phase out when an individual income reaches $523,600 and $1,047,200 for married filing joint taxpayers. See Instructions Form 6251 and Publication 17.

Line 2 Excess Advanced Premium Tax Credit (Form 8962)

Although there is no penalty for not having health insurance, if the taxpayer purchased health care through the Marketplace, the individual must complete Form 8962 to calculate if they need to repay the premium tax credit repayment.

Using Form 8962, the Premium Tax Credit (PTC) is a credit that can help individuals and their families pay for their health insurance if they have enrolled in a qualified health plan through the Marketplace. The Marketplace is an exchange for those who need qualified health care to purchase qualifying plans, and a taxpayer may be able to claim the Premium Tax Credit if an individual and his or her tax family (as defined below) enrolled through the Marketplace for a qualified health plan. For more information, see Publication 974 and Instructions Form 8962. The Premium Tax Credit is reported on both Form 1040 and Form 1040NR.

Terms to know for PTC purposes:

- **Tax Family:** Consists of individuals whom the taxpayer (and spouse if Married Filing Jointly) claims as a dependent on his or her tax return. A family's size is the number of qualifying individuals on his or her tax family.
- **Household Income:** Household income is the modified gross income of the taxpayer (and spouse if filing a joint return) plus the modified AGI of each individual claimed as a dependent who is required to file a tax return because his or her income meets the threshold to file. Household income does not include the modified AGI of dependents who are only filing a current year tax return to claim a refund of their federal withholding.
- **Modified AGI:** Modified AGI is the AGI on the tax return plus certain income that is not subject to tax, such as foreign earned income, tax-exempt interest, and the portion of Social Security benefits that is not taxable.
- **Coverage Family:** The coverage family includes all individuals in the tax family who are enrolled in a qualified health plan and are not eligible for minimum essential coverage (MEC) beyond the coverage in the individual market. Individuals included in the coverage family may change from month to month. If an individual in the tax family is not enrolled in a qualified health plan or is enrolled in a qualified health plan but is eligible for minimum essential coverage, he or she is not part of the coverage family. The Premium Tax Credit is available to pay the coverage of those included in the coverage family.

- **Monthly Credit Amount**: The amount of tax credit for a month. The PTC for the year is the sum of all monthly credit amounts. The monthly credit amount is the least of the following:
    - The enrollment premiums for the month for one or more qualified health plans in which any individual in the tax family was enrolled.
    - The applicable, monthly amount of the Second Lowest Cost Silver Plan (SLCSP) premium after the monthly contribution amount has been subtracted.
    - To qualify for the monthly credit amount, at least one tax family member must be enrolled in a qualified health plan on the first day of the month. The monthly credit will not apply if the tax family was not enrolled in a qualified health plan on the 1st of the month. For more instructions see Instructions Form 8962.
- **Enrollment Premiums**: Total monthly premiums for one or more qualified health plans that any tax family member enrolled in. Form 1095-A reports the enrollment premiums. The tax professional should ask to see all forms related to health coverage.
- **Applicable Second Lowest Cost Silver Plan (SLCSP)**: The Second Lowest Cost Silver Plan is, as the name suggests, the plan in the silver category (discussed further in the "Marketplace Plan Levels" Section) that costs the second least. It is not the cheapest but the second-cheapest plan. It is important to know the premium of the SLCSP offered in your area, because that premium is one of the things used to calculate the PTC. The SLCSP premium is a different premium than the enrollment premium described above.
- **Monthly Contribution Amount**: The monthly contribution is also one of the things used to calculate the Premium Tax Credit amount. The monthly contribution is the amount of income that taxpayers are responsible to pay as their monthly premiums.
- **Qualified Health Plan**: A qualified health insurance plan (also referred to as a policy) purchased through the Marketplace at the bronze, silver, gold, or platinum level. Catastrophic health plans and stand-alone dental plans purchased through the Marketplace, as well as all plans purchased through SHOP (Small Business Health Options Programs), are not qualified health plans for the purposes of the PTC.

Minimum Essential Coverage (MEC)

Minimum essential coverage includes government-sponsored programs, eligible employer-sponsored plans, individual market plans, and any other coverage that the Department of Health and Human Services designates as minimum essential coverage:

- Health plans offered in the individual market.
- Grandfathered health plans.
- Government-sponsored programs.
- Employer-sponsored plans.
- Other health coverage plans designated as minimum essential coverage by the Department of Health and Human Services.

Señor 1040 Says: Minimum essential coverage does not include coverage consisting solely of excepted benefits. Excepted benefits include stand-alone vision and dental plans (except pediatric dental coverage), workers' compensation coverage, and coverage limited to a specified disease or illness. A taxpayer may have any of these types of coverage and still qualify for the PTC on their qualified health plan.

The following "essential health benefits" must be provided to be a qualified health plan:

- Ambulatory patient services.
- Emergency services.
- Hospitalization.
- Maternity and newborn care.
- Mental health and substance abuse.
- Prescription drugs.
- Rehabilitative services and devices.
- Laboratory services.
- Preventive and wellness services and chronic disease management.
- Pediatric services, including oral and vision care.

The Individual Shared Responsibility Provision requires the taxpayer and each member of his or her family to do one of the following:

- Have qualifying health coverage.
- Qualify for a health coverage exemption.
- Make a shared responsibility payment when filing their federal income tax return.

Many people already have minimum essential coverage and do not have to do anything more than maintain the coverage and report their coverage when they file their tax return. If the taxpayer is covered by any of the following types of plans, they are considered covered under the health care law and do not have to pay a penalty or get a health coverage exemption:

- Any Marketplace plan or any individual insurance plan they already have.
- Any job-based plan, including retiree plans and COBRA coverage.
- Medicare Part A or Part C.
- Most Medicaid coverage.
- The Children's Health Insurance Program (CHIP).
- Most individual health plans bought outside the Marketplace, including "grandfathered" plans (not all plans sold outside the Marketplace qualify as minimum essential coverage).
- Dependents under the age of 24 who are covered under a parent's plan.
- Self-funded health coverage offered to students by universities for plan or policy years that started on or before Dec. 31, 2014 (check with your university to see if the plan counts as minimum essential coverage).
- Health coverage for Peace Corps volunteers.
- Certain types of veteran's health coverage through the Department of Veterans Affairs.
- Department of Defense Nonappropriated Fund Health Benefits Program.
- Refugee Medical Assistance.
- State high-risk pools for plan or policy years that started on or before December 31, 2014 (check with your high-risk pool plan to see if it qualifies as minimum essential coverage).

For a more detailed list of types of plans that do and do not count as minimum essential coverage, see Instructions Form 8965, *Health Coverage Exemptions*, from the IRS.

Marketplace Plan Levels

The ACA requires that all new policies, including those plans that are sold on the exchange (except stand-alone dental, vision, and long-term care plans), comply with one of the four benefit categories set up by the Patient Protection and Affordable Care Act (PPACA). PPACA established four levels of coverage based on the concept of "actuarial value," which is the share of health care expenses the plan covers for a typical group of enrollees. As plans increase in actuarial value, they would cover a greater share of enrollee's medical expenses overall, though the details could vary across different plans. The levels of coverage provided for in the PPACA are central to the coverage that individuals will get and how each will ultimately perceive the effects of the health reform law.

The four Marketplace levels are:

Bronze	60%
Silver	70%
Gold	80%
Platinum	90%

For people with low and modest incomes, the ACA provides reduced cost sharing if enrollees select a plan from the silver tier in the federal or state marketplace. The cost-sharing reductions are accomplished by requiring insurers to create variants of each standard silver plan, with each variant meeting a successively higher actuarial value. The federal government reimburses insurance companies for the loss of profit resulting from reducing costs for their customers. This act of reimbursement is also referred to as a "subsidy".

As the percentage of expenses paid by the health plan increases, the percentage of expenses paid by the individual decreases. The health plans that cover more medical expenses usually have a higher monthly payment, but individuals will pay less whenever they receive medical care. Individuals can choose to pay a higher monthly premium so that when they need medical care, they pay less. The taxpayer could choose to pay a lower monthly premium, but the taxpayer would pay more when he or she needs medical care.

Employer-sponsored Coverage

If the taxpayer and other members of the tax family had the opportunity to enroll in a plan that is MEC offered by their employer for 2022, the taxpayer is considered eligible for MEC under the plan for a month only if the offer of coverage met a minimum standard of affordability and provided a minimum level of benefits, referred to as "minimum value." The coverage offered by an employer is generally considered affordable for the taxpayer and qualifying family members allowed to enroll in the coverage. Share of the annual cost for self-only coverage, which is sometimes referred to as the employee required contribution, is not more than 9.78% of household income.

Other Taxes

Example: Don was eligible to enroll in his employer's coverage for 2021 but instead applied for coverage in a qualified health plan through the Marketplace. Don provided accurate information about his employer's coverage to the Marketplace, and the Marketplace determined that the offer of coverage was not affordable, and that Don was eligible for APTC. Don enrolled in the qualified health plan for 2021. Don got a new job with employer coverage that he could have enrolled in as of September 1, 2021, but chose not to. Don did not return to the Marketplace to determine if he was eligible for APTC for the months September through December 2021, and remained enrolled in the qualified health plan. Don is not considered eligible for employer-sponsored coverage for the months January through August of 2021 because he gave accurate information to the Marketplace about the availability of employer coverage, and the Marketplace determined that he was eligible for APTC for coverage in a qualified health plan. The Marketplace determination does not apply, however, for the months September through December of 2021. This is because Don did not provide information to the Marketplace about his new employer's offer of coverage. Whether Don is considered eligible for employer-sponsored coverage and ineligible for the PTC for the months September through December of 2021 is determined under the eligibility rules described under Employer-Sponsored Plans in Pub. 974 *Premium Tax Credit (PTC)*. If taxpayer cannot get benefits under an employer-sponsored plan until after a waiting period has expired, taxpayer is not treated as being eligible for that coverage during the waiting period. See Pub. 974 *Waiting periods and other periods without access to benefits section*.

Advance Payments of the Premium Tax Credit

If the taxpayer purchased insurance through the Health Insurance Marketplace, they may be eligible for an Advanced Premium Tax Credit (APTC) to help pay for the insurance coverage. Receiving too little or too much in advance will affect the taxpayer's refund or balance due. To avoid owing a balance, the taxpayer should contact the insurance provider to report changes in income or family size to the Marketplace as soon as possible.
If the taxpayer and members of their family enrolled in Marketplace coverage, Form 1095-A should be received from the Marketplace with the months of coverage and the amounts of APTC paid. If the taxpayer received a Form 1095-A showing APTC, Form 8962 must be filed, even if the taxpayer is not otherwise required to file. The taxpayer's Premium Tax Credit is determined by reference to the premium amount for the second lowest cost silver plan offered by an exchange in the rating area where the taxpayer resides.

The Premium Tax Credit is limited to the amount of premium paid for the chosen plan. The credit may be payable in advance, with the payments going directly to the insurance company. A taxpayer who is eligible for an advanced assistance payment may decline it and receive the full amount of the credit on the tax return. Eligibility and the amount of the credit itself are affected by the family size and household income. A married couple must file a joint return to claim the credit. If a married couple files Married Filing Separately, they are not eligible for the credit. If taxpayers file separately because they are victims of domestic abuse, then see Notice 2014-23 for the criteria.

A taxpayer is allowed an advanceable and refundable credit to help subsidize the purchase of health insurance. The taxpayer must have household income of at least 100% but not more than 400% of the federal poverty line for a family of the size involved. The taxpayer must not receive health insurance under an employer-sponsored plan (including COBRA) or certain government plans such as Medicare.

Individuals purchasing health insurance through the Marketplace may choose to receive the credit in advance. With this choice, the government would make payments to the health insurance provider for the taxpayer. The difference between the advanced credit and the allowable credit may be claimed or paid when the taxpayer files their current tax return.

Household income means an amount equal to the sum of the following items:

- The taxpayer's Modified Adjusted Gross Income (MAGI).
- The MAGI of all other individuals who are both of the following:
  - Counted in family size.
  - Required to file an income tax return for the year under IRC §1 without regard to the exception for a child whose parents elect to use IRC §1(g)(7).

Remember, Modified Adjusted Gross Income (MAGI) is adjusted gross income, plus all the following:

- The amount excluded under IRC §911, *Foreign-Earned Income Exclusion*.
- Tax-exempt interest income.
- The excluded portion of Social Security benefits.

Individuals not legally present in the U.S. or incarcerated are excluded as applicable taxpayers. An applicable taxpayer will be eligible for the credit only for months at least one member of the taxpayer's family is any of the following:

- Is enrolled in a qualified health plan through an exchange.
- Is not eligible for coverage through a government program such as Medicaid, Medicare, Children's Health Insurance Program (CHIP), certain benefits for veterans and their families, and health coverage for Peace Corps volunteers (TRICARE).
- Is not able to get affordable coverage through an employer plan that provides minimum value.

For taxpayers who receive advance credits, the actual credit may not equal the amounts of credits paid in advance. The difference may occur when:

- The taxpayer does not apply for the advanced credit or does not apply until after beginning to pay the premium.
- The taxpayer's income is different from the income that was used to compute the advanced credit.
- The number of dependents changed during the year.
- The marital status changed during the year.

Even if one is not otherwise required, a taxpayer must file a tax return if the individual received an advanced credit during the tax year, or if the taxpayer declined the advanced credit to try to receive the refundable credit instead.

Other Taxes

Excess Advanced Premium Tax Credit Repayment

The Premium Tax Credit helps pay health insurance premiums that were purchased through the Health Insurance Marketplace. If the advanced payments of this credit were made for coverage for the taxpayer, spouse, or dependents, Form 8962 would be used. If the advanced payments were more than the Premium Tax Credit, the taxpayer has an excess to be repaid, which is reported on Schedule 2, line 46, and added to their tax liability, meaning that paying their taxes will also repay that excess. An additional tax liability could be caused by the taxpayer or spouse having an increase in income and not reporting the change to the Marketplace. If the advanced payments exceed the credit allowed, the income tax liability imposed for the tax year is increased by the difference.

Shared Policy Allocation

For any month during the year that the taxpayer, spouse, or dependents do not have minimum essential coverage and do not qualify for a coverage exemption, the taxpayer will have to make an individual shared responsibility payment with his tax return. The annual payment amount is either a percentage of taxpayer's household income or a flat dollar amount, whichever is greater, but it is capped at the national average premium for a bronze level health plan available through the Marketplace. Taxpayer will owe 1/12th of the annual payment for each month the taxpayer, spouse, or dependents don't have either coverage or an exemption.

If a taxpayer, spouse, or dependent did not have coverage, and the taxpayer's income was below the tax filing threshold for their filing status (Single, Married Filing Jointly, etc.), the taxpayer could qualify for a coverage exemption and would not be required to make a payment. Taxpayers do not have to file a return solely to claim this exemption. If taxpayers choose to file a tax return, they should not make a payment with their return; instead, they should complete Part II of Form 8965, *Coverage Exemptions for Your Household Claimed on Your Return*, to claim the coverage exemption.

Part 1 Review Questions

To obtain the maximum benefit from this chapter, LTP recommends that you complete each of the following questions, and then compare them to the answers with feedback that immediately follow. Under governing self-study standards, vendors are required to present review questions intermittently throughout each self-study course.

These questions and explanations are not part of the final examination and will not be graded by LTP.

OT1.1
Betty is subject to alternative minimum tax (AMT). Which form is used to calculate her AMT?

   a. Form 6251
   b. Form 4868
   c. Form 8863
   d. Form 8801

OT1.2
A taxpayer may qualify for an exemption to claim the exclusion from the "shared responsibility". Which form would the taxpayer use to report the exclusion?

a. Form 8611
b. Form 8965
c. Form 8828
d. Form 8834

OT1.3
Which of the following is not true about Form 8962, *Premium Tax Credit*?

a. It's a credit that can help individuals and their families pay for their health insurance.
b. Reported on Schedule 2, line 2, and calculated using Form 8962.
c. It's a credit that provides health insurance for the taxpayer and his/her family.
d. Taxpayer may be able to claim the premium tax credit if an individual and his or her tax family enrolled through the Marketplace for a qualified health plan.

OT1.4
Which of the following is not true about the Advance Premium Tax Credit (APTC)?

a. Helps pay for the insurance coverage.
b. Receiving too little or too much in advance will affect the taxpayer's refund or balance due.
c. To avoid a balance due, report changes in income or family size to the Marketplace as soon as possible.
d. The Advance Premium Tax Credit is considered a refundable credit.

OT1.5
What is the alternative minimum tax (AMT) exemption amount for married filing jointly?

a. $73,600
b. $114,600
c. $99,950
d. $518,400

OT1.6
What is the alternative minimum tax (AMT) exemption amount for married filing separately?

a. $57,300
b. $99,950
c. $73,600
d. $518,400

Other Taxes

Part 1 Review Questions Answers

OT1.1
Betty is subject to alternative minimum tax (AMT). Which form is used to calculate her AMT?

   a. Form 6251
   b. Form 4868
   c. Form 8863
   d. Form 8801

Feedback: Review section *Line 1 Alternative Minimum Tax.*

OT1.2
A taxpayer may qualify for an exemption to claim the exclusion from the "shared responsibility". Which form would the taxpayer use to report the exclusion?

   a. Form 8611
   b. Form 8965
   c. Form 8828
   d. Form 8834

Feedback: Review section *Shared Policy Allocation.*

OT1.3
Which of the following is not true about Form 8962, *Premium Tax Credit*?

   a. It's a credit that can help individuals and their families pay for their health insurance.
   b. Reported on Schedule 2, line 2, and calculated using Form 8962.
   c. It's a credit that provides health insurance for the taxpayer and his/her family.
   d. Taxpayer may be able to claim the premium tax credit if an individual and his or her tax family enrolled through the Marketplace for a qualified health plan.

Feedback: Review section *Line 2, Form 8962: Premium Tax Credit.*

OT1.4
Which of the following is not true about the Advance Premium Tax Credit (APTC)?

   a. Helps pay for the insurance coverage.
   b. Receiving too little or too much in advance will affect the taxpayer's refund or balance due.
   c. To avoid a balance due, report changes in income or family size to the Marketplace as soon as possible.
   d. The Advance Premium Tax Credit is considered a refundable credit.

Feedback: Review section *Advance Payments of the Premium Tax Credit.*

OT1.5

What is the alternative minimum tax (AMT) exemption amount for married filing jointly?

a. $73,600
b. $114,600
c. $99,950
d. $518,400

Feedback: Review section *Line 1 Alternative Minimum Tax.*

OT1.6

What is the alternative minimum tax (AMT) exemption amount for married filing separately?

a. $57,300
b. $99,950
c. $72,900
d. $518,400

Feedback: Review section *Line 1 Alternative Minimum Tax.*

Part 2 Taxes for Self-Employment

The self-employed individual pays both the employer and the employee tax. Most taxpayers who receive a W-2 don't pay much attention to their paycheck. This part will discuss what taxes the self-employed individual must pay, as well as how they must pay their Social Security and Medicare tax and the amount that needs to be paid.

Line 4 Self-Employment tax. Attach Schedule SE

This will be covered in "*Federal Business Income*" chapter.

Line 5 Social Security and Medicare Tax on Unreported Tip Income (Form 4137)

Form 4137 is used to calculate the Social Security and Medicare tax on tips not reported to the taxpayer's employer. This concept was covered previously in Chapter 5, "Federal Income". Please refer to that section to review the information. If this form is used and needed, mark box A on this line, attach the form to the return, and report the amount on line 58 in the space provided.

Line 6 Uncollected Social Security and Medicare Tax (Form 8919)

If the taxpayer was an employee but was treated as an independent contractor by the employer, Form 8919, *Uncollected Social Security and Medicare Tax on Wages*, is used to figure and report the taxpayer's share of uncollected Social Security and Medicare taxes due on compensation. Filing this form ensures that the Social Security and Medicare taxes will be credited to the correct Social Security record.

Form 8919 must be filed if all the following apply:

➢ The taxpayer performed services for a firm.

- ➤ The firm did not withhold the taxpayer's share of Social Security and Medicare taxes from the employee's pay.
- ➤ The pay from the firm was not for services as an independent contractor.
- ➤ One of the reasons listed below and taken from the Form 8919 under "Reason Codes" applies to the taxpayer.

> **A**—The taxpayer filed Form SS-8, *Determination of Worker Status for Purposes of Federal Employment Taxes and Income Tax Withholding* and received a determination letter stating that the taxpayer was an employee of the firm. A taxpayer would file Form SS-8 if their income was reported to them on the 1099-MISC or Form 1099-NEC, but the IRS determined that the income should have been reported to the taxpayer on a W-2.
>
> **C**—The taxpayer received other correspondence from the IRS that states, "I am an employee."
>
> **G**—The taxpayer filed Form SS-8 with the IRS and has not received a reply.
>
> **H**—The taxpayer received Form W-2 and Form 1099-NEC from his or her employer for the tax year 2021, but the amount on Form 1099-NEC should have been included as wages on Form W-2. Do not file Form SS-8 if code *H* was selected on Form 8919.

Line 8 Additional Tax on IRAs and Other Similar Plans and Accounts

The calculated amount from Form 5329 is reported on Line 8 of the Schedule 2. Form 5329 is used to report additional taxes on the following items:

- ➤ IRAs
- ➤ Other qualified retirement plans
- ➤ Modified endowment contracts
- ➤ Coverdell ESAs
- ➤ QTPs
- ➤ Archer MSAs
- ➤ HSAs
- ➤ ABLE accounts

Form 5329 should be filed if any of the following apply:

- ➤ The taxpayer received a distribution from a Roth IRA and either the amount on line 25c, Form 8606, *Nondeductible IRAs*, is more than zero, or the distribution includes a recapture amount that is subject to the 10% additional tax, or the qualified first-time home buyer receives the distribution for the purchase.
- ➤ The taxpayer received a distribution subject to tax on early distributions from a qualified retirement plan other than a Roth IRA.
- ➤ The taxpayer received a distribution subject to the tax on early distributions from a qualified retirement plan other than a Roth IRA, and the taxpayer meets an exception to the tax, and code 1 (which shows that an early distribution penalty must be assessed) is in box 7 of the 1099-R.

- The taxpayer received a distribution subject to the tax on early distributions from a qualified retirement plan other than a Roth IRA and meets the exception, and code 7 (which shows that the distribution was normal and deserves no penalty) is in box 7 of the 1099-R.
- The taxpayer received taxable distributions from Coverdell ESAs or QTPs.
- The contributions for 2021 to traditional IRAs, Roth IRAs, Coverdell ESAs, Archer MSAs, or HSAs exceed the maximum contribution limit, or the taxpayer had a tax due from an excess on line 15 of 2021 Form 5329.
- The taxpayer did not receive the required minimum distribution (RMD) from his or her qualified retirement plan.

The additional tax on an early distribution is included in the taxpayer's gross income and is an additional 10%, although there are some exceptions to the rule. The additional 10% tax on an early withdrawal does not apply to any of the following:

- A qualified disaster distribution.
- A qualified HSA funding distribution from an IRA.
- A distribution from a traditional or SIMPLE IRA that was converted to a Roth IRA.
- An in-plan Roth rollover.
- A distribution of certain excess IRA contributions.

The following qualified retirement plan rollover guidelines are in effect as of January 1, 2021:

- If the qualified retirement plan loan is offset due to termination or severance from employment, the taxpayer has until the due date, including extensions, to both file his or her tax return and to roll over the plan's offset amount.
- If the qualified retirement plan has been wrongfully levied by the IRS, the amount returned plus interest may be contributed to the account or to an IRA as long as the plan allows rollovers, but it may not be contributed to an endowment contract, which is beyond the scope of this course. The taxpayer has until the due date to make the contribution; no extensions can be filed.

In many instances, individuals who fail to take a required minimum distribution (RMD) on time do so inadvertently. IRA custodians and trustees are required to provide IRA owners with an RMD statement indicating their need to take an RMD, but circumstances may prevent an IRA owner from doing so in a timely manner. Individuals need to withdraw the proper amount by April 1st of the year after they turn 72, or by December 31st of any subsequent year. Anyone who does not will be subject to a 50% excess accumulation penalty tax on the amount not withdrawn. IRA beneficiaries who fail to take a required death distribution timely are subject to the same penalty amount.

Although IRA owners must be notified, the rules do not, however, require an RMD statement to be provided to beneficiaries; in some cases, a beneficiary may not know that he or she must take an RMD. A beneficiary that fails to timely take an RMD should discuss the completion of IRS Form 5329, *Additional Tax on Qualified Plans (Including IRAs) and Other Tax-Favored Accounts* with his or her tax professional to either pay or ask for a waiver of the 50% excess accumulation penalty tax.

An excess accumulation as it relates to traditional IRA, Simplified Employee Pensions (SEP), Savings Incentive Match Plans for Employees of Small Employers (SIMPLE), and beneficiary Individual Retirement Accounts (IRAs) is defined as an amount remaining in an IRA as a result of an account owner or beneficiary failing to timely satisfy a required minimum distribution (RMD).

Failing to withdraw the RMD by the applicable deadline may result in owing the IRS an additional tax of 50% on the RMD. The taxpayer can request a waiver of the fee from the IRS with reasonable cause by including a letter of explanation with Form 5329 on his or her tax return. The taxpayer should complete lines 52 and 53 of Form 5329 using the form's instructions. Enter "RC" and the requested waiver amount in parentheses on the dotted line next to line 54. Subtract the requested amount from the "shortfall" (the amount of taxes owed before figuring in the waiver's amount) and enter the result on line 54 (the amount will flow to line 55) and pay the tax due on line 55. See Instructions Form 5329.

Line 9 Household Employment Taxes

Taxpayers who employ household workers may be required to pay and withhold employment taxes from their employees. Employment taxes include Social Security tax, Medicare tax, federal unemployment tax, federal income tax withholding, and state employment taxes. To determine if the worker is self-employed, the worker must provide his or her own tools and offer services to the general public in an independent business.

Some examples of household workers include: babysitters, caretakers, cleaning people, domestic workers, drivers, health aides, housekeepers, maids, nannies, private nurses, private chefs, and yard workers. A worker who performs childcare services in their home is generally not the taxpayer's employee. Household workers are not considered to be the taxpayer's employees but are instead considered self-employed if their services are offered to the general public in an independent business.

Example: Melchior has made an agreement with Ezra to care for his lawn. Melchior runs a lawn care business and offers his services to the general public. Melchior provides his own tools and supplies, and he hires and pays his employees. Neither Melchior nor his employees are Ezra's household employees.

Form 1040, Schedule H, *Household Employment Taxes*, must be used to report household employment taxes if the taxpayer pays any of the following wages to the employee:

> - Social Security and Medicare wages of $2,100 or more.
> - Federal Unemployment Tax Act (FUTA) wages.
> - Wages from which federal income taxes were withheld.

If the taxpayer pays more than $2,100 in a calendar year to a household employee, the taxpayer must pay Social Security and Medicare taxes for that employee and withhold (or pay) the employee's portion of those taxes.

The taxpayer, who is the employer, is not required to withhold federal income taxes for household employees unless the employee asks to have withholdings taken out and the employer agrees to withhold. If such an agreement is reached, the employer must have the employee(s) complete Form W-4, *Employee's Withholding Allowance Certificate*. As with the other employment taxes, withheld federal income taxes may be reported on Schedule H. An extension for the personal return does not extend the due date for the payment of these taxes. Schedule H is reported on Form 1040, Schedule 2, line 9. Schedule H can be a standalone form if the taxpayer is not filing a yearly tax return. If a paid tax preparer completed the form for the taxpayer, then he or she would complete the Paid Preparer Use Only section on Schedule H.

Line 10 First-Time Homebuyer Credit Repayment (Form 5405)

If the taxpayer purchased his or her residence in 2008 and qualified for the first-time homebuyer credit, the taxpayer may have to repay the credit that was received on the 2008 tax return. The credit that was received in 2008 was an interest-free loan to the taxpayer and is to be repaid over a 15-year period. If the taxpayer purchased his or her home prior to April 8, 2008, and did not own another main home for 36 months prior to the date of purchase and received the credit, he or she will have to repay the loan.

If the taxpayer sold or converted the main home prior to repayment of the first-time homebuyer credit, the remaining portion of the loan must be repaid in the year the taxpayer sells or converts the property. This repayment is reported using Form 5405 on Form 1040, Schedule 2, line 10.

Example: In June 2017, Watson claimed the credit for the home he purchased in August 2011. Watson moved out and converted his home to a rental in 2021; Watson will have to repay the remaining portion of the first-time homebuyer credit on his 2021 tax return because he sold it before the end of the 15-year repayment period.

Line 11 Additional Medicare Tax (Form 8959)

The taxpayer may be subject to a 0.9% additional Medicare tax that applies to Medicare wages, railroad retirement act compensation, and self-employment income over the filing status threshold. This tax is an employee tax, not an employer tax. The employer is responsible for withholding the additional tax once the taxpayer's compensation exceeds $200,000 (regardless of filing status) in a calendar year. The taxpayer cannot request their employer to stop the withholding of the additional tax. If the taxpayer has wages as well as self-employment income, the threshold is reduced on the self-employment income, but not below zero.

Filing Status	Threshold Amount
Married Filing Jointly	$250,000
Married Filing Separately	$125,000
Single	$200,000
Head of Household	$200,000
Qualifying Widow(er) with Dependent Child	$200,000

The above threshold amounts are not indexed for inflation.

Example: Kathy, a single filer, has $130,000 in self-employment income and $0 in wages. Kathy is not liable for the Additional Medicare Tax and does not have to file Form 8959.

Other Taxes

Example: George and Jean are married and filing a joint return. George has $190,000 in wages and Jean has $150,000 in compensation subject to railroad retirement taxes. Neither George nor Jean has wages or compensation that exceed $200,000 because their employers do not combine the wages and railroad retirement compensation to determine whether they are in excess of the $250,000 threshold for a joint return. George and Jean are not liable for the additional tax.

Example: Carl, a single filer, has $220,000 in self-employment income and $0 in wages. Carl must file Form 8959 as he is liable to pay the additional Medicare Tax on $20,000 of his $220,000 income ($220,000 minus the threshold of $200,000).

Taxes that might be reported on line 11 include the following:

- Additional Medicare tax.
- Net Investment Income tax.
- Additional tax on health savings accounts (HSA) distribution.
- Additional tax on Archer MSA distributions.
- Additional tax on Medicare Advantage MSA distributions.
- Additional tax on an HSA because the taxpayer did not remain eligible for the testing period.
- Recapture of the following credits:
    o Investment Credit.
    o Low Income Housing Credit.
    o Indian Employment Credit.
    o New Markets Credit.
    o Credit for Employer-Provided Childcare Facilities.
    o Alternative Motor Vehicle Credit.
    o Alternative Fuel Vehicle Refueling Property Credit.
    o Qualified Plug-In Electric Drive Motor Vehicle Credit.
- Recapture of a federal mortgage subsidy.
- Section 72(m)(5) excess benefits tax.
- Uncollected Social Security and Medicare or RRTA tax on tips or group-term life insurance.
- Golden parachute payments.
- Tax on the accumulated distribution of trusts.
- Excise tax on insider stock compensation from an expatriated corporation.
- Interest on the tax due on installment income from the sale of certain residential lots and timeshares.
- Interest on the deferred tax on gain from certain installment sales with a sales price over $150,000.
- Additional tax on recapture of a charitable contribution deduction relating to a fractional interest in tangible personal property.
- Look-back interest under section 167(g) or 460(b).
- Additional tax on income received from a nonqualified deferred compensation plan that fails to meet the requirements of IRC §409A.
- Additional tax on compensation received from a nonqualified deferred compensation plan described in IRC §457A, but only if the compensation would have been includable as income in an earlier year if the amount had been determinable before 2014.
- Tax on non-effectively connected income for any part of the year that the taxpayer was a nonresident alien.

> Any interest amount from Form 8261, line 16f, relating to distributions from, and dispositions of, stock of an IRC §1291 fund.
> Any interest amount from Form 8261, line 24, identified as "1294INT".

Line 12 Net Investment Income Tax (NIIT)

Reported using Form 8960, NIIT is a 3.8% tax on the lesser of net investment income or the excess of the taxpayer's modified adjusted gross income amount that is over the filing status threshold. NIIT generally includes income and gain from passive activities. For the purposes of the NIIT, a passive activity, as defined by §469 of the Internal Revenue Code, includes rental activity whether the taxpayer materially participated or not. The activity must also be a trade or business as defined under §162 of the Internal Revenue Code and be non-passive before the income can be excluded from NIIT. Individuals who have NIIT and modified adjusted gross income (MAGI) over the following thresholds will owe 3.8%:

Filing Status	Threshold Amount
Married filing jointly	$250,000
Married filing separately	$125,000
Single	$200,000
Head of Household (with qualifying person)	$200,000
Qualifying widow(er) with dependent child	$250,000

Taxpayers should be aware that these threshold amounts are not indexed for inflation. If an individual is exempt from Medicare taxes, he or she may still be subject to NIIT if the taxpayer has NIIT and the modified adjusted gross income is over the applicable thresholds.

Unless these items result from the ordinary course of a trade or business that is neither a passive activity nor a trade or business of trading in financial instruments or commodities, investment income includes: gross income from interest, dividends, capital gains, rental and royalty income, nonqualified annuities, income from businesses involved in the trading of financial instruments or commodities, and income from businesses that are passive activities to the taxpayer. Net investment income tax does not include distributions from a qualified retirement plan, wages, unemployment compensation, operating income from a non-passive business, Social Security, alimony, tax-exempt interest, self-employment income, or Alaska Permanent Fund distributions.

The Alaska Permanent Fund is a dividend that is paid to all qualifying residents of Alaska. The dividend is based upon a five-year average of the Permanent Fund's performance, which is based on the stock market and other factors. The dividend is taxable on the recipients' federal tax returns.

The net investment income tax will not apply to any amount of gain that is excluded from gross income for regular income tax purposes. The pre-existing statutory exclusion in IRC §121 exempts the first $250,000 (or $500,000 in the case of a married couple filing jointly) of gain recognized on the sale of a principal residence from gross income for regular income tax purposes and, thus, from the NIIT. For more information on NIIT, go to www.irs.gov and see the FAQs for the NIIT.

The following gains are examples of items that are taken into consideration when computing NIIT:

- Gains from sale of stocks, bonds, and mutual funds.
- Capital gain distributions from mutual funds.
- Gain from the sale of investment real estate, including the gain on the sale of a second home that is not the taxpayer's primary residence.
- A gain from the sale of interest in partnerships and S corporations (to the extent that the partner or shareholder was a passive owner).

Distributions are considered when determining the modified adjusted gross income threshold. Distributions from a nonqualified retirement plan are included in net investment income. Form 8960 will be filed if the taxpayer has net investment income tax. For more information, refer to IRS Regulation Sections 1.1411-1 through 1.1411-10.

Additional Taxes

The following are other taxes reported on Form 1040, Schedule 2, line 17:

- Form 8611   *Recapture of Low-Income Housing Credit*
- Form 8828   *Recapture of Federal Mortgage Subsidy*
- Form 8853   *Archer MSAs and Long-Term Care Insurance Contracts*
- Form 4255   *Recapture of Investment Credit*
- Form 8889   *Health Savings Account*

Line 18 Total Additional Taxes

Add the amounts of lines 4 through 17z and report the total on line 18. This is the total amount of Additional Taxes. Report this amount on Form 1040, line 23, to add the amount toward the taxpayer's total tax liability.

Line 20 Net Tax Liability Installment

This line reports the amount calculated from Form 965-A. This is beyond the scope of this course. See Instructions Form 965-A for more information.

Kiddie Tax (Form 8615)

Although the Form 8615 is not included on Schedule 2 as an additional tax, it is an additional tax to the parent. If the parent claims their child's unearned income, the child would not file a tax return. Claiming the child's unearned income would change the parents tax liability and could affect the taxpayers adjusted gross income (AGI). The election is made annually. The parent can claim their child's unearned income if the child meets the following conditions:

1. The child had $2,200 or more of unearned income.
2. The child is required to file a tax return.
3. The child either:
    a. Was under age 18 at the end of 2021.
    b. Was age 18 at the end of 2021 and didn't have earned income that was more than half of their support.

Other Taxes

   c. Was a full-time student at least age 19 and under age 24 at the end of 2021 and did not have earned income that was more than half of their support.
4. At least one of the child's parents was alive at the end of 2021.
5. The child does not need to file a joint return for 2021.

A "child" regarding the kiddie tax rules includes legally adopted children and stepchildren. These rules apply whether the child is or is not a dependent. If neither of the child's parents were living at the end of the year, none of the rules apply.

Support includes all amounts spent to provide the child with food, lodging, clothing, education, medical and dental care, recreation, transportation, and similar necessities. To calculate the child's support, count support provided by parents and their child, and others who support the child. Scholarship received by the child is not considered support for the child if he or she is a full-time student.

The Setting Every Community Up for Retirement Act (SECURE ACT) of 2019 repealed the TCJA changes made for Kiddie Tax. For tax year 2020 and beyond, the law reverts the kiddie tax back to the parent's marginal tax rate. See Publication 919 and IRC Section 1(g).

Part 2 Review Questions

To obtain the maximum benefit from this chapter, LTP recommends that you complete each of the following questions, and then compare them to the answers with feedback that immediately follow. Under governing self-study standards, vendors are required to present review questions intermittently throughout each self-study course.

These questions and explanations are not part of the final examination and will not be graded by LTP.

OT2.1
Cesar pays Rosa $200 weekly to clean his house. Rosa does not live with Cesar, but she does clean other individuals' houses as well. Which of the following scenarios best describes Cesar's tax responsibility?

   a. Cesar is required to withhold employment taxes for Rosa.
   b. Cesar is required to pay withholding taxes for Rosa.
   c. Cesar is not required to withhold employment taxes for Rosa.
   d. Cesar is not required to pay or withhold employment taxes for Rosa.

OT2.2
Which of the following taxpayers would report other taxes on Schedule 2, Line 1?

   a. Yesenia, who earned $75,000 as gross wages.
   b. Paul, who earned $12,000 as gross wages and $75,000 from self-employment.
   c. Jim, who earned $10,000 in interest and $360,000 as gross wages.
   d. Kathy, who only had Social Security benefits.

Other Taxes

OT2.3
Ezekiel, a single filer, has $220,000 in self-employment income and $0 in wages. Ezekiel must file Form 8959 as he is liable to pay the .9% Additional Medicare Tax. What is the Additional Medicare Tax threshold amount for single taxpayers?

   a. $230,000
   b. $250,000
   c. $200,000
   d. $125,000

OT2.4
Jerimiah, a single filer, has $420,000 in self-employment income and $0 in wages. Jerimiah must file Form 8959 as he is liable to pay the .9% Additional Medicare Tax. What is the Additional Medicare Tax threshold amount for single taxpayers?

   a. $230,000
   b. $250,000
   c. $200,000
   d. $125,000

OT2.5
Esther is 4-years-old and lives with her parents. They would like to claim the income that she earned while being a movie star on the local television station. The earned income was $2,310.45. Which of the following would describe what Esther and her parents need to do?

   a. Esther's parents should not claim her earned income.
   b. Esther would need to file her own tax return as a dependent on another return.
   c. Esther does not need to file since she is under the reporting amount.
   d. Esther cannot be claimed as a dependent on her parents' return.

OT2.6
Stephen would like to include his son Richard's interest and dividend income (including capital gain distributions) on his personal tax return. Which of the following would not allow Stephen to report the income?

   a. Richard is 18-years-old.
   b. Richard's gross income is $7,500.
   c. Richard had income only from interest and dividends.
   d. Richard is 22-years-old and a part-time student.

Part 2 Review Question Answers

OT2.1
Cesar pays Rosa $200 weekly to clean his house. Rosa does not live with Cesar, but she does clean other individuals' houses as well. Which of the following scenarios best describes Cesar's tax responsibility?

   a. Cesar is required to withhold employment taxes for Rosa.
   b. Cesar is required to pay withholding taxes for Rosa.
   c. Cesar is not required to withhold employment taxes for Rosa.
   d. Cesar is not required to pay or withhold employment taxes for Rosa.

Feedback: Review section *Line 7a – Household Employment Taxes*.

OT2.2
Which of the following taxpayers would report other taxes on Schedule 2, Line 1?

a. Yesenia, who earned $75,000 as gross wages.
b. Paul, who earned $12,000 as gross wages and $75,000 from self-employment.
c. Jim, who earned $10,000 in interest and $360,000 as gross wages.
d. Kathy, who only had Social Security benefits.

Feedback: Review section *Line 8: Taxes from Other IRS Forms.*

OT2.3
Ezekiel, a single filer, has $220,000 in self-employment income and $0 in wages. Ezekiel must file Form 8959 as he is liable to pay the .9% Additional Medicare Tax. What is the Additional Medicare Tax threshold amount for single taxpayers?

a. $230,000
b. $250,000
c. $200,000
d. $125,000

Feedback: Review section *Form 8959: Additional Medicare Tax.*

OT2.4
Jerimiah, a single filer, has $420,000 in self-employment income and $0 in wages. Jerimiah must file Form 8959 as he is liable to pay the .9% Additional Medicare Tax. What is the Additional Medicare Tax threshold amount for single taxpayers?

a. $230,000
b. $250,000
c. $200,000
d. $125,000

Feedback: Review section *Form 8959: Additional Medicare Tax.*

OT2.5
Esther is 4-years-old and lives with her parents. They would like to claim the income that she earned while being a movie star on the local television station. The earned income was $2,310.45. Which of the following would describe what Esther and her parents need to do?

a. Esther's parents should not claim her earned income.
b. Esther would need to file her own tax return as a dependent on another return.
c. Esther does not need to file since she is under the reporting amount.
d. Esther cannot be claimed as a dependent on her parents' return.

Feedback: Review section *Kiddie Tax.*

Other Taxes

OT2.6
Stephen would like to include his son Richard's interest and dividend income (including capital gain distributions) on his personal tax return. Which of the following would not allow Stephen to report the income?

   a. Richard is 18-years-old.
   b. Richard's gross income is $7,500.
   c. Richard had income only from interest and dividends.
   d. **Richard is 22-years-old and a part-time student.**

Feedback: Review section *Kiddie Tax*.

Takeaways

"Other taxes" consist of different types of taxes. Some of the taxes have forms that are attached to the federal Form 1040, while others are reported on Schedule 2. The IRS has expanded Schedule 2 by detailing certain additional taxes, which have their own line on Schedule 2. For example, on page 2 of Schedule 2, line 17 is for additional tax items such as Health Savings Account, Archer Medical Savings Account, and recapturing deductible credits.

AMT is a separate tax that is added to the income tax. Under tax law, certain deductions could give taxpayers a beneficial treatment for those who qualify for the tax deduction. The purpose of the minimum tax credit is to prevent the double taxation of deferral preference adjustments. AMT is a tax imposed in addition to the regular income tax to recapture the reductions resulting from the use of special tax relief provisions of the tax law. The repayment of the Premium Tax Credit is based on the amount of the premium paid and the taxpayer's income.

TEST YOUR KNOWLEDGE!
Go online to take a practice quiz.

Chapter 7 Payments and Tax Credits

Introduction

A nonrefundable tax credit reduces the taxpayer's tax liability to pay. Unlike a deduction, which reduces the amount of income subject to taxation, a credit directly reduces the tax itself. There are two types of credits: nonrefundable, which cannot reduce tax liability below zero, and refundable, which can reduce tax liability below zero, resulting in the need for a refund.

Objectives

At the end of this lesson, the student will:

> ➤ Explain how a nonrefundable credit affects the taxpayer's tax liability.
> ➤ Name the refundable credits.
> ➤ Recognize the Earned Income Credit (EIC) qualifications.
> ➤ Identify who qualifies for the additional child tax credit.
> ➤ Know the rules for the refundable portion of the American opportunity credit (AOC).
> ➤ Recognize when a dependent qualifies for the Other Dependent Credit (ODC).

Resources

Form 1040	Publication 17	Instructions Form 1040
Form 1098-T	Publication 503	Instructions Form 1098-T
Form 1116	Publication 505	Instructions Form 1116
Form 2441	Publication 514	Instructions Form 2441
Form 8396	Publication 524	Instructions Form 8396
Form 8801	Publication 596	Instructions Form 8801
Form 8812	Publication 972	Instructions Form 8812
Form 8863	Publication 4933	Instructions Form 8863
Form 8867	Publication 4935	Instructions Form 8867
Form 8880	Tax Topic 601, 602, 607, 608, 610	Instructions Form 8880
Form 8959	Schedule 3	Instructions Form 8959
Schedule EIC	Instructions Schedule 3	Instructions Schedule EIC
Schedule R		Instructions Schedule R

Table of Contents

Introduction	261
Part 1 Nonrefundable Credits	264
Foreign Tax Credit	264
Form 2441: Child and Dependent Care	265
Child of Divorced or Separated Parents	266
Earned Income Test	266
Work-Related Expense Requirement	267
Joint Return Requirement	267
Rules for Students Spouses Who Are Not Able to Care for Themselves	267
Employer Dependent Care Assistance	268
Expenses Not for Care	269
Payments to Relatives or Dependents	269
Dependent Care Provider Information	269
Form 8863: Education Credits	270
Lifetime Learning Credit	270
American Opportunity Credit (AOC)	271
No Double Benefit Allowed	272
Adjustment to Qualified Education Expenses	272
Scholarships and Fellowships	273
Who Claims the Expenses?	273
Expenses Paid by the Dependent	273
Expenses Paid by the Taxpayer	273
Expenses Paid by Others	274
Academic Period	274
Eligible Education	274
Claiming Credits for More than One Eligible Student	275
Form 1098-T	275
Tuition Payments Statement	277
Form 8880: Retirement Savings Contributions Credit	277
Form 5695: Residential Energy Credits	277
Part 1 Review Questions	278
Part 1 Review Questions Answers	279
Part 2 Other Nonrefundable Credits	280
Form 8396: Mortgage Interest Credit	280
Form 1098-MA	282
Schedule R: Credit for the Elderly or Disabled	282
Income Limits for Schedule R	283
How to Calculate the Credit	284
Adoption Credit or Exclusion	284
Child Tax Credits	284
Qualifying Child for Child Tax Credit	285
Qualifying Person for the ODC	285
Improperly Claiming the CTC, ODC, or ACTC	286
Part 2 Review Questions	286
Part 2 Review Questions Answers	287
Part 3 Payments and Refundable Tax Credits	288
Federal Income Tax Withheld	289
Estimated Tax Payments	289
Amount Overpaid	289
Returns with Refunds	291
Direct Deposit	291

- Direct Deposit Limits 291
- Amount Paid with a Request for Extension 292
- Excess Social Security or Railroad Retirement Tax Withheld 292
- Earned Income Credit (EIC) 292
- Community Property 293
- Minister's Housing 294
- Earned Income Rules 294
- Valid Social Security Number 294
- Uniform Definition of a Qualifying Child 295
- Foster Child 295
- A Qualifying Child of More than One Person 296
- Tie-Breaker Rules 296
- Special Rule for Divorced or Separated Parents 296
- The Taxpayer as a Qualifying Child of Another Person 297
- EIC for Taxpayers without Qualifying Children 297
- Schedule EIC Worksheets 297
- EIC Disallowed 297
- EIC Taxpayer Penalties 298
- Claiming a Child in Error...299
- Nontaxable Combat Pay Election for EIC 299
- Part 3 Review Questions 299
- Part 3 Review Questions Answers 301

Takeaways 302

Payments and Tax Credits

Part 1 Nonrefundable Credits

Nonrefundable credits reduce the taxpayer's income tax. The credits are computed based on the order found on Form 1040, Schedule 3, Part I.

Foreign Tax Credit

The foreign tax credit intends to reduce the double tax burden that could occur to a foreign source of income taxed by the foreign country and the United States. Generally, the credit for foreign taxes paid or accrued to a foreign country or U.S. possession will qualify for the tax credit reported on Form 1040, Schedule 3, line 1. If the taxpayer claims a foreign tax credit using Schedule 3, Form 1116, *Foreign Tax Credit*, it must be attached to the tax return. The other way that the taxpayer could claim the credit is as an itemized deduction on Schedule A under "other taxes."

Do not complete Form 1116 if the taxpayer qualifies for any of the following:

- All foreign gross income is from interest and dividends and reported on Form 1099-INT, 1099-DIV, or Schedule K-1.
- Total foreign taxes were not more than $300 ($600 if married filing jointly).
- All foreign source gross income was "passive category income."

2021 Schedule 3

Form 2441: Child and Dependent Care

Dependent care benefits are payments the employer paid directly to either the taxpayer or the care provider for taking care of the qualifying dependent(s) while the taxpayer worked. Dependent care benefits are pre-taxed contributions made based on the fair market value of care in a daycare facility provided by or sponsored by the employer under a Flexible Spending Arrangement (FSA).

"Care" is the cost of attending a facility to qualifying individual(s) outside the taxpayer's home. It does not include food, lodging, education, clothing, or entertainment. If a dependent care facility provides the care, the center must meet all the applicable state and local regulations. A dependent care facility is a place that offers care for more than six individuals who do not live there and receives a fee, payment, or grant for providing those services for any individual. Include the cost of a day camp, but not the cost of an overnight camp, summer school, or tutoring program.

The taxpayer can take a nonrefundable credit of up to 50% of the qualifying expenses for the care of a qualified dependent when the expenditures are work-related. The percentage of credit goes down as income goes up, with 20% of eligible expenses as the least amount allowed. Expenses are limited to $8,000 for one and $16,000 for two or more qualified dependents. Child and dependent care is reported on Form 2441 and flows to Form 1040, Schedule 3, line 2.

A qualifying person is:

- A qualifying child under 13 and claimed as a dependent. If a child turns 13 during the tax year, you can still prorate their care for the portion of the year the child was not 13.
- A disabled spouse who wasn't physically or mentally able to care for him or herself.
- Any disabled person who wasn't physically or mentally able to care for him or herself and whom the taxpayer can claim as a dependent unless one of the following is true:
    - The disabled individual had a gross income of $4,400 or more.
    - The disabled individual filed a joint return.
    - The disabled individual or spouse, if filing a joint tax return, could be claimed as a dependent on another individual's 2021 tax return.

To be able to claim the child and dependent care expenses, the taxpayer must meet all of the following requirements:

- The care must be for one or more qualifying persons who are identified on Form 2441.
- If filing a joint return, the taxpayer (and spouse if filing a joint return) must have earned income during the year.
- The taxpayer must pay child and dependent care expenses to allow the taxpayer and spouse to file jointly, work, or look for work.
- The taxpayer must make payments for child and dependent care to someone who cannot be claimed as a dependent on the taxpayer's return.
- The filing status may be Single, Head of Household, or Qualifying widow(er) with a dependent child. If married, they must file a joint return (unless an exception applies).
- The taxpayer must fill out Form 2441 to identify the provider's name, TIN, the cost of care, and the address of the location where the care was provided and attach the form to their tax return.

Payments and Tax Credits

> ➤ If the taxpayer excludes or deducts dependent care benefits provided by a dependent care benefit plan, the total amount excluded or deducted must be less than the dollar limit for qualifying expenses ($8,000 per child up to $16,000).

Below is the current chart used to calculate the child and dependent care credit. Calculate the credit amount by multiplying the percentage on the right against the credit's monetary limit ($8,000-$16,000) and which percentage, based on the taxpayer(s) combined income. For tax year 2021, the income increase was part of the American Rescue Plan Act. The following is just a snapshot of the percentage chart.

Income	Percentage
$0 – $125,000	50%
$143,000 –145,000	40%
$163,000 – $165,000	30%
$183,000 – $400,000	20%
$418,000 – $420,000	10%
$438,000 – No limit	0%

For example, a taxpayer and his spouse each made $50,000 for a combined income of $100,000, and they paid $8,500 for childcare for one child. Because they paid $8,500 for childcare and only for one child, they will be allowed to use $8,000 of that expense to calculate their credit amount because that is the credit limit no matter how much they paid on childcare. Because their combined income was under $125,000, they will calculate their credit amount using the 50% section from the chart. Therefore, the 50% deduction is calculated as follows: $8,000 × .50 = $4,000. Their credit amount is $4,000.

If all other details were the same, but they had only spent $2,000 on childcare, their credit amount would be 50% of that two thousand, not three. This is because they did not spend enough to reach the credit limit, meaning their credit amount would be $1,000 ($2,000 × .50 = $1,000).

Child of Divorced or Separated Parents

In addition to meeting the qualifying person requirements, additional rules apply in the case of divorced or separated parents. The parent who has physical custody of the child for the more significant portion of the year is the only parent who can claim the credit, regardless of how much support the other parent provides or if the dependency exemption is released.

Earned Income Test

The taxpayer and spouse (if filing jointly) must have earned income to claim the credit. Earned income includes wages, salary, tips, other taxable employee compensation, and net earnings from self-employment. A loss from self-employment reduces income. If the taxpayer has nontaxable combat pay not included in earned income, they may include the income to calculate the child and dependent credit. If both the taxpayer and spouse have nontaxable combat pay, both will have to make the election. A good tax professional should calculate the credit both ways for the taxpayer and see which results in the higher credit amount.

Señor 1040 Says: Remember Child and Dependent Care Expenses are a different credit than the Additional Child Tax Credit.

Work-Related Expense Requirement

Child and dependent care expenses must be work-related to qualify for the credit. You can consider work-related expenses only if the following are true:

> - Dependent care allows the taxpayer(s) to work or look for work.
> - The expenses are for a qualifying person's care.

Example 1: Darlene works during the day, and her spouse, Craig, works at night and sleeps while Darlene is working. Their five-year-old son, Trevor, goes to daycare so Craig can sleep. Their expenses are work-related because the care allows Craig to sleep to perform his job adequately.

Example 2: Darlene and Craig get a babysitter on Craig's night off, so they can go out to eat and spend some time together. This expense is not work-related because the care is not directly facilitating Darlene or Craig's ability to work or look for work.

Joint Return Requirement

Usually, married couples file a joint return to take the child and dependent care credit. However, if the taxpayer and spouse are legally separated or living apart, they may still take the credit. For a married taxpayer who is separated, all the following must apply to be eligible for the credit:

> - The taxpayer must file their own, separate return.
> - The taxpayer's home was the qualifying individual's home for more than half the year.
> - The taxpayer paid more than half the cost of home upkeep for the year.
> - The taxpayer's spouse did not live in their home during the last six months of the year.

Rules for Students Spouses Who Are Not Able to Care for Themselves

A married couple is treated as having earned income for any month that one was a full-time student or attended a school during any five months of the tax year (the months do not have to be consecutive) or is physically or mentally disabled or unable to care for himself. This definition of "school" does not include night school or a correspondence school.

If the taxpayer or spouse was a full-time student for at least five months or was disabled, they are considered to have earned an income of $250 per month (or $500 if more than one qualifying person was cared for during the tax year). This is done to help taxpayers who have little-to-no earned income qualify for the Child and Dependent Care Credit, because credits can only be claimed if the taxpayer or spouse has earned income.

Payments and Tax Credits

Employer Dependent Care Assistance

If the employer provides dependent care benefits excluded from income (such as those received under a cafeteria plan), the taxpayer must subtract that amount from the applicable dollar limit of the Child and Dependent Care Credit. Dependent care benefits include the following:

- Amounts the employer paid directly to the taxpayer or the taxpayer's provider while the taxpayer worked.
- The fair market value of care in a daycare facility provided or sponsored by the employer.
- Pre-tax contributions made under a dependent flexible spending arrangement.

Box 10 reports dependent care benefits on the taxpayer's W-2. If a partner received benefits, they would appear in box 13 on the K-1, Form 1065 with code O.

The amount excluded from income is limited to the smallest of the following:

- The total amount of dependent care benefits received during the year.
- The total amount of qualified expenses incurred during the year.
- The taxpayer's earned income.
- The spouse's earned income.
- $5,000 or $2,500 if married filing separately.

For example, if the taxpayer with an earned income of $43,000 qualifies for the child and dependent care credit and pays $3,000, of which the employer reimburses $1,000, the taxpayer's basis for childcare for one child is $2,000, and he or she would have $1,000 in eligible benefits:

Maximum allowed	$3,000
Benefits excluded from income*	−1,000
Reduced limit for figuring credit	$2,000
	× .50
Childcare credit allowed	$1,000

*This amount shows on Form W-2 in box 10, and when it shows, you must complete the second page of Form 2441, even if the taxpayer has no additional eligible benefits.

Señor 1040 Says: Make sure to always check if there is an amount in box 10 of the W-2 for Dependent Care Payments.

If dependent care assistance exceeds the amount paid for dependent care, the excess amount becomes income to the taxpayer and is reported on line 1 of Form 1040. The letters "DCB" (dependent care benefit) should be written on the dotted line in the space before the entry block for line 1.

You can also pay for the care provided in the home with the dependent care benefits. The taxpayer may have to withhold taxes (FICA and FUTA) for the dependent care provider if dependent care is in the taxpayer's home. The taxpayer is not required to withhold taxes if the dependent care provider is self-employed.

Due to the COVID-19 pandemic, the Taxpayer Certainty and Disaster Relief Act of 2020 allows Cafeteria Plans to permit a carryover of unused dependent care benefits funds. See also Notice 2021-15.

Expenses Not for Care

Care expenses do not include the taxpayer's money for food, lodging, clothing, education, or entertainment. Expenses for a child in nursery school, preschool, or similar programs for children below the kindergarten level are considered expenses for care. Expenses to attend kindergarten or higher schooling are not expenses for childcare. In most situations, expenses for before or after-school care are expenses for care; you must do more research for the exceptions to this. Do not use the summer school and tutoring programs as dependent care expenses. The cost of sending the dependent to an overnight camp is not considered work-related; however, the cost of a day camp may be a work-related expense.

Payments to Relatives or Dependents

Payments made to relatives for dependent care, which enable the taxpayer to work when the relative lives in the taxpayer's home, may still apply as a dependent care payment. However, if any of the following apply, the payments cannot be counted as payment for dependent care:

- The dependent is claimed as the taxpayer's dependent (or spouse filing jointly).
- The child was under 19 at the end of the year, even if they were not the taxpayer's dependent.
- If the person was not the taxpayer's spouse during the year.
- If the person providing the care is the other parent of the qualifying person and if the qualifying person is the taxpayer's child, and if the child is under the age of 13.

Dependent Care Provider Information

When completing Form 2441, you will need the following information about the individual or organization that provides care for the taxpayer's qualifying child or dependent:

- The provider's name.
- The provider's address.
- The provider's identification number (EIN or SSN).

If the taxpayer cannot provide all the required information, the credit may not be allowed. The taxpayer can show that they exercised due diligence by getting and keeping the provider's completed Form W-10, *Dependent Care Provider's Identification and Certification*.

The taxpayer may also supply a statement from the employer if the employer's dependent care plan is the provider. The taxpayer might supply a letter or invoice if it shows the required information. If the provider refuses to give the information to the taxpayer, the taxpayer should provide the information they have available, attach a statement explaining the provider's refusal to supply the information, and explain what attempts you made to obtain the information. To ensure the IRS does not disallow the credit, the taxpayer should complete due diligence on the care provider to ensure that all the information is accurate.

Payments and Tax Credits

> *Señor 1040 Says:* Encourage the taxpayer to maintain records about their childcare provider and store them along with their tax returns.

Tax Tip: If the dependent care provider cares for the dependent in the taxpayer's home, the provider may be considered a household employee. As a tax professional, you should ask questions about dependent care and document your questions and answers from the taxpayer.

Form 8863: Education Credits

Education credits are available for taxpayers who pay expenses for postsecondary education. To claim the education credit, the student must receive Form 1098-T from the student's school and provide that form to the tax preparer. The two education credits are the American opportunity credit (AOC) and the lifetime learning credit; report them on Form 8863, *Education Credits*. Lifetime learning is a nonrefundable credit, and the American opportunity is a partially refundable credit. You must meet the following requirement to be eligible for either credit:

- Education credits are not available to taxpayers filing MFS.
- Education expenses paid for the taxpayer, the spouse, or the dependents (if another taxpayer can claim the student, the student cannot claim the credit on their tax return. Any expenses the student paid are paid by the taxpayer who claimed the student as a dependent).
- Do not consider meals, lodging, student activities, athletics, transportation, insurance, and personal living expenses as qualified expenses.
- Qualified education expenses generally do not include any noncredit course expenses or any course of instruction or education involving sports, games, or hobbies. However, if the course of instruction is part of the student's degree program, these expenses can qualify.
- Treat prepayments for an academic period that begins during the first three months of the following year as if the academic period begins in the year of the prepayment.
- The taxpayer can claim an education credit for qualified education expenses that were not refunded when the student withdraws.
- If the taxpayer or spouse was a nonresident alien for any part of the year, they could not claim a credit unless they qualify and elect to be a resident alien.
- The amount on Form 1040, line 1, is $90,000 or more ($180,000 or more if MFJ).

Lifetime Learning Credit

The lifetime learning credit is available at any time for the taxpayer, the taxpayer's spouse, or the taxpayer's dependent. The maximum allowed credit is $2,000 or 20% of the first $10,000 of qualified tuition and related expenses paid for all students during the year in which the taxpayer claimed them on the same tax return. Qualified expenses include tuition and fees required for enrollment at an eligible post-secondary program. Expenses incurred to acquire or improve the taxpayer's job skills are eligible expenses.

An expense related to a course that involves sports, games, or hobbies is not a qualified expense unless it is part of the student's degree program. Taxpayers must reduce their qualified expense by any education assistance from the post-secondary program, scholarships, or amounts to compute the lifetime learning credit.

The lifetime learning credit is not based on the student's workload. Expenses for graduate-level courses are eligible. The amount of credit a taxpayer can claim does not increase based on the number of students for whom the taxpayer paid qualified expenses. The student does not have to be enrolled at least half-time in the course of study to be eligible for the credit. The nonrefundable portion of the education credits is reported on Form 8863, line 19, and is carried to Form 1040, Schedule 3, line 3. To qualify for the lifetime learning credit, the taxpayer's modified adjusted gross income (MAGI) should be less than $136,000 for taxpayers filing MFJ or less than $68,000 for all others.

Remember, modified adjusted gross income (MAGI) is adjusted gross income, plus all of the following:

> ➤ The amount excluded under IRC §911, *Foreign-Earned Income Exclusion*.
> ➤ Tax-exempt interest income.
> ➤ The excluded portion of Social Security benefits.

American Opportunity Credit (AOC)

The American opportunity credit (AOC) is a credit of up to $2,500, up to 40% of which may be refundable. Base the credit on 100% of the first $2,000 and 25% of the next $2,000. To qualify for the AOC, the taxpayer's MAGI must be less than $180,000 for taxpayers filing MFJ and $90,000 for all others.

Qualified expenses include tuition and fees for enrollment at an eligible post-secondary program and expenses for books, supplies, and equipment needed for a course of study, whether or not the student purchases the materials from the education institution. The student must carry at least half the normal full-time workload for the course of study the student enrolled in. The student must also be free of federal or state felony offenses consisting of the possession or distribution of a controlled substance. The refundable portion of the education credit is found on Form 8863, line 8, and reported on Form 1040, page 2, line 29.

For example, Donna and Doug are first-year students at an eligible post-secondary program. They must have certain books and other reading materials to use in their mandatory first-year classes. Doug bought his books directly from a friend, and Donna purchased hers at the college bookstore. Although Donna and Doug purchased their books through different avenues, the cost of both purchases is qualifying education expenses since books qualify for the American opportunity credit.

You can claim the American opportunity credit for a student who meets all the following requirements:

> ➤ The student has not completed their first four years of postsecondary education determined by the eligible post-secondary program.

Payments and Tax Credits

The student has not claimed the American opportunity credit or the Hope Scholarship Credit for any prior four tax years.
- For at least one academic period beginning in 2021, the student did the following:
  - Was enrolled in a program that leads to a degree certificate or other credential
  - Carried at least one-half of the normal full-time workload for their course of study.
- The student does not have any federal or state felony conviction for possessing or distributing a controlled substance.

When the professional interviews the taxpayer to determine if they qualify for the American opportunity credit, be sure to ask the following questions:

- Did the student receive Form 1098-T?
- Has the Hope Scholarship Credit or American opportunity credit been claimed for this student for four tax years before 2021?
- Was the student enrolled at least half-time for at least one academic period that began (or treated as begun) in 2021 at an eligible education institution in a program leading toward a postsecondary degree, certificate, or other recognized postsecondary education credential?
- Did the student complete the first four years of postsecondary education before 2021?
- Was the student convicted of a felony for possession or distribution of a controlled substance before the end of 2021?

Asking and documenting these questions are part of the tax professional's due diligence.

No Double Benefit Allowed

The taxpayer cannot do any of the following:

- Deduct higher education expenses on their income tax return and claim an education credit based on the same expenses.
- Claim more than one credit based on the same qualified education expenses.
- Claim a credit based on expenses paid with tax-free scholarship, grant, or employer-provided education assistance.
- Claim a credit based on the same expenses used to figure the tax-free portion of a distribution from a Coverdell education savings account (ESA) or a qualified tuition program (QTA).
- Claim a lifetime learning credit in the same year the tuition and fees deduction was claimed.

Adjustment to Qualified Education Expenses

If taxpayers pay qualified education expenses with certain tax-free funds, they cannot claim a credit for those amounts. Taxpayers must reduce the qualified education expense by the amount of any tax-free education assistance.

Tax-free education assistance includes the following:

- The tax-free parts of scholarships and fellowships.
- The tax-free portion of Pell grants.
- Employer-provided education assistance.

- Veterans' education assistance.
- Received other nontaxable (tax-free) payments (other than gifts or inheritances) as educational assistance.

Scholarships and Fellowships

A scholarship is generally an amount paid or allowed for the benefit of a student to attend a post-secondary program. The student may be either an undergraduate or a graduate student. A fellowship is paid for the benefit of an individual to aid in the pursuit of study or research. How the student pays for their expenses with the fellowship money determines the taxable portion. A scholarship or fellowship qualifies as tax-free if the following conditions are met:

- The fellowship or scholarship does not exceed qualifying expenses.
- The funds are not designated for other purposes such as room and board and cannot be used for qualified education expenses.
- It does not represent payment for teaching, research, or other services required as a condition for receiving the scholarship.

Señor 1040 Says: When a student receives a scholarship, make sure that it is not taxable to the student. Do research on how the funds were used by the student. If they were not used for qualifying expenses, the funds could be taxable to the student.

Who Claims the Expenses?

If there are qualified education expenses for the taxpayer's dependent for a year, the taxpayer can claim an education credit for the dependent's expenses for the current year. For the taxpayer to claim an education credit for their dependent's expenses, the taxpayer must also claim an exemption. The taxpayer does this by listing the dependent's name and other required information on Form 1040.

Expenses Paid by the Dependent

If the taxpayer claims an exemption on their tax return for an eligible student who is the taxpayer's dependent, treat any expenses paid or deemed paid by the dependent as if the taxpayer paid them. Include these expenses when figuring the amount of the taxpayer's education credit.

Expenses Paid by the Taxpayer

If the taxpayer claimed an exemption for a dependent who is an eligible student, only the taxpayer could include any expenses paid when figuring the amount of the education credit. If neither the taxpayer nor anyone else claims an exemption for the dependent, the dependent can include any expenses paid when figuring the education credit.

Expenses Paid by Others

Someone other than the taxpayer, the taxpayer's spouse, or the taxpayer's dependent (such as a relative or former spouse) may make a payment directly to an eligible post-secondary program to pay for an eligible student's qualified education expenses. In this case, treat the student as receiving the payment from the other person and, in turn, paying the college. The taxpayer paid the expenses if they claimed an exemption on their return for the student.

Example: In 2021, Laura Hardy directly pays an eligible college for her grandson's qualified education expenses. To claim an education credit, her grandson, Thomas, is treated as receiving the money as a gift from his grandmother and, in turn, paying his qualified education expenses himself. Unless someone else claims Thomas's tax return exemption, only Thomas can use the payment to claim an education credit. If anyone, such as Thomas's parents, claims an exemption for Thomas on their tax return, that person may be able to use the expenses to claim an education credit. If anyone else claims an exemption for Thomas, Thomas cannot claim an education credit.

Academic Period

An academic period includes a semester, trimester, quarter, or another period of study determined by the college or university.

Eligible Education

An eligible post-secondary program is any college, university, vocational school, or other postsecondary educational institution eligible to participate in a student aid program administered by the Department of Education. It includes virtually all accredited, public, nonprofit, and proprietary (privately owned profit-making) postsecondary colleges. The education institution should tell the taxpayer if it is an eligible college or university.

Certain colleges and universities outside the United States also participate in the U.S. Department of Education's Federal Student Aid (FSA) programs. You can find a list of these foreign schools on the Department of Education's website at www.fafsa.ed.gov/index.htm. Click "Find my school codes," complete the two items on the first page, click "Next," and then follow the remaining instructions to search for a foreign school.

Be aware that not all eligible education institutions treat certain Coverdell education savings accounts (529 Plans) the same way, nor do they consider the same things when determining if a scholarship or fellowship grant is not taxable. To determine if you can use the Coverdell education savings account for the college, university, vocational school, or another postsecondary education institute, the school in question must participate in a student aid program administered by the U.S. Department of Education. The education institution can be an accredited public, nonprofit, or proprietary postsecondary institution. Beginning in 2018, this includes any private, religious, or public school for kindergarten through 12th grade as determined by state law. To determine if scholarships and fellowship grants are tax-free, the education institution must maintain a regular facility and curriculum and normally have a regularly enrolled body of students where it carries on its educational activities.

Claiming Credits for More than One Eligible Student

The taxpayer can claim only one credit (per student) for each eligible student but can claim different credits for different students. For example, suppose a taxpayer pays qualified education expenses for more than one student in the same year. In that case, the taxpayer can choose to take the American opportunity credit for one student and the lifetime learning credit for the other.

Form 8863, Part III, must be completed for each individual claiming education credits on the tax return before completing Part I and Part II. Form 1098-T must be given to the tax preparer; making sure you receive this form is part of the tax professional's due diligence.

Form 1098-T

To help figure the education credit reported on Form 8863, the taxpayer should receive Form 1098-T from their school. Generally, an eligible education institution (such as a college or university) must send Form 1098-T (or an acceptable substitute) to each enrolled student by January 31st of each year. An institution may choose to report payments received (box 1) or billed (box 2) for qualified education expenses. Form 1098-T should provide other information from the institution, including adjustments made for prior years, the amount of scholarships, grants, reimbursements, or refunds provided, and whether the taxpayer was enrolled at least half-time or was a graduate student.

The eligible educational institution may ask for a completed Form W-9S, *Request for Student's or Borrower's Taxpayer Identification Number and Certification*, or some similar statement to obtain the student's name, address, and taxpayer identification number.

The lender does not have to file Form 1098-T or furnish a statement for the following:

> - Students enrolled in a degree program who take courses with no academic credit.
> - Nonresident alien students, unless requested by the student.
> - Students whose qualified tuition and related expenses are entirely waived or paid with scholarships.
> - Students for whom the eligible education institution do not maintain separate financial accounting and whose qualified tuition and related expenses are covered by a formal billing arrangement between an institution and the student's employer or a governmental entity such as the Department of Veterans Affairs or the Department of Defense.

To calculate qualified tuition and related expenses, eligible education institutions may report either the payments received or billed. They must use the same reporting method for all calendar years unless the IRS grants permission to the education institution to change the reporting method.

All filers of Form 1098-T may truncate the student's identification number on payee statements. When completing the tax return, you must use the institution's EIN. Tax preparers should review their clients' Form 1098-T and keep a copy in each taxpayer's file.

Payments and Tax Credits

[Form 1098-T Tuition Statement 2021 shown]

Box 1: The school enters the amount of qualified tuition and related expenses from all sources during the calendar year here. The amount in box 1 is the total amount received by the taxpayer minus any reimbursements or refunds made during the tax year. Do not reduce this amount by scholarships or grants (reported separately in box 5).

Box 2: Reserved for future use.

Box 3: Reserved for future use.

Box 4: Adjustments made for a prior year. Enter reimbursements or refunds of qualified tuition and expenses made in 2021 related to payments received for any prior year after 2002. See Instructions Form 1098-T.

Box 5: This box shows the total amount received for scholarships or grants administered and processed during the calendar year. Remember, if the amount in box 5 is larger than the amount in box 1, do not claim the education credit for the taxpayer.

Box 6: Adjustments to Scholarships or Grants for a prior year. Enter the amount of any reduction reported for any prior year after 2002.

Box 7: If this box is checked, the amount in box 1 or 2 includes amounts the taxpayer paid before the end of the current year for the next year's tuition.

Box 8: A checkmark in this box indicates that the student was at least a half-time student during any academic period that began during the tax year. Although each university determines who and what is considered a "part-time student," the part-time student workload must be equal to or exceed the standards established by the Department of Education under the Higher Education Act.

Box 9: If this box is checked, the taxpayer is a graduate student. A graduate student must be enrolled in a program or programs leading to a graduate-level degree, graduate-level certificate, or another recognized graduate-level educational credential.

Box 10: If the insurer of the qualified tuition and related expenses made reimbursements to the student, enter the amount here.

Some eligible educational institutions combine all fees for an academic period into one amount. Contact the institution if the student does not receive or have access to a statement showing amounts for qualified education expenses and personal expenses. The institution must provide this information to the taxpayer and report the amount paid or billed for qualified education expenses on Form 1098-T.

Tuition Payments Statement

When an eligible education institution provides a reduction in tuition to an employee of the institution or a spouse or dependent child of an employee, the amount of the reduction may or may not be taxable. If taxable, the employee received a payment and, in turn, paid the educational institution on behalf of the student.

Form 8880: Retirement Savings Contributions Credit

The Retirement Savings Contributions Credit is based on the first $2,000 contributed to IRAs, 401(k)s, and certain other retirement plans. Use Form 8880, *Credit for Qualified Retirement Savings Contributions*, to calculate the credit. The taxpayer can contribute until the tax return's due date; filing an extension does not change the due date for making these contributions. This credit reduces the taxpayer's income tax dollar-for-dollar and is reported on Form 1040, Schedule 3, line 4. To claim this credit for 2021, the taxpayer's MAGI must be less than $33,000 if Single or MFS, $49,500 if filing Head of household, or $66,000 if married filing jointly or Qualified widow(er) with a dependent. Report this credit on Form 1040, Schedule 3, line 4. If a taxpayer claims the credit, attach Form 8880 to Form 1040.

Form 5695: Residential Energy Credits

If taxpayers made energy-saving improvements to their main home in the United States, they might be able to claim the residential energy efficient property credit and report it on Form 1040, Schedule 3, line 5. The credit and its ability to carry forward any portion are still available from 2017 to 2022. The following residential energy efficient property credits are available for the 2021 tax year if the taxpayer made such improvements to the main home located in the United States:

- Qualified solar electric property credit.
- Qualified solar water heating property credit.
- Qualified small wind energy property credit.
- Qualified geothermal heat pump property credit.
- Qualified biomass fuel property costs.

If the taxpayer is a condominium owner or a tenant-stockholder in a cooperative housing corporation and has paid their proportionate share of the cost, the taxpayer could qualify for the credit. There is a 30% credit for installing qualified solar water-heating property, qualified solar electric property, geothermal heat pumps, and small wind-energy property. The credit applies for property placed in service during 2021, which is 26% for 2021 and 2022.

Payments and Tax Credits

Part 1 Review Questions

To obtain the maximum benefit from this chapter, LTP recommends that you complete each of the following questions and then compare them to the answers with feedback that immediately follows. Under governing self-study standards, vendors must present review questions intermittently throughout each self-study course.

These questions and explanations are not part of the final examination and will not be graded by LTP.

TCPP1.1
Jerry has three qualifying children for the federal dependent care expense. What is the maximum amount Jerry can claim?

   a. $3,000
   b. $1,500
   c. $6,000
   d. No limit

TCPP1.2
Tiffany has two children. Hunter, age 12, and Suzy, age 11. At what age will Tiffany be unable to claim the child and dependent care expense?

   a. 12
   b. 13
   c. 14
   d. 18

TCPP1.3
Jenny files married filing separately. How much will she be able to claim for her education credit?

   a. $0
   b. $4,000
   c. $1,500
   d. $3,000

TCPP1.4
Doug and his wife Brittney are full-time students at a qualifying school. For tax purposes, they earned income if they are full-time students for how many months?

   a. 12
   b. 7
   c. 5
   d. 4

TCPP1.5
Which of the following is a nonrefundable tax credit?

    a. Lifetime learning credit
    b. Earned Income Tax Credit
    c. Additional Child Tax Credit
    d. Federal income tax withheld

Part 1 Review Questions Answers

TCPP1.1
Jerry has three qualifying children for the federal dependent care expense. What is the maximum amount Jerry can claim?

    a. $3,000
    b. $1,500
    c. $6,000
    d. No limit

Feedback: Review section *Form 2441: Child and Dependent Care.*

TCPP1.2
Tiffany has two children. Hunter, age 12, and Suzy, age 11. At what age will Tiffany be unable to claim the child and dependent care expense?

    a. 12
    b. 13
    c. 14
    d. 18

Feedback: Review section *Form 2441: Child and Dependent Care.*

TCPP1.3
Jenny files married filing separately. How much will she be able to claim for her education credit?

    a. $0
    b. $4,000
    c. $1,500
    d. $3,000

Feedback: Review section *Form 8863: Education Credits.*

TCPP1.4
Doug and his wife Brittney are full-time students at a qualifying school. For tax purposes, they earned income if they are full-time students for how many months?

    a. 12
    b. 7
    c. 5
    d. 4

Feedback: Review section *Form 8863: Education Credits.*

Payments and Tax Credits

TCPP1.5

Which of the following is a nonrefundable tax credit?

    a. **Lifetime learning credit**
    b. Earned Income Tax Credit
    c. Additional Child Tax Credit
    d. Federal income tax withheld

Feedback: Review section *Part 1: Nonrefundable Credits*.

Part 2 Other Nonrefundable Credits

Form 1040, Schedule 3, Line 6, reports the combined amount of the following credits:

- The general business credit; calculate this credit using Form 3800.
- Credit for prior year minimum tax; calculate this credit using Form 8801.
- Mortgage interest credit; calculate this credit using Form 8396.
- Credit for the elderly or disabled; calculate this credit using Schedule R.
- Adoption credit; calculate this credit using Form 8839.
- Carryforward of the District of Columbia first-time homebuyer credit; calculate this credit using Form 8859.
- Credit to holders of tax credit bonds; calculate this credit using Form 8912.

Research may be needed to report the above credits.

Form 8396: Mortgage Interest Credit

Taxpayers claim the mortgage interest credit if a state, local governmental unit, or agency under a qualified mortgage credit certificate program issues them a Mortgage Credit Certificate (MCC).

If the mortgage is equal to or smaller than the certified indebtedness amount (in other words, the loan) shown on the MCC, multiply the certified credit rate shown on the MCC by all interest paid on the mortgage during the year.

If the mortgage amount is larger than the certified indebtedness amount shown on the MCC, multiply the certified credit percentage rate shown on the MCC by the interest allocated to the certified indebtedness amount shown on the MCC to calculate the credit.

Señor 1040 Says: Certificates issued by the Federal Housing Administration, Department of Veterans Affairs, and Farmers Home Administration (as well as Homestead Staff Exemption Certificates) do not qualify for the credit.

The home to which the certificate relates must be the taxpayer's primary residence, and the home must be within the jurisdiction of the governmental agency that issued the certificate. The taxpayer could not claim the credit if the interest were paid to a related party. If the taxpayer refinances the mortgage, be aware that the certificates must be reissued to the taxpayer and meet all the following conditions:

➢ The owner and the property cannot change.
➢ The new certificate must entirely replace the existing certificate. The holder cannot retain any portion of the outstanding balance of the previous certificate.
➢ The certified indebtedness on the new certificate cannot exceed the outstanding balance shown on the certificate.
➢ The credit rate of the new certificate cannot exceed the credit rate of the old certificate.
➢ The new certificate cannot result in a larger amount on line 3 than would otherwise have been allowable under the previous certificate for any tax year.

The taxpayer may have an unused mortgage credit to carry forward up to the next three tax years or until they use it completely, whichever comes first. They have to use the current year's credit before using any carryforward credits. If using the carryforward credits from more than one year, begin with the carryforward credit from the earliest prior year (i.e., 2020 before 2019, 2019 before 2018). If the certificate credit is more than 20%, do not carry forward amounts over $2,000. To complete Form 8396, *Mortgage Interest Credit*, see the form's instructions.

Figure the 2020 credit and carry any excess forward to 2020 on Form 8396, *Mortgage Interest Credit*, and attach Form 8396 to Form 1040. On Form 8396, be sure to include any credit carried forward from the prior three tax years. Use the current-year credit before prior-year credits are applied. Include the credit in the total amount of other credits reported on Schedule 3, line 6; check box c and write in "Form 8396" to show which nonrefundable credit was included on that line. A tax professional should keep a copy of the MCC in the taxpayer's files, as the IRS may want to see the certificate at a future point in time.

Form 1098, *Mortgage Interest Statement*, is required to include the amount of the outstanding principal, the loan origination date, and the property's address. The owner of an inherited property may not treat the property as having a different basis than was reported by the state for estate tax purposes. IRC §6035 requires estates that file an estate tax return to issue payee statements listing the property's value reported on the estate tax return to all persons inheriting property from the estate. These changes apply to all estate tax returns filed after February 29, 2016. For more information, see Notice 2015-57 and IRC §6035.

If the taxpayer purchased and sold the home within nine years, the homeowner may recapture some credit. In this case, one must file Form 8828, *Recapture of Federal Mortgage Subsidy*; you must do more research on this topic.

Payments and Tax Credits

Form 1098-MA

If the taxpayer has received mortgage assistance payments allocated from the Housing Finance Agency Innovation Fund for the Hardest Hit Housing Markets (HFA Hardest Hit Fund) or the Emergency Homeowner's Loan Program, report the amount paid by the homeowner and the assistance payments on Form 1098-MA.

> *Señor 1040 Says:* Do not confuse Mortgage Interest Credit with Mortgage Assistance Payments. They are not the same credit.

Schedule R: Credit for the Elderly or Disabled

The Credit for the Elderly or Disabled is a nonrefundable credit based on the taxpayer's filing status, age, and income. A person is permanently and totally disabled if the taxpayer cannot engage in any substantial gainful activity due to a physical or mental condition or if a qualified physician determined that the condition has lasted or can be expected to last continuously for at least a year or until death. If the taxpayer is under 65, a physician's statement must be attached to the tax return. The statement must certify that the taxpayer was permanently and totally disabled on the date of retirement.

The base amount is reduced by most nontaxable pension and Social Security benefits and by half of the AGI that exceeds the base amount. To claim this credit, the taxpayer must meet the following criteria:

- Be age 65 or older by the end of the tax year.
- Meet the following conditions if under the age of 65 at the end of the tax year:

- o Retired on permanent and total disability: they must have been permanently and totally disabled on or before January 1, 1976, or January 1, 1977, if the taxpayer retired before 1977.
- o Received taxable disability benefits in the current tax year.
- o Have reached the employer's mandatory retirement age (when the employer's retirement program requires an employee to retire) on or before January 1 of the tax year in question.

If the taxpayer is under the age of 65, they must have a physician's statement certifying that they were permanently and totally disabled on the date of retirement. Do not file the statement with the taxpayer's Form 1040; however, the taxpayer must keep it for their records. The instructions for Schedule R include a template statement taxpayers can provide to their physicians to complete and keep for their records. The taxpayer's income cannot exceed the limits listed below to qualify for the credit, so many taxpayers will not be able to take advantage of it.

Señor 1040 Says: Be aware that when preparing a Schedule R to determine a taxpayer's eligibility for the elderly or disabled credit, the Social Security income must be considered as well even though it is not taxable.

Income Limits for Schedule R

If the taxpayer's income exceeds the following limits, the taxpayer cannot claim the credit.

If filing status is:	The taxpayer cannot take the credit if the amount from Form 1040, or Form 1040-SR, line 8b, is:	Or the taxpayer received:
Single, Head of Household, or Qualifying widow(er) with dependent child	$17,500 or more	$5,000 or more of nontaxable Social Security or other nontaxable pensions, annuities, or disability income
Married Filing Jointly if only one spouse qualifies for the credit	$20,000 or more	$5,000 or more of nontaxable Social Security or other nontaxable pensions, annuities, or disability income
Married Filing Jointly if both spouses qualify for the credit	$25,000 or more	$7,500 or more of nontaxable Social Security or other nontaxable pensions, annuities, or disability income
Married Filing Separately and the taxpayer did not live with spouse any time during the year	$12,500 or more	$3,750 or more of nontaxable Social Security or other nontaxable pensions, annuities, or disability income

Example 1. Adam retired on disability as a salesperson, and he now works as a daycare provider assistant earning minimum wage. Although he does different work, Adam is a daycare provider assistant on ordinary terms for minimum wage. Thus, he cannot take the credit because he is engaged in a substantial gainful activity.

Example 2. Jess retired on disability and took a job with a former employer on a trial basis. The trial period lasted for some time, during which Jess was paid at a rate equal to minimum wage. Due to Jess's disability, he performed light-duty of a nonproductive, make-work nature. Unless the activity is both substantial and gainful, Jess is not engaged in a substantial, gainful activity. The activity was gainful because Jess's payment was at or above the minimum wage rate. However, the activity was not substantial because the duties were of a nonproductive, make-work nature. More information is needed to determine if Jess can engage in a substantial gainful activity.

How to Calculate the Credit

If the taxpayer checked box 6, the total amount entered on line 11 would be $5,000. If the taxpayer checked boxes 2, 4, or 9, then enter the total amount of disability income received. If the taxpayer checked box 5, enter the total amount of disability income received from the taxpayer and spouse on line 11.

Adoption Credit or Exclusion

The maximum adoption credit amount a taxpayer can receive from their employer is $14,440. Suppose the taxpayer's modified adjusted gross income (MAGI) is between $216,660 and $256,660; in that case, the credit may be reduced based on income. A taxpayer can use the adoption credit for foreign and domestic adoptions in most circumstances. Some states have determined that if a child has special needs, the taxpayer may receive the maximum amount of the credit unless they claimed some expenses in a prior year. Use Form 8839.

Child Tax Credits

The child tax credit (CTC) is a nonrefundable credit for taxpayers who have a qualifying child. ARPA made major changes to the Child Tax Credit (CTC). For tax year 2021, the credit increased from $2,000 to $3,000 per child between the ages of 6 and 17 at the end of 2021. Children under the age of 6 will receive $3,600 per qualifying child.

The phaseout amounts have been increased to $150,000 for married taxpayers filing a joint return and qualifying widow(ers). Head of household phaseout is $112,500 and $75,000 for all other taxpayers. The taxpayer's tax liability and modified AGI limits the child tax credit. If the child were not issued a valid Social Security number, they would not qualify the taxpayer for either credit. This credit is reported on Form 1040, line 19.

To be a qualifying child for the child tax credit and the additional child tax credit, the child must be a citizen, national, or resident of the United States. The taxpayer completes the substantial presence test (Part I) if the taxpayer has a dependent that has an ITIN and if the taxpayer is claiming the child tax credit for the dependent. If the dependent does not qualify for the child tax credit, the taxpayer cannot include that dependent in the calculation for the credit. However, the dependent may still qualify for the Other Dependent Credit (ODC).

The Additional Child Tax Credit (ACTC) is a refundable credit available for taxpayers with qualifying children. It cannot claim the full child tax credit due to a tax liability limitation. The maximum refund amount per child is $1,400. Due to the TCJA, the earned income threshold has decreased from $3,000 to $2,500. The taxpayer should use Schedule 8812, Parts II-III to calculate the additional child tax credit. Part I of the schedule is independent of Parts II-III. For the child tax credit and the additional child tax credit, TCJA increased the gross income phaseout amount to $400,000 for joint filers and $200,000 for all other filers. This credit is reported on Form 1040, line 28.

ARPA made major changes to the Child Tax Credit (CTC). For tax year 2021, the credit increases from $2,000 to $3,000 per child between the ages of 6 and 17 at the end of 2021. Children under the age of 6 will receive $3,600 per qualifying child. The phaseout amounts have been increased to $150,000 for married taxpayers filing a joint return and qualifying widow(ers). Head of Household phaseout is $112,500 and $75,000 for all other taxpayers.

Advanced payments of this credit could be taken monthly from July through December. The credit could be up to 50% of the taxpayer's child tax credit based on the 2019 or 2020 tax return. The advanced payments are only available for taxpayers living in the United States for at least six months of the year. Claiming the Advanced Child Tax Credit using a U.S. address may affect the taxpayer's Child Tax Credit and make the taxpayer return the advanced payments. If the taxpayer does not qualify for the ACTC, the TCJA thresholds apply. Taxpayers who received the advanced payments will be mailed an IRS Letter 6419 declaring the amount of the advanced payments received. If the taxpayer files a joint return, each spouse would receive a letter claiming half of what was sent. The tax preparer needs both letters to report the accurate amount.

Qualifying Child for Child Tax Credit

For a child to qualify for the child tax credit, they must meet the following conditions:

- ➤ The child is the son, daughter, stepchild, eligible foster child, brother, sister, stepbrother, stepsister, half-brother, half-sister, or a descendent of any of these.
- ➤ The child was 17 and under for tax year 2021 only.
- ➤ The child did not provide over half of their support.
- ➤ The child lived with the taxpayer for more than half of 2021.
- ➤ The child is claimed as a dependent on the taxpayer's return.
- ➤ The child does not file a joint return for the year or only files to claim a refund of withheld income tax or if the dependent paid estimated payments.
- ➤ The child was a U.S. citizen, U.S. national, U.S. resident alien, or adopted by a U.S. citizen, U.S. national, or U.S. resident alien.

Qualifying Person for the ODC

An individual qualifies for the Other Dependent Credit (ODC) if they meet the following conditions:

- ➤ The taxpayer claims the individual as a dependent on their tax return.
- ➤ The dependent is ineligible for the CTC or the ACTC.
- ➤ The dependent was a U.S. citizen, U.S. national, U.S. resident alien or adopted by a U.S. citizen, U.S. national, or U.S. resident alien.
- ➤ They have a TIN on or before the due date of the 2021 tax return.

Payments and Tax Credits

Example: Levi is claiming his 10-year-old nephew Fernando, who lives in Mexico and qualifies as Levi's dependent. Because Fernando is not a U.S. citizen, U.S. national, or a U.S. resident alien, Levi cannot use Fernando to claim the Other Dependent Credit (ODC) unless Levi adopts him, and Fernando comes to live with Levi in the United States.

Improperly Claiming the CTC, ODC, or ACTC

If the taxpayer has claimed any of these credits in error, they may be prohibited from claiming these credits for two years. If the error is determined to be fraud, they may be prohibited from claiming the credit for 10 years. The taxpayer may also have to pay penalties and interest. If the tax preparer committed the error and the IRS determines that the error was intentional, the tax preparer will be charged penalties and interest and may be prohibited from preparing returns for as long as the IRS decides it is appropriate.

CTC or ACTC tax returns after 2015 that were denied or reduced for any reason except a clerical or mathematical error will have to file Form 8862 and attach the form to their tax return. Beginning in 2018, the ODC has been added to both the due diligence questionnaire and part III of Form 8862, *Information to Claim Certain Credits After Disallowance*.

Part 2 Review Questions

To obtain the maximum benefit from this chapter, LTP recommends that you complete each of the following questions and then compare them to the answers with feedback that immediately follows. Under governing self-study standards, vendors are required to present review questions intermittently throughout each self-study course.

These questions and explanations are not part of the final examination and will not be graded by LTP.

TCPP2.1
Which of the following is a nonrefundable credit?

a. American opportunity act
b. Mortgage Interest Credit
c. Earned income tax credit
d. Residential energy credit

TCPP2.2
Olivia is single and wants to know if she qualifies for the Credit for the Elderly or Disabled. To qualify for the credit, Olivia's adjusted gross income cannot be more than _____ to qualify.

a. $17,000
b. $17,500
c. $20,000
d. $25,000

TCPP2.3
Which of the following is only for tax year 2021?

a. Child Tax Credit increase
b. Refundable Advanced Child Tax Credit
c. Other Dependent Credit is refundable
d. Child Tax Credit is refundable

TCPP2.4
Russel is a single dad and has three children between the ages of 7 – 17. He also claims a son in Mexico is living in the United States. IRS determined that he filed a fraudulent tax return. Which of the following could happen to Russel?

1. Russel could be prohibited from claiming credits for two years.
2. Russel could be prohibited from claiming credits for ten years.
3. Russel will be charged penalties and interest.
4. Russel could be prohibited from claiming credits for eight years.
5. Russel will have to file Form 8862 for two years.
6. Russel will have to file Form 8862 for ten years.

1, 3 & 5
1 – 4
1, 2, 3, 5 & 6
2, 4, & 6

Part 2 Review Questions Answers

TCPP2.1
Which of the following is a nonrefundable credit?

a. American opportunity act
b. Mortgage Interest Credit
c. Earned income tax credit
d. Residential energy credit

Feedback: Review section *Part 2: Other Nonrefundable Credits.*

TCPP2.2
Olivia is single and wants to know if she qualifies for the Credit for the Elderly or Disabled. To qualify for the credit, Olivia's adjusted gross income cannot be more than_____to qualify.

a. $17,000
b. $17,500
c. $20,000
d. $25,000

Feedback: Review section *Schedule R: Credit for the Elderly or Disabled.*

TCPP2.3
Which of the following is only for tax year 2021?

   a. Child Tax Credit increase
   b. Refundable Advanced Child Tax Credit
   c. Other Dependent Credit is refundable
   d. Child Tax Credit is refundable

Feedback: Review section *Part 2: Other Nonrefundable Credits.*

TCPP2.4
Russel is a single dad and has three children between the ages of 7 – 17. He also claims a son in Mexico is living in the United States. IRS determined that he filed a fraudulent tax return. Which of the following could happen to Russel?

   1. Russel could be prohibited from claiming credits for two years.
   2. Russel could be prohibited from claiming credits for ten years.
   3. Russel will be charged penalties and interest.
   4. Russel could be prohibited from claiming credits for eight years.
   5. Russel will have to file Form 8862 for two years.
   6. Russel will have to file Form 8862 for ten years.

1, 3, & 5
1 – 4
1, 2, 3, 5 & 6
2, 4, & 6

Feedback: Review section *Part 2: Other Nonrefundable Credits.*

Part 3 Payments and Refundable Tax Credits

In the tax industry, the term "refundable credit" refers to a credit that allows the taxpayer to lower their tax liability dollar-for-dollar to zero and below, resulting in a refund. When the refundable credit exceeds the amount of taxes owed, it could result in a tax refund.

A refundable tax credit is a tax credit that is treated as a payment and can be refunded to the taxpayer by the IRS. Refundable tax credits offset certain taxes that are normally not reduced. Refundable credits can produce a larger federal tax refund than the amount of money a person paid during the year. Refundable tax credits, like payments, are applied toward a person's tax obligation, and any overpayments are refunded back to the individual. Withholding for federal income taxes and estimated taxes are also refundable credits, as these are prepayments toward a person's annual tax liability that can and will be refunded to the taxpayer if they withhold too much.

Federal Income Tax Withheld

Form 1040, page 2, line 25, reports the federal income tax withheld from all income reported by forms such as the W-2, W-2G, 1099-R, 1099-NEC, SSA-1099, and Schedule K. The amount of tax withheld is on Form W-2 in box 2 and on the Form 1099 series in box 4. If the taxpayer had federal tax withheld from Social Security benefits, it is in box 6 of Form SSA-1099. If the taxpayer had additional Medicare tax withheld by their employer, that amount shows on Form 1040, Schedule 2, line 11. Calculate the additional Medicare tax on Form 8959 and attach it to the return.

Estimated Tax Payments

Form 1040, page 2, line 26, reports any estimated tax payments made in the current tax year and any overpayments applied from the prior year's tax return. If a taxpayer and their spouse have divorced during the current tax year and made estimated payments together, enter the former spouse's SSN in the space provided on the front of Form 1040. The taxpayer should attach a statement to Form 1040 explaining that the divorced couple made the payments together; that statement should also contain proof of payments, the name, and SSN of the individual making the payments.

Estimated tax payments are also referred to as quarterlies since the payments are due in four equal payments. If the due dates fall on a Saturday, Sunday, or a legal holiday, estimated payments are due on the next business day. Estimated payments are due on the following dates:

- April 15th
- June 15th
- September 15th
- January 15th (of the following year)

Amount Overpaid

The taxpayer can receive their overpayment as a paper check from the U.S. Treasury Department or through a direct deposit from the U.S. Treasury Department into a checking or savings account. After filing the tax return electronically, the taxpayer can go to www.irs.gov and click "Where's My Refund?" to receive information that is available about their return within 24 hours after its acceptance. If the overpayment amount is different than what the taxpayer was expecting, the taxpayer should receive an explanation from the IRS within two weeks after depositing the refund.

Form 1040, page 2, line 34, states if there was an overpayment of current-year taxes and indicates how the taxpayer would like to receive the overpayment refund. Enter on Line 35a the desired refund amount the taxpayer wants. They can select a portion of that amount as a refund and forward the rest as estimated tax payments for the following tax year. Use line 36 to enter the desired estimated payments. The taxpayer can also elect to carry forward their entire refund amount. If the taxpayer wants to carry out overpayments to the following year, enter the amount they would like to have applied on Form 1040, line 36. Suppose a couple filed MFJ, and a taxpayer's spouse wants the overpayment applied to her account. In that case, the refund amount splits to the taxpayer's account and the spouse's separate account. The taxpayer can include up to three bank accounts on Part I in Form 8888. Use Part II to purchase U.S. Series I Savings Bonds.

Payments and Tax Credits

Example: Pat made estimated payments for the current tax year of $11,000 and overpaid her quarterlies by $4,500. Pat wants $2,000 refunded, so enter $2,000 on Line 36. Pat would like the remaining $2,500 applied to next year's estimated payments, so enter the $2,500 amount on Line 35a.

If the taxpayer wants to deposit the entire overpayment directly, submit a valid routing number and account number. A routing number is a nine-digit number that indicates which financial institute receives the direct deposit refund. The account number is specific to the taxpayer. The first two digits of the routing number have to be 01 through 12 or 21 through 32. Some financial institutions have a separate routing number for direct deposits. If there is no entry on Form 1040, Page 2, line 35b or line 35d, the taxpayer will receive a paper check.

The routing number on a deposit slip may differ from the routing number on the bottom of a personal check. If the tax preparer is entering the numbers from the bottom of the check, make sure you do not enter the check number when entering the account number. On Form 1040, be sure to indicate whether the account is a checking or savings account. The IRS will allow the taxpayer to have their direct deposit split between multiple accounts, but not all software supports the use of Form 8888 to do so.

If any of the following happen, the financial institution rejects the direct deposit, and the IRS sends a paper check to the taxpayer instead:

➢ Any numbers or letters on lines 35b or 35d are crossed out, or some type of correction material (such as correction tape or white-out) has been used.
➢ The taxpayer's financial institution(s) will not allow a joint return to be deposited to an individual account; The U.S. Treasury Department is not responsible if the financial institution rejects the direct deposit.
➢ Three direct deposits have already been made to that account.
➢ The name on the account does not match the name on the tax refund.

Señor 1040 Says: The IRS is not responsible for a lost refund if the account information is entered incorrectly. The taxpayer is responsible for making sure that his or her routing number and account number are accurate, and that the financial institution will accept the direct deposit.

Returns with Refunds

When individual taxpayers have an overpayment on their current-year tax return, they have several options for receiving the overpayment:

- They can apply the overpayment to next year's estimated tax return.
- They can receive a paper check.
- They can receive a direct deposit.
- Although not all software supports it, they can divide the refund amount into different bank accounts.

Direct Deposit

Taxpayers may have refunds deposited into their checking or savings accounts. The tax professional must have the taxpayer's account number, routing number, and the financial institution's name to directly deposit the refund. All this information is on a taxpayer's check.

Form 8888, *Allocation of Refund*, allows the taxpayer to split and deposit refunds into multiple accounts. You can file Form 8888 electronically. A qualified account can be a checking or savings account or other accounts such as a money market account or an IRA. The taxpayer should not try to deposit money into an account not in their name directly. This form is limited to three accounts and can also be used to purchase U.S. Series I Savings Bonds.

Direct Deposit Limits

The IRS has imposed a limit of three direct deposits that can be electronically deposited into a single financial account or loaded on a pre-paid debit card. Any further deposits will be converted to a paper check and mailed to the taxpayer within four weeks. Taxpayers will receive a notification via mailed letter that their account has exceeded the direct deposit limit.

The IRS has imposed this direct deposit limit to prevent criminals from obtaining multiple refunds. The new limitations also protect taxpayers from tax preparers who illegally obtain their tax preparation fees by using Form 8888 to split the refund into multiple accounts. Tax preparers who do this will be subject to a fine.

Señor 1040 Says: The IRS will send refunds under $1 only if requested in writing.

Payments and Tax Credits

If the taxpayer files a joint return and either the taxpayer or the spouse has an offset of bad debt to pay, the other spouse may be an injured spouse, a term and concept that is beyond the scope of this course. If the IRS took one spouse's refund to pay the other spouse's tax liability, the injured spouse would file Form 8379 to see if they meet the conditions to get their portion of the refund back from the IRS.

Amount Paid with a Request for Extension

If the taxpayer used Form 4868 to file an extension and is making a payment, report the payment amount with the extension on Form 1040, Schedule 3, line 10. Do not include the taxpayer's fees when the individual pays by debit or credit card.

> *Señor 1040 Says:* If the taxpayer itemizes his deductions and paid by credit or debit card, the convenience fees are no longer a deduction on Schedule A.

Excess Social Security or Railroad Retirement Tax Withheld

When a taxpayer has more than one employer, it is possible that the employers withhold too much for Social Security or Railroad Retirement Tax Act (RRTA) benefits. If that is the case, the taxpayer may claim the excess payment on Form 1040, Schedule 3, line 9, as a refundable credit. If, however, one employer withholds too much tax for Social Security or Railroad Retirement Tax Act, the employer makes the adjustment for the employee. Even if the employer does not refund the extra withholding to the employee, the taxpayer cannot adjust their income tax form but must instead file Form 843 to claim the refund.

The taxpayer is entitled to the credit if they had more than one employer and exceeded the following withholding limits for 2021:

- $142,800 in wages subject to Social Security and tier 1 RRTA withholding taxes of $8,853.60 or less.
- $106,200 in wages subject to tier 2 RRTA withholding tax of $5,203.80 or less. This rule applies only to railroad employees. To calculate the over-withholding, see the worksheet for railroad retirement tax withholding in Publication 505, *Tax Withholding and Estimated Tax*.

All wages are subject to Medicare tax withholding.

Earned Income Credit (EIC)

The earned income credit (EIC), also referred to as earned income tax credit (EITC), is a refundable tax credit for low- to moderate-income working individuals and families. When the EIC exceeds the amount of taxes owed, it results in a refundable credit. Report the EIC on Form 1040, page 2, line 27.

Twenty-eight states and the District of Columbia have an EITC program. Most use federal eligibility rules, and their version of the credit parallels major elements of the federal structure. In most states and localities, the credit is refundable (as is federal), although, in a few areas, the EITC is used only to offset taxes owed. For more information, go to www.irs.gov/eitc. The taxpayer must have earned income during the tax year to be eligible for the earned income tax credit. If a married couple is filing a joint return, and only one spouse worked, both would still meet the earned income requirement.

Remember, earned income is income the taxpayer received for working and includes the following types of income:

- Wages, salaries, tips, and other types of taxable employee pay.
- Net earnings from self-employment.
- Gross income received as a statutory employee.
- Union strike benefits.
- Long-term disability benefits received before reaching the minimum retirement age.

Unearned income includes the following:

- Interest and dividends.
- Pensions and annuities.
- Social Security and railroad retirement benefits (including disability benefits).
- Alimony and child support.
- Welfare benefits.
- Workers' compensation benefits.
- Unemployment compensation.
- Income while an inmate.
- Workfare payments (see Publication 596 for a definition).

A taxpayer and their spouse, if filing jointly, must have a valid SSN to qualify for the earned income tax credit. If the SSN says, "Not valid for employment," and if the SSN was issued so that the taxpayer or spouse could receive aid from a federally funded program, they do not qualify to receive earned income credit. If the SSN says, "Valid for work only with INS authorization," or "Valid only with DHS authorization," then the SSN is valid, but only if the authorization has not expired.

Community Property

Taxpayers who live in a community property state could qualify for Head of Household if the couple has lived apart for at least the last six months of the year. A taxpayer's earned income for EIC does not include any amount earned by their spouse, even though income belongs to the spouse under the state's community property laws and is not earned income for EIC purposes. The taxpayer, however, must include it with all their earned income on the federal tax return. The same rules apply to taxpayers living in Nevada, Washington, and California who are Registered Domestic Partners (RDP's).

The IRS may ask the taxpayer to provide additional documentation to prove that the qualifying dependents belong to the taxpayer. The IRS might ask for the following documents:

- Birth certificate.
- School records.
- Medical records.

During the initial interview, tax professionals should inform their clients what they might need if the IRS audits their claim for EIC. If a taxpayer receives an audit letter, the letter will include the taxpayer's name, address, telephone number, and the name of the IRS employee responsible for the taxpayer's audit. This process will delay the client's refund. If the taxpayer is found to fraudulently claim the EIC, the taxpayer will be denied the credit for the current tax year and for the next nine years after that.

Minister's Housing

The housing allowance provided to a minister as part of the minister's pay is generally not subject to income tax. Still, net earnings from self-employment include this pay; therefore, it is earned income for EIC.

Earned Income Rules

To qualify for EIC, the taxpayer's adjusted gross income (AGI) must be below a certain amount, and the taxpayer (and spouse if married filing jointly) must meet the following requirements:

- Have a valid Social Security number (if filing MFJ, the spouse must also have a valid SSN).
- Have earned income from employment or self-employment income.
- Not file as Married filing separately (MFS).
- File MFJ as a U.S. citizen, as a resident alien all year, or as a nonresident alien married to a U.S. citizen.
- Not file Form 2555 or Form 2555-EZ.
- Not have investment income over $10,000.
- Have a qualifying child who meets the four dependent tests (age, relationship, residency, and joint return; see "Qualifying Child" below).
    - Be at least age 25 and under age 65 at the end of the year.
    - Live in the United States for more than half the year.
    - Not qualify as a dependent of another person.
- The AGI must be less than:
    - $51,464 ($57,414 MFJ) with three or more qualifying children.
    - $47,915 ($53,865 MFJ) with two qualifying children.
    - $42,158 ($48,108 MFJ) with one qualifying child.
    - $21,430 ($27,380 MFJ) with no qualifying children.

The maximum EIC that a married filing joint taxpayer can receive with three or more qualifying children is $6,728.

Valid Social Security Number

The qualifying child must have a valid Social Security number (SSN) issued by the Social Security Administration (SSA) unless a child died in the same year they were born. Social Security cards with the legend "not valid for employment" are issued to aliens who are not eligible to work in the United States but who need an SSN so they can get a federally funded benefit such as Medicaid. Suppose the immigration status of a taxpayer or spouse has changed to U.S. citizen or permanent resident. In that case, the taxpayer should ask the SSA for a new Social Security card without the legend. If the SSN says, "valid for work only with INS authorization or DHS authorization," this is considered a valid SSN, and the taxpayer may qualify for the credit. Taxpayers with an ITIN do not qualify for EIC.

Uniform Definition of a Qualifying Child

The Working Families Tax Relief Act of 2004, amended in 2008, added the joint return test and standardized the definition of a qualifying child for the five child-related tax benefits. The tax law also defined exceptions and special rules for dependents with a disability, children of divorced parents, and adopted children (always treated as the taxpayer's child), including a child lawfully placed with the taxpayer for adoption.

Taxpayers that have missing or kidnapped children that a non-family member abducted may still claim the child. The IRS treats a kidnapped child as living with the taxpayer for more than half of the year if the child lived with the taxpayer for more than half of the part of the year before the date of the kidnapping, even if that length of time does not amount to half of a year. For example, if they kidnap a child on March 1, the parent can still claim the child if they lived with the taxpayer for at least half of the two months (January and February) preceding the date of the kidnapping.

Although there are five tests to claim a dependent, a qualifying child must meet only four of the dependent tests to qualify for the EIC:

- Relationship
- Age
- Residency
- Joint return

To review these tests' rules and guidelines, please refer to "The Filing Status, Dependents, and Deductions" Chapter.

Foster Child

To receive the EIC, a person is the taxpayer's foster child if the child is placed with the taxpayer by a judgment, decree, other order of any court of competent jurisdiction, or by an authorized placement agency such as a state or local government agency, a tax-exempt organization licensed by a state, an Indian tribal government, or an organization authorized by an Indian tribal government to place Indian children.

Example: Allison, who is 12-years-old, was placed in the taxpayer's care two years ago by an authorized agency responsible for placing children in foster homes. Allison is the taxpayer's eligible foster child because she was placed there by an authorized licensed agency.

A Qualifying Child of More than One Person

Sometimes a child meets the rules to be a qualifying child of more than one person. However, only one person can use a qualifying child to claim the EIC. If two eligible taxpayers have the same qualifying child, they can decide who will take all the following related tax benefits:

- The child's exemption.
- The child tax credit.
- Head of Household filing status.
- The credit for child and dependent care expenses.
- The exclusion for dependent care benefits.
- The Earned Income Credit.

Only one taxpayer can claim these benefits, and they must claim either all of them or none of them. Do not divide the benefits between the two competing taxpayers. The tie-breaker rule applies if the taxpayer and the other person(s) cannot agree and if more than one person claims the EIC or other benefits using the same child. However, the tie-breaker rule does not apply if the other person is the taxpayer's spouse and files a joint return.

If the taxpayer and someone else have the same qualifying child, but the other person cannot claim the EIC because the taxpayer is not eligible or because his or her earned income or AGI was too high, the child is a qualifying child for the taxpayer. Suppose a taxpayer's EIC is denied because the qualifying child is treated as the qualifying child of another person for the current tax year. In that case, they can attempt to claim the EIC if they have another, separate qualifying child. However, the taxpayer cannot take the EIC using the qualifying child that another individual claimed.

Example: Pedro has two children, Nora from his first marriage to Darla and a son named Francisco from his current marriage to Martha. Even if Pedro and Darla agree to let Darla claim the EIC for Nora, Pedro can still claim the EIC for his son Francisco, and Pedro is not prohibited from claiming Francisco simply because he chose to give up his claim to Nora.

Tie-Breaker Rules

The tie-breaker rules covered in Chapter 4 also apply to the EIC.

Example: 25-year-old Jeannie and her five-year-old son, Billy, lived with Jeannie's mother, Sarah, all year. Jeannie is unmarried, and her AGI is $8,100. Her only source of income was from a part-time job. Sarah's AGI was $20,000 from her job. Billy's father did not live with Billy or Jeannie. Billy is a qualifying child of both Jeannie and Sarah since he meets the relationship, age, residency, and joint return tests. Jeannie and Sarah must decide who will claim Billy as their dependent. If Jeannie does not claim Billy as a qualifying child for the EIC or Head of household filing status, Jeannie's mother can claim Billy as a qualifying child for each of those tax benefits for which she qualifies. Remember that the dependent test for support does not apply to the EIC.

Special Rule for Divorced or Separated Parents

The special rules covered in Chapter 4 that apply to divorced or separated parents trying to claim an exemption for a dependent do not apply to the EIC. For more information, see Publication 501 and Publication 596.

The Taxpayer as a Qualifying Child of Another Person

To review how to determine if a taxpayer is a qualifying child of another person, refer to Chapter 4. If the taxpayer (or spouse filing a joint return) is a qualifying child of another person, the taxpayer or spouse cannot claim the EIC. This rule is true even if the person for whom the taxpayer or spouse is a qualifying child does not claim the EIC or meet all the rules to claim the EIC. Write "No" beside line 64a (Form 1040) to show that the taxpayer does not qualify.

Example: Max and his daughter, Letty, lived with Max's mother all year. Max is 22-years-old and attended a trade school full time. Max had a part-time job, earned $5,100, and had no other income. Because Max meets the relationship, age, and residency tests, he is a qualifying child of his mother, and she can claim the EIC if she meets all the other requirements. Because the taxpayer is his mother's qualifying child, he cannot claim the EIC for his daughter.

EIC for Taxpayers without Qualifying Children

Taxpayers who do not have qualifying children may also be eligible for the EIC. To be eligible for the EIC, the taxpayer must meet the following conditions:

- The taxpayer must be at least 18-years-old at the end of 2021 (the age requirement changed for tax year 2021. If the taxpayer is filing a joint return; however, it is not required that both the taxpayer and the spouse meet the age requirement).
- The taxpayer must not be dependent on another person.
- The taxpayer must not be the qualifying child of another person.
- The taxpayers must have resided in the United States for more than half of the year.
- Maximum income should be more than $21,430 or $27,380 if married filing jointly.

Schedule EIC Worksheets

Taxpayers eligible for the EIC with qualifying children must complete Schedule EIC. Schedule EIC requires including the child's name, Social Security number, year of birth, the number of months lived in the home located in the United States, and the child's relationship to the taxpayer. Schedule EIC must be attached to the taxpayer's Form 1040. The taxpayer's income must be less than the threshold amounts to qualify for EIC. Worksheets are available to help with the calculations of the EIC, and completing the EIC worksheets is essential to determining the amount of credit a taxpayer may claim on their return. The completed worksheet should be placed in the client's file and not be attached to the federal tax return. The IRS has the EIC worksheets on its website. If the taxpayer files Form 1040 Schedule SE, the taxpayer must complete EIC Worksheet B, found in Instructions Form 1040. Generally, all other taxpayers would figure their earned income by using Worksheet A of the Form 1040 Instructions.

EIC Disallowed

There are circumstances when the IRS does not allow the EIC. Some of the most common reasons for disallowance of the EIC include:

- Claiming a child who does not meet all the qualifying child tests.
- The Social Security numbers are mismatched or incorrect.

- o Example: A couple is married during the current tax year, and they file their tax return under the spouse's married name; however, the wife did not change her name with the Social Security Administration, so her Social Security number is assigned with her maiden name listed, making the information on the return incorrect.
➤ Filing as Single or Head of Household when the taxpayer is married.
➤ Over- or underreporting income.

If the taxpayer's EIC has been denied or reduced for any year after 1996 for any reason other than a mathematical error, the taxpayer will have to complete Form 8862, *Information to Claim Earned Income Credit after Disallowance,* and attach it to their tax return. When interviewing the taxpayer, the tax preparer should ask if the taxpayer has ever received a notice from the IRS or filed Form 8862 in any year after 1996. If the taxpayer has received a notice that the EIC was denied or reduced from a previous tax year, the preparer should complete Form 8862 to claim the credit again if the taxpayer is eligible.

The purpose of Form 8862 is to claim the EIC after it has been disallowed or reduced in an earlier year. Form 8862 must be attached to the tax return if all the following apply:

➤ The EIC was reduced or disallowed for any reason other than a mathematical or clerical error for a year after 1996.
➤ The taxpayer wants to claim the EIC and meet all the requirements.

The taxpayer must attach Schedule EIC and Form 8862 to the return if the taxpayer has any qualifying children. The taxpayer may be asked for additional information before a refund is issued. If the IRS contacts the taxpayer to request additional information, and the taxpayer does not provide the necessary information or documentation, the taxpayer will receive a statutory notice of deficiency from the IRS. The notice explains that an adjustment will be assessed unless the taxpayer files a petition in the tax court within 90 days. If the taxpayer fails to reply to the IRS or file a petition within 90 days, the IRS will deny their petition for the EIC and assess to determine how much tax they might owe.

EIC Taxpayer Penalties

The IRS may penalize the taxpayer if it determines that the taxpayer has been negligent or has disregarded rules or regulations relating to the EIC. The taxpayer may be prohibited from claiming EIC for the next two years if they are found negligent. If the taxpayer has fraudulently claimed the credit, the taxpayer will be prohibited from claiming the credit for the next ten years.

The tax preparer may be assessed penalties for not performing their due diligence.

Example: Brittni claimed the EIC on the 2020 tax return that she filed in February 2021. The IRS determined that she was not entitled to the EIC due to fraud. She received a statutory notice of deficiency in September 2021, telling her the adjustment amount that would be assessed unless she filed a petition in the tax court within 90 days. The IRS determined that Brittni did not file her petition, and she was prohibited from claiming the EIC on her return, for ten years, until 2031. In that year, she will have to complete and attach Form 8862 to her return to claim the credit again.

Claiming a Child in Error

The most common error is to claim a child that is not a qualifying child and does not meet the tests. The knowledge requirement for paid tax preparers states that the preparer must apply a reasonable standard (as defined by Circular 230 and the Form 8867 Instructions) to the information received from the client. If the information provided by the client appears to be incorrect, incomplete, or inconsistent, then the paid preparer must make additional inquiries of the client until they are satisfied that they have gathered the correct and complete information.

Example 1: Cindy tells Jack, her tax preparer, that she is 22-years-old and has two sons, aged 10 and 11. Jack may need to ask Cindy the following questions:

- Are these Cindy's biological children, foster sons, or adopted sons?
- Was Cindy ever married to the children's father?
- Were the children placed in Cindy's home for adoption or as foster children?
- Did the father live with Cindy?
- How long have the children lived with Cindy?
- Does Cindy have any records to prove that the children lived with her, such as school or medical records?

Example 2: Maria tells Andres, her tax preparer, that last year she filed Single and claimed the EIC for her child, but that this year she has two children to claim for EIC. Andres may need to ask Maria the following questions:

- You claimed one child last year. What changed?
- How many months did the children live with you?
- Do you have any records to prove the children living with you, such as school or medical records?

Nontaxable Combat Pay Election for EIC

Nontaxable combat pay for armed forces members is only considered earned income for the EIC if they elect to include nontaxable combat pay in earned income to increase or decrease the EIC. Figure the credit with and without the nontaxable combat pay before making the election. If the taxpayer makes the election, they must include all nontaxable combat pay as earned income. Examples of nontaxable military pay are combat pay, basic allowance for housing (BAH), and the basic allowance for subsistence (BAS). Combat pay is reported on Form W-2 in box 12 with code Q.

Part 3 Review Questions

To obtain the maximum benefit from this chapter, LTP recommends that you complete each of the following questions and then compare them to the answers with feedback that immediately follows. Under governing self-study standards, vendors are required to present review questions intermittently throughout each self-study course.

These questions and explanations are not part of the final examination and will not be graded by LTP.

Payments and Tax Credits

TCPP3.1
Refundable credits are considered payments toward the taxpayer's liability. Which of the following does not lower the taxpayer's liability?

a. Earned Income Tax Credit
b. Excess CASDI
c. Additional Child Tax Credit
d. American Opportunity Credit

TCPP3.2
Estimated payments are due in four equal payments. Which of the following is not a due date for estimated tax payments?

a. April 15th
b. September 15th
c. June 15th
d. December 15th

TCPP3.3
Which of the following is a refundable tax credit?

a. Lifetime learning credit
b. Child tax credit
c. Retirement savings contribution credit
d. Additional child tax credit

TCPP3.4
Which of the following could qualify the taxpayer for EIC?

a. 6-year-old with an ITIN
b. 12-year-old with an SSN and lives in Mexico
c. 30-year-old and partially disabled
d. A 23-year-old full-time student attending a qualifying college

TCPP3.5
Which taxpayer would not qualify for EIC?

a. Dependent with a valid ITIN
b. Cannot file MFS
c. Investment income under $3,400
d. Have earned income

TCPP3.6
Which taxpayer could qualify for EIC?

a. 68-year-old single with an income of $10,395
b. MFJ with two children and an income of $59,292
c. MFJ with three children, an income of $19,589, and qualifying children do not live with the taxpayer
d. HH with one child, age 23, and going to school full-time, with an income of $17,422

Part 3 Review Questions Answers

TCPP3.1
Refundable credits are considered payments toward the taxpayer's liability. Which of the following does not lower the taxpayer's liability?

a. Earned Income Tax Credit
b. Excess CASDI
c. Additional Child Tax Credit
d. American Opportunity Credit

Feedback: Review section *Part 3: Refundable Tax Credits and Payments.*

TCPP3.2
Estimated payments are due in four equal payments. Which of the following is not a due date for estimated tax payments?

a. April 15th
b. September 15th
c. June 15th
d. December 15th

Feedback: Review section *Estimated Tax Payments.*

TCPP3.3
Which of the following is a refundable tax credit?

a. Lifetime learning credit
b. Child tax credit
c. Retirement savings contribution credit
d. Additional child tax credit

Feedback: Review section *Child and Dependent Credits.*

TCPP3.4
Which of the following could qualify the taxpayer for EIC?

a. 6-year-old with an ITIN
b. 12-year-old with an SSN and lives in Mexico
c. 30-year-old and partially disabled
d. A 23-year-old full-time student attending a qualifying college

Feedback: Review section *Qualifying Child for Child Tax Credit.*

TCPP3.5
Which taxpayer would not qualify for EIC?

a. Dependent with a valid ITIN
b. Cannot file MFS
c. Investment income under $3,400
d. Have earned income

Feedback: Review section *Child and Dependent Credits.*

TCPP3.6
Which taxpayer could qualify for EIC?

   a. 68-year-old single with an income of $10,395
   b. MFJ with two children and an income of $59,292
   c. MFJ with three children, an income of $19,589, and qualifying children do not live with the taxpayer
   d. **HH with one child, age 23, and going to school full-time, with an income of $17,422**

Feedback: Review section *Earned Income Rules*.

Takeaways

A tax credit reduces the amount of tax the taxpayer is liable for. Unlike a deduction, which reduces the amount of income subject to tax, a tax credit directly reduces the taxpayer's liability. A tax credit is a sum deducted from the total amount a taxpayer owes. There are two categories of tax credits: nonrefundable and refundable.

There are a variety of credits and deductions for the taxpayer. This lesson covered a few credits that allow taxpayers to lower their tax liability to zero and below and possibly receive a refund from the credits. A refundable credit is a tax credit treated as a payment and can thus be refunded to the taxpayer by the IRS. Refundable credits can help offset certain types of taxes that normally cannot be reduced and can even produce a federal refund.

TEST YOUR KNOWLEDGE!
Go online to take a practice quiz.

Chapter 8 Itemized Deductions

Introduction

When computing taxable income, personal expenses cannot be claimed as itemized deductions; however, tax rules do allow for some deductions that are essential for daily living. These specific expenses are deductible as itemized deductions. A *standard deduction* is a set amount that the taxpayer can claim based on their filing status. *Itemized deductions* are shown on the tax return using Schedule A, *Itemized Deductions*. The taxpayer must decide whether to itemize deductions or use the standard deduction and should choose whichever option is best for their tax situation.

Itemized deductions are beneficial if the total amount is higher than the standard deduction. Some taxpayers must itemize deductions because they do not qualify for the standard deduction. Taxpayers not eligible to use the standard deduction include nonresident aliens and individuals who file a tax return for a period of less than 12 months. When a married couple files individual returns, if one spouse itemizes deductions, the other spouse must also itemize deductions. Even if standard deductions deliver the best option for them. See Publication 501, *Exemptions, Standard Deduction, and Filing Information*.

Objectives

At the end of this lesson, the student will:

- Explain which deductions are limited to the 7.5% floor.
- Identify which taxpayer is eligible to use Form 2106 after December 31, 2017, until December 31, 2025.
- Classify which taxpayer is eligible to use Form 3903 after December 31, 2017, until December 31, 2025.

Resources

Form 1040	Publication 17	Instructions Form 1040
Form 2106	Publication 463	Instructions Form 2106
Form 4684	Publication 502	Instructions Form 4684
Form 4952	Publication 526	Instructions Form 4952
Form 8283	Publication 529	Instructions Form 8283
Schedule A	Publication 530	Instructions for Schedule A
Publication 1771	Publication 936	Tax Topics 501–506, 508–515
Publication 597		

Table of Contents

Introduction	303
Part 1 Itemized Deductions	306
TCJA and Itemized Deductions	306
Itemizing While Married Filing Separate	306
Medical and Dental Expenses	307
Spouse and Dependent Medical Expenses	308
Medical Expense Reimbursement	308
Taxes Paid	309
State and Local General Sales Tax (SALT)	309
General Sales Tax	310
Real Estate Taxes	310
Personal Property Taxes	311
Other Taxes	311
Nondeductible Taxes and Fees	311
Home Mortgage Interest and Points	311
Grandfathered Debt	312
Mortgage Insurance Premiums	313
Form 1098: 2021	314
Part 1 Review Questions	314
Part 1 Review Questions Answers	315
Part 2 Charity and Casualty and Theft Losses	316
Gifts to Charity	317
Cash Contributions	317
Other Than by Cash or Check	318
Car Expenses	318
Canadian, Israeli, and Mexican Charities	319
Taxpayer Must Keep Records	319
Other Itemized Deductions	319
Gambling Losses	319
Casualty and Theft Losses	320
Disasters and Casualties	320
Disaster Relief	321
Tips on Reconstructing Tax Records for a Disaster	321
Other Helpful Agencies	321
Figuring Loss	322
Determining the Decrease in Fair Market Value	322
Casualty and Theft Losses of Income-Producing Property	323
Business Records	323
Investment Interest	323
Fines or Penalties	324
Part 2 Review Questions	324
Part 2 Review Questions Answers	325
Part 3 Form 2106: Employee Business Expenses and Other Expenses	326
Taxing Employee Expenses	327
Tax Home	328
Temporary Assignment or Job	328
Meals	328
Travel and Transportation Expenses	328
Entertainment	329
Business Gifts	329
Business Recordkeeping	330

- Reimbursements 330
- Other Expenses 330
- Tax Preparation Fees 330
- Education 330
- Part 3 Review Questions 331
- Part 3 Review Questions Answers 331

Takeaways 332

Part 1 Itemized Deductions

TCJA and Itemized Deductions

The Tax Cuts and Jobs Act (TCJA) has eliminated the overall limitation of itemized deductions based on the taxpayer's adjusted gross income. This was referred to as the deductions being "phased out" or "limited." The TCJA also changed the limitations that can impact the total itemized deduction amount; for example, the total amount that can be deducted from the state and local income tax on Schedule A, line 5, is now capped at $10,000 ($5,000 for MFS); taxpayers may not be able to include all of their expenses as deductions.

For example, in 2017, George's itemized deductions for his state and local taxes was $17,000. George's financial situation did not change, and he expected to be able to deduct the same amount in 2018. However, even though George would still have qualified for a $17,000 itemized deduction under the old rules, George will only receive a $10,000 deduction on line 5 under the TCJA. His deduction amount is capped. Taxpayers should itemize or consider itemizing if they meet the following criteria:

- Taxpayer would get a higher amount of deductions by itemizing.
- The taxpayer had large unreimbursed medical or dental expenses that amounted to more than 7.5% of their adjusted gross income.
- The taxpayer paid mortgage interest.
- The taxpayer paid points to discount the interest rate.
- The taxpayer had casualty or theft losses that were declared during a federal disaster.
- The taxpayer made contributions to qualified charities and has receipts for recordkeeping.
- The total of the taxpayer's itemized deductions is higher than the standard deduction to which the taxpayer is entitled.
- The taxpayer paid state and local taxes (may be capped).
- The taxpayer paid property taxes (may be capped).

Itemizing While Married Filing Separate

If taxpayers are filing MFS and one spouse itemizes, the other spouse is obligated to itemize, even if the spouse's total deductions may be less than the standard deduction to which he or she would otherwise be entitled. If one spouse later amends the return, the other spouse must also amend his or her return. To formally agree to the amendments, both taxpayers must file a "consent to assessment" for any additional tax that one might owe as a result of the amendment. In the case of a spouse who qualifies to file as Head of household, this rule will not apply. The spouse who qualifies as Head of household is not required to itemize deductions even if the spouse who is required to file MFS decides to itemize their deductions. However, if the spouse filing Head of household decides to itemize deductions, the spouse filing MFS is required to itemize deductions.

Señor 1040 Says: If the taxpayer is MFS and both the spouse and taxpayer elect to deduct sales tax and the spouse elects to use the optional sales tax tables, the taxpayer must use that table to figure the state and local general sales tax deduction (SALT).

Itemized Deductions

Medical and Dental Expenses

Medical care expenses can be deducted if amounts are paid for the diagnosis, cure, treatment, or prevention of a disease or condition affecting any part or function of the body. Procedures such as facelifts, hair transplants, hair removal, and liposuction are generally not deductible. Cosmetic surgery is only deductible if it is to improve a deformity arising from or directly related to a congenital abnormality, a personal injury from an accident or trauma, or a disfiguring disease. Medications are only deductible if prescribed by a doctor. The taxpayer can deduct any medical and dental expenses that exceed 7.5% of the taxpayer's AGI as shown on Form 1040, page 1, line 11. The 7.5% has been made a permanent floor.

Examples of deductible medical expenses include the following:

- Personal protective equipment (PPE)
    - Masks
    - Hand sanitizer
    - Wipes
- Medical insurance premiums
- Medicare
- Dental treatment
- Prescription medicines
- Medical service fees
- Mileage
- Taxi
- Ambulance
- Cost of other needed transportation
- Medical care
- Legal abortions
- Acupuncture
- Seeing eye guide dogs care cost
- Eye exams
- Eyeglasses
- Contact lenses
- Solutions to clean contact lenses
- Eye surgery for nearsightedness
- Hospital fees
- Lab fees
- X-rays
- Psychiatric care
- Hearing aids and batteries
- Other medical aids
- Nursing care
- Artificial limbs & teeth
- Birth control pills
- Chiropractor services
- Inpatient care meals
- Lodging during hospital treatments while away from home for inpatient and outpatient care
- Capital expenses for medical equipment

Improvements to the home may be deducted if their main purpose is to provide a medical benefit. The deduction is limited to the difference between the increase in the fair market value of the home and the cost of the improvements.

Itemized Deductions

Examples of nondeductible medical expenses include over-the-counter medications, bottled water, diaper services, expenses for general health items, health club dues (unless related to a specific medical condition), funeral expenses, illegal operations and treatments, weight-loss programs (unless recommended by a doctor for a specific medical condition), and swimming pool dues. However, prescribed therapeutic swimming costs are deductible.

Other nondeductible items are insurance premiums paid for life insurance; loss of earnings, limbs, or sight; guaranteed payments for days the taxpayer is hospitalized for sickness or injury; and the medical insurance coverage portion of the taxpayer's auto insurance. Cafeteria plans are not deductible unless the premiums are included in box 1 of Form W-2.

The medical mileage rate for 2021 is 16 cents per mile and for 2022 it is 18 cents per mile.

Spouse and Dependent Medical Expenses

The taxpayer is allowed to claim medical expenses that were paid for their spouse. To claim the expenses, they must have been married at the time the spouse received medical treatment or at the time the expenses were paid. If the taxpayer and spouse do not live in a community property state and file separate returns, each would claim only their paid medical expenses. If the taxpayer and spouse live in a community property state and file separate returns, the medical expenses must be divided equally if they were paid out of community funds.

The taxpayer is allowed to claim medical expenses that were paid for their dependent(s). To claim these expenses, the individual must have been a dependent at the time the medical treatment was completed or when the expenses were paid. An individual would qualify as a dependent if all the following are true:

- The individual was a qualifying child or a qualifying relative.
- The individual was a U.S. citizen or a resident of the United States, Canada, or Mexico.
- The dependent gross income was $4,300 or more.

Medical expenses can be deducted for any individual who is a dependent of the taxpayer, even if the taxpayer cannot claim the exemption for the individual on his or her return.

Example: James, age 66, has an AGI of $35,000; 7.5% of $35,000 is $2,625.00, and James had medical expenses of $2,700; therefore, James would be able to deduct $75.00 for medical expenses. The $75.00 is the difference between his expenses and the 7.5% "floor" needed to deduct medical expenses.

Example: Ryan, age 35, has an AGI of $40,000; 7.5% of $40,000 is $3,000, and Ryan had medical expenses of $2,500; therefore, Ryan will not be able to deduct his medical expenses since they are not over $3,000.

Medical Expense Reimbursement

Taxpayers can deduct only their medical amounts paid during the taxable year. If the taxpayer receives a reimbursement for a medical expense, the taxpayer must reduce their total medical deduction for the year. If taxpayers are reimbursed for more than their medical expenses, they may have to include the excess as income. If the taxpayer paid the entire premium for medical insurance, the taxpayer would not include the excess reimbursement as gross income.

Premiums paid for qualified long-term care insurance contracts can be deducted within limits for long-term care insurance.

Qualified long-term care premiums are limited to the following and are reported on Schedule A for 2021:

Age	Amount
Age 40 or under	$450
Age 41–50	$850
Age 51–60	$1,690
Age 61–70	$4,520
Age 71 or over	$5,640

2022 long-term care rates are the same as above.

Fees paid to retirement or nursing homes designed for medical care and/or psychiatric care are deductible. Meals, lodging, and prescriptions are deductible only if the individual is in the home primarily to get medical care. If the main reason the individual is in the home is personal, meals and lodging are not deductible.

Improvements made to the taxpayer's home due to a medical condition may increase the fair market value of the house. Some examples are:

- Construction of entrance or exit ramps
- Widening doorways or hallways
- Lowering cabinets and countertops
- Installing lifts
- Modifying stairways
- Adding handrails or grab bars in the home

If the cost of the improvement is more than the new fair market value, then the difference is a medical expense.

Example: Caroline had a lift installed in her two-story house for medical reasons. The cost of the lift was $12,000. The increase in her fair market value was $10,000. Therefore, she can deduct $2,000 as a medical expense.

Taxes Paid

Certain taxes such as state, local, or foreign taxes, real estate taxes, and personal property taxes can be deducted by the taxpayer. Property taxes can only be deducted by the owner of the property. Real estate taxes are deductible on Schedule A for all property owned by the taxpayer; it is not limited to personal residences like mortgage interest. Deeded time-shares may have a deductible real estate tax as well.

State and Local General Sales Tax (SALT)

State and local tax amounts withheld from wages are reported on line 5 of Schedule A, and the taxpayer may deduct the amounts of the following state and local taxes to reduce the taxpayer's federal tax liability:

- State and local taxes withheld from wages during the current tax year.

Itemized Deductions

- State estimated tax payments made during the current year.
- State and local taxes paid in the current tax year for a prior tax year.
- Mandatory contributions made to the California, New Jersey, or New York Non-occupational Disability Benefit Fund.
- Mandatory contributions made to the Rhode Island Temporary Disability Fund or Washington State Supplemental Workmen's Compensation Fund.
- Mandatory contributions to the Alaska, California, New Jersey, or Pennsylvania state unemployment funds.
- Mandatory contributions to state family leave programs such as the New Jersey Family Leave Insurance (FLI) program and the California Paid Family Leave program.

Interest and penalties for paying taxes late are never a deduction. For tax returns after December 31, 2017, and before January 1, 2026, the state and local tax (SALT) is capped at $10,000 or $5,000 if the taxpayer is married filing separate.

General Sales Tax

If the taxpayer selects to deduct state and local sales tax, the taxpayer will check box 5a on Schedule A. The taxpayer can deduct either actual expenses or an amount figured using the Optional State Sales Tax Tables. If the Optional State Sales Tax Tables is chosen, taxpayer must check the sales tax tables for their local jurisdictions and follow the calculation instructions found at www.irs.gov/individuals/sales-tax-deduction-calculator. If the filing status is MFS and one spouse elects to use the sales tax, the other spouse must use the sales tax method as well. Actual receipts showing general sales taxes paid should be kept. See Schedule A Instructions.

Señor 1040 Says: The taxpayer can either deduct state and local general sales taxes or state and local income taxes; not both.

Real Estate Taxes

State, local, or foreign real estate taxes paid for real estate owned by the taxpayer are deducted on line 6 of Schedule A, only if the taxes are based on the assessed value of the property. If the taxpayer's real estate taxes are included in the mortgage and paid out of an escrow account, the amount paid by the mortgage company is the deducted amount.

After December 31, 2017, the taxpayer is no longer able to deduct foreign personal or real property taxes. If the taxes are based on the assessed value of the property, state and local real estate taxes paid on real estate owned by the taxpayer are deducted on line 5b of Schedule A. Items such as leasing solar equipment that has been added to the taxpayer's property tax bill is not a real estate tax deduction.

If the monthly mortgage payment includes an amount placed in an escrow account for real estate taxes, the taxpayer may not be able to deduct the total amount placed in escrow. Only deduct the real estate taxes that the third party actually paid to the taxing authority. If the third party does not notify the taxpayer of the amount of real estate tax paid, the taxpayer should contact the third party or the taxing authority to report the correct amount on the return. If the taxpayer bought or sold real estate during the year, the real estate taxes charged to the buyer should be reported on the settlement statement and in box 5 of Form 1099-S.

Personal Property Taxes

Personal property taxes are deducted on line 5c of Schedule A. The taxpayer should deduct state or local tax that is imposed yearly based on the value of the property. After December 31, 2017, the taxpayer must deduct personal property taxes on line 5c of Schedule A. The taxpayer should be careful not to include refunds, rebates, interest, or penalties as taxes paid.

Example: Lourdes pays a yearly registration fee for her car. Part of her fee is based on value, and the other part is based on the weight of the car. Lourdes can only deduct the part of the fee that was based on the value of the car, not the part based on the weight of the car.

Other Taxes

The taxpayer can claim a credit for foreign taxes as a nonrefundable credit on Form 1040, Schedule 3, line 1, or take it as an itemized deduction on Schedule A under "other taxes." The taxpayer may or may not have to complete Form 1116, *Foreign Tax Credits*. After December 31, 2017, the taxpayer must deduct other taxes on line 6 of Schedule A. Other taxes consist of foreign taxes earned from overseas investments and not from real property owned abroad.

Nondeductible Taxes and Fees

Nondeductible miscellaneous taxes and fees:

- ➢ Federal income tax and most excise taxes.
- ➢ Employment tax, such as Social Security, Medicare, federal unemployment, and railroad retirement taxes.
- ➢ Federal estate tax.
- ➢ Fines and penalties.
- ➢ Gift tax.
- ➢ License fees (such as for a marriage or driver's license).
- ➢ Certain state and local taxes such as the gasoline tax, car inspections, and other improvements to personal property.

Home Mortgage Interest and Points

Home acquisition debt is a mortgage that a taxpayer took out to buy, build, or substantially improve a qualified home. A qualified loan is a loan used to acquire the taxpayer's primary residence or a second home, and the loan must be secured by the individual property.

A home mortgage is any loan that is secured for the taxpayer's main home or second home. To make the mortgage interest deductible, the loan must be secured and can be a first or second mortgage, a home improvement loan, or a home equity loan. For loans acquired before the TCJA went into effect on December 15, 2017, the interest on up to $1 million of debt ($500,000 for Married filing separately) that was used for acquiring, constructing, or substantially improving the residence is deductible.

If the taxpayer has a primary home and a second home, the home acquisition and home equity debt dollar limit apply to the total mortgage on both homes.

For home loans secured after December 15, 2017, the deductible amount is limited to $750,000 ($375,000 for Married filing separately). Taxpayers may use the 2017 threshold amounts if the following are true:

- if the home acquisition debt was taken on prior to December 16, 2017
- if they entered into a written, binding contract on or before December 15, 2017, in order to close on a principal residence before January 1, 2018
- if they purchased the property before April 1, 2018.

If a taxpayer refinances a home acquisition loan that was acquired before the TCJA went into effect, the refinanced loan is subject to the same provisions as the original, pre-TCJA loan, but only up to the amount of the balance of the original loan. Any additional debt not used to buy, build, or substantially improve the home is not a home acquisition debt. For example, Cheryl took out a home equity line of credit for $100,000. She used $10,000 to redo the master bedroom and then used the rest to go on a world cruise. The $10,000 could be used as home acquisition debt, she is unable to use the world cruise as home acquisition debt. That could be considered income to Cheryl. See Publication 936.

Grandfathered Debt

If the taxpayer took out a mortgage on their home before October 14, 1987, or refinanced the loan, it may qualify as grandfathered debt. Grandfathered debt does not limit the amount of interest that can be deducted. All the interest paid on this loan is fully deductible home mortgage interest. However, the grandfathered debt amount could limit the home acquisition debt. For example, Sergio took out a first mortgage of $200,000 to buy a house in 1986. The mortgage was a 7-year balloon note, and the entire balance on the note was due in 1993. Sergio refinanced the debt in 1993 with a new 30-year mortgage. The refinanced debt is treated as grandfathered debt for the entire 30 years of the loan.

The main home is the property where the taxpayer lives the most. The second home is a similar property. The main or second home could be a boat or recreational vehicle, both must provide basic living accommodations, which include a sleeping space, a toilet, and cooking facilities. Mortgage interest and points are reported to the taxpayer on Form 1098 and entered on line 8 of Schedule A.

Form 1098, *Mortgage Interest Statement*, usually includes the paid amounts of mortgage interest, real estate taxes, and points (defined below). Mortgage companies will often "sell" mortgages during the year. If this occurs, the taxpayer could receive a Form 1098 from each mortgage company.

Señor 1040 Says: Remember to ask your clients if they paid more than one mortgage company. If they have more than one Form 1098, ask if this was for a second mortgage or if they bought and sold homes during the year.

Mortgage interest paid to an individual not issued on Form 1098 is reported on line 8b of Schedule A. The recipient's name and Social Security number or employer identification number are required. Failure to provide this information may result in a $50 penalty.

Points, often called loan origination fees, maximum loan charges, loan discounts, or discount points, are prepaid interest. Points that the seller pays for on behalf of the borrower are treated as being paid by the borrower, allowing the borrower, not the seller, to deduct these points as interest.

The full amount of paid points cannot be 100% deducted in the year of purchase or refinance. Points are considered prepaid interest and are generally deducted over the life of the mortgage on an annual basis. The taxpayer can fully deduct points in the year paid if they meet the following tests:

1. The primary home secures the loan.
2. Where the loan was originated a proven business practice is paying loans.
3. Points paid were less than the points that are charged in the area.
4. Cash method of accounting was used.
5. The points were not used to pay such items as appraisal fees, attorney fees, and property taxes.
6. The loan is used to purchase or build the main home.
7. Points were based on a percentage of the principal amount of the mortgage.
8. The funds provided at or before closing, plus any points the seller paid, were at least as much as the points charged.
9. On the buyers closing statement the amount is clearly indicated as points charged for the mortgage. The points may be shown as paid from either the buyer's or seller's funds.

Points paid when borrowing money for a refinance are normally deductible over the life of the loan, to qualify to deduct the point in the year of the refinance, the taxpayer must qualify for the first 6 of the above list. If the taxpayer pays off a mortgage early, the taxpayer can deduct the remaining points in the year the loan was paid off. Points are currently deductible only if paid from the taxpayer's funds. Financed points must be deducted over the life of the loan. If the taxpayer refinances and ends the loan, the remaining points are deducted when the life of the loan ends.

Mortgage Insurance Premiums

Mortgage Insurance Premiums has been extended through December 31, 2021. Mortgage insurance premiums paid by a taxpayer in connection with acquisition indebtedness on a qualified residence are treated as qualified residence interest and are deductible. Box 4 of Form 1098 will show the amount the taxpayer paid for insurance premiums paid in 2021.

Itemized Deductions

Qualified mortgage insurance is mortgage insurance provided by the Department of Veterans Affairs, the Federal Housing Administration, or the Rural Housing Service. These fees are known as funding fees or a guarantee fee. The taxpayer cannot deduct mortgage insurance premiums if the amount on Form 1040, line 8b, is more than $109,000 ($54,500 if married filing separately). The *Mortgage Insurance Premium Worksheet* should be used to figure the deduction. The worksheet can be found in Instructions Form 1040, Schedule A.

Form 1098: 2021

Part 1 Review Questions

To obtain the maximum benefit from this chapter, LTP recommends that you complete each of the following questions, and then compare them to the answers with feedback that immediately follows. Under governing self-study standards, vendors are required to present review questions intermittently throughout each self-study course.

These questions and explanations are not part of the final examination and will not be graded by LTP.

IDP1.1
Pam is 65; at which percentage will she begin deducting her federal medical expenses?

    a. More than 10% of her adjusted gross income.
    b. More than 8% of her adjusted gross income.
    c. She cannot claim medical expenses because of her age.
    d. 7.5% of her adjusted gross income.

IDP1.2

Which of the following is not a deductible medical and dental expense?

   a. Artificial limbs
   b. False teeth
   c. Eyeglasses
   d. Maternity clothes

IDP1.3

John and his wife Cynthia are filing MFS. John is itemizing his deductions. Which of the following is true?

   a. Cynthia must file single and take the standard deduction.
   b. Cynthia must file head of household.
   c. Cynthia must itemize her deductions.
   d. Cynthia must itemize only if she has enough deductions.

IDP1.4

Which of the following taxes can be deducted on federal Schedule A, lines 5-7?

   a. Fines and penalties
   b. Real estate taxes
   c. Federal income tax withholding
   d. Tattoo removal

IDP1.5

Catherine's total taxes paid on Schedule A, line 5e, are $14,500. How much will she deduct?

   a. $10,000
   b. $12,500
   c. $12,200
   d. $24,400

Part 1 Review Questions Answers

IDP1.1

Pam is 65; at which percentage will she begin deducting her federal medical expenses?

   a. More than 10% of her adjusted gross income.
   b. More than 8% of her adjusted gross income.
   c. She cannot claim medical expenses because of her age.
   d. 7.5% of her adjusted gross income.

Feedback: Review section *Medical and Dental Expenses*.

Itemized Deductions

IDP1.2
Which of the following is not a deductible medical and dental expense?

a. Artificial limbs
b. False teeth
c. Eyeglasses
d. Maternity clothes

Feedback: Review section *Medical and Dental Expenses*.

IDP1.3
John and his wife Cynthia are filing MFS. John is itemizing his deductions. Which of the following is true?

a. Cynthia must file single and take the standard deduction.
b. Cynthia must file head of household.
c. Cynthia must itemize her deductions.
d. Cynthia must itemize only if she has enough deductions.

Feedback: Review section *Itemizing While Married Filing Separate*.

IDP1.4
Which of the following taxes can be deducted on federal Schedule A, lines 5-7?

a. Fines and penalties
b. Real estate taxes
c. Federal income tax withholding
d. Tattoo removal

Feedback: Review section *Real Estate Taxes*.

IDP1.5
Catherine's total taxes paid on Schedule A, line 5e, are $14,500. How much will she deduct?

a. $10,000
b. $14,500
c. $12,200
d. $24,400

Feedback: Review section *State and Local General Sales Tax (SALT)*.

Part 2 Charity and Casualty and Theft Losses

There are two ways to donate to a bonified nonprofit: cash and noncash. The taxpayer could receive a tax benefit based on the amount of the contribution and the taxpayer's adjusted gross income. Casualty is when the taxpayer has lost property by destruction that is sudden or unexpected. Theft is when an individual takes another individual's belongings with the intent to deprive the owner.

Gifts to Charity

Contributions made to "qualified domestic organizations" by individuals and corporations are deductible as charitable contributions. Contributions of money or property, such as clothing, to qualified organizations may be deducted. Dues, fees, or bills to clubs, lodges, fraternal orders, civic leagues, political groups, for-profit organizations, or similar groups are not deductible. Gifts of money or property given to an individual are also not deductible, even if they were given for altruistic reasons. Raffle tickets or church bingo games would not be a deductible expense (they may count as gambling expenses). Another nondeductible item are Super Bowl squares by qualified domestic organizations. If the taxpayer received a benefit (for example, a gift of $60) from the donation, the donation amount must be reduced by the value of the benefit.

Cash Contributions

Cash contributions include those paid by cash, checks, electronic funds transfer, debit card, credit card, or payroll deduction. Cash contributions are not deductible regardless of the amount unless the taxpayer keeps one of the following:

- A bank record that shows the name of the qualified organization, the date of the contribution, and the amount of the contribution. Bank records may include:
    - A canceled check.
    - A bank or credit union statement.
    - A credit card statement.
- A receipt or a letter or other written communication from the qualified organization showing the name of the organization, the date of the contribution, and the amount of the contribution.
- The payroll deduction records or a pledge card or other document prepared by the organization. The document from the organization must show the name of the organization.

The tax professional should not overlook charitable contributions made through payroll deductions; they would appear on the taxpayer's last check stub or W-2. Make sure that the payroll deductions are not pretax contributions. Pretax contributions are not deductible. Advise your clients to make donations with checks, not cash. Make sure they get a receipt for all cash donations.

For payroll deduction contributions, one must keep the following:

- A pay stub, Form W-2, or other document furnished by the taxpayer's employer that shows the date and amount of the contribution.
- A pledge card or other document prepared by or for the qualified organization that shows the name of the organization.

The written communication must include the name of the charity, the date of the contribution, and the amount of the contribution. If the contribution was more than $250, the taxpayer should receive a statement from the charitable organization. When figuring the $250 or more, do not combine separate donations. The charitable organization must include the following on the letter or statement:

- The amount of money that was contributed and a description of any property that was donated.

> Whether or not the organization provided goods or services to the taxpayer in return, a description and estimate value of the taxpayer's contribution must be included.

If the taxpayer is unable to use Schedule A and does charitable contributions, they can deduct $300 on line 12b of Form 1040, or $600 for those filing jointly.

If the taxpayer overstates their charitable deductions and that results in understating their tax liability, the taxpayer could be assessed a penalty of 20% of the total deduction amount if more than 10% of the amount is owed. The taxpayer could also have to pay the underpayment of penalty for understating the amount if more than $5,000.

Other Than by Cash or Check

If the taxpayer gives items such as clothing or furniture, the taxpayer will be able to deduct the fair market value (FMV) at the time of the donation. The FMV is what a willing buyer would pay to purchase when both the buyer and seller are aware of the condition of the sale. If the noncash deduction amount is over $500, the taxpayer must fill out Form 8283. If the contribution is a motor vehicle, boat, or airplane, the organization accepting the donation must issue the taxpayer Form 1098-C with the required information for the taxpayer to attach it to Form 8283. If the deduction is over $5,000, for one item, the taxpayer must get an appraisal of the donated property.

When taxpayers donate noncash items, they must keep a list of the items donated as well as obtain and keep the receipt. Donated items are priced according to their resale value, not the price of the item when it was purchased. See Instructions Schedule A.

If noncash charitable contributions are made with a value of more than $500, the taxpayer is required to complete Form 8283, *Noncash Charitable Contributions*, and attach it to the return. Use Section A of Form 8283 to report noncash contributions for which the taxpayer claimed a deduction of $5,000 or less per item (or group of similar items). Also, use Section A to report contributions of publicly-traded securities. Complete Section B, Form 8283, for each deduction over $5,000 claimed for one item or group of similar items. A separate Form 8283 must be submitted for separate contributions over $5,000 to different organizations. The organization that received the property must complete and sign Part IV of Section B.

The IRS may disallow deductions for noncash charitable contributions if they are more than $500 and if Form 8283 is not submitted with the return. See Publication 526 and Schedule A Instructions.

Car Expenses

If the taxpayer claims expenses directly related to the use of their car when providing services to a qualified organization, the taxpayer must keep reliable written records of expenses. For example, the taxpayer's records might show the name of the organization the taxpayer was serving and the dates the car was used for a charitable purpose. The taxpayer would use the standard mileage rate of 14 cents a mile, records must show the miles driven for the charitable purpose.

Canadian, Israeli, and Mexican Charities

The taxpayer may be able to deduct contributions to certain charitable organizations under the income tax treaty United States has with Mexico, Canada, and Israel. These organizations must meet tests like the ones used to qualify U.S. organizations to receive deductible contributions. The organization would be able to tell the taxpayer if they meet the necessary test. See Publication 526.

Taxpayer Must Keep Records

Records prove the amount of the contributions one makes during the year. The types of records to keep depends on the amount of the contributions and whether they include any of the following:

> - Cash contributions.
> - Noncash contributions.
> - Out-of-pocket expenses when volunteering.

Organizations are usually required to give a written statement if they receive a payment that is more than $75 and is partly a contribution and partly a payment made in exchange for goods or services. The statement should be kept with the taxpayer's records. See Revenue Procedure 2006-50, 2006-47 I.R.B. 944.

Other Itemized Deductions

The following items can be claimed on Schedule A, line 16:

> - Gambling losses up to the extent of gambling winnings.
> - Casualty and theft losses from income-producing property.
> - An ordinary loss attributable to a contingent payment debt instrument or an inflation-indexed debt instrument.
> - Amortizable premiums on taxable bonds purchased before October 23, 1986.
> - Certain unrecovered investments in a pension.
> - Impairment-related work experience of persons with disabilities.
> - Federal estate tax on income with the respect of a decedent.
> - Deductions for repayment of amounts under a claim of right if over $3,000. See Publication 525.

See Instructions Schedule A.

Gambling Losses

The taxpayer must report the full amount of any gambling winnings for the year. The taxpayer will deduct gambling losses for the year on line 16, Schedule A (Form 1040). The taxpayer may claim gambling losses up to the amount of gambling winnings. Taxpayers cannot reduce gambling winnings by gambling losses and report the difference; they must report the full amount of their winnings as income and claim their losses up to the amount of winnings as an itemized deduction. Therefore, the taxpayer's records should show winnings separately from losses. The taxpayer must keep an accurate diary or similar record of losses and winnings. The diary should contain at least the following information:

- ➤ The date and type of specific wages or wagering activity.
- ➤ The name and address or location of the gambling establishment.
- ➤ The names of other persons present with the taxpayer at the gambling establishment.
- ➤ The amount(s) won or lost.

Casualty and Theft Losses

A casualty is the damage, destruction, or loss of property resulting from an identifiable event that is sudden, unexpected, or unusual. A loss on deposits can occur when a bank, credit union, or other financial institution becomes insolvent or bankrupt. When property is damaged or destroyed as a result of hurricanes, earthquakes, tornadoes, fires, vandalism, car accidents, and similar events, it is called a casualty loss. A casualty loss must be sudden and unexpected, so damages that occur over time do not qualify. Theft is the unlawful taking and removing of money or property with the intent to deprive the owner.

Before January 1, 2018, if theft occurred, the taxpayer completed Form 4684, *Casualty and Theft*, and attach it to the return. The loss calculated on Form 4684 was transferred to line 15 of Schedule A. The IRS allowed taxpayers who used Schedule A to deduct these losses with limited coverage.

A casualty loss amount equals the least of the following:

- ➤ The decrease in the fair market value (FMV) of the property as result of the event (in other words, the difference between the property's fair market value immediately before and after the casualty).
- ➤ The adjusted basis in property before the casualty loss, minus any insurance reimbursement.

After figuring a casualty or theft loss and subtracting any reimbursements, one must figure how much of the loss is deductible. To claim a loss as a deduction, each loss amount must have been greater than $100 or greater than 10% of the amount on Form 1040, line 8b, reduced by $100.

After December 31, 2017, theft losses can no longer be claimed, and casualty losses can only be claimed if they are the result of an event that was officially declared a federal disaster by the President of the United States. Apart from this, casualty losses are still calculated using the same methods explained above. Form 4684, *Casualty and Theft*, must still be attached to the tax return. If the taxpayer has a net qualified disaster loss on Form 4684, line 15, and has not itemized deductions, the taxpayer may qualify for an increased standard deduction

Disasters and Casualties

If damage from a casualty is to personal, income-producing, or business property, taxpayers may be able to claim a casualty loss deduction on their tax return. Taxpayers must generally deduct a casualty loss in the year it occurred. However, if the property was damaged as a result of a federally declared disaster, taxpayers can choose to deduct that loss on their return for the tax year immediately preceding the year in which the disaster happened. A federally declared disaster is a disaster that took place in an area declared by the President to be eligible for federal assistance. Taxpayers can amend a tax return by filing Form 1040X, *Amended U.S. Individual Incomime Tax Return*.

Disaster Relief

The following website is where a taxpayer and tax professional can find the list of presidentially declared disaster areas: https://www.irs.gov/newsroom/tax-relief-in-disaster-situations.

Tips on Reconstructing Tax Records for a Disaster

Reconstructing records after a disaster may be essential for tax purposes and for obtaining federal assistance or insurance reimbursement. After a disaster, taxpayers might need certain records to prove their loss. The more accurately a loss is estimated, the more loan and grant money may be available.

Below are tips to help the taxpayer gather the necessary information to reconstruct their records regarding their personal residence and real property. A piece of real estate is not just the land but is also anything built on, growing on, or attached to the land.

- Take photographs or videos as soon as possible after the disaster. This establishes the extent of the damage.
- Contact the title company, escrow company, or bank that handled the purchase of the home to get copies of the original documents. Real estate brokers may also be able to help.
- Use the current property tax statement for land-versus-building ratios if available. If they are not available, owners could get copies from the county assessor's office.
- The basis or fair market value of the home needs to be established. This can be completed by reviewing comparable sales within the neighborhood or by contacting an appraisal company or visiting a website that provides home valuations.
- The mortgage company copies of appraisals or other information needed regarding cost or fair market value in the area.
- Insurance policies list the value of the building, which initiates a base figure for replacement value insurance.
- If improvements were made to the home, contact the contractors who did the work to see if records are available. Get statements from the contractors that state their work and its cost.
    - Get written accounts from friends and relatives who saw the house before and after any improvements. See if any of them have photos taken at get-togethers.
    - If there is a home improvement loan, get paperwork from the institution that issued the loan. The amount of the loan may help establish the cost of the improvements.
- For inherited property, check court records for probate values. If a trust or estate existed, contact the attorney who handled the estate or trust.
- If no other records are available, check the county assessor's office for old records that might address the value of the property.

Other Helpful Agencies

There are several agencies that can help determine the fair market value of most cars on the road. The following are available online resources:

- Kelley Blue Book: www.kbb.com.

Itemized Deductions

- ➢ National Automobile Dealers Association: www.nadaguides.com.
- ➢ Edmunds: www.edmunds.com.

Call the car dealer where the vehicle was purchased and ask for a copy of the contract. If this is not available, give the dealer the details and ask for a comparable price. If the taxpayer is making payments on the car, another source is the lien holder.

It can be difficult to reconstruct records showing the fair market value of some types of personal property. Here are some things to consider when categorization lost items and their values:

- ➢ Look on mobile phones for pictures that were taken in the home that might show the damaged property in the background before the disaster.
- ➢ Check websites that could establish the cost and fair market value of lost items.
- ➢ Support the valuation with photographs, videos, canceled checks, receipts, or other evidence.
- ➢ If items were purchased using a credit or debit card, contact the credit card company or bank for past statements.

If there are no photos or videos of the property, a simple method to help remember what items were lost is to sketch pictures of each room that was impacted:

- ➢ Draw a floor plan showing where each piece of furniture was placed – include drawers, dressers, and shelves.
- ➢ Sketch pictures of the room looking toward any shelves or tables showing their contents.
- ➢ These do not have to be professionally drawn, just functional.
- ➢ Take time to draw shelves with memorabilia on them.
- ➢ Be sure to include garages, attics, closets, basements, and items on walls.

Figuring Loss

Taxpayers may have to reconstruct their records to prove a loss and the amount thereof. To compute loss, determine the decrease in FMV of the property resulting from the casualty or disaster or determine the adjusted basis of the property – this is generally the amount that the property is now worth after events have added to or lessened the value of the amount that was originally paid for the property.

Taxpayers may deduct whichever of these two amounts is smaller after subtracting the amount of any reimbursement provided the taxpayer. Certain deduction limits apply. See Publication 547, *Casualties, Disasters and Thefts*, for details on limits and Publication 551, *Basis of Assets*, for basis information.

If the casualty loss deduction causes a taxpayer's deductions for the year to be more than their income for the year, there may be a net operating loss. For more information, see Publication 536, *Net Operating Losses (NOLs) for Individuals, Estates and Trusts*.

Determining the Decrease in Fair Market Value

Fair market value (FMV) is generally the price for which the property could be sold to a buyer. The decrease in FMV used to figure the amount of a casualty loss is the difference between the property's fair market value immediately before and after the casualty. FMV is generally determined through an appraisal.

Casualty and Theft Losses of Income-Producing Property

Taxpayers can no longer claim a business casualty loss of income-producing property as an itemized deduction. If preparing a tax return from before 2018, use the following information to complete Form 4684:

> ➤ Loss from other activities from Schedule K-1 (Form 1065-B), box 2.
> ➤ Federal estate tax on income with respect to a decedent.
> ➤ Amortizable bond premium on bonds acquired before October 23, 1986.
> ➤ Deduction for repayment of amounts under a claim of right if over $3,000 (see Publication 525).
> ➤ Certain unrecovered investments in a pension.
> ➤ Impairment-related work expenses for a disabled person (see Publication 529).

Business Records

> ➤ To create a list of lost inventories, get copies of invoices from suppliers. Whenever possible, the invoices should date back at least one calendar year.
> ➤ Check for photos on mobile phones, cameras, and videos of buildings, equipment, and inventory.
> ➤ Gathering information about income, get copies from the bank statements. The deposits should reflect what the sales were for the given time period.
>   - Get copies of last year's federal, state, and local tax returns. This includes sales tax reports, payroll tax returns, and business licenses from the city or county. These should reflect gross sales for a given time period.
> ➤ If there are no photographs or videos available, sketch an outline of the inside and outside of the business location and then start to fill in the details of the sketches. For example, for the inside of the building, record where equipment and inventory were located. For the outside of the building, map out the locations of items such as shrubs, parking, signs, and awnings.
>   - If the business was pre-existing, go back to the broker for a copy of the purchase agreement. This should detail what was acquired.
>   - If the building was newly constructed, contact the contractor or a planning commission for building plans.

Investment Interest

Investment income is income that comes from interest payments, dividends, and capital gains collected upon the sale of a security or other assets, and any other profit made through an investment vehicle of any kind. Generally, individuals earn most of their total net income each year through regular employment income.

An investment interest expense is any amount of interest that is paid on loan proceeds used to purchase investments or securities. Investment interest expenses include margin interest used to leverage securities in a brokerage account and interest on a loan used to buy property held for investment.

The deductions for investment expenses could be limited by the at-risk rules and the passive activity loss limits. It does not include any interest related to passive activities or to securities that generate tax-exempt income. Investment expense deduction is limited to investment income. An example of investment income is interest and ordinary dividend income. Property held for investment purposes includes property that produces interest, dividends, annuities, or royalties that were not earned in the ordinary course of a trade or business. Alaska Permanent Fund dividends are not investment income.

Investment interest does not include any qualified home mortgage interest or any interest taken into account in computing income or loss from a passive activity. The deduction for investment interest expense is limited to the amount of net investment income.

Example: Sandy had interest income in the amount of $800. She also had ordinary dividend income in the amount of $325. Sandy's investment interest expense for the year was $695. Sandy will be allowed to deduct the full amount of investment interest expense on her Schedule A since her investment income exceeds her investment interest expense.

When claiming investment interest, Form 4952 should be completed and attached to the tax return. Form 4952 does not have to be completed if the following apply:

> ➤ Taxpayer interest expense is not more than the investment income from interest and ordinary dividends minus qualified dividends.
> ➤ The taxpayer has no other deductible investment expenses.
> ➤ The taxpayer had non-disallowed interest expense for the year.

Report Investment interest on Schedule A, line 9. See Publication 550.

Señor 1040 Says: Alaska Permanent Fund dividends, including those reported on Form 8814, are not investment income.

Fines or Penalties

The taxpayer cannot deduct their fines or penalties paid to a governmental unit for violating a law. This includes all fines and penalties paid in an actual settlement or a potential liability. Fines or penalties include parking tickets, tax penalties, and penalties deducted from teachers' paychecks after an illegal strike.

Part 2 Review Questions

To obtain the maximum benefit from this chapter, LTP recommends that you complete each of the following questions, and then compare them to the answers with feedback that immediately follows. Under governing self-study standards, vendors are required to present review questions intermittently throughout each self-study course.

These questions and explanations are not part of the final examination and will not be graded by LTP.

IDP2.1
Alberta has the following records of charitable contributions: $1,200 check to her church; $600 payroll after-tax dollars to local charity; and $400 fair market value of household items to a qualifying homeless shelter. How much can she deduct for her cash contributions on Schedule A, Itemized Deductions?

a. $1,200
b. $400
c. $1,800
d. $2,200

IDP2.2
Which of the following is not a type of investment income?

a. Interest earned
b. Dividend distributions
c. Capital gains
d. Interest paid on a loan

IDP2.3
Mark has received several W-2G's totaling $7,000. Mark shows proof of his gambling losses totaling over $22,000. What amount of his gambling loss can Mark deduct?

a. He can deduct $22,000 on his current year tax return.
b. He can deduct $7,000 on his current year tax return.
c. He can deduct $7,000 on his current year tax return and the remaining $5,000 the following year.
d. He does not have to report the gambling winnings or the losses.

IDP2.4
Which form needs to be completed and attached to the tax return when claiming a "Casualty and Theft Loss"?

a. Form 2106
b. Form 8889
c. Form 4684
d. Form 3903

Part 2 Review Questions Answers

IDP2.1
Alberta has the following records of charitable contributions: $1,200 check to her church; $600 payroll after-tax dollars to local charity; and $400 fair market value of household items to a qualifying homeless shelter. How much can she deduct for her cash contributions on Schedule A, Itemized Deductions?

a. $1,200
b. $400
c. $1,800
d. $2,200

Feedback: Review sections *Gifts to Charity, Cash Contributions, and Other Than by Cash or Check.*

Itemized Deductions

IDP2.2

Which of the following is not a type of investment income?

a. Interest earned
b. Dividend distributions
c. Capital gains
d. Interest paid on a loan

Feedback: Review section *Investment Interest.*

IDP2.3

Mark has received several W-2G's totaling $7,000. Mark shows proof of his gambling losses totaling over $22,000. What amount of his gambling loss can Mark deduct?

a. He can deduct $22,000 on his current year tax return.
b. He can deduct $7,000 on his current year tax return.
c. He can deduct $7,000 on his current year tax return and the remaining $5,000 the following year.
d. He does not have to report the winnings or the losses.

Feedback: Review section *Gambling Losses.*

IDP2.4

Which form needs to be completed and attached to the tax return when claiming a "Casualty and Theft Loss"?

a. Form 2106
b. Form 8889
c. Form 4684
d. Form 3903

Feedback: Review section *Casualty and Theft Losses.*

Part 3 Form 2106: Employee Business Expenses and Other Expenses

Prior to January 1, 2018, the following section is no longer reported on the federal return. This section is to help those who prepare returns in the states that did not conform to the Tax Cuts and Jobs Act. The amount is still calculated on the federal Schedule A, to arrive at the state deduction amount.

Form 2106 is still used by Armed Forces reservists, qualified performing artists, fee-basis state or local government officials, and employees who will be claiming impairment-related work expenses such as traveling more than 100 miles from home to perform their services. See Instructions Form 2106.

The suspension of miscellaneous itemized deductions under section 67(a), employees, who do not fit into the above classifications may not use Form 2106. The information in the next section has been provided to assist those preparing taxes in the states that did not conform to section 67(a) and still need to calculate the federal deduction to arrive at the state deduction amount. The following states do not conform:

Itemized Deductions

- Alaska
- Arkansas
- California
- Georgia
- Hawaii
- Iowa
- Minnesota
- Montana
- New York

An employee may deduct unreimbursed expenses that are paid and incurred during the current tax year. The expenses must be incurred for conducting trade or business as an employee, and the expenses must be ordinary and necessary. An expense is considered ordinary if it is common and necessary in the taxpayer's trade or business. Self-employed taxpayers do not use this form to report their business expenses. For example, a nurse may be required to provide malpractice insurance and is often required to wear a uniform. Since the employer does not reimburse these expenses, the nurse may be able to deduct those items on Schedule A as a miscellaneous deduction subject to the 2% AGI limitation.

An employee may deduct the following unreimbursed business expenses on Schedule A as a miscellaneous deduction subject to the 2% AGI limitation:

- Employee's business bad debt.
- Education that is employment related.
- Licenses and regulatory fees.
- Malpractice or professional insurance premiums.
- Occupational taxes.
- Passport for a business trip.
- Subscriptions to professional journals and trade magazines related to the taxpayer's trade or business.
- Travel, transportation, entertainment, gifts, and car expenses related to the taxpayer's trade or business.
- Tools used in a trade or business.
- Memberships for professional associations.
- Uniforms, work clothing, or protective wear, as well as their cleaning and maintenance.

Do not include on Form 2106 any educator expenses that were taken on Form 1040, Schedule 1, line 11.

Taxing Employee Expenses

Tax treatment of employee business expenses depends on whether the expenses are categorized as reimbursed expenses or non-reimbursed expenses. Business expenses incurred by an employee under a reimbursement arrangement with an employer are normally not shown on the tax return. Unreimbursed business expenses are deductible as miscellaneous itemized deductions. The definition of trade or business does not include the performance of services as an employee.

The taxpayer can deduct certain expenses as miscellaneous itemized deductions on Schedule A. The taxpayer can deduct the expenses that exceed 2% of their adjusted gross income. The calculation is determined by subtracting 2% of the AGI from the total amount of qualifying expense.

Tax Home

The taxpayer's main place of doing business is considered their tax home. If the taxpayer does not have a regular or main place of business due to the nature of work, the taxpayer's tax home may be the place where one regularly lives. To determine one's main place the length of time must be taken into consideration. See Tax Topic # 511.

Temporary Assignment or Job

The taxpayer may regularly work at their tax home and at another location. If the assignment is temporary, the taxpayer's tax home does not change. If the assignment is indefinite, the taxpayer must include in any income amounts received from his or her employer for living expenses, even if they were considered travel expenses. An indefinite assignment is a job that is expected to last a year or more, even if it does not end up lasting that long.

To determine the difference between a temporary and an indefinite assignment, look at when the taxpayer began working. A temporary assignment usually lasts for one year or less, although a temporary assignment could turn into an indefinite assignment, requiring the tax home to change. An indefinite assignment can be a series of short assignments to the same location for a certain amount of time. If the time spent at that location becomes a sufficiently lengthy period of time, then the temporary could turn to indefinite.

If the taxpayer is a federal employee participating in a federal crime investigation or prosecution, the taxpayer is not limited to the one-year rule but must meet other requirements to deduct the expenses.

If the taxpayer returns home from a temporary assignment, the taxpayer is not considered to be away from home. If the taxpayer takes a job that requires a move with the understanding that they will keep the job after the probationary period, the job is considered "indefinite". The expense for lodging and meals is not deductible.

Meals

Deductions can be determined by using the actual meal expense for the standard meal allowance. If there is no reimbursement for meal expenses, then only 50% of the standard meal allowance is deductible, and that 50% is subject to the 2% floor. Employees who travel out of town for extended periods of time may elect to take a per diem rate. The federal per diem rate depends on the location.

A transportation worker is defined as an individual whose work involves moving people or goods by plane, bus, ship, truck, etc. Transportation workers can deduct a special per-day allowance for meals and incidentals if their work requires that they travel away from home to areas with different federal per diem rates. Unlike other traveling employees, a Department of Transportation (DOT) worker is allowed to deduct up to 80% of the meal.

Travel and Transportation Expenses

If the taxpayer travels away from their tax home for business, the expenses could be deducted on Form 2106. Business-related travel expenses must be ordinary and necessary expenses of traveling away from home for the business or job. Expenses cannot be lavish or extravagant. A taxpayer is traveling away from home if:

> The taxpayer's duties require one to be away from the general area of their tax home for substantially longer than an ordinary day's work.
> The taxpayer needs sleep or rest to meet the demands of his or her work while away from home.

Travel by airplane, train, or bus is generally deductible. Fares paid for taxis, airport limousines, buses, or other types of transportation used between the airport, bus station or hotel, can be deducted including those used between the hotel and the client visited. Necessary trips are also deductible. Cleaning expenses, business calls, tips, and other necessary expenses related to the trip are also deductible.

Employees who drive their own vehicles are permitted to deduct either the actual expenses or the standard mileage rate for unreimbursed mileage. If the taxpayer is partially reimbursed, only the portion that is unreimbursed is reportable. See Publication 463, *Travel, Entertainment, Gift, and Car Expenses*.

Entertainment

Entertainment expenses must be ordinary and necessary. This includes activities generally considered to provide entertainment, recreation, or amusement to clients, customers, or employees. Expenses for entertainment that are lavish or extravagant are not deductible. An expense is not considered lavish or extravagant if the expense is reasonably based on facts and circumstances related to the business.

Entertainment expense deductions are limited to 50% of the actual expense and are further reduced by the 2% floor. "Entertainment" includes any activity that generally is considered to provide diversion, amusement, or recreation. It does not include club dues and membership fees to country clubs, airline clubs, and hotel clubs. The taxpayer may deduct entertainment expenses only if they are ordinary and necessary. Deducting entertainment expenses must meet either the "directly related" test or the "associated" test.

The "directly related" entertainment test, must meet the following conditions:

> Expenses must be directly related to business either before, during, or after the entertainment or associated with the active conduct of business.
> The taxpayer and client engaged in business during the entertainment period.
> The entertainment was more than a general expectation of getting income or some other specific business benefit in the future.

To meet the "associated" test, the entertainment must be associated with the active conduct of the taxpayer's trade or business and occur directly before or after a substantial business discussion. Daily lunch or entertainment expenses with subordinates or coworkers are not deductible, even if business is discussed.

Business Gifts

Gifts can be given to the client directly or indirectly. The taxpayer can deduct up to $25 per client per year for business gifts. Items do not include those that cost $4 or less, have the taxpayer's name imprinted on them, and are distributed (for example, pens, pencils, cases, etc.). Any item that could be considered a gift or entertainment is considered entertainment. Packaged food and beverage items are treated as gifts.

Business Recordkeeping

If audited, taxpayers must prove their deductions to the IRS. It is important to keep all receipts related to the tax return. Records of expenses should include the following:

- Amount paid.
- Time, date, and place.
- The purpose of the business discussion or the nature of the expected business benefit.
- People in attendance.

Reimbursements

Reimbursements paid by an employer's accountable plan are not reported in box 1 of Form W-2. Excess reimbursements paid by a nonaccountable plan are included in the employees' wages in box 1 of the W-2. See Instructions Form 2106.

Other Expenses

The taxpayer can deduct certain other expenses as miscellaneous itemized deductions subject to the 2% of adjusted gross income limit. The following are examples of deductible expenses:

- Expenses to manage, conserve, or maintain property held for producing taxable gross income (such as office space rented to maintain investment property).
- Attorney fees and legal expenses paid to collect taxable income.
- Appraiser fees to determine the value of a donated party.
- Fees paid to determine the value of a casualty loss.

The taxpayer can deduct investment fees, custodial fees, trust administration fees, and other expenses paid for managing investments that produce taxable income.

Tax Preparation Fees

Tax preparation fees are deductible to the taxpayer. If the taxpayer paid the preparation fee by using a debit or credit card and a convenience fee was charged, the taxpayer cannot deduct the convenience fee as a part of the overall cost of preparing the return.

Education

The taxpayer can deduct qualifying education tuition and expenses. The education must be required by the employer or the law to keep one's salary, status, or job or to maintain or improve skills required in the taxpayer's present job in order to be deductible. Education that qualifies the taxpayer for his or her first job in a specific field is not deductible on Schedule A, nor is education that enables the taxpayer to change jobs; however, these may be deductible as a lifetime learning credit.

Deductible expenses include tuition, textbooks, registration fees, supplies, transportation (standard mileage or actual expenses), lab fees, the cost of writing papers or dissertations, student cards, insurance, and degree costs.

Part 3 Review Questions

To obtain the maximum benefit from this chapter, LTP recommends that you complete each of the following questions, and then compare them to the answers with feedback that immediately follows. Under governing self-study standards, vendors are required to present review questions intermittently throughout each self-study course.

These questions and explanations are not part of the final examination and will not be graded by LTP.

IDP3.1

Which form is used to report employee business expenses for years prior to 2018?

a. Form 2441
b. Form 2106
c. Schedule C
d. Form 1040-EZ

IDP3.2

Which of the following states did not conform to TCJA?

a. Alaska, Arkansas, Alabama, and California
b. New York, New Jersey, Montana, and Iowa
c. Hawaii, Arkansas, Montana, and Georgia
d. Minnesota, Georgia, Texas, and Florida

IDP3.3

Which of the following best describes "Tax Home"?

a. Taxpayer does not work regularly at their tax home.
b. Taxpayers' employment was in a different city for 42 weeks.
c. Taxpayer worked regularly at a temporary assignment.
d. Taxpayer is a federal employee investigating crimes.

Part 3 Review Questions Answers

IDP3.1

Which form is used to report employee business expenses for years prior to 2018?

a. Form 2441
b. Form 2106
c. Schedule C
d. Form 1040-EZ

Feedback: Review section *Part 3: Form 2106 Employee Business Expenses.*

Itemized Deductions

IDP3.2
Which of the following states did not conform to TCJA?

   a. Alaska, Arkansas, Alabama, and California
   b. New York, New Jersey, Montana, and Iowa
   c. Hawaii, Arkansas, Montana, and Georgia
   d. Minnesota, Georgia, Texas, and Florida

Feedback: Review section *Part 3: Form 2106 Employee Business Expenses.*

IDP3.3
Which of the following best describes "Tax Home"?

   a. Taxpayer does not work regularly at their tax home.
   b. Taxpayers' employment was in a different city for 42 weeks.
   c. Taxpayer worked regularly at a temporary assignment.
   d. Taxpayer is a federal employee investigating crimes.

Feedback: Review section *Part 3: Form 2106 Employee Business Expenses.*

Takeaways

The taxpayer must decide to use the itemized deduction or the standard deduction. The standard deduction is a dollar amount that reduces the amount of income on which the taxpayer is taxed. The itemized deduction can be greater than the standard deduction. Some taxpayers must itemize their deductions because they do not qualify to use the standard deduction or because one's spouse chose to itemize their deductions.

TEST YOUR KNOWLEDGE!
Go online to take a practice quiz.

Chapter 9 Schedule C

Introduction

This chapter presents an overview of Schedule C, which includes income and expenses. Business income or loss that is reported on Schedule C is reported on Form 1040, Schedule 1, line 3. Sole proprietorship is not a legal entity; it refers to a person who owns a business and is personally responsible for its debts. Sole proprietorship is a popular business structure due to the simplicity, ease of setup, and nominal start-up costs. Ultimately, a sole proprietor would register the business name with the state and city, obtain local business licenses, and then open for business. A drawback of being a sole proprietor is that the owner is 100% personally liable for the business's income and/or debt.

Objectives

At the end of this lesson, the student will:

- ➢ Identify the differences between accounting periods and accounting methods.
- ➢ Understand the guidelines between an independent contractor and an employee.
- ➢ Recognize what determines start-up costs.
- ➢ Identify how to classify employees.

Resources

Form 1040	Publication 15	Instructions Form 1040
Form 1099-NEC	Publication 15-A	Instructions Form 1099-NEC
Form 3115	Publication 334	Instructions Form 3115
Form 4562	Publication 463	Instructions Form 4562
Form 4797	Publication 535	Instructions Form 4797
Form 8829	Publication 536	Instructions Form 8829
Schedule C	Publication 538	Instructions for Schedule C
Schedule SE	Publication 544	Instructions Schedule SE
	Publication 551	Publication 946
	Publication 560	Publication 527
	Publication 587	

Table of Contents

Introduction	333
Part 1 Business Entity Types	335
Sole Proprietorship	335
Husband and Wife Qualified Joint Venture (QJV)	335
Single-member Limited Liability Company (LLC)	336
Accounting Periods	336
Calendar Year	336
Fiscal Year	336
Change in Tax Year	336
Accounting Methods	337
Cash Method	337
Accrual Method	338
Combination (Hybrid) Method	338
Independent Contractors	338
Statutory Employees	339
Statutory Nonemployees	340
Identification Numbers	340
Schedule SE: Self-Employment Tax	340
Schedule C	341
Schedule C, Part I, Income	343
Schedule C, Part II, Expenses	345
Part 1 Review Questions	349
Part 1 Review Questions Answers	350
Part 2 Line 30: Business Use of the Home	352
Form 8829: Office in the Home	352
Administrative or Management Activities	353
Simplified Option for Home Office Deduction	354
Regular and Exclusive Use	355
Principal Place of Business	355
Expenses	356
Schedule C, Part III, Cost of Goods Sold	357
Schedule C, Part V, Other Expenses	359
Part 2 Review Questions	361
Part 2 Review Questions Answers	362
Part 3 Qualified Business Income	363
Qualified Business Income (QBI)	363
20% Deduction for a Pass-Through Qualified Trade or Business	364
Issues in Calculating the Deduction	364
Specified Service Trade or Business	365
Taxpayers with Income Above the Threshold	365
QBI and the W-2	365
QBI and Property	365
Service Trade Disqualifier	366
Pass-Through Entities	367
Sec. 199A Overview	367
Recordkeeping	368
Benefits of Recordkeeping	368
Part 3 Review Questions	369
Part 3 Review Questions Answers	370
Takeaways	371

Part 1 Business Entity Types

There are many different types of business entities with their own sets of rules, regulations, and guidelines within the U.S. tax laws. The following entity type could apply to Schedule C, E, and/or F.

Sole Proprietorship

A sole proprietor is an individual owner of a business or a self-employed individual. Taxable income is reported on Schedule C and flows to Form 1040, Schedule 1, line 3. A business owner could have to pay self-employment tax reported, which is reported on Schedule SE.

A sole proprietorship reports the income and expenses from the owner's business on Schedule C, *Profit or Loss from a Business*. An individual is self-employed if the following apply:

- Conducts a trade or business as a sole proprietorship.
- Is an independent contractor.
- Is in business for himself or herself in any other way.

Self-employment can include work in addition to regular full-time business activities. It can also include certain part-time work done at home or in addition to a regular job.

Minimum Income Reporting Requirements for Schedule C Filers

If the taxpayer's net earnings from self-employment are $400 or more, the taxpayer is required to file a tax return. If net earnings from self-employment were less than $400, the taxpayer may still have to file a tax return if he or she meets other filing requirements.

Husband and Wife Qualified Joint Venture (QJV)

A husband and wife cannot be sole proprietors of the same business. If they are joint owners, they are partners and should file a partnership return using Form 1065, *US Partnership Return of Income*. They can be partners, but "sole" means one, and for the purposes of a business, the IRS does not recognize spouses as one.

If the taxpayer and spouse each materially participated in the business as the only members of a jointly owned and operated business, and if they file a joint return, they can elect to be taxed as a qualified joint venture (QJV) instead of a partnership. This election does not generally increase the total tax on the joint return, but it does give the self-employment credit for each taxpayer's Social Security earnings.

To make the QJV election, the spouses must divide all their income and expenses between them and file two separate Schedule Cs. Once the election has been made, it can only be revoked with IRS permission. The election will remain in effect if the spouses file as a qualified joint venture. If the taxpayer and spouse do not qualify in one year, then they will need to resubmit the paperwork to qualify as a qualified joint venture for the next year.

Schedule C

If the spouses own an unincorporated business and if they live in a state, foreign country, or a U.S. possession that has community property laws, the income must be treated as either a sole proprietorship or a partnership. Alaska, Arizona, California, Idaho, Louisiana, Nevada, New Mexico, Texas, Washington, and Wisconsin are the only states with community property laws.

Single-member Limited Liability Company (LLC)

For federal income tax purposes, a single-member LLC is not a separate entity. The single-member LLC would report income directly on the related Schedule as a sole-proprietor. A sole member of a domestic LLC would need to submit Form 8832 to the IRS prior to filing a corporation return if it is electing to treat the LLC as a corporation.

Accounting Periods

An accounting period is the fixed time that covers the company's financial statements. A tax year is an annual accounting period used for keeping records as well as for reporting income and expenses. An accounting period cannot be longer than 12 months, and options include:

- ➤ The standard calendar year.
- ➤ A fiscal year, which is a 12-month period that can end on the last day of any month except December.

Taxpayers generally choose the calendar-year accounting period for their individual income tax returns. Business owners must choose their accounting period before filing their first business schedule

Calendar Year

A calendar tax year is the 12 consecutive months from January 1st to December 31st. Sole proprietors must adopt the calendar year if any of the following apply:

- ➤ The taxpayer does not keep books or records.
- ➤ The taxpayer has no annual accounting period.
- ➤ The taxpayer's present tax year does not qualify as a fiscal year.
- ➤ The taxpayer's use of the calendar tax year is required under the Internal Revenue Code (IRC) or the Income Tax Regulations.

Fiscal Year

A fiscal year is 12 consecutive months ending on the last day of any month except December. A "52 to 53-week tax year" is a fiscal year that varies from 52 to 53 weeks. It does not have to end on the last day of the month. For more information on fiscal years, who might choose them, and why, see Publication 538.

Change in Tax Year

To change the type of tax year used, the taxpayer should file Form 1128, *Application to Adopt, Change, or Retain a Tax Year*. See Instructions Form 1128 for more information.

Accounting Methods

Accounting methods are sets of rules used to determine when income and expenses are reported on a return. The accounting method chosen for the business must be used throughout the life of the business. If the owner wants to change the accounting method, approval from the IRS must be obtained. The two most common methods are cash and accrual. Businesses that have inventory must use the accrual accounting method.

The following are acceptable accounting methods:

> - The cash method.
> - The accrual method.
> - Special methods of accounting for certain items of income and expenses.
> - The combination (hybrid) method, using elements of two or more of the above.

Taxpayers should choose whichever system best reflects their income. If the taxpayer does not choose an accounting method that clearly reflects their income, the IRS may recalculate the income to reflect the correct accounting method, which could involve penalties and interest. Taxpayers must use the same accounting method when figuring their taxable income and keeping their books. However, business owners can use a different accounting method for each business they operate. See Publication 538, *Accounting Periods and Methods*.

Cash Method

If one uses the cash method, all items must be reported as income in the year in which they are actually or constructively received. Income is constructively received when it becomes or is made available to the taxpayer without restrictions, such as through a bank account; the income does not necessarily have to be in the taxpayer's physical possession.

When using the cash method, all expenses are deducted in the year they are paid. This is the method most individual taxpayers use. Exceptions to the rule include prepaid expenses—for example, insurance or tuition. If expenses were paid in advance, they are generally deductible only in the year to which the expense applies.

Example: In the beginning of 2021, Chandler paid his business insurance expenses in advance for 2021, 2022, and 2023. For his 2021 tax return, he will only be able to claim the portion of those expenses that were used for 2021. He will only be able to claim the portion of the expense used for 2022 and 2023 on his tax returns for those respective years.

Cash method is the simplest accounting method, and taxpayers must use this method if they do not keep regular or adequate books.

The following three types of taxpayers are unable to use the cash method:

> - C corporations.
> - Partnerships that have a C corporation as a partner.
> - Tax shelters.

Schedule C

Accrual Method

If the accrual method is used, income is reported when earned, whether it has been actually or constructively received. Similarly, expenses are deducted when acquired rather than when paid. Businesses with inventory are required to use the accrual method to track the business' cost-of-goods-sold. Once this accounting method has been chosen, the taxpayer cannot change to a different accounting method without IRS permission.

If a business owner chooses the accrual method, the amount of gross income would be reported at the earliest of the following events:

- When payment was received.
- When the income is due.
- When the business earned the income.
- When title was passed to the business.

Example: Ruben is a calendar-year taxpayer who uses the accrual method and owns a dance studio. He received payment on October 1, 2021, for a one-year contract for 48 one-hour lessons beginning on October 1, 2021. Ruben gave eight lessons in 2022. Ruben would include one-sixth (8/48) of the payment in his 2022 income and the remaining five-sixths (40/48) would be reported in his 2021 tax year because, under the accrual method, income is reported when it has been earned, not when it has been actually or constructively received.

Combination (Hybrid) Method

The taxpayer can choose any combination of cash, accrual, and special methods of accounting if the combination clearly shows the taxpayer's income and expenses and if the method is used consistently. The combination (or hybrid) method is often used when a company possesses some kind of inventory that is not essential to accounting for income. The combination method cannot be used in the following cases:

- If inventory is necessary to account for income, the accrual method must be used.
- If the cash method for figuring income is used, the cash method must also be used for expenses. It cannot be combined with another method.
- If the taxpayer uses an accrual method for reporting expenses, then the accrual method of income must be used for everything else as well.
- If the taxpayer uses a combination method that includes the cash method, treat that combination method as the cash method.

Independent Contractors

An independent contractor is an individual who is hired by employers on a per-contract basis where the employer only has the right to control or direct the result of the work but cannot dictate what or how the result will be achieved. This classification permits the taxpayer to certain tax benefits and full responsibility for their employment taxes. An independent contractor can itemize all ordinary and necessary business expenses by using the appropriate schedule.

To be considered an independent contractor, the taxpayer should set their own hours and work schedule, be responsible for having their own tools or equipment, and usually work for multiple individuals or companies.

If a taxpayer is an independent contractor, the taxpayer would not fill out Form W-4, *Employee's Withholding Allowance Certificate,* nor will taxes be withheld from the taxpayer's paycheck. The independent contractor is responsible for paying self-employment tax (Social Security and Medicare) and making estimated tax payments to cover both the self-employment tax and their income tax.

Taxpayers are considered employees and not independent contractors if the following apply:

- Must comply with their employer's work instructions.
- Receive training from the employer or the employer's designee.
- Provide services that are integral to the employer's business.
- Provide services that are personally rendered.
- Hire, pay, and supervise workers for the employer.
- Have an ongoing working relationship with the employer.
- Must follow set hours of work.
- Work full time for the employer.
- Work on the employer's premises.
- Work in a sequence set by the employer.
- Submit regular reports to the employer.
- Receive payments of regular amounts at regular intervals.
- Receive payments for business or travel expenses.
- Rely on employer to provide tools and materials.
- Do not have a major investment in resources for providing services.
- Do not make a profit or suffer a loss from services provided.
- Work for one employer at a time.
- Do not offer services to the general public.
- Can be fired by the employer.
- May quit anytime without incurring liability.
- Are statutory employees.

If one qualifies as a statutory employee for income tax purposes, the box titled "Statutory Employee" on Form W-2, *Wage and Tax Statement*, will be checked. Income, as well as both ordinary and necessary business expenses, are reported on Schedule C.

Statutory Employees

A statutory employee is an independent contractor who is nevertheless still treated as an employee due to some statute. This applies to the following occupational groups, all of whom qualify as statutory employees under U.S. law:

- Agent drivers or commissioned drivers limited to those who distribute food, beverages (other than milk products), and laundry or dry-cleaning services for someone else.
- Full-time life insurance salespeople who work for one company.
- A home worker who follows the guidelines of his or her employer using materials furnished by that employer and returning them as designated by the employer.

Schedule C

> Traveling or city salespeople who sell for one principal employer. The goods sold must be merchandise for resale or supplies for use in the buyer's business operation. The customers must be retailers, wholesalers, contractors, or operators of hotels, restaurants, or other businesses dealing with food or lodging.

To make sure the salespeople are employees under the usual common-law rules, individuals must be evaluated separately. If a salesperson does not meet the tests for a common-law employee, then they may be considered a statutory employee. See Publication 15 and Publication 535.

A statutory employee is very limited and must meet specific criteria to meet the definition. Tax preparers should watch for incorrectly marked Forms W-2 and advise people with incorrectly marked forms to have their employers reissue a corrected Form W-2. If the taxpayer does not wish to do this, the tax professional should prepare the return using the information reported on Form W-2.

Statutory Nonemployees

Statutory nonemployees are treated as self-employed for federal tax purposes, including income and employment taxes. The following are considered statutory nonemployees:

> Direct sellers.
> Qualified real estate agents.
> Certain types of caretakers.

Identification Numbers

Generally, the taxpayer can use their SSN or taxpayer identification number (TIN) on the appropriate schedule. However, the taxpayer must have an employer identification number (EIN) if either applies:

> The taxpayer pays wages to one or more employees.
> The taxpayer files pension or excise tax returns.

Taxpayers can obtain an EIN by completing Form SS-4, *Application for Employer Identification Number*. A new EIN must be obtained if either the entity type or the ownership of the business changes. If the business has employees, the employer (or their delegate) must see the SSN to verify the name and number as it appears on the Social Security card. The employer (or their delegate) must have each employee complete Form W-4. See Publication 17 and SS-4 Instructions.

Schedule SE: Self-Employment Tax

Social Security and Medicare taxes become a little more complicated for self-employed taxpayers. Normally, the standard 12.4% tax for Social Security and 2.9% tax for Medicare is split between employees and their employer; an employee pays half this amount, and the employer matches it. Self-employed individuals, however, are simultaneously the employee and the employer and thus must pay the full 15.3% tax for Social Security and Medicare by themselves. This is called the self-employment tax (SE), and self-employed taxpayers must pay it because they do not have Social Security and Medicare taxes withheld from their earnings.

The self-employment tax is not as overwhelming as it might seem, however. For example, the 15.3% self-employment tax is figured from 92.35% of the taxpayer's net profit; it is not figured from their gross income or even from their total net profit, just 92.35% of it. Taxpayers who have net profit of $400 do not need to pay self-employment tax. If net earnings are more than $400, self-employment tax needs to be paid. Self-employed taxpayers are allowed to deduct half of the self-employment tax as an adjustment to income on Form 1040, Schedule 1, line 15.

Reported on Form 1040, Schedule 2, line 4, the SE tax applies to everyone who has self-employment income with net earnings of $400 or more. Self-employment income consists of income from self-employed business activities that are reported on Schedule C, E, and F, as well as income received by clergy and employees of churches and religious organizations. There are three ways to figure net earnings from self-employment:

- The regular method.
- The nonfarm optional method.
- The farm optional method.

The regular method must be used unless the taxpayer qualifies to use either one or both optional methods. To calculate net earnings (sometimes referred to as "actual earnings") using the regular method, multiply the self-employment earnings by 92.35% (.9235).

Taxpayers who make estimated tax payments to cover the self-employment tax they expect to owe. The due dates of estimated tax payments are:

- April 15th.
- June 15th.
- September 15th.
- January 15th of the upcoming calendar year.

If any of these dates fall on a holiday or weekend, the payment is due the next business day.

Schedule C

Schedule C, *Profit or Loss from Business*, is used for the sole proprietor or the sole owner of an LLC to report the business income and expenses for the current tax year. If the business owner owns multiple businesses, then a separate Schedule C must be filed for each business.

Completing Schedule C

Schedule C is a very detailed form that categorizes the income and expense of the business. The first portion requires basic information about the business and its type.

Line A: Enter the business or professional activity that provided the principal source of income reported on line 1 of the Schedule C. If the taxpayer owned more than one business, each business must complete a separate Schedule C or appropriate form. If the general field or activity is wholesale or retail trade or services connected with production services, state the type of customer or client. For example, "wholesale of hardware to retailers," or "appraisal of real estate for lending institutions."

Schedule C

Portion of 2021 Schedule C

Line B: Enter the six-digit code found in the instructions for Schedule C to designate the type of business. If the taxpayer's company-type is not listed, find a similar principal business or professional activity code. No matter how unsure you are about which code to use, try not to use business code 999999, *Unknown Business*; businesses with this code are significantly more likely to be audited by the IRS due to the lack of information provided by using that code.

Line C: Enter the business name.

Line D: Enter the employer ID number (EIN). The taxpayer would have obtained this number by filling out and submitting Form SS-4 online to the IRS. If there is no EIN, enter the taxpayer's SSN at the top of the page where indicated. Remember: as a sole proprietorship, the company only needs an EIN in the following cases:

- ➢ The company has a qualified retirement plan.
- ➢ The company is required to file an employment, an excise, or an alcohol, tobacco, or firearms return.
- ➢ At least part of the company involves paying gambling winnings.

Line E: Business address. Enter the physical address of the business, not a P.O. Box number. If the business has a suite or room number, make sure that it is entered as well. If the business was conducted from the taxpayer's home, and if it is the same address used on Form 1040, page 1, do not complete this line.

Line F: Select which accounting method was used by the business during the tax year.

Line G: Material Participation

"Material participation" is when an owner of a passive activity takes part in the business's operations even though they typically wouldn't. A business is a passive activity if the owner does not regularly participate in the day-to-day operations of the business. Rental activity is the most common type of passive activity, but it is far from the only kind. If the business experienced a passive activity loss, the loss may be limited by reducing the percentage of the business's income that can be taxed, but only if the taxpayer can show that they materially participated in the business.

To be able to limit losses by claiming "material participation", the taxpayer must meet any of the seven material participation tests from the requirements listed below. These generally cover any work done in connection with an activity in which one owned an interest at the time the work was completed. However, work is considered participation if it is work that the owner would not customarily do in the same type of activity, and if one of the main reasons for doing the work was to avoid the disallowance of losses or credits from the activity under the passive activity rules.

If the taxpayer meets any of these tests, check "Yes" on line G; otherwise, check "No." For the purposes of the passive activity rules, any of the following requirements must be met to be considered to have materially participated:

1. The taxpayer substantially participated in the activity on a regular and continuous basis for more than 500 hours during the tax year.
2. The taxpayer substantially participated in the activity of all individuals, even including those who do not own an interest in the activity.
3. The taxpayer participated during the tax year as much as any other person in the company.
4. Taxpayer participated for more than 100 hours during the tax year but did not materially participate.
5. The taxpayer materially participated in the activity for any 5 of the prior 10 tax years.
6. The taxpayer is in a personal service activity in which the taxpayer materially participated for any three prior tax years. A personal service activity is an activity that involves performing personal services in the fields of health, law, engineering, architecture, accounting, consulting, or any other trade or business in which capital is not a material income-producing factor.
7. Taxpayer meets the test if any person other than the taxpayer did the following:
   a) Received compensation for performing management services in connection with the activity.
   b) Spent more hours during the tax year doing other activities than he or she spent performing management services in connection with the activity, regardless of whether the person was compensated for the service.

Line H: If the business was started or acquired in the current tax year, check the box.

Line I: If the taxpayer made any payments that would require the taxpayer to file Form(s) 1099, check yes; otherwise, check no.

Schedule C, Part I, Income

Gross Income Receipts

Self-employment income is income earned from the performance of personal services that cannot be classified as wages because an employer-employee relationship does not exist between the payer and the payee because they are the same person. Self-employment tax is imposed on any U.S. citizen or resident alien who has self-employment income. If one is self-employed in a business that provides services (where products are not a factor), the gross income goes on line 7 of Schedule C and includes amounts reported on Form 1099-MISC, Form 1099-K, and Form 1099-NEC.

Different Kinds of Income

The taxpayer must report on their tax return all income received in business unless it is excluded by law. In most circumstances, income will be in the form of cash, checks, and credit card charges. Bartering is another form of income, and its fair market value must be included as income.

Example: Ernest operates a plumbing business and uses the cash method of accounting. Jim owns a computer store and contacts Ernest to discuss fixing the clogged pipes in his store in exchange for a laptop for Ernest's business. This is business-to-business bartering. If Ernest accepts the deal, he must report the fair market value of the laptop as income because it was the "income" he received in exchange for his service.

Miscellaneous Income

If one is self-employed in a business involving manufacturing, merchandising, or mining, the gross income on line 7 of Schedule C is the total sales from that business, minus the cost of goods sold, and plus any income from investments and incidental or outside operations or sources. If the taxpayer is involved in more than one business, a separate Schedule C is filed for each business (for example, newspaper delivery and computer consulting). Other income commonly includes bank interest, rebates, and reimbursements from government food programs for a daycare provider.

Part I Income

#	Description	
1	Gross receipts or sales. See instructions for line 1 and check the box if this income was reported to you on Form W-2 and the "Statutory employee" box on that form was checked	1
2	Returns and allowances	2
3	Subtract line 2 from line 1	3
4	Cost of goods sold (from line 42)	4
5	**Gross profit.** Subtract line 4 from line 3	5
6	Other income, including federal and state gasoline or fuel tax credit or refund (see instructions)	6
7	Gross income. Add lines 5 and 6	7

Portion of 2021 Schedule C

Line 1: Enter the gross receipts for the year from the trade or business. Include all amounts received, even if the income was not reported on Form(s) 1099.

Line 2: Enter returns and allowances for the year from the trade or business. Even though this amount will be subtracted later, make sure it is entered here as a positive number. A sales return is a refund given to the taxpayer's customers who returned defective, damaged, or unwanted products.

Line 6: Report all amounts from finance reserve income, scrap sales, bad debts recovered, interest (on notes and accounts receivable), state gasoline or fuel tax refunds received in 2021. Prizes and awards related to the trade or business and other miscellaneous business income are also reported on line 6.

Schedule C, Part II, Expenses

To be a deductible business expense, the tangible or nontangible item must be either ordinary or necessary. An ordinary expense is an expense that is common, standard, and accepted in the taxpayer's industry. A necessary expense is one that is helpful and appropriate for the taxpayer's trade or business. An expense does not have to be indispensable to be considered necessary. The taxpayer needs to keep records of their expenses no matter how minimal the payment is. Documentation is the key if the taxpayer is ever audited for proof of expenses.

Portion of 2021 Schedule C

The following examples are expenses that can be deducted:

Line 8: Advertising. Advertising is communicating with the general public to promote a product or service that the business provides. All advertising expenses can generally be deducted if the expense is related to the business. Advertising for purposes of influencing legislation is not deductible as this is considered lobbying, which is beyond the scope of this course.

Line 9: Car and Truck Expenses. Expenses used for business can be deducted as a business expense. Vehicle expenses include gasoline, oil, repairs, license tags, insurance, and depreciation. For 2021, the mileage rate for claiming expenses was 56 cents per mile and for 2022 the rate will be 58.5 cents per mile. The standard mileage rate for each mile of business use can be used for the taxpayer's owned or leased vehicle. The standard mileage rate cannot be used if five or more cars or light trucks are used at the same time.

The taxpayer may choose between using the actual expenses incurred by using the vehicle or using the standard mileage rate. Report the expense amount on Schedule C, Part II, line 9. The taxpayer should include the following in his or her daily business mileage log:

➢ Beginning mileage.
➢ Ending mileage.
➢ Commuting mileage.

Schedule C

Business meals for 2021 are 100% deductible only if the properly-applied rules from Revenue Procedure 2019-48 are used. The rule is for expenses incurred after December 31, 2020, and before January 1, 2022, the food and/or beverages must be provided by a restaurant. A restaurant means a business that prepares and sells food and beverages to retail customers for immediate consumption, regardless of whether the food or beverages are consumed on the restaurant's premises. A restaurant does not include a business that primarily sell prepackaged food or beverages not for immediate consumption, such as:

- A grocery store
- Specialty food store
- Beer, wine, or liquor store
- Drugstore
- Convivence store
- Newsstand
- A vending machine or kiosk

See Notice 2021-25.

When determining the 100% meal deduction, the following applies:

- Business meals that don't qualify for the 100% deduction, such as those that were purchased from a grocery store, may still qualify for the 50% deduction.
- The 100% meals deduction applies to amounts paid or incurred after December 31, 2020, and before January 1, 2023.

Remember, ordinary business-related meals are 50% deductible if business travel is either overnight or long enough to require the taxpayer to stop for sleep or rest to properly perform his or her duties. The taxpayer should note the destination and the reason for travel on a daily business mileage document.

Line 10: Commissions and Fees. A commission is a service charge for providing advice on an investment purchase for the taxpayer. The commission must be ordinary and necessary for the type of business the taxpayer claims. Expenses paid for services rendered by a nonemployee could be considered commissions or fees. If more than $600 is paid to one individual, Form 1099-NEC and/or 1099-MISC must be filed, and a copy of the form should be issued to the independent contractor by January 31st of the following year. A copy of the form must be sent to the taxpayer who rendered the work; a copy must also be sent to the IRS along with Form 1096, which is beyond the scope of this course. See Instructions Form 1099(s).

Line 11: Contract Labor. Contract labor includes payments to individuals that are not employees, such as independent contractors. Report the payment amounts on this line.

Line 12: Depletion. Depletion is only deducted when a taxpayer has an economic interest in mineral property such as oil, gas, and standing timber reported on this line.

Line 13: Depreciation. Depreciation is the annual deduction that is allowed or allowable on all qualified business property reported on this line. If the taxpayer has timber depletion, they will use Form T. See Publication 535.

Line 14: Employee Benefit Programs. Employee benefit programs are an expense for the business owner and include retirement plans, disability insurance, life insurance, education assistance, and vacation and holiday pay. Expenses for employees such as accident plans, health plans, dependent-care expenses, and group life insurance plans can be deducted on this line.

Line 15: Insurance. The following business insurance premiums may be deducted on this line:

- Liability insurance.
- Malpractice insurance.
- Casualty insurance, such as fire or theft.
- Workers' compensation insurance.
- Disability insurance that covers the business's overhead expenses if the sole proprietor becomes unable to work.
- Bond insurance.
- Insurance to cover inventory and merchandise.
- Credit insurance.
- Business interruption insurance.

One who is self-employed may qualify to deduct up to 100% of the medical insurance premiums paid for themselves and qualifying family members. To take the deduction, the insurance plan must be established under the business, and the business must make a profit. See Publication 535.

Line 16: Interest. The following are examples of deductible interest reported on this line:

- The portion of mortgage interest related to the business.
- If auto is used in business, business percentage of the auto loan interest.
- Interest capitalization.
- Interest on business purchases.

See Publication 535.

Line 17: Legal and professional fees. The following are examples of deductible legal and professional expenses on this line:

- Bookkeeping and accounting fees.
- Tax preparation fees for business tax preparation.
- Business-related attorney's fees.

See Publication 334 and 535.

Line 18: Office Expense. Office expenses that are not included in office-in-home expenses are deducted here. The following are examples of deductible expenses on this line:

- Postage
- Office supplies

Line 19: Pension and profit-sharing plans. Deduct the contribution portion of an employee's pension or profit-sharing plan that is paid as a benefit to the employee using this line. See Publication 560.

Schedule C

Line 20: Rent or lease. Schedule C, Part II, line 20a, is used for the lease of vehicles, machinery, and equipment rentals. Part II, line 20b, is used for leasing other rental property, such as rent for an office, building, or warehouse. See Publication 560.

Line 21: Repairs and maintenance. Repairs and maintenance of equipment, offices, buildings, or structures are deductible expenses and should include the cost of labor and supplies on this line.

Line 22: Supplies. Ordinary and necessary expenses that are not included in inventory should be deducted on this line.

Line 23: Taxes and licenses. The following are examples of deductible expenses on this line:

- License and regulatory fees for the trade or business.
- Real estate and personal property taxes on business assets.
- State and local sales taxes imposed for the selling of goods or services.
- Social Security and Medicare taxes paid to match employee wages.
- Paid federal unemployment tax.
- Federal highway use tax.
- Contributions to a state unemployment insurance fund or to a disability benefit fund if the contributions are considered taxes under state law.

Do not deduct the following:

- Federal income tax, including the self-employment tax.
- Estate and gift taxes.
- Taxes used to pay for improvements, such as paving and sewers.
- Taxes on the taxpayer's primary residence.
- State and local sales taxes on property purchased for use in the business.
- State and local sales taxes imposed on the buyer that were required to be collected and paid to state and local governments.
- Other taxes and licenses fees not related to the business.

See Publication 535.

Line 24a: Travel. The following are examples of ordinary and necessary business travel expenses that can be deducted on this line:

- Business airfare.
- Hotels for business trips.
- Taxi fares and tips while on business.

Example: Gladys lives in Seattle, Washington, and is a paid tax practitioner. She went to the Latino Tax Fest to learn the latest tax law and updates. The Fest was held on Tuesday, Wednesday, and Thursday. Gladys flew from Seattle to Las Vegas, Nevada, on Sunday and then flew home on Friday. Her ordinary and necessary expenses are the above costs that were incurred during the days of the convention, not the costs that were incurred on Sunday, Monday, and Friday. Her meals and hotel room on Sunday, Monday, and Friday are not a business expense.

See Publication 463.

Line 24b: Meals. Include expenses for meals while traveling away from home on this line.

Line 25: Utilities. Utility expenses include water, gas, electric, and telephone costs. Business telephone expenses do not include the base rate for any personal phone lines into the taxpayer's house, even if they are used for the business. If the taxpayer has additional costs related to the business use of the phone, such as long-distance calls, the taxpayer can deduct those expenses on this line. If the taxpayer has a dedicated second phone line for business, all expenses may be deducted regarding the second phone line via this line.

Line 26: Wages. The gross amount paid in wages (minus employment credits) to employees is deducted from the business' gross income. If the self-employed taxpayer paid themselves out of the profits of the business, those "wages" are not deductible as an expense on line 26. This is considered a *draw* and is not a deductible expense.

Line 27: Other Expenses. Other expenses are deducted in Part V of Schedule C, and the total amount of any deductions in Part V is reported here. Other expenses include any expense that is not described elsewhere and is both ordinary and necessary in the operation of the taxpayer's business.

Part 1 Review Questions

To obtain the maximum benefit from this chapter, LTP recommends that you complete each of the following questions, and then compare them to the answers with feedback that immediately follows. Under governing self-study standards, vendors are required to present review questions intermittently throughout each self-study course.

These questions and explanations are not part of the final examination and will not be graded by LTP.

SC1.1
Which of the following best describes a self-employed taxpayer?

a. An in-home caregiver who is paid by the family.
b. An individual who owns their own corporate company.
c. An individual who owns their own company.
d. An individual who is the general partner of a partnership.

SC1.2
Which business entity may be required to pay self-employment tax?

a. Partnership
b. Corporation
c. Schedule C filer
d. Qualified Joint Ventures

SC1.3
Which accounting period ends in December?

a. Calendar
b. Fiscal
c. Both
d. None

Schedule C

SC1.4
Which of the following would require a self-employed individual to obtain an Employer Identification Number (EIN)?

   a. Pays wages to his employees.
   b. Files Schedule C.
   c. Files Form 1099-MISC.
   d. Pays independent contractors.

SC1.5
Which of the following is not considered a legal and professional fee?

   a. Bookkeeping
   b. Accounting fees
   c. Tax preparation fees
   d. Home mortgage interest

SC1.6
Which of the following is considered a legal and professional fee?

   a. Business-related attorney's fees
   b. Postage
   c. Office supplies
   d. Taxes and licenses

SC1.7
Which of the following is not an accounting method?

   a. Cash method
   b. Accrual method
   c. Combination method
   d. First in, first out

Part 1 Review Questions Answers

SC1.1
Which of the following best describes a self-employed taxpayer?

   a. An in-home caregiver who is paid by the family.
   b. An individual who owns their own corporate company.
   c. **An individual who owns their own company.**
   d. An individual who is the general partner of a partnership.

Feedback: Review section *Sole Proprietorship*.

SC1.2
Which business entity may be required to pay self-employment tax?

   a. Partnership
   b. Corporation
   c. Schedule C filer
   d. Qualified Joint Ventures

Feedback: Review section *Schedule SE: Self-Employment Tax.*

SC1.3
Which accounting period ends in December?

   a. Calendar
   b. Fiscal
   c. Both
   d. None

Feedback: Review section *Accounting Periods.*

SC1.4
Which of the following would require a self-employed individual to obtain an Employer Identification Number (EIN)?

   a. Pays wages to his employees.
   b. Files Schedule C.
   c. Files Form 1099-MISC.
   d. Pays independent contractors.

Feedback: Review section *Identification Numbers.*

SC1.5
Which of the following is not considered a legal and professional fee?

   a. Bookkeeping
   b. Accounting fees
   c. Tax preparation fees
   d. Home mortgage interest

Feedback: Review section *Line 17: Legal and Professional Fees.*

SC1.6
Which of the following is considered a legal and professional fee?

   a. Business-related attorney's fees
   b. Postage
   c. Office supplies
   d. Taxes and licenses

Feedback: Review section *Line 17: Legal and Professional Fees.*

Schedule C

SC1.7

Which of the following is not an accounting method?

a. Cash method
b. Accrual method
c. Combination method
d. First in, first out

Feedback: Review section *Accounting Methods*.

Part 2 Line 30: Business Use of the Home

Report the total amount of expenses from business use of the home on Line 30 of the Schedule C. This amount is typically determined by completing Form 8829, unless the taxpayer elects to use the simplified method.

Portion of 2021 Schedule C

Form 8829: Office in the Home

Self-employed taxpayers may be able to use Form 8829, *Expenses for Business Use of Your Home*, to claim deductions for certain expenses for business use of their home. To qualify for these deductions, the taxpayer must show that they used a space (such as an office) in the home exclusively and regularly for business. The amount of deduction a taxpayer can receive is based on what percent of the house's total square footage is being used for the business.

Example: Monica has an office she uses exclusively to manage and run her catering business. To receive a deduction for her home business expenses, Monica would divide the square footage of her office by the total square footage of her home to find the percentage of expense she can deduct. If her office is 130-square-feet and her home is 1,000-square-feet, then the percentage of her expenses she can deduct would be 13%.

Daycare providers would use Form 8829 to report expenses based on the number of hours spent caring for children or disabled dependents. The time also includes time spent cleaning the house before and after children arrive or leave as well as time spent preparing activities for the children.

Portion of 2021 Schedule 8829

If childcare providers do not use their entire home for childcare, they will use a combination of hours and square feet to determine business use. The home portion does not have to meet the exclusive-use test if the use is for an in-home daycare facility.

Business expenses that apply to a part of the taxpayer's home may be a deductible business expense if the part of the home was exclusively used on a regular basis in all of the following ways:

- As the principal place of business for any of the taxpayer's trade or business.
- As a place of business used by patients, clients, or customers to meet or deal during the normal course of trade or business.
- In connection with the trade or business if the office is a separate structure that is not attached to the taxpayer's home.

Some exceptions to the "space rule used on a regular basis" are certain daycare facilities and storage spaces used for inventory or product samples. The tax professional must determine whether the office in the home qualifies as the taxpayer's principal place of business.

To qualify the office in the home as the primary place of business, the following requirements must be met:

- The taxpayer uses the home exclusively and regularly for administrative or management activities of the taxpayer's trade or business.
- The taxpayer has no other fixed location where the taxpayer conducts substantial administrative or management activities of his or her trade or business.

Administrative or Management Activities

There are many activities that can be considered administrative or managerial in nature. Some of the most common include the following:

- Billing customers, clients, or patients.
- Keeping books and records.
- Ordering supplies.
- Setting up appointments.

Schedule C

> Writing reports or forwarding orders.

If the following activities are performed at another location, the taxpayer would be disqualified from being able to claim the home office deduction:

> The taxpayer conducts administrative or management activities at other locations other than the home.
> The taxpayer conducts administrative or management activities at places that are not fixed locations of his or her business, such as in a car or a hotel room.
> The taxpayer occasionally conducts administrative or management activities at an outside location not at his or her home.
> The taxpayer conducts substantial non-administrative or non-management business activities at a fixed location outside of the home.
> The taxpayer has suitable space to conduct administrative or management activities outside of his or her home but chooses to work at home for these activities.

Example: Fernando is a self-employed plumber. Most of Fernando's time is spent installing and repairing plumbing at customers' homes and offices. He has a small office in his home that he uses exclusively and regularly for the administrative or management activities of his business, such as calling customers, ordering supplies, and keeping his books. Fernando writes up estimates and records of work completed at his customers' premises but does not conduct any substantial administrative or management activities at any fixed location other than his home office. Fernando does not do his own billing. He uses a local bookkeeping service to bill his customers.

Because it is the only fixed location where he does his administrative and managerial activities, Fernando's home office qualifies as his principal place of business for deducting expenses for its use. The fact that a bookkeeper does his billing is not important, as it does not change or impact where Fernando does his business administrative and managerial activities.

Simplified Option for Home Office Deduction

Taxpayers may use a simplified option to figure the home office business deduction. Revenue Procedure 2013-13 provides an optional safe harbor method that taxpayers may use, which is an alternative to the calculation, allocation, and substantiation of actual expenses for purposes of satisfying the Internal Revenue Code section 280A. These rules do not change the home office criteria for claiming business use but instead simplify the ruling for recordkeeping and calculation.

The major highlights of the simplified option are as follows:

> Standard deduction of $5-per-square-foot of home used for business with a maximum 300-square-feet.
> Allowable home-related itemized deductions claimed in full on Schedule A.
> No home depreciation deduction or later recapture of depreciation for the years the simplified option is used.

When selecting a method, the taxpayer must choose to use either the simplified method or the regular method for any taxable year and can make that choice by using their selected method on their tax return. However, once the method has been chosen for the year, it cannot be changed. If the methods are used in different tax years, the correct depreciation table must be used. Year-by-year determination is acceptable.

The deduction under the safe harbor method cannot create a net loss; it is limited to the business' gross income reduced by deductions unrelated to the home office deduction. Any excess is disallowed and cannot be carried over or back, unlike the carryover of unallowed expenses that is available to offset income from that activity in the succeeding year when using the actual expense method.

Regardless of the method that is used to claim the home office, the space must be regularly and exclusively used as the taxpayer's principal place of business. If the taxpayer used the simplified method for tax year 2021, and they chose not to use it for 2022, taxpayer may have an unallowed expense from a prior year carryover to the current year. See Instructions Form 8829.

Regular and Exclusive Use

The portion of the home that is used must be used exclusively for conducting business.

Example: Nadine teaches piano lessons in her home. She has a piano in her spare bedroom and a grand piano in her living room. She uses the piano in her spare bedroom to teach her students and the grand piano for the students' recitals. Nadine does not use the spare bedroom for anything else except teaching students and storing music books related to her students. Her spare bedroom is used exclusively and regularly for business, but her grand piano is not; it is only used for recitals for her students. Therefore, she would only be able to claim the spare bedroom as a deduction and not the living room.

Like everything with tax law there are exceptions to the rule; the taxpayer does not have to meet the exclusive use test if either of the following applies:

- If the taxpayer uses part of their home for storage of inventory or sample product(s), he or she may deduct business use of the home expense if the following conditions are met:
  - The taxpayer sells products at wholesale or retail as his or her trade or business.
  - The taxpayer keeps inventory in his or her home for the trade or business.
  - His or her home is the only fixed location for the trade or business.
  - The storage space is used on a regular basis.
  - The space used can be identifiable as a separate suitable space for storage.
- The taxpayer uses part of the home as a daycare facility.

Principal Place of Business

If the taxpayer conducts business outside of the home and uses his or her home substantially and regularly to conduct business, he or she may qualify for a home office deduction. The taxpayer can also deduct expenses for a separate freestanding structure such as a studio or a barn, but the regular and exclusive use test must apply. To determine if the place used is the primary place of business, the following factors must be considered:

- The relative importance of the activities performed at each location where the taxpayer conducts his or her business.
- The amount of time spent at each location where the taxpayer conducts business.

Schedule C

Portion of 2021 Form 8829

In Publication 587, *Business Use of Your Home*, the IRS provides a simplified method to determine the expenses related to using your home for business.

Expenses

There are three types of expenses included in the operation of a home when considering an office in the home:

- Direct expenses incurred only for the business part of the home such as painting and repairs in the area used for business. These expenses are fully deductible.
- Indirect expenses for running the home such as insurance, utilities, and general repairs (e.g., roof, HVAC, etc.). These expenses are deducted based on the percentage of business use of the home.
- Unrelated expenses only for parts of the home not used for businesses such as lawn care and painting a room not used for business. These expenses are not deductible.

Direct expenses include the following:

- Business portion of casualty losses.
- Insurance: indirect insurance covers the entire home while direct insurance covers the business; rider insurance policies (which are beyond the scope of this course) can be a direct expense.
- Business rent.
- Business repairs for the home.

- Business portion of real estate taxes.
- Business portion of home mortgage interest.

Samples of indirect expenses include:

- *Security system:* The cost to maintain and monitor the system is considered an indirect cost. However, the taxpayer may depreciate the percentage of the system that relates to his business.
- *Utilities and services:* Including electricity, gas, trash removal, and cleaning services.
- *Telephone:* The basic local service charge, including taxes for the first line into the home, is a nondeductible personal expense. Long distance phone calls and the cost of a secondary home phone line used exclusively for business are both deductible expenses.
- *Depreciation:* If the taxpayer owns the home, he or she may deduct depreciation. For more information, see Publication 587. Before calculating the depreciation deduction, the following information is needed:
    - The month and year the taxpayer began using the home for business.
    - The adjusted basis and fair market value of the home at the time the taxpayer began using it for business; the cost of the home plus any improvements, minus casualty losses or depreciation deducted in earlier years; land is never considered part of the adjusted basis.
    - The cost of improvements before and after the taxpayer began using the home for business.
    - The percentage of the home used for business.

The following are expenses that cannot be deducted:

- Bribes and kickbacks.
- Charitable contributions.
- Demolition expenses or losses.
- Dues paid to business, social, athletic, luncheon, sporting, airline, and hotel clubs.
- Lobbying expenses.
- Penalties and fines paid to a governmental agency for breaking the law.
- Personal, living, and family expenses.
- Political contributions.
- Repairs that add value to the home or increase the property life.

Schedule C, Part III, Cost of Goods Sold

The cost of goods sold is used when a business has inventory or produces a product. Inventory must be calculated at the beginning and end of the year.

Schedule C

Portion of 2021 Schedule C

The following items are used to calculate a business's cost of goods sold:

Line 35: Beginning inventory. This should be the same as last year's closing inventory, unless the business was started in the current tax year.

Line 36: Purchases. The amount of reported purchases on this line is the completed products or raw materials used for manufacturing, merchandising, or mining plus the cost of shipping minus the cost of items for personal use.

Line 37: Cost of labor. The cost of labor used in the actual production of the goods. The cost of labor is not wages, which are reported on Schedule C, Part II, line 26, *Wages*. The cost of labor is mainly used in manufacturing or mining, since the labor can be properly charged to the cost of goods sold. A manufacturing business can properly allocate indirect and direct labor to the expense of the cost of goods. A direct expense would be the labor to fabricate raw material into a saleable product.

Line 38: Materials and Supplies. Materials used in the actual production or processing of the goods such as hardware and chemicals are charged to the cost of goods sold.

Line 39: Other Costs. A proportion of overhead expenses related to creating a product. Containers and freight used for raw materials are examples of other costs.

Line 41: Ending Inventory. The counted inventory at the end of the tax year is used as the beginning inventory for the following year's return.

Inventory is an itemized list of goods, with valuations, held for sale or consumption in a manufacturing or merchandising business. Inventory should include all finished or partly finished goods and only those raw materials and supplies that have been acquired for sale or that will physically become a part of merchandise intended for sale. How companies valuate inventory varies from business to business. See Publication 334 for more information.

Schedule C, Part IV, Information on Your Vehicle

Portion of 2021 Schedule C

The taxpayer would enter the information of the vehicle in Part IV to be able to claim the related expenses. Commuting is generally considered travel between home and work. Part IV is used to calculate the standard mileage rate for the taxpayer's vehicle. If more than one vehicle was used, attach a statement containing the same information included in Schedule C, Part IV. The following circumstances may not meet the commuting rules:

> - The taxpayer has at least one regular location away from home, and the travel is to a temporary work location in the same trade or business. See Pub 463.
> - The travel is to a temporary work location outside the location where he or she lives and normally works.
> - The home is the principal place of business, and the travel is to another work location in the same trade or business, regardless of whether the location is regular or temporary and regardless of the distance. See IRC Section 280A(c)(1)(A).

For more information on recordkeeping rules for vehicles, see Publication 463.

Schedule C, Part V, Other Expenses

Other expenses are deducted in Part V, Schedule C. Other expenses include any expense that is not included elsewhere and is both ordinary and necessary in the operation of the taxpayer's business. Once all other expenses have been reported, figure the total amount, and report it on line 48 and line 27a.

Portion of 2021 Schedule C

Schedule C

Any ordinary and necessary business expense that was not deducted elsewhere on Schedule C would be reported in this section. List the type and amount of each expense separately in the spaces provided. If more space is needed, use another sheet of paper. Other expenses can include the following:

- Amortization that began in 2021; Form 4562 will need to be attached.
- Bad business debt that was previously reported as income. If the bad debt is paid off after writing the amount off as a deduction or expense, the business must include the reduction amount that they had received as income on their next return.
- At-risk loss deduction.
- Business start-up costs.
- Costs of making commercial buildings energy efficient.
- Deductions for removing barriers to individuals with disabilities and the elderly.
- Excess farm loss.
- Film and television production expenses.
- Forestation and reforestation costs.

Do not include the following as other expenses:

- Charitable contributions.
- Cost of business equipment or furniture.
- Replacements or permanent improvements to property.
- Personal, living, and family expenses.
- Fines or penalties paid to a government for violating any law.

Bad Debts from Sales or Services

The business owner accrues bad debt when he or she is unable to collect money they are owed by customers. The only kind of debt that can be reported on the tax return is bad business debt. Bad debt that is unrelated to business is not a reportable entry. Bad debt is loss that was either of the following:

- Created or acquired in the taxpayer's trade or business.
- Closely connected to the taxpayer's trade or business when the debt became partly or 100% valueless.

Debts are deductible only when they become totally worthless. When using the cash method of accounting, bad debts cannot be deducted unless the amount was previously included as income. Bad business debts are usually the result of credit card sales to customers.

Start-Up Costs

Start-up costs are the expenses incurred before a business begins due to starting or purchasing a business. Taxpayers can elect to deduct up to $5,000 of start-up costs and up to $5,000 of organizational expenditures that were paid or incurred during the tax year in which the trade or business began. Start-up or organizational expenditures that are not deductible in the year in which the trade or business began must be capitalized and amortized over the course of the 15 years following the business or trade's beginning. See Pub 535.

The following are examples of start-up costs:

- Survey of market.

- Advertisements for the opening of the business.
- Training wages.
- Travel and other expenses incurred to secure distributors, suppliers, etc.
- Consulting fees and professional fees connected with starting a business.
- Legal fees.
- Net operating loss (NOL).

A net operating loss is incurred when business expenses and expenditures exceed business income. Sometimes the loss is great enough to offset income from other tax years. For more information, see Publication 536, *Net Operating Losses (NOLs) for Individuals, Estates and Trusts*.

Part 2 Review Questions

To obtain the maximum benefit from this chapter, LTP recommends that you complete each of the following questions, and then compare them to the answers with feedback that immediately follow. Under governing self-study standards, vendors are required to present review questions intermittently throughout each self-study course.

These questions and explanations are not part of the final examination and will not be graded by LTP.

SC2.1
Which federal form is used with Schedule C to report home office expenses?

a. Form 2106
b. Form 8829
c. Form 4562
d. Form 8889

SC2.2
Which of the following is not a major highlight of the new federal simplified option method?

a. Standard deduction of $15-per-square-foot of home used for business, with a maximum of 300-square-feet.
b. Allowable home-related itemized deductions claimed in full on Schedule A.
c. No home depreciation deduction or later recapture of depreciation for the years the simplified option is used.
d. Standard deduction of $5-per-square-foot of home used for business, with a maximum of 300-square-feet.

SC2.3
Which of the following is not used to calculate cost of goods?

a. Beginning and ending inventory
b. Vehicle mileage
c. Cost of labor
d. Materials

SC2.4
Which of the following is not used to calculate cost of goods?

a. Cost of labor
b. Materials and supplies
c. Ending inventory only
d. Bad debts

SC2.5
Which of the following is a simplified option for the home office deduction?

a. Standard deduction of $5-per-square-foot with a maximum of 300-square-feet
b. Claiming a home deprecation deduction on Form 8829
c. All home-related itemized deductions are claimed on the Schedule C
d. Setting up business appointments

SC2.6
Which of the following is not a simplified option for the home office deduction?

a. Standard deduction of $5-per-square-foot with a maximum of 300-square-feet
b. Cannot claim a home deprecation deduction
c. All home-related itemized deductions are claimed on the Schedule A
d. Billing customers, clients, or patients

Part 2 Review Questions Answers

SC2.1
Which federal form is used with Schedule C to report home office expenses?

a. Form 2106
b. Form 8829
c. Form 4562
d. Form 8889

Feedback: Review section *Form 8829: Office in the Home.*

SC2.2
Which of the following is not a major highlight of the new federal simplified option method?

a. Standard deduction of $15-per-square-foot of home used for business, with a maximum of 300-square-feet.
b. Allowable home-related itemized deductions claimed in full on Schedule A.
c. No home depreciation deduction or later recapture of depreciation for the years the simplified option is used.
d. Standard deduction of $5-per-square-foot of home used for business, with a maximum of 300-square-feet.

Feedback: Review section *Simplified Option for Home Office Deduction.*

SC2.3
Which of the following is not used to calculate cost of goods?

a. Beginning and ending inventory
b. Vehicle mileage
c. Cost of labor
d. Materials

Feedback: Review section *Schedule C, Part III, Cost of Goods Sold.*

SC2.4
Which of the following is not used to calculate cost of goods?

a. Cost of labor
b. Materials and supplies
c. Ending inventory only
d. Bad debts

Feedback: Review section *Schedule C, Part III, Cost of Goods Sold.*

SC2.5
Which of the following is a simplified option for the home office deduction?

a. Standard deduction of $5-per-square-foot with a maximum of 300-square-feet.
b. Claiming a home deprecation deduction on Form 8829.
c. All home-related itemized deductions are claimed on the Schedule C.
d. Setting up business appointments.

Feedback: Review section *Simplified Option for Home Office Deduction.*

SC2.6
Which of the following is not a simplified option for the home office deduction?

a. Standard deduction of $5-per-square-foot with a maximum of 300-square-feet.
b. Cannot claim a home deprecation deduction.
c. All home-related itemized deductions are claimed on the Schedule A.
d. Billing customers, clients, or patients.

Feedback: Review section *Simplified Option for Home Office Deduction.*

Part 3 Qualified Business Income

Qualified Business Income (QBI)

Qualified business income deduction (QBI) is a tax deduction that allows eligible self-employed and small-business owners to deduct up to 20% of their qualified business income on the tax return. Taxpayers' total taxable income for 2021 must be under $164,900 for single filers or $329,800 for joint filers to qualify.

Schedule C

Qualified Business Income (QBI) is the net amount of income, gain, deduction, and loss with respect to any qualified business of the taxpayer. Qualified items of income, gain deduction, and loss include items that are effectively connected with the conduct of a U.S. trade or business and are included in determining the business's taxable income for the tax year.

The Section 199A Qualified Business Income Deduction, enacted as part of the Tax Cuts and Jobs Act in 2017, was meant to provide a tax benefit to smaller flow-through businesses in response to the large decrease in the C corporation tax rate from 35% to 21%.

The initial step in calculating the Sec. 199A deduction begins with determining the QBI, which is determined separately for each of the taxpayer's qualified businesses. Certain investment items are excepted from QBI, including short-term and long-term capital gains and losses, dividends, and interest income not properly allocable to a trade or business. QBI also does not include reasonable compensation payments to a taxpayer for services rendered to a qualified business, guaranteed payments to a partner for services rendered to a business, and, to the extent provided in regulations, a Sec. 707(a) payment to a partner for services rendered to the business (Sec. 199A(c)).

20% Deduction for a Pass-Through Qualified Trade or Business

The combined QBI amount serves as a placeholder: it is the amount of the Section 199A deduction before considering a final overall limitation. Under this overall limitation, a taxpayer's QBI deduction is limited to 20% of the taxpayer's taxable income in excess of any net capital gain. The combined QBI amount is the sum of the deductible QBI amounts for each of the taxpayer's qualified businesses. The deductible QBI amount of a qualified business is generally 20% of its QBI, but the deductible QBI amount may be limited when the business is a specified service trade or business or by a wage and capital limitation. See Sec. 199A(b).

The calculation of a taxpayer's Sec. 199A deduction depends on whether the taxpayer's taxable income is below a lower taxable income threshold ($164,900, or $329,800 if filing a joint return). When computing taxable income for this purpose, the Sec. 199A deduction is ignored.

If a taxpayer has income below the lower threshold, calculating the Sec. 199A deduction is straightforward. The taxpayer first calculates the deductible QBI amount for each qualified business and combines the deductible QBI amounts to determine the combined QBI amount. If the taxpayer has only one qualified business, the combined QBI amount is the deductible QBI amount for that business. The taxpayer then applies the overall taxable income limitation to the combined QBI. Thus, the taxpayer's Sec. 199A deduction is equal to the lesser of the combined QBI amount or the overall limitation (20% × taxpayer's taxable income in excess of any net capital gain).

Issues in Calculating the Deduction

If the taxpayer has taxable income above the higher threshold amount, two issues arise in the calculation of the Sec. 199A deduction. First, a business of the taxpayer will not be treated as a qualified business, and the income of the business of the taxpayer will not be included in QBI if the business meets the definition of a specified service trade or business (see below). Thus, the Sec. 199A deduction will be denied in full for the business. Second, if a business is a qualified business (i.e., it is not a specified service trade or business), the deductible QBI amount for the business is subject to a W-2 wage and capital limitation. Taxpayers with taxable income that is over the phaseout amount are unable to use Sec. 199A deduction for the business income that is a specified service trade or business.

Specified Service Trade or Business

A specified service trade or business is defined in Sec. 199A(d)(2) as "any trade or business which is described in section 1202(e)(3)(A) (applied without regard to the words 'engineering, architecture,') ... or which involves the performance of services that consist of investing and investment management, trading, or dealing in securities (as defined in section 475(c)(2)), partnership interests, or commodities (as defined in section 475(e)(2))."

Sec. 1202(e)(3)(A) defines a "qualified trade or business" as:

> "…any trade or business involving the performance of services in the fields of health, law, engineering, architecture, accounting, actuarial science, performing arts, consulting, athletics, financial services, brokerage services, or any trade or business where the principal asset of such trade or business is the reputation or skill of 1 or more of its employees or owners."

Thus, service trades or businesses (e.g., engineering, architecture, manufacturing, etc.) that are not specified service trades or businesses are eligible for the deduction regardless of the taxpayer's taxable income, but businesses providing specified services (e.g., law, accounting, consulting, investment management, etc.) of taxpayers who have taxable income above the higher taxable income threshold limit are excluded from the deduction.

Taxpayers with Income Above the Threshold

If a taxpayer has taxable income above the higher taxable income threshold and owns a business that is not a specified service trade or business, the QBI deductible amount for the business is subject to a limitation based on W-2 wages or capital (capital here is measured as the unadjusted basis of certain business assets) (Sec. 199A(b)(2)(B)). The deductible QBI amount for the business is equal to the *lesser* of 20% of the business's QBI or the *greater* of 50% of the W-2 wages for the business or 25% of the W-2 wages plus 2.5% of the business's unadjusted basis in all qualified property. Thus, two alternative limitations under Sec. 199A(b)(2) may limit the deductible QBI amount for each business that is included in a taxpayer's combined QBI amount (a pure 50% wage test or a combined 25% wage and capital test).

QBI and the W-2

W-2 wages are total wages subject to wage withholding, elective deferrals, and deferred compensation paid during the tax year that are attributable to QBI (Sec. 199A(b)(4)). However, amounts not properly included in a return filed with the Social Security Administration on or before the 60th day after the due date (including extensions) for that return are not included (Sec. 199A(b)(4)(C)). A partner's allocable share of W-2 wages is required to be determined in the same manner as the partner's share of wage expenses.

QBI and Property

The basis of qualifying property is calculated as the unadjusted basis immediately after acquisition of that property. Qualifying property is tangible property or depreciable property that was held by and available for use in the business at the close of the tax year, or was used in the production of QBI at any time during the year and the "depreciable period" has not ended before the close of the tax year (Sec. 199A(b)(6)).

Schedule C

The depreciable period starts on the date the property is first placed in service and ends the last day of the last full year of the applicable recovery period under Sec. 168 (disregarding Sec. 168(g)) or 10 years after the beginning date, whichever is later. This rule allows "qualified property" to include property that has exhausted its modified accelerated cost recovery system (MACRS) depreciation period if it is still in its first 10 years of service. The statute directs Treasury to provide anti-abuse rules to prevent the manipulation of the depreciable period of qualified property through related-party transactions and for determining the unadjusted basis immediately after the acquisition of qualified property in like-kind exchanges and involuntary conversions.

Service Trade Disqualifier

A taxpayer potentially loses all or part of the Sec. 199A deduction if taxable income rises too high and the income is from a specified service business. The income phaseout amounts are as follows (adjusted for inflation in 2021):

- Single $164,900 - $214,900 partial phase out of Sec. 199A
              $214,901+ complete phase out of Sec. 199A
- MFJ $329,800 - $429,800 partial phase out of Sec. 199A
              $429,801+ complete phase out of Sec. 199A

A taxpayer potentially loses all or part of the Sec. 199A deduction if taxable income rises too high and the income is from a specified service business, which includes "fields of health, law, accounting, actuarial science, performing arts, consulting, athletics, financial services, brokerage services, or any trade or business where the principal asset of the business is the reputation or skill of one or more of its employees or owners."

Taxpayer earnings under the threshold amount could qualify for the Sec. 199A deduction even if the income is from a specified service business.

- Single   < $164,900
- MFJ   < $329,800

Taxpayer earnings over the threshold amount qualify for a lesser amount or for none of the Sec. 199A deduction.

- Single $214,901+
- MFJ $429,801+

The terminology "within the United States" means taxpayers only receive the 20% deduction on business income earned exclusive in the U.S. and on rental income from property located inside the U.S. The taxpayer only counts W-2 wages for businesses or real estate located within the U.S. If depreciable property figures into the formula, the property must be located inside the U.S. Therefore, if an entrepreneur has qualified business income from within and outside the U.S., separate the two before calculating Sec. 199A deduction.

Pass-Through Entities

The pass-through deduction is available regardless of which deduction method is chosen itemized or standard deduction. The deduction cannot exceed 20% of the excess of a taxpayer's taxable income over net capital gain. If QBI is less than zero, it is treated as a loss from a qualified business in the following year.

For pass-through entities other than sole proprietorships, the deduction cannot exceed whichever of the following is greater:

- 50% of the W-2 wages with respect to the qualified trade or business ("W-2 wage limit").
- The sum of 25% of the W-2 wages paid with respect to the qualified trade or business *plus* 2.5% of the unadjusted basis of all "qualified property" immediately after acquisition.

Qualified property is any tangible, depreciable property that is held by and available for use in a qualified trade or business.

For a partnership or S corporation, each partner or shareholder is treated as having W-2 wages for the tax year in an amount equal to his or her allocable share of the W-2 wages of the entity for the tax year. A partner's or shareholder's allocable share of W-2 wages is determined in the same way as the partner's or shareholder's allocable share of wage expenses. For an S corporation, an allocable share is the shareholder's pro rata share of an item. However, the W-2 wage limit begins phasing out in the case of a taxpayer with taxable income exceeding $329,800 for married individuals filing jointly ($164,900 for other individuals). The application of the W-2 wage limit is phased in for individuals with taxable income exceeding these thresholds over the next $100,000 of taxable income for married individuals filing jointly (or $50,000 for other individuals).

Sec. 199A Overview

To get the savings, a business owner may want to make operational, legal, and accounting changes early in the year.

The three major concepts with the Sec. 199A deduction are as follows:

- It benefits the following "pass-through entities":
    - Sole proprietorships.
    - Partnerships.
    - S corporations.
    - Real estate investment trusts (REITs).
    - Qualified cooperatives.
- It shelters taxable income that would otherwise be taxed as ordinary income subject to the highest individual tax rates.
- The bigger the benefit, the more complex the rules.

Schedule C

Recordkeeping

This section will cover basic recordkeeping for all business returns. A tax professional should emphasize to their clients the importance of recordkeeping and to keep business and personal accounts separate. If a taxpayer has a loss on their business return, remind the taxpayer of the hobby rules. The taxpayer does not want to lose expense deductions due to poor recordkeeping; this is where the tax professional should spend time with their clients to educate them on how to track income and expenses. A good recordkeeping system includes a summary of all business transactions. These transactions in books are called journals and ledgers and can be kept electronically or as hard copies (paper). If paper records are kept, they must be locked up. The electronic records must be backed up in case of a computer crash and should be password protected.

Benefits of Recordkeeping

Everyone in business must keep appropriate and accurate records. Recordkeeping will help the taxpayer:

- Monitor the progress of their business.
- Prepare an accurate financial statement.
- Classify receipts.
- Track deductible business expenses.
- Prepare the tax return.
- Support reported income and expenses on the tax return.

Records show the taxpayer if the business is improving, which items sell the best, and insights to increase the success of the business. Records are needed to prepare accurate financial statements, which include profit and loss, balance sheets, and any other financial statements. Taxpayers should identify receipts at the time of purchase. It is easier to get into the habit of tracking receipts when received rather than dealing with them when preparing the tax return. A tax professional should teach clients how to identify and track receipts.

Kinds of Records to Keep

The taxpayer should choose the recordkeeping system that is best for their business. The system should match the accounting method of the taxpayer's tax year. The recordkeeping system should include a summary for all the taxpayer's business transactions. For example, recordkeeping should show gross income as well as deductions and credits for the business. Supporting documentation for consistent transactions, such as purchases, sales, and payroll, should be maintained. It is important to retain documentation that supports the entries in the journal, ledgers, and the tax return. Records for travel, transportation, and gift expenses fall under specific recordkeeping rules. For more information see Publication 463. There are also specific employment tax records the employer must keep. For a complete list, see Publication 51 (Circular A).

Assets used in business can be property, such as machinery and equipment used to conduct business. Records of the asset are used to figure depreciation and the gain or loss when the asset is sold. Records should show the following information:

- When and how the business asset was acquired.

- The purchase price of the business asset.
- The cost of any business improvements.
- Section 179 deduction.
- Business deductions taken for depreciation.
- Business deductions taken for casualty losses, such as losses resulting from fires, storms, or natural disasters.
- How the business asset was used.
- When and how the business asset was disposed.
- The selling price of the asset or the business.
- The expense of the business asset.

The following are examples of records that might show the information from the above list:

- Purchase and sales business invoices.
- Business purchase of real estate closing statements (HUD-1).
- Canceled business checks.
- A business' bank statements.

Maintaining Records

Tax records should be kept as needed for the administration of any provision of the Internal Revenue Code. Business records should be kept that support an item of income or deduction appearing on the return until the period of limitations is finished. Generally, that time frame is a 3-year period, although certain records must be kept longer than 3 years.

Employment records must be kept for at least 4 years after the date the tax becomes due or is paid. Records that pertain to assets such as property should be kept as long as the taxpayer owns the business asset. Other creditors, such as an insurance company, may require the business records to be kept longer than the IRS.

Part 3 Review Questions

To obtain the maximum benefit from this chapter, LTP recommends that you complete each of the following questions, and then compare them to the answers with feedback that immediately follow. Under governing self-study standards, vendors are required to present review questions intermittently throughout each self-study course.

These questions and explanations are not part of the final examination and will not be graded by LTP.

SC3.1
Jade started a new business in 2021. Which of the following is not considered to be self-employment income?

a. Income from Schedule E
b. Income from Schedule F
c. Income from Schedule C
d. Income from wages

Schedule C

SC3.2
Which of the following chooses the recordkeeping system?

   a. Taxpayer
   b. Internal Revenue Service
   c. Franchise Tax Board
   d. Taxpayer's banker

SC3.3
Which of the following best describes how long to keep records?

   a. Employment records need to be kept for at least 6 years.
   b. Business records should be kept if an item of income or deduction appear on the tax return.
   c. Business records that pertain to property should be kept for at least 10 years.
   d. Computer software that was purchased for the business does not need to be kept.

Part 3 Review Questions Answers

SC3.1
Jade started a new business in 2021. Which of the following is not considered to be self-employment income?

   a. Income from Schedule E
   b. Income from Schedule F
   c. Income from Schedule C
   d. Income from wages

Feedback: Review section *Schedule C, Part I, Income.*

SC3.2
Which of the following chooses the recordkeeping system?

   a. Taxpayer
   b. Internal Revenue Service
   c. Franchise Tax Board
   d. Taxpayer's banker

Feedback: Review section *Kinds of Record to Keep.*

SC3.3
Which of the following best describes how long to keep records?

   a. Employment records need to be kept for at least 6 years.
   b. Business records should be kept if an item of income or deduction appear on the tax return.
   c. Business records that pertain to property should be kept for at least 10 years.
   d. Computer software that was purchased for the business does not need to be kept.

Feedback: Review section *How long to Keep Records.*

Takeaways

Business income is derived from a multitude of sources using Schedules C, E, and F. How business income is calculated and which deductions and expenses are reported can vary based on the type of business, the method of accounting used, and many other factors. It is essential that the tax professional be familiar with the concepts when preparing business returns.
There are four common tax errors for business taxpayers:

1. Not paying enough estimated tax.
2. Depositing employment taxes.
3. Filing tax returns and payroll returns late.
4. Not separating business and personal expenses.

See Publication 15, 505, 535, and Circular E for more information.

TEST YOUR KNOWLEDGE!
Go online to take a practice quiz.

Chapter 10 Schedule E

Introduction

Rental income is any payment received for the use or occupation of real estate or personal property. The payment that is received is taxable to the taxpayer and is generally reported on Schedule E. Each Schedule E can report three properties. If the taxpayer has more than three properties, additional Schedule E's would be used. Schedule E is not used to report personal income and expenses. The taxpayer should not use Schedule E to report renting personal property, that is not a business. To report other income, use Schedule 1, lines 8 – 24b.

Objectives

At the end of this lesson, the student will:

- Know the types of income reported on Schedule E.
- Realize the difference between repairs and improvements.
- Recognize where to find the rental property depreciation chart.

Resources

Form 1040	Publication 17	Instructions Form 1040
Form 4562	Publication 527	Instructions Form 4562
Form 4797	Publication 534	Instructions Form 4797
Form 6198	Publication 544	Instructions Form 6198
Form 8582	Publication 925	Instructions Form 8582
Schedule E	Publication 946	Instructions for Schedule E
		Tax Topics 414, 415, 425, 704

Table of Contents

Introduction	372
Reporting Rental Income	375
Types of Rental Income	375
Advance Rent	375
Canceling a Lease	375
Expenses Paid by Tenant	375
Property or Services (instead of rent)	375
Security Deposits	376
Rental Property Also Used as Home	376
Fair Rental Value of Portion of Building Used as a Home	376
Part Interest	376
Lease with Option to Buy	376
Husband and Wife Qualified Joint Venture (QJV)	377
Types of Property	378
Types of Expenses	378
Expenses That Cannot be Claimed	381
Claiming Deductions When Renting Out the House or Part of the Home	382
Other Expenses	382
Depreciation	382
Insurance Premiums Prepaid	382
Interest	382
Expenses Paid to Obtain a Mortgage	382
Legal and Other Professional Fees	383
Local Benefit Taxes	383
Transportation and Travel Expenses	383
Pre-rental Expenses	383
Rental of Equipment	383
Uncollected Rent	384
Vacant Rental Property	384
Points	384
Repairs and Improvements	384
Repairs	384
Improvements	384
Recordkeeping	385
Not Rented for Profit	385
Rental of Vacation Homes and Other Dwelling Units	385
Dividing Expenses for Vacation Homes and Other Dwelling Units	386
Fair Rental Price	386
Use as Main Home Before or After Renting	386
Property Changed to Rental Use	387
Dividing Expenses for Property Changed to Rental Use	387
Depreciation	387
Passive Activity Limits	388
At-Risk Rules	388
Passive Activity Limits	388
Real Estate Professional	388
Limited Partnership Interests	389
Active Participation	389
Rental Property Sales	389
Property That Can Be Depreciated	390
Property Owned	390
Property Having a Determinable Useful Life	391
Property Lasting More than One Year	391
Property used in Business or Income-Producing Activity	391
Property That Cannot Be Depreciated	392
Excepted Property	392

- The Beginning and Ending of Depreciation 392
- Placed in Service 392
- Royalties 392
- Partnership or S Corporation Income 393
- Office in Home 394
- Part I Review Questions 394
- Part 1 Review Questions Answers 395

Takeaways 396

Reporting Rental Income

If the taxpayer rents buildings, rooms, or apartments and provides heat and electric, trash collection, etc., the taxpayer should report the income and expenses in Part I of Schedule E. Do not use Schedule E to report a not-for-profit activity.

If the taxpayer provided significant services primarily for the tenant's convenience, such as regular cleaning, changing linens, or maid service, the taxpayer reports the rental income and expenses on Schedule C (Form 1040), *Profit or Loss from Business*, or Schedule C-EZ, *Net Profit from Business*. Significant services do not include the furnishing of heat and light, cleaning of public areas, trash collection, etc. If the taxpayer provides significant services, the taxpayer may have to pay self-employment tax on the income.

Types of Rental Income

Cash or the fair market value of property received for the use of real estate or personal property is taxable rental income. Individuals who operate on the "cash basis" report their rental income as income when it is constructively received and deduct expenses as they are paid. In addition to normal rent, many other things may be considered rent.

Advance Rent

Advance rent is any amount collected by the taxpayer before the time it is due. This income is reported in the year the taxpayer receives it, regardless of the accounting method and when the income was due.

Example: On March 18, 2021, Matthew signed a 10-year lease to rent Martha's property. During 2021, Martha received $9,600 for the first year's rent and $9,600 as rent for the last year of the lease. Martha must include $19,200 as rental income in 2021 ($9,600 + $9,600 = $19,200).

Canceling a Lease

If the tenant paid the landlord to terminate the lease, the amount received is considered rent. The amount paid from the tenant is included in the year received, regardless of the accounting method.

Expenses Paid by Tenant

If the occupant pays any of the owner's expenses, the payments are rental income. The taxpayer must include them as income and can deduct the rental expenses if they are deductible.

Example: Anet pays the water and sewage bill for Fernando's rental property and deducts the amount from her rent payment. Under her terms of the lease, Anet is not required to pay those bills. Fernando would deduct the amount Anet paid for the water and sewage bill as a utility expense, and include the amount as rental income.

Property or Services (instead of rent)

If the taxpayer receives property or services as rent instead of money, the fair market value of the property or service is included as rent income.

Example: Lynn enjoys painting and she is Leonard's tenant. Lynn offers to paint the rental property in lieu of paying two months' rent. Leonard accepts the offer. Leonard will include in his rental income the amount that Lynn would have paid for two months' rent. Leonard can deduct the same amount that was included as rent as a rental expense.

Security Deposits

Do not include a security deposit as income when received if the owner returns it at the end of the lease. If the owner keeps part or all of the security deposit during any year because the tenant did not perform under the terms of the lease, the owner must include the amount in income for that year.
If a security deposit is to be used as the final rent payment, it is advance rent. The taxpayer would include it in income in the year received.

Rental Property Also Used as Home

If the taxpayer rented property that is also used as his or her home and it is rented for fewer than 15 days during the tax year, do not include the rent received as income. Rental expenses may not be deducted.

Fair Rental Value of Portion of Building Used as a Home

Fair rental value for property is an amount that a person who is not related to the owner would be willing to pay for rental use. If any part of the building or structure is occupied by the taxpayer for personal use, the gross rental income includes the fair rental value of the part occupied for personal use. See Publication 946, *Residential Rental Property*.

Part Interest

If the taxpayer is a partial owner in a rental property, the taxpayer must report their percentage of the rental income from the property.

Lease with Option to Buy

If the rental agreement offers the tenant the right to purchase the property, the payments received under the agreement are considered rental income. If the tenant exercises the right to purchase the property, the payments received for the period after the date of sale are considered part of the selling price.

Husband and Wife Qualified Joint Venture (QJV)

A husband and wife cannot be sole proprietors of the same business. If they are joint owners, they are partners and should file a partnership return on Form 1065, *U.S. Return of Partnership Income.* They can be partners, but "sole" means one. For purposes of a business, the IRS does not recognize spouses as one.

If the taxpayer and spouse each materially participated in the business as the only members of a jointly owned and operated business and file a joint return, they can elect to be taxed as a qualified joint venture instead of a partnership. Generally, this election does not increase the total tax on the joint return, but it gives the credit for each taxpayer's social security earnings. If Form 1065 was filed for a prior year, the partnership terminates the year immediately preceding the year the joint venture election takes effect.

To make the election, the taxpayers must divide all income and expenses and file two separate Schedule E. Once the election is made, it can only be revoked with IRS permission. The election remains in effect for as long the spouses file as a qualified joint venture. If the taxpayer and spouse do not qualify in one year, then the next year they will need to redo the paperwork to become a qualified joint venture.

Community Income Exception

If the spouses own an unincorporated business and they live in a state, foreign country, or a U.S. possession that has community property laws, the income and deductions are reported as follows:

1. If only one spouse participates in the business, all of the income from that business is self-employment earnings of the spouse who carried the business.
2. If both spouses participate, the income and the deductions are allocated to the spouses based on their distributive shares.
3. If either or both spouses are partners in a partnership, see Publication 541.
4. If the taxpayer and spouse elected to treat the business as a qualifying joint venture, both taxpayer and spouse must file separate Schedule C or C-EZ and a separate Schedule SE.

Schedule E

Community property law states are Arizona, California, Idaho, Louisiana, Nevada, New Mexico, Texas, Washington, and Wisconsin.

Types of Property

```
Type of Property:
1 Single Family Residence    3 Vacation/Short-Term Rental   5 Land        7 Self-Rental
2 Multi-Family Residence     4 Commercial                   6 Royalties   8 Other (describe)
```

Like determining a filing status, rental property(s) need to be classified as well. Single family residence means any building situated on one lot with a single dwelling, and sharing no common wall, foundation, or other interconnection. Types of single-family residences are mobile homes, homes, and mansions. Use code 1 for these structures.

Multi-family residence is a classification of housing where multiple separate housing units for residential inhabitants are contained within one building. This includes duplex, tri-plex, condos, and/or apartments. Use code 2 for these structures.

Commercial buildings include offices, hotels, malls, retail stores, etc. Use code 4 for these structures.

Land is never depreciated, but property may need to report income for renting out the land. Use code 5 for this use. Items considered rent income include renting the land to a farmer to grow crops; this would not be reported on Schedule F, but Schedule E. Basis for land is the price determined by the county as land value. It is also found on the property statement.

Royalties is income derived from the use of the owner's property. A royalty payment must relate to the use of a valuable right. A valuable right could be items such as precious minerals (gold, silver, etc.) and crude oil.

Self-rental is when the owner of the property rents the business to their business. This is regarded as materially participates, therefore any net income for the property is deemed to be nonpassive.

Types of Expenses

```
Expenses:
 5  Advertising
 6  Auto and travel (see instructions)
 7  Cleaning and maintenance
 8  Commissions
 9  Insurance
10  Legal and other professional fees
11  Management fees
12  Mortgage interest paid to banks, etc. (see instructions)
13  Other interest
14  Repairs
15  Supplies
16  Taxes
17  Utilities
18  Depreciation expense or depletion
19  Other (list) ▶
20  Total expenses. Add lines 5 through 19
```

Deductible rental expenses are expenditures that are incurred in renting the property. The taxpayer would deduct all ordinary and necessary expenses such as:

Advertising – line 5

Generally, advertising is considered an ad in a local paper, online, or other means of advertising to cause a potential renter to inquire about the property. The price paid is the amount entered on this line.

Auto and Travel – line 6

Taxpayer can deduct ordinary and necessary auto and travel expenses related to the rental activity. The taxpayer should keep track of the miles to and from the rental. Generally, the mileage that is ordinary and necessary is collecting rent, working on the rental, etc. The standard mileage rate is used for the current tax year. Taxpayer can claim the mileage only if they:

1. Owned the vehicle and used the standard mileage rate for the first year placed in service.
2. Leased the vehicle and are using the standard mileage rate for the entire lease period.

Señor 1040 Says: The taxpayer cannot deduct car rental or lease payments, depreciation, or the actual auto expense if the standard mileage rate is used.

Cleaning and Maintenance – line 7

The day-to-day maintenance of the property is an allowed expense provided it is only for common areas and day-to-day cleanliness. These expenses are also limited to the days that are allowable rental days and not personal use days.

Commissions – line 8

Fees or commission paid to agents who collect the rent, maintain the rental, or find tenants could be reported on line 8.

Insurance – line 9

Insurance for the rental property and the rider policy if the taxpayer has one.

Legal and Other Professional Fees – line 10

You can't claim legal fees charged as part of buying or selling the property. The only exception is if the taxpayer is in the business of renting properties, and the total legal expenses for the current tax income year are $10,000 or less.

The taxpayer can claim fees paid to an accountant for managing their accounts and the tax return preparation and tax advice. Fees involved for setting up the rental property are not a deduction.

Schedule E

Management Fees – line 11

Property management services are reported on line 11 and may lower the taxpayer's liability. The taxpayer may claim the entire cost of the services, but must keep all invoices or statements the property management company issues as evidence of the deduction's eligibility.

Part of property management is to maintain the paperwork between the tenant and the landlord. This can come in handy during tax season, especially for landlords who are not particularly organized or good at bookkeeping. When the management company prepares the paperwork for the tax preparer, it can deliver a more accurate tax return.

Mortgage Interest Paid to Banks – line 12

The taxpayer can claim the interest charged on money borrowed to buy the rental property, but not the entire mortgage payment.

If the taxpayer borrowed money against the rental and did not use it for the rental, the interest is not a deduction on Schedule E.

Other Interest – line 13

If the taxpayer paid interest on the rental income to an individual and did not receive Form 1098, enter the amount on line 13 and not on line 12. Attach to the return a statement that shows the name and address of the person who received the income. On the dotted line next to line 13 enter "See attached."

Repairs – line 14

The taxpayer can claim costs for repairs to the property or general maintenance. However, if the taxpayer is doing the work themselves, only claim the materials and not the time it took to repair the property. If the work is more of an improvement than a repair, then the taxpayer cannot claim the cost as an expense. The distinction between repairs and improvements can be tricky. If the taxpayer is unsure whether work done on the property is a repair or maintenance, then the tax professional would need to ask questions to help the taxpayer determine the difference.

Supplies – line 15

"Materials and supplies" are tangible property used or consumed in the business operations that fall within any of the following categories:

> - Tangible items that cost less than $200.
> - Personal property with an economic useful life of 12 months or less.
> - Spare parts that have been acquired to maintain or repair a unit of tangible property.

The cost of such items may be deducted in the year the item is used or consumed. To use this deduction, the taxpayer should keep records of when items are used or consumed for the rental property.

Schedule E

Cleaning and repair supplies are fully deductible, and some materials are as well. Supplies used in maintenance or to complete repairs are reported under supplies and not added to line 14. Materials on the other hand are generally not "used up" and sometimes become a part of the property. Materials used for improvements are usually depreciated, but materials used for repairs are considered supplies and can be deducted.

For example, the taxpayer changed the roof on their rental property. Nails and tar would be considered repair supplies, while roof shingles would be considered as repair materials. The supplies get deducted, and the materials are added to the basis and depreciated separately over 27.5 years.

If the roof replacement was a repair and not an improvement (replacing a leaky roof), the roof shingles would be considered repair supplies, and would be deducted in the year the expenses were incurred.

Taxes – line 16

This line reports the property tax paid on the property. Like the primary home, one cannot claim the bonds or other add-on taxes that are not related to the property.

Utilities – line 17

Utilities that can be claimed are what the taxpayer pays, such as water, electricity, etc. If the renter is the one paying these expenses, it is not a landlord deduction.

Depreciation – line 18

Depreciation is the annual deduction one must take to recover the cost or other basis of business or investment property having a useful life. Depreciation starts when the taxpayer puts the property into service.

Other Expenses – line 19

What is claimed on this line is any ordinary and necessary expenses not included in lines 5 - 18.

Expenses That Cannot be Claimed

The taxpayer cannot claim deductions for capital expenses, private expenses, or expenses that do not relate to the rental. Capital expenses are the costs of buying a capital asset or increasing its value, for example the cost of buying the property and making improvements. Private expenses are things purchased for their own benefit, rather than to generate rental income.

Rental income expenses that are unable to be used on the taxpayer's personal income tax return:

- Purchase price of a rental property.
- Capital portion of mortgage repayments.
- Interest on money borrowed for any purpose other than financing a rental property.
- The costs of making additions or improvements to the property.
- The costs of repairing or replacing damaged property, if the work increases the property's value.
- Real estate agent fees (commissions) charged as part of buying or selling the property.

Claiming Deductions When Renting Out the House or Part of the Home

The general rule is to claim expenses related to the rental activity only. One cannot claim private living costs or capital expenses. Private living costs include the taxpayer's day-to-day costs, such as food, electricity, or gas. Capital expenses include buying furniture for the rented room or the cost of improving that portion of the property. The taxpayer can claim depreciation on capital expenses. Expenses the taxpayer may be able to claim include electricity, gas, telephone and internet, insurance, or rates that are related to the rental portion. If the taxpayer is living in the house, these expenses will need to be apportioned.

Renting Out the House - Apportionment

If the taxpayer rents out the house on an occasional basis, the taxpayer can claim the percentage of expenses for the time the house is rented. This may apply where the taxpayer rents out the house or property while away for a short period of time. The percentage of expenses claimed must match the amount of time in the tax year the house was rented out.

Renting Out a Room - Apportionment

If the taxpayer is renting out part of the home, the taxpayer can only claim expenses that relate to that part of the property. The taxpayer can only claim expenses for the time the room was rented out and occupied. Expenses could be claimed as a percentage based on the total area of the home and the rented room area.

Other Expenses

Depreciation

Depreciation is a capital expense. Depreciation begins when the property has been placed in service.

Insurance Premiums Prepaid

If the owner prepays an insurance premium for more than one year in advance, the payment will be applied for the year it was used.

Example: Gary paid $1,200 for his insurance on April 15, 2021, for 2021 and 2022. Gary will apply $600 for insurance in 2021 and $600 for insurance in 2022. He cannot take the entire amount in 2021.

Interest

Mortgage interest paid on the rental building could be deducted in the year paid. If the taxpayer owns a partial interest in a rental property, part of the rental expenses for that property can be deducted based on the taxpayer's percentage interest.

Expenses Paid to Obtain a Mortgage

Expenses that include mortgage commissions, abstract fees, and recording fees are capital expenses and are added to the basis of the property.

Legal and Other Professional Fees

These fees include legal and other professional fees such as tax preparation and expenses paid to resolve a tax underpayment related to rental activities. Federal taxes and penalties are not deductible.

Local Benefit Taxes

A deduction cannot be taken for charges of local benefits that increase the value of the rental property. Examples of such charges are putting in streets, sidewalks, or water and sewer systems. These charges are capital expenditures that cannot be depreciated. The charges may be added to the basis of the property. Local benefit taxes may be deducted if they are for maintaining, repairing, or paying interest charges for the benefits.

Transportation and Travel Expenses

Taxpayers can deduct ordinary and necessary local transportation expenses if they incur them while collecting rental income or to manage, conserve, or maintain the rental property. If taxpayers use a personal vehicle for maintaining rental activities, the deduction of the expenses is either by actual expenses or the standard mileage rate. For 2021 the business mileage rate is 56 cents per mile. For tax year 2022, the rate is 58.5 cents per mile.

The taxpayer can deduct the ordinary and necessary expenses of traveling away from home if the primary purpose of the trip was to collect rental income or to manage, conserve, or maintain rental property. The taxpayer must properly allocate expenses between rental and nonrental activities.
Information needed to record auto expenses accurately:

- Beginning mileage
- Ending mileage
- Commuting mileage
- Business mileage (notes about the destination and reason for travel should be made)
- Separate records for each rental property

If the taxpayer rents only part of the property, the expenses must be allocated between the part rented and the part that is not rented.

Pre-rental Expenses

The taxpayer can deduct ordinary and necessary expenses for managing, conserving, or maintaining rental property from the time it is made available for rent.

Rental of Equipment

The taxpayer could deduct the rent paid for equipment that is used for rental purposes. Nevertheless, if the lease contract is a purchase contract, the taxpayer cannot deduct these payments.

Uncollected Rent

If the taxpayer uses the cash-basis, the taxpayer cannot deduct uncollected rent since the cash-basis taxpayer was never included in income. If the taxpayer is an accrual-basis taxpayer, the taxpayer must report the income when it is earned. If the taxpayer is unable to collect the rent, one may be able to deduct it as a bad-debt business expense.

Vacant Rental Property

If the taxpayer holds property for rental purposes, the taxpayer may be able to deduct ordinary and necessary expenses for managing, conserving, or maintaining rental property from the time it became available for rent. Loss of rental income is not deductible.

Points

Points are used to describe certain charges paid or treated as paid by a borrower to obtain a home mortgage. Points are not added to the basis of the property.

Repairs and Improvements

Repairs

Maintains the good condition of the rental property. Repairs do not add to the value of the property or substantially prolong its life. The following are examples of repairs:

- Repainting the property inside and out.
- Fixing gutters or floors.
- Fixing leaks.
- Plastering a hole in a wall.
- Replacing broken windows.

If repairs are made during an extensive remodeling of the property, the whole job is an improvement. Improvements add value to the property and prolong the property's useful life. Improvements to property must be capitalized. The capitalized costs can generally be depreciated as if the improvements were separate property.

Example: Janice purchased an old Victorian house. The house needed many repairs, such as re-plastering, repainting, replacing broken windows, replacing roof tiles, and fixing leaks. After taking several months to complete the repairs, Janice was finally able to place the property on the market for rent. The remodeling of the property is considered an improvement, not a repair.

Improvements

Any expense that is paid to improve the property must be capitalized. An improvement adds value or prolongs the property life, restores the property, and/or adapts the property to a new or different use. Examples include:

> *Betterment* includes expenses for fixing a pre-existing defect or condition or for enlarging or expanding the property.

Restoration includes expenses for replacing a substantial structural part of the property, repairing damage to the property, or rebuilding the property to a like-new condition.

Adaptation includes expenses for altering the property to a use that is not consistent with the intended ordinary use of the property.

Recordkeeping

Keeping records is a way to show proof of any deduction that has been claimed on the tax return. Generally, one should keep the records for at least three years from the date of filing the tax return and claiming the deduction.

The taxpayer must keep records regarding travel and transportation expenses. The record-keeping requirements for travel and transportation expenses are the same as the requirements discussed in earlier chapters.

The taxpayer must also keep records regarding expenses and days of rental use. Records should be kept if the taxpayer or a member of the family used the rental property for personal purposes. The taxpayer should keep records of days he or she personally spent on repairing or maintaining the property.

Not Rented for Profit

If the property is not rented with the intent of making a profit, the expenses can be deducted only up to the amount of income. In this situation, the income is reported on Schedule 1, lines 8 – 24b. The mortgage interest, real estate taxes, and casualty losses are deducted on the appropriate lines of Schedule A. Other expenses are deducted on Schedule A, line 22, and are subject to the 2% floor. If the taxpayer rents the home fewer than 15 days a year, the taxpayer does not have to report any of the rental income and cannot deduct any of the expenses.

Rental of Vacation Homes and Other Dwelling Units

If the taxpayer uses a dwelling as both a home and a rental unit, expenses must be divided between personal use and rental use. The taxpayer uses a dwelling as a home if he or she uses it for personal use more than the greater of:

- 14 days
- 10% of the total days it is rented to others at a fair rental price

Personal use consists of any day the unit is used by:

- The taxpayer or other person who has an interest in it unless rented to another owner as the main home under a shared equity financing agreement.
- A family member or member of any other family who has an interest in it unless the family member uses the dwelling as his or her main home and pays fair rental price.
- Anyone under an arrangement that lets the taxpayer use some other dwelling unit even if that person pays a fair rental price.
- Anyone who uses the dwelling at less than a fair rental price.

Schedule E

Days spent substantially working full time to repair or maintain the property do not count as personal days. If any part of a building or structure is occupied by the taxpayer for personal use, its gross rental income includes the fair rental value of the part occupied for personal use.

Dividing Expenses for Vacation Homes and Other Dwelling Units

If a unit is used for both rental and personal use, the expenses must be divided between the two. Any day that the unit is rented at the fair market value and used for both rental and personal use, the expenses are considered business use. Any day that the unit is available for rent but not actually rented is not a day of rental use.

Example: A ski lodge is available for rent from November 1 through March 31 (a total of 151 days, using 28 days for February). The taxpayer's family uses it for 14 days in October. No one rents it the first week of November or at any time in March. The person who rented it the first week in December was called home on an emergency and let the taxpayer's daughter use it for two days. The remainder of the year the lodge is closed and not used by anyone.

$\quad$ Rental Days: $151 - 38 = 113$

The lodge was available for 38 days in which it was not rented. Days used by taxpayer and/or the taxpayer's family on which fair rental price was received count as rental days. The use by the taxpayer's daughter in December is recorded as rental days.

$\quad$ Total Use: $113 + 14 = 127$

Personal Use: Percentage on rental is $113/127 = 89\%$. The deductible portion of any expenses is 89%. If the taxpayer does not have a profit from the rental, deductible expenses are limited.

Fair Rental Price

A fair rental price for property is an amount that a person who is not related to the taxpayer would be willing to pay. The rent charged is not a fair rental price if it is substantially less than rent charged for other similar properties. Ask the following questions when comparing one property to another:

- Is it used for the same purpose?
- Is it approximately the same size?
- Is it in approximately the same condition?
- Does it have similar furnishings?
- Is it in a similar location?

If any one of the answers are no, the properties are not similar.

Use as Main Home Before or After Renting

Do not count personal days when the property was used as a main home or after renting or offering it for rent in either of the following:

1. The taxpayer rented or tried to rent the property for 12 or more consecutive months.

2. The taxpayer rented or tried to rent the property for a period of less than 12 consecutive months, and the period ended because the property was sold or exchanged.

This special rule does not apply when dividing expenses between rental and personal use.

Property Changed to Rental Use

If the taxpayer converts their home or other property (or a part of it) to rental use at any time other than at the beginning of the year, the taxpayer must divide the yearly expenses (such as depreciation, taxes, and insurance) between rental use and personal use. The taxpayer can deduct as rental expenses only the portion of the expenses that was for the part of the year the property was used or held for rental purposes. The taxpayer cannot deduct insurance or depreciation for the part of the year the property was held for personal use. The taxpayer can deduct home mortgage interest and real estate taxes as an itemized deduction on Schedule A for the part of the year the property was used for personal purposes.

Dividing Expenses for Property Changed to Rental Use

If an expense is for both personal and rental use, the expense must be divided between personal and rental use. Any reasonable method can be used to divide the expense. For example, it may be reasonable to divide the cost of some items, such as water, based on the number of people using them. However, the two most common methods for dividing expenses are:

1. Dividing an expense based on the number of rooms in the home
2. Dividing an expense based on the square footage of the home

Depreciation

Depreciation is the annual deduction for recovery of the purchase price of the fixed-asset expenditure. Property used for business should be depreciated. The amount of depreciation taken each year is determined by the basis of the property, the recovery period for that property, and the depreciation method. The recovery period for residential rental property under MACRS is 27.5 years and is used for property placed in service after 1986.

Depreciation for rental property (in the year placed in service) is reported on Form 4562, *Depreciation and Amortization*, and flows to Schedule E.

Depreciation that was not taken in one year cannot be taken in a following year, but an amended return (Form 1040X) can be filed for the year in which it was not taken (if no more than three years prior). If depreciable property is sold, its basis for determining gain or loss will be reduced by depreciation "allowed or allowable," even if not deducted. Land is never depreciated.

Section 179 deductions cannot be used to depreciate rental property. The rental property can be depreciated if all of the following requirements are met:

➢ The taxpayer owns the property.
➢ The taxpayer uses the property as an income-producing activity.
➢ The property has a determinable useful life.
➢ The property is expected to last more than one year.

Schedule E

Passive Activity Limits

Passive activity is an activity in which the taxpayer did not materially participate during the tax year. The two types of passive activity:

1. Trade or business not materially participated in
2. Rental activities even if the taxpayer participated in

Material participation is the involvement in the activity of the business on a regular, continuous, and substantial basis. The taxpayer can claim a passive loss only against active income. Any excess passive activity loss can be carried forward to future years until used, or until it can be deducted in the year when the taxpayer disposes of the activity in a taxable transaction.

At-Risk Rules

The at-risk rules place a limit on the amount that can be deducted as a loss from rental real estate activity. Losses from holding real property (other than mineral property) placed in service before 1987 are not subject to the at-risk rules.

Generally, any loss from an activity subject to the at-risk rules is allowed only to the extent of the total amount at risk in the activity at the end of the tax year. The taxpayer is considered at-risk in an activity to the extent that cash and the adjusted basis of other property contributed to the activity and certain amounts borrowed for use in the activity.

The taxpayer may need to complete Form 6198 to figure their loss if:

- The taxpayer has a loss from the activity that is a trade or business or for production of income
- The taxpayer is not at-risk in this activity.

Passive Activity Limits

Rental real estate activities are passive activities; exceptions may apply for certain real estate professionals. Rental activity is when the taxpayer receives income mainly for the use of tangible property, rather than for services. Deductions or losses from passive activities are limited. Taxpayers cannot offset their income with passive activity income; passive activity income can only offset passive activity loss. The excess loss or credit is carried forward to the next tax year.

Real Estate Professional

Generally, rental activities are passive activities even if the taxpayer materially participates. However, the activity may not be passive if all of these are true:
- The taxpayer is a real estate professional
- During the year the individual materially participated in the rental activities
- Participates more than 750 hours in performing personal services in the trade or business
- Spends half of the time performing personal services in real property

Qualified activities include developing, redeveloping, constructing, reconstructing, acquiring, converting, operating, managing, leasing, or selling real property. A taxpayer materially participates in an activity if for the tax year the taxpayer was involved in its operation on a regular, continuous, and substantial basis during the year. If the taxpayer meets these requirements, the rental business is not a passive activity. If the taxpayer has multiple properties, each one is treated separately unless the taxpayer chooses to treat them as one activity. Personal services that were performed as an employee cannot be counted. If the taxpayer files a joint return, the hours cannot be added together to fulfill the requirements.

Limited Partnership Interests

If the taxpayer held property in a limited partnership as a limited partner, the taxpayer does not materially participate in rental real estate. Failure to meet the minimum-hours threshold may result in the passive activity amount being limited. Proper recordkeeping is the key to making sure that if the taxpayer is ever audited, the taxpayer does not lose their passive activity loss (PAL).

Active Participation

If a taxpayer owned at least 10% of the rental property and made management decisions in a significant and bona fide sense, he or she is considered to have active participation. Management decisions include approving new tenants, deciding on rental terms, approving expenditures, and similar decisions. In most cases, all rental real estate activities are passive activities. For this purpose, a rental activity is an activity from which income is received mainly for the use of tangible property rather than for services.

Example: Christian is single and had the following income and losses during the tax year:

Salary	$56,954
Lottery winnings	$10,000
Rental loss	($3,450)

The rental loss resulted from a residential rental house that Christian owned. Christian made all the management decisions including collecting rent, making repairs, or hiring someone to complete the repairs, and approving the current tenant. Christian actively participated in the rental property management; therefore, he can use the entire loss of $3,450 to offset his other income.

Rental Property Sales

When rental property or other business assets are sold, the gain or loss must be reported on Form 4797, *Sales of Business Property*. If the property sold includes land, both the land and the property must be reported on Form 4797. Each property is reported separately in the appropriate part of Form 4797. The different sections of Form 4797 are as follows:

Part I: Used to report sales of the section 1231 portion of a real estate transaction. This includes land and all long-term property sold at a loss. A transaction reported here are not required to report in Part III.

Part II: Used to report sales of business property that are not reported in Part I or Part III.

Schedule E

Part III: Used to calculate the recapture of depreciation and certain other items that must be reported as ordinary income on the disposition of property. The property includes sections 1245, 1250, 1252, 1254, and 1255 property sales. This includes most long-term property that was depreciated and sold at a gain.

Depreciation should be calculated (and deducted on the appropriate form) for the period prior to the sale. If the taxpayer sells or exchanges property used partly for business or rental purposes and partly for personal purposes, the taxpayer must figure the gain or loss on the sale or exchange as though two separate pieces of property were sold. The taxpayer must divide the selling price, selling expenses, and the basis of the property between the business or rental part and the personal part. The taxpayer must subtract depreciation that was taken or could have taken from the basis of the business or rental part. Gain or loss on the business or rental part of the property may be a capital gain or loss or an ordinary gain or loss. Any gain on the personal part of the property is a capital gain. The taxpayer cannot deduct a loss on the personal part.

Depreciation is the annual deduction that allows taxpayers to recover the cost or other basis of their business or investment property over a certain number of years. Depreciation begins when a taxpayer places property in service for use in a trade or business or to produce income. The property ceases to be depreciable when the taxpayer has fully recovered the property's cost or other basis or when the property has been retired from service, whichever comes first.

Property That Can Be Depreciated

Most types of tangible property can be depreciated. Examples of tangible property are:

- Buildings
- Vehicles
- Machinery
- Furniture
- Equipment
- Storage facilities

Land is tangible property and can never be depreciated. Some intangible items that can be depreciated are:

- Copyrights
- Patents
- Computer software if life value is more than one year.

Property that needs to be depreciated must meet the following requirements:

- Must be the taxpayer's own property.
- Must be used in the taxpayer's business or income-producing activity.
- Property must have a determinable useful life.
- The property is expected to last more than one year.

Property Owned

To claim depreciation, one must be the owner of the property, even if the property has debt. Leased property can be claimed only if ownership in the property includes the following:

- The legal title to the property.
- The legal obligation to pay for the property.
- The responsibility to pay maintenance and operating expenses.
- The duty to pay any taxes on the property.
- The risk of loss if the property is destroyed, condemned, or diminished in value through obsolescence or exhaustion.

Example: Amanda made a down payment on a rental property and assumed Terrance's mortgage. Amanda owns the property and can depreciate it.

If the property is held as a business or investment property as a life tenant, the taxpayer may depreciate the property.

Property Having a Determinable Useful Life

Property must have a determinable useful life to be depreciated. It must be something that wears out, decays, is used up, becomes obsolete, or loses its value from natural causes.

Property Lasting More than One Year

To depreciate property, the useful life must be one year or more.

Example: Ms. Lady maintains a library for her tax business. She purchases yearly technical journals to use in her tax business. The library would be depreciated, but the technical journals do not have a useful life of more than one year. The technical journals can be taken as a yearly business expense.

Property used in Business or Income-Producing Activity

To claim depreciation on property one must use it in their business or an income-producing activity. If the taxpayer uses the property to produce an investment use, then the income is taxable. One cannot depreciate property that one uses solely for personal activities.

If the property has a multiple use business and personal purpose, the portion that is used as business may be depreciated. For example, the taxpayer cannot deduct deprecation on a car used only for commuting to and from work or used for personal shopping trips and family vacations. Records must be kept showing business and personal use of the property.

Inventory cannot be depreciated. Inventory is any property that is held primarily for sale to customers in the ordinary course of business. If the owner is in the rent-to-own business, certain property held in that business may be considered as depreciable instead of inventory. See Publication 946.

Containers for the products one sells are part of inventory and is not depreciable. Containers used to ship products can be depreciated if the life expectancy is more than one year and meet the following requirements:

1. Qualify as property used in business
2. Title to the containers does not pass to the buyer

Property That Cannot Be Depreciated

Land does not wear out; therefore, it cannot be depreciated. The cost of land generally includes clearing, grading, planting, and landscaping. Although land is never depreciated, certain improvements to the land can be depreciated, such as landscaping.

Excepted Property

The following property cannot be depreciated even if the requirements are met:

1. Property placed in service and disposed of in the same year.
2. Equipment used to build capital improvements.
3. Section 197 intangibles that must be amortized.
4. Certain term interests.

The Beginning and Ending of Depreciation

Depreciation begins when the property is placed in service for use in a trade or business or to produce income. Depreciation ends when the cost (or other basis) has been fully recovered or when it has been retired from service, whichever comes first.

Placed in Service

Property is placed in service when it is ready and available for a specific use for a business activity, an income-producing activity, a tax-exempt activity, or a personal activity. Even if the property is not being used, it is still placed in service when it is ready and available for its specific use.

Example 1: Joel purchased a machine in December of last year for his business. The machine was delivered but not installed. Joel had the machine installed and ready for use in February of the current tax year. The machine would be placed in service in February of the current year.

If the property has been converted from personal to business use, the "placed in service" date is the date it was converted to business use or to an income-producing activity. In other words, depreciation begins when the property has been placed in service.

Example 2: Nicolas purchased a home as his primary residence in 2016, and in 2021 he converted it to a rental property. He placed the home in service in 2021; therefore, Nicolas would start depreciation when it was placed in service as an income-producing property.

Royalties

Portion of Schedule E

Royalty income is reported on Schedule E as ordinary income. The following are examples of royalty income:

- Copyrights on literary, musical, or artistic works.
- Patents on inventions.
- Gas, oil, and mineral properties.
- Depletion, if the taxpayer is the owner of an economic interest in mineral deposits or oil and gas wells.
- Coal and iron ore.

Like rental income, expenses reduce this income. If the taxpayer was self-employed as a writer, inventor, artist, etc., income and expenses should be reported on Schedule C.

If the taxpayer is in business as a self-employed writer, artist, or musician, or if they hold an operating oil, gas, or mineral interest, the income and expenses would be reported on Schedule C. Royalties from copyrights and patents, oil and gas, and mineral properties are taxable as ordinary income and are reported on page 1 of Schedule E.

Taxable rental income and taxable income from royalties is reported on Schedule E and reported on Form 1040, line 17. However, income from renting hotel rooms or other retail property where the renter provides significant additional services is not reported on Schedule E; it is reported as business income on Schedule C.

Partnership or S Corporation Income

Portion of Schedule E

Income a taxpayer receives from a partnership or an S corporation is taxable. Neither the partnership nor the S corporation pays taxes. The taxes are "passed through" to the partners or shareholders, who report the income, as well as some of the expenses, on their individual tax returns. This income is reported on Schedule E, page 2.

Taxpayers should receive a Schedule K-1 from the partnership or S corporation, which will show the income and expenses the taxpayers would report on their individual returns.

Part II on page 2 of Form 1040, Schedule E is used to report partnership and shareholders of a subchapter S corporation income from the Schedule K-1. If the taxpayer actively participates in their partnership's business, it is nonpassive income or nonpassive loss. Partnership income is reported to each partner on Schedule K-1.

Schedule E

Office in Home

If the taxpayers use an area of their home as an office to manage or maintain records for their rental property, they are allowed to deduct expenses for an office in the home. Schedule E filers should complete the "office in the home" worksheet used by employees to calculate their home office expenses. The taxpayer should deduct the home office expenses on Schedule E under the "Other" heading.

Part I Review Questions

To obtain the maximum benefit from this chapter, LTP recommends that you complete each of the following questions, and then compare them to the answers with feedback that immediately follows. Under governing self-study standards, vendors are required to present review questions intermittently throughout each self-study course.

These questions and explanations are not part of the final examination and will not be graded by LTP.

SE1.1
Marlene paid $4,000 for real estate taxes on her rental property located at 1850 Happy Street, Jersey City, New Jersey. She paid $6,850 of real estate taxes on her primary residence. Marlene has household employees for whom she paid social security taxes of $1,300 and state income tax of $2,500. What amount of real estate tax will Marlene deduct on her Schedule E?

a. $14,650
b. $6,850
c. $4,000
d. $1,300

SE1.2
Candy paid her landlord $3,000 to cancel her lease. What amount is included in her landlord's income for the year?

a. $1,500
b. $2,000
c. $3,000
d. $0

SE1.3
Property _____ to be depreciable when the taxpayer has fully recovered the property's cost or other basis.

a. ceases
b. contains
c. commences
d. completes

SE1.4
Royalty income is reported on which of the following as ordinary income?

   a. Schedule E, page 1
   b. Schedule E, page 2
   c. Royalty income is not reportable
   d. Form 1040, line 21

SE1.5
Depreciation is a(n) _____ allowance for the wear and tear of the property.

   a. annual
   b. monthly
   c. quarterly
   d. taxpayer's choice

Feedback:

Part 1 Review Questions Answers

SE1.1
Marlene paid $4,000 for real estate taxes on her rental property located at 1850 Happy Street, Jersey City, New Jersey. She paid $6,850 of real estate taxes on her primary residence. Marlene has household employees for whom she paid social security taxes of $1,300 and state income tax of $2,500. What amount of real estate tax will Marlene deduct on her Schedule E?

   a. $14,650
   b. $6,850
   c. $4,000
   d. $1,300

Feedback: *Please read Part 1.*

SE1.2
Candy paid her landlord $3,000 to cancel her lease. What amount is included in her landlord's income for the year?

   a. $1,500
   b. $2,000
   c. $3,000
   d. $0

Feedback: *Please read Part 1.*

SE1.3
Property _____ to be depreciable when the taxpayer has fully recovered the property's cost or other basis.

   a. ceases
   b. contains
   c. commences
   d. completes

Feedback: *Please read Part 1.*

SE1.4
Royalty income is reported on which of the following as ordinary income?

   a. **Schedule E, page 1**
   b. Schedule E, page 2
   c. Royalty income is not reportable
   d. Form 1040, line 21

Feedback: *Please read Part 1.*

SE1.5
Depreciation is a(n) _____ allowance for the wear and tear of the property.

   a. **annual**
   b. monthly
   c. quarterly
   d. taxpayer's choice

Feedback: *Please read Part 1.*

Takeaways

There are two types of residential activities: rental-for-profit activity and not-for-profit rental activity. This chapter discussed the types of income reported on Schedule E and the different property types. Special rules limit the amount of rental expense deductions that may be taken by an individual taxpayer on a residence that is rented out for part of a year and used for personal use during other parts of the year. Because of passive activity rules, income is required to be classified as active, passive, or non-passive. Active income is attributable to the direct efforts of the taxpayer such as salary, commissions, wages, etc.

TEST YOUR KNOWLEDGE!
Go online to take a practice quiz.

Chapter 11 Farm Income

Introduction

Income received from the operation of a farm or from rental income from a farm is taxable. Farmers determine their taxable income from farming and related activities by using Schedule F. Profit or loss from farm income is first reported on Schedule F and then "flows" to Form 1040, Schedule 1, line 6. A farm could qualify to be a qualified joint venture (discussed in Schedule C chapter).

Objectives

At the end of this lesson, the student will:

> ➢ Understand basic farm income.
> ➢ Know when a taxpayer should file Schedule F.

Resources

Form 1040	Publication 17	Instructions Form 1040
Form 4797	Publication 51 (Circular A)	Instructions Form 4797
Form 4835	Publication 225	Instructions Form 4835
Form 8990	Publication 334	Instructions Form 8990
Schedule F	Publication 463	Instructions Schedule F
	Publication 536	
	Publication 538	

Table of Contents

Farm Income	397
Introduction	397
Part I: Schedule F	399
Where to Report Sales of Farm Products	399
Completing Schedule F	400
Schedule F Profit or Loss Framing	401
Part I: Farm Income Cash Method	401
Sales Caused by Weather-Related Conditions	401
Rents (Including Crop Share)	402
Income Averaging for Farmers	402
Elected Farm Income (EFI)	403
Line 1 Sale of purchased livestock and other resale items	403
Items Purchased for Resale	403
Line 3 Cooperative Distributions	403
Line 4 Agriculture Payments	404
Line 5 CCC (Commodity Credit Corporation Loans)	404
Line 8 Other Types of Income	405
Canceled Debt	405
Schedule F Part II Farm Expense Cash and Accrual Method	406
Line 10, Car and Truck Expenses	407
Line 14, Depreciation	407
Line 17, Fertilizer and Lime	407
Line 20, Insurance	407
Line 21, Interest	408
Line 22, Labor Hired	408
Line 25, Repairs and Maintenance	408
Line 29, Taxes	408
Line 32 Other Expenses	408
Other Nondeductible Expenses	411
Losses from Operating a Farm	411
Not-for-Profit Farming	411
Farmers and Fisherman Estimated Payments	411
Part 1 Review Questions	412
Part 1 Review Questions Answers	413
Takeaways	414

Part I: Schedule F

Livestock income from breeding, draft, sport, or dairy purposes such as beef, pork, dogs, or cats are reportable on Schedule F.

Taxpayers are in the business of farming if they cultivate, operate, or manage a farm for profit, either as an owner or tenant. A farm can include livestock, dairy, poultry, fish, fruit, and truck farms. It can also include plantations, ranches, ranges, and orchards. See Publication 225.
A farmer must keep records to prepare an accurate tax return. Tax records are not the only type of records needed for a farming business. The taxpayer should keep records that measure the farm's financial performance.

Income reported on Schedule F does not include gains or losses from sales or other farm assets dispositions such as:

- Land
- Depreciable farm equipment
- Buildings and structures
- Livestock held for draft, breeding, sport, or dairy purposes

Taxpayers are in the business of farming if they cultivate, operate, or manage a farm for profit, either as an owner or tenant. A farm can include livestock, dairy, poultry, fish, fruit, and truck farms. It can also include plantations, ranches, ranges, and orchards. See Publication 225.

A farmer must keep records to prepare an accurate tax return. Tax records are not the only type of records needed for a farming business. The taxpayer should keep records that measure the farm's financial performance.

Where to Report Sales of Farm Products

When livestock, produce, grains, or other products raised on the taxpayer's farm are for sale or bought for resale, the entire amount received is income and reported on Schedule F.

When farm products are bought for resale, the profit or loss is the difference between the selling price and the basis in the product. The year that the payment was received is the year that the income is reported.

Item Sold	Schedule F	Form 4797
Farm products raised for sale	X	
Farm products bought for resale	X	
Farm products not held primarily for sale, such as livestock held for draft, breeding, sport, or dairy purposes (bought or raised)		X

Example: In 2020, Avery purchased 20 feeder calves for $6,000 with the intent to resell them. Avery sold them in 2021 for $11,000. The $11,000 sale is reported as sales, and the $6,000 purchase price is reported as basis, resulting in $5,000 reported as profit on the 2022 tax return.

Farm Income

$11,000	Sales price (reported on Schedule F, line 1a)
–$ 6,000	Purchase price (basis, reported on Schedule F, line 1b)
$5,000	Profit (reported on Schedule F, line 1c)

Livestock held for draft, breeding, sport, or dairy purposes may result in ordinary capital gain or loss when sold depending upon the circumstances and needs to be reported on Form 4797. Animals that are not held for primary sale are considered business assets of the farm.

Completing Schedule F

Portion of 2021 Schedule F

As with any return, interviewing the taxpayer before entering the information is necessary. The SSN or the EIN must be entered in the appropriate area. Line B is the principal agricultural activity codes. Like a Schedule C, Schedule F has specific codes. Select the code that best describes the taxpayer's majority source of income. For example, Alberto owns a dairy farm. He receives income from milk production and selling male calves. Alberto receives most of the income from the dairy cattle and milk production. The code is used to determine where the farmer makes most of the income. Principal Agricultural Activity Codes are located on Schedule F, Part IV.

Line C Accounting Method: The two accounting methods are Cash and Accrual. "Other" and/or Hybrid is not an option for farm income. Check the appropriate box. Using the cash accounting method taxpayer would complete Parts I and II. Income is reported in the year in which it was actually or constructively received. If payment on an expenditure such as prepaid expense creates an intangible asset that has a useful life that extends beyond 12 months of the end of the taxable year, that expense may not be deductible. See Publication 225.

If the accrual method is used, Parts II, III, and Part I, line 9 must be completed. Income is reported in the year it was earned, and expenses are deducted in the year they are incurred, even though they were paid in a prior year. Taxpayers who use the accrual method will use the cash basis for deducting business expense owed to a related cash-basis taxpayer. See Publication 538.

Certain farming collectives are unable to use the cash method of accounting.

A farming syndicate may be a partnership, LLC, S corporation, or any other enterprise other than a C corporation if:

> ➢ The interests in the business have at any time been offered for sale in a way that would require registration with any federal or state agency.

> More than 35% of the losses during any tax year are allocable to limited partners or limited entrepreneurs. A limited partner is one who can lose only the amount invested or required to be invested in the partnership. A limited entrepreneur is a person who does not take any active part in managing the business.

Line E is a yes or no question. Line E asks if the taxpayer materially participated in the activity. The taxpayer must meet the seven tests to qualify for material participation. To qualify for farming material participation, the taxpayer must own an interest at the time work is performed in connection with the activity.

Line F asks if any payments made in the current tax year requires Form 1099 to be filed. See General Instructions for Certain Information Returns if more information is needed. If the taxpayer paid more than $600 in rents, services, and prizes, then Form 1099-MISC would be filed.

Schedule F Profit or Loss Framing

Like Schedule C & E, farm income has specific line items for income and expenses that are industry related. This section is designed for the tax preparer to become aware of types of farm income. For more information, see Instructions Schedule F.

Part I: Farm Income Cash Method

Portion of 2021 Schedule F

Sales Caused by Weather-Related Conditions

If the farmer sells or exchanges more livestock, including poultry, than normal due to a drought, flood, or other weather-related conditions, the farmer may qualify to postpone the reporting until the following year. All the conditions must be met:

> - The principal trade or business is farming
> - The accounting method is the cash method
> - The taxpayers must be able to show that under their usual business practices, they would not have sold or exchanged the additional animals in that year except for the weather-related conditions

Farm Income

> ➢ The weather-related condition caused an area to be designated as eligible for assistance by the federal government

If sales or exchanges were made before the area became eligible for federal assistance due to weather-related conditions, the taxpayer could qualify if the weather-related condition caused the area to be designated. To qualify for the disaster the president of the United States must declare the area as a disaster.

Señor 1040 Says: A weather-related sale or exchange of livestock (other than poultry) held for draft breeding or dairy purposes may be an involuntary conversion. See Publication 225.

Example: Bernie is a calendar-year taxpayer, and he normally sells 100 head of beef cattle a year. As a result of the disaster, Bernie sold 250 head during 2020. Bernie realized $70,200 from the sale. On August 9, 2020, as a result of the drought, the affected area was declared a disaster area eligible for federal assistance. Bernie can postpone a portion ($42,120) of the income until 2021. ($70,200 ÷ 250 = $280.80 × 150 = $42,120).

Rents (Including Crop Share)

Rent received for farmland us is rental income and not reported on Schedule F. However, if the farmer materially participates in the farming operations on the land, the rent received is farm income.

If the taxpayer pastures someone else's livestock and takes care of them for a fee, the income is from the farming business. That income must be reported as "other" income on Schedule F. If the pasture is strictly rented out without providing services, the income is to be reported on Schedule E as rental income.

Rent received in the form of crop shares is income in the year the shares were converted to money or the equivalent. The accounting method used—cash or accrual—does not matter. Whether the material participation in operating the farm is crop sharing or livestock, the rental income is included in self-employment income.

Crop-sharing lease arrangements that involve a loss may be subject to the limits under the passive-loss rules.

Income Averaging for Farmers

Taxpayers can use income averaging to figure their tax for any year in which they were engaged in a farming business as an individual, a partner in a partnership, or a shareholder in an S corporation. Services performed as an employee are disregarded in determining whether an individual is engaged in a farming business. However, a shareholder of an S corporation engaged in a farming business may treat compensation received from the corporation that is attributable to the farming business as farm income. Corporations, partnerships, S corporations, estates, and trusts cannot use income averaging.

Elected Farm Income (EFI)

EFI is the amount of income from the farming business that is elected to be taxed at base-year rates. EFI can be designated as any type of income attributable to the farming business. However, EFI cannot be more than the taxable income, and EFI from a net capital gain attributable to the farming business cannot be more than the total net income. If the taxpayer is using income averaging, that is figured on Schedule J. See Publication 225.

Line 1 Sale of purchased livestock and other resale items

Income from farming reported on Schedule F includes amounts taxpayers receive from cultivating, operating, or managing a farm for gain or profit, either as an owner or tenant. Income is included but not limited to:

> - Income from operating a nursery specializing in growing ornamental plants.
> - Income from the sale of crop shares if the taxpayer materially participated in producing the crop.
> - Operating a stock, dairy, poultry, fish, fruit, or truck farm and income from operating a plantation, ranch, range, orchard, or grove.

Both the actual cash received, and the fair market value of goods or income constructively received, are reported on lines 1 through 8. If the taxpayer ran the farm and received rents based on crop share or farm production, that income is reported as rents. If the taxpayer sold livestock due to drought, flood, or other weather-related conditions, the taxpayer could elect to report the income from the sale in the year after the year of sale.

For example, Caleb uses the cash method, and sold three Holstein heifers due to weather-related circumstances in 2021. Caleb chose to report the income in the year after the sale, which would be 2022. For Caleb to make the election, all the following must apply:

1. Caleb's main business is farming.
2. Caleb can show he sold the livestock due to a weather-related event.
3. Caleb's farm area qualified for federal aid.

Items Purchased for Resale

If the cash method is used, deduct the ordinarily deducted cost of the livestock and other items purchased for resale only in the year of sale. Deduct this cost, including freight charges for transporting the livestock to the farm, on Part I of Schedule F.

Example: The cash method of accounting is used, and in 2021 Sandy purchased 50 steers that she will sell in 2022. She cannot deduct the cost of the steers on her 2021 return. She will deduct the cost in Part I of her 2022 Schedule F.

Line 3 Cooperative Distributions

Distributions from a farm cooperative are reported on Form 1099-PATR on line 3a. Taxpayer may receive multiple Form 1099-PATR, report the total distribution from all cooperatives. Distributions include:

> - Patronage dividends

Farm Income

- Nonpatronage distributions
- Per-unit retain allocations
- Redemptions of nonqualified written notices of allocation
- Per-unit retain certificates

Line 4 Agriculture Payments

Government payments received on Form 1099-G or Form CCC-1099-G are reported on line 4a. Any of the following sources are reported:

- Price loss coverage payments.
- Agriculture risk coverage payments.
- Coronavirus Food Assistance Program Payments.
- Coronavirus Food Assistance Program Payments
- Market Facilitation Program Payments.
- Market gain from the repayment of a secured Commodity Credit Corporation (CCC) loan for less than the original loan amount.
- Diversion payments.
- Cost-share payments.
- Payments in the form of materials (such as fertilizer or lime) or services (such as grading or building dams).

The taxpayer reports crop insurance proceeds in the year received. Federal crop disaster payments are treated as proceeds for crop insurance proceeds. If 2021 was the year of the crop damage, the taxpayer can elect to include certain proceeds in their 2022 income. To make this election check the box on 6c.

Crop insurance proceeds received in a prior year and elected to be treated in the current year's income, would be reported on line 6d. All other income that does not have a designated line on which to report is reported on line 8. Types of income could include, but are not limited to:

- Illegal federal irrigation subsidies
- Bartering income
- Income from Form 1099-C
- State gasoline or fuel tax refunds received in current tax year

See Schedule F Instructions for a complete list.

Line 5 CCC (Commodity Credit Corporation Loans)

Loans are generally not reported as income. However, if the production was pledged in part to secure a CCC loan, then treat the loan as if it were a sale of the crop and report the loan proceeds as income in the year received. Approval is not needed from the IRS to adopt this method of reporting CCC loans. Once the CCC loan is reported as income for the year received, all CCC loans in that year and subsequent years are reported the same way.

If pledged crops are forfeited to the CCC in full payment of the loan, then the individual may receive a Form 1099-A, *Acquisition or Abandonment of Secured Property*. In box 6 of Form 1099-A, one would see "CCC," and the amount of the outstanding loan would also be indicated on the form. See Publication 225.

Line 8 Other Types of Income

- Bartering Income.
- Income from canceled debt.
- State gasoline or fuel tax refunds received.
- Income from line 2 that includes Biofuel Producer Credit (Form 6478).
- Income from line 8 that includes Biodiesel and Renewable Diesel Fuels Credit (Form 8864).
- 2020 Schedule 3 credit for federal tax paid on fuels.
- Recapture of excess depreciation on listed property including Section 179 expense deduction.
- Inclusion amount on leased property when the business drops 50% or less.
- Any recapture of a deduction or credit for clean-fuel vehicle.
- Any income from breeding fees.
- Gain or a loss on commodity sales.
- Any credit amount from qualified sick and family leave wages.

Canceled Debt

If a debt is canceled or forgiven other than as a gift or bequest to the taxpayer, the individual must include the canceled amount in gross income for tax purposes. Discharge of qualified farm indebtedness is one of the exceptions to the general rule. It is excluded from taxable income; report the canceled amount on Schedule F, line 10, if the canceled debt was incurred in the farming business. If the debt is a nonbusiness debt, report the canceled amount as "other income" on Form 1040, line 21.

The taxpayer can elect to defer income from a discharge of business indebtedness that occurred after 2008 and before 2011. If the election is made, generally the deferred income is included in gross income ratably over a five-year period beginning in 2014 (for calendar-year taxpayers), and the exclusions listed below do not apply.

1. The cancellation takes place in a bankruptcy case under Title 11 of the U.S. Code.
2. The cancellation takes place due to insolvency.
3. The canceled debt is qualified farm debt.
4. The canceled debt is a qualified real property business debt in the case of a taxpayer other than a C corporation (see Publication 334 for more details).
5. The canceled debt is a qualified principal residence discharged after 2006 and before 2014.

See Publication 4492-B for more information.

Exclusions do not apply in any of the following situations:

- If a canceled debt is excluded from income because it takes place in a bankruptcy case, the exclusion in situations 2, 3, 4, and 5 above do not apply
- If a canceled debt is excluded from income because it takes place when the taxpayer is insolvent, the exclusion in situations 3 and 4 above do not apply to the extent of insolvency
- If a canceled debt is excluded from income because it is the taxpayer's qualified principal residence indebtedness, the exclusion in situation 2 above does not apply unless the taxpayer elects to apply situation 2 instead of the exclusion for qualified principal residence indebtedness

Farm Income

For more information about canceled debt, see Publication 225 and 982.

Income from the farming business is the sum of any farm income or gain minus any farm expenses or losses allowed as deductions in figuring taxable income. However, it does not include gain or loss from the sale or other disposition of land or from the sale of development rights, grazing rights, or other similar rights.

Schedule F Part II Farm Expense Cash and Accrual Method

Part II of the Schedule F lists some common farm expenses that are typically deductible. Current costs are expenses that do not have to be capitalized or included in inventory costs. The deduction for the cost of livestock feed and certain other supplies may be limited. If the taxpayer has an operating loss, the taxpayer may not be able to deduct the loss.

Certain expenses paid throughout the year may be part personal and part business. Some shared expenses could include expenses for gasoline, oil, fuel, water, rent, electricity, telephone, automobile upkeep, repairs, insurance, interest, and taxes. Shared expenses need to be allocated correctly between personal and business. The personal portion is not deductible; the business portion would be deducted on Schedule F.

Ordinary and necessary costs of operating a farm for profit are deductible business expenses. Current costs are expenses that do not have to be capitalized or included in inventory costs. However, the deduction for the cost of livestock feed and certain other supplies may be limited. If the taxpayer has an operating loss, the taxpayer may not be able to deduct this loss. The following are not deductible:

- Personal or living expenses.
- Expenses used to raise a family.
- Animal expenses used by the taxpayer to raise the animal.
- Repaid expenses.
- Inventory losses.
- Personal losses.

Portion of 2021 Schedule F

Prepaid farm supplies are amounts paid during the tax year for the following items:

> ➤ Feed, seed, fertilizer, and similar farm supplies not used or consumed during the year. Do not include amounts paid for farm supplies that would have been consumed if not for a fire, storm, flood, other casualty, disease, or drought.
> ➤ Poultry (including egg-laying hens and baby chicks) bought for use (or for both use and resale) in the farm business. Include only the amount that would be deductible in the following year if the taxpayer had capitalized the cost and deducted it ratably over the lesser of 12 months or the useful life of the poultry.
> ➤ Poultry bought for resale and not resold during the year.

Line 10, Car and Truck Expenses

Only expenses that are used for business can be deducted as a business expense. Items include gasoline, oil, repairs, license tags, insurance, and depreciation. For 2014, the standard mile rate is 56 cents per mile. The standard mileage rate for each mile of business use can be used for the taxpayer's owned or leased vehicle. The standard mileage rate cannot be used if five or more cars or light trucks are used at the same time.

Line 14, Depreciation

When property is acquired to be used in the farm business and expected to last more than one year, do not deduct the entire cost in the year. The cost is recovered over more than one year and deducted each year on Schedule F as depreciation or amortization. For more information, research depreciation and amortization.

Line 17, Fertilizer and Lime

In the year paid or incurred, the cost of fertilizer, lime, and other materials applied to farmland to enrich, neutralize, or condition the land can be an expense. The cost to apply the material is also an expense. Remember, if items are prepaid, more research will be needed.

Line 20, Insurance

Ordinary and necessary cost of insurance for the farm business is a business expense. Premiums can include payment for the following types of insurance:

> ➤ Fire, storm, crop, theft, liability, and other insurance on farm business assets
> ➤ Health and accident insurance on farm employees
> ➤ Workers' compensation insurance set by state law that covers claims for job-related bodily injuries or diseases suffered by employees on the farm, regardless of fault
> ➤ Business interruption insurance
> ➤ State unemployment insurance on farm employees (deductible as taxes if they are considered taxes under state law)

Self-employed health insurance can be deducted as well as medical, dental, and qualified long-term care insurance coverage for the taxpayer, the spouse, and dependents when figuring adjusted gross income.

Line 21, Interest

Interest paid on farm mortgages and other obligations incurred in the farm business can be deductible. If the cash method of accounting is used, deduct interest paid during the tax year. Interest paid with other funds received from the original lender through another loan, advance, or other arraignment similar to a loan cannot be deducted until payments are made on the new loan. Under the cash method, if interest is prepaid before it is due, the deduction is taken in the tax year in which the interest is due.

Line 22, Labor Hired

Reasonable wages paid for regular farm labor, piecework, contract labor, and other forms of labor hired to perform the farming operations can be paid in cash or in noncash items such as inventory, capital assets, or assets used in business. The cost of boarding farm labor is a deductible labor cost. Other deductible costs incurred for farm labor could include health insurance, workers' compensation insurance, and other benefits.

Line 25, Repairs and Maintenance

Most expenses for repair and maintenance are deductible. However, repairs or an overhaul to depreciable property that increases the asset's value or adapts it to a different use is a capital expense.

Line 29, Taxes

Real estate and property taxes on farm business assets such as farm equipment, animals, farmland, and farm buildings can be deducted in the year paid. The taxes on the part of the farm used for personal use are not a deductible expense on the business; those expenses may be deductible on Schedule A.

State and local general sales tax on non-depreciable farm business items are deductible as part of the cost of those items. Include state and local general sales tax imposed on the purchase of the assets for use in the farm business as part of the cost that is depreciable.

Individuals cannot deduct state and federal income taxes as farm business expenses. Individuals can deduct state and local income taxes only as an itemized deduction on Schedule A. Federal income tax is not a deduction. One-half of the self-employment tax is figured as an adjustment to income on Form 1040.

Line 32 Other Expenses

Travel Expenses

Ordinary and necessary expenses can be deducted if they are incurred while traveling away from home for farm business. Lavish and extravagant expenses cannot be deducted. For tax purposes, the farm business's location is considered the location of the farm and the taxpayer is traveling away from the farm if:

- Duties require the taxpayer to be absent from the farm for substantially longer than an ordinary workday
- Sleep and rest are required to meet the demands of work while away from home

Following are some examples of deductible travel expenses:

- Air, rail, bus, and car transportation
- Meals and lodging
- Dry cleaning and laundry
- Telephone and fax
- Transportation between hotel and temporary work or business meeting location
- Tips for any expenses

Remember, ordinary business-related meals are 50 percent deductible if business travel is overnight or long enough to require the taxpayer to stop for sleep or rest to properly perform his or her duties.

The following list is not a complete list but includes some expenses that may be deducted as farm expense on Part II of Schedule F. These expenses must be for business purposes and paid in the year used (if using the cash method) or incurred (if using the accrual method).

- Accounting fees
- Advertising
- Business travel and meals
- Commissions
- Consultant fees
- Crop-scouting expenses
- Dues to cooperatives
- Educational expenses (to maintain and improve farming skills)
- Farm-related attorney fees
- Farm magazines
- Ginning
- Insect sprays and dusts
- Litter and bedding
- Livestock fees
- Marketing fees
- Milk assessment
- Record-keeping expenses
- Service charges
- Small tools expected to last one year or less
- Stamps and stationery
- Subscriptions to professional, technical, and trade journals that deal with farming

Marketing Quota Penalties

Marketing quota penalties can be deducted as an "other expense" on Schedule F. These penalties are paid for marketing crops in excess of farm marketing quota. If the penalty is not paid but the purchaser of the crop deducts it from the payment, include the payment in gross income. Do not take a separate deduction for the penalty.

Capital Expenses

A capital expense is a payment or a debt incurred for the acquisition, improvement, or restoration of an asset that is expected to last more than one year. Include the expense in the basis of the asset. Uniform capitalization rules also require the asset to be capitalized or included in certain inventory expenses.

Business Use of Home

Business use of the home can be deducted if part of the home is exclusively and regularly used as:

- The principal place of business for any trade or business
- A place to meet or deal with patients, clients, or customers in the normal course of the trade or business
- In connection with a trade or business, if using a separate structure that is not attached to the home

An office in the home will qualify as the principal place of business for deducting expense for its use if both of the following requirements are met:

- The taxpayer uses it exclusively and regularly for the administrative or management activities of the trade or business.
- The taxpayer has no other fixed location where one conducts substantial administrative or management activities of the trade or business.

The IRS has provided a simplified method to determine the expense use for your home, which has been discussed in chapter 6. For more information, see Publication 587.

Business Start-Up and Organizational Costs

The taxpayer can elect to deduct up to $5,000 of business start-up costs and $5,000 of organizational costs paid or incurred after October 22, 2004. The $5,000 deduction is reduced by the amount of the total start-up or organizational costs exceeding $50,000. Any remaining costs must be amortized.

Crop Production Expenses

The uniform capitalization rules require the taxpayer to capitalize expense incurred in producing plants. However, for certain taxpayers who are required to use the accrual method of accounting, the capitalization rules do not apply to plants with a pre-productive period of two years or less. See Uniform Capitalization Rules in Publication 225, chapter 6 for more information.

Timber

Capitalize the cost of acquiring timber; do not include the cost of the land. Generally, one must capitalize the direct costs incurred in reforestation; however, one can elect to deduct some forestation and reforestation costs.

Christmas Tree Cultivation

If the taxpayer is in the business of planting and cultivating Christmas trees to sell when they are more than 6 years old, capitalize expense incurred for planting and stump culture and add them to the basis of the standing trees. The taxpayer would recover these expenses as part of the adjusted basis when the trees are sold as standing trees, or as a depletion allowance when the trees are cut.

Breeding Fees

If the accrual method is used, breeding fees need to be capitalized and allocated to the cost of the basis of the calf, foal, etc. Breeding fees can be an expense on Schedule F.

Other Nondeductible Expenses

Personal expenses and certain other items on the tax return cannot be deducted even if they are farm related. The taxpayer cannot deduct certain personal and living expenses, including rent and insurance premiums paid on property used as the taxpayer's primary residence. The cost of maintaining personal vehicles or other items used for personal use or the cost of purchasing or raising produce or livestock consumed by the taxpayer and his or her family is not deductible.

Losses from Operating a Farm

If the farm expenses are more than the farm income, the taxpayer has a loss from the operation of the farm. The amount of the loss one can deduct when figuring the taxable income may be limited. To figure the deductible loss, the following limits must be applied:

- The at-risk limits
- The passive activity limits

If the deductible loss after applying the limits is more than the income for the year, there may be a net operating loss. See Publication 536 for more information. This is beyond the scope of this course.

Not-for-Profit Farming

If the taxpayer operates a farm for profit, all ordinary and necessary expenses of carrying on the business of farming can be deducted on Schedule F. If the farming activity or other activity the taxpayer is engaged in or invests in is not-for-profit, the income from the activity is reported on Form 1040, line 21, and the expenses are deducted on Schedule A. Losses from not-for-profit farming can be limited.

Farmers and Fisherman Estimated Payments

If the taxpayer is a California resident and they are either a farmer or fisherman, there is a special provision for them. If 2/3 of the gross income for 2020 and 2021 was from farming or fishing, the entire estimated tax for 2021 was due on January 18, 2022. If the 2/3 rule still applies for 2021 and 2022, the entire estimated payment would be on January 16, 2023.

Farm Income

Part 1 Review Questions

To obtain the maximum benefit from this chapter, LTP recommends that you complete each of the following questions, and then compare them to the answers with feedback that immediately follows. Under governing self-study standards, vendors are required to present review questions intermittently throughout each self-study course.

These questions and explanations are not part of the final examination and will not be graded by LTP.

SF1.1
Which of the following farm assets could produce a gain or a loss for the taxpayer?

   a. Land
   b. Depreciable farm equipment
   c. Buildings and structures
   d. Livestock

SF1.2
When farm products are sold, they are reported on_____.

   a. Schedule F
   b. Form 4797
   c. Form 8949
   d. Form 1040

SF1.3
Sales from dog breeding is reported on____.

   a. Schedule A
   b. Schedule C
   c. Schedule E
   d. Schedule F

SF1.4
EFI stands for _____.

   a. Electronic filing income
   b. Electronic farm income
   c. Elected farm income
   d. Elected filing income

SF1.5
Dog breeding sales is reported on____.

   a. Is a hobby
   b. Does not need to be reported
   c. Schedule E
   d. Schedule F

Part 1 Review Questions Answers

SF1.1
Which of the following farm assets could produce a gain or a loss for the taxpayer?

   a. Land
   b. Depreciable farm equipment
   c. Buildings and structures
   d. Livestock

Feedback: Review section *Schedule F, Farm Income.*

SF1.2
When farm products are sold, they are reported on_____.

   a. Schedule F
   b. Form 4797
   c. Form 8949
   d. Form 1040

Feedback: Review section *Schedule F, Farm Income.*

SF1.3
Sales from dog breeding is reported on____.

   a. Schedule A
   b. Schedule C
   c. Schedule E
   d. Schedule F

Feedback: Review section

SF1.4
EFI stands for _____.

   a. Electronic filing income
   b. Electronic farm income
   c. Elected farm income
   d. Elected filing income

Feedback: Review section

SFI.5

Dog breeding sales is reported on____.

   a. Is a hobby
   b. Does not need to be reported
   c. Schedule E
   d. Schedule F

Feedback: Review section

Takeaways

Taxpayers are in the business of farming if they cultivate, operate, or manage a farm for profit, either as an owner or tenant. A farm includes livestock, dairy, poultry, fish, fruit, and truck farms. The farm can also include plantations, ranches, ranges, and orchards.

TEST YOUR KNOWLEDGE!
Go online to take a practice quiz.

Chapter 12 Depreciation

Introduction

Depreciation is an annual deduction that allows taxpayers to recover the cost or other basis of their business or investment property over a specified number of years. Depreciation is an allowance for the wear and tear, decline, or uselessness of a property and begins when a taxpayer places property in service for use in a trade or business. The property ceases to be depreciable when the taxpayer has fully recovered the property's cost or other basis or when the property has been retired from service, whichever comes first. Depreciation is reported on Form 4562.

Objectives

At the end of this lesson, the student will:

> ➢ Describe when property cannot be depreciated.
> ➢ Recognize when depreciation begins and ends.
> ➢ Identify which method of depreciation to use for the property.

Resources

Form 1040	Publication 544	Instructions Form 1040
Form 4562	Publication 551	Instructions Form 4562
Form 3115	Publication 946	Instructions Form 3115

Table of Contents

- Introduction 415
- Part 1 Defining Depreciation and Depreciation Methods 417
  - Depreciation 417
  - Section 179 417
  - Bonus Depreciation 417
  - The Beginning and End of Depreciation 418
  - Property That Can Be Depreciated 418
  - Property Owned 419
  - Property Having a Determinable Useful Life 419
  - Property Lasting More than One Year 419
  - Property Used in Business or an Income-Producing Activity 419
  - Property That Cannot Be Depreciated 420
  - Property Acquired by Like-kind Exchanges 420
  - De minimis Safe Harbor Election 421
  - Depreciation Methods 421
  - Modified Accelerated Cost Recovery System (MACRS) 421
  - Straight Line Method 423
  - Part 1 Review Questions 423
  - Part 1 Review Questions Answers 424
- Part 2 Depreciation Basis and Depreciation under MACRS 425
  - Basis of Depreciable Property 425
  - Cost Basis 425
  - Other Basis 425
  - Adjusted Basis 425
  - Figuring Depreciation Under MACRS 426
  - GDS Property Classifications 426
  - Which Convention Applies? 427
  - Changing Accounting Methods 428
  - Idle Property 429
  - Cost or Other Basis Fully Recovered 429
  - Retired from Service 429
  - Understanding the Table of Class Lives and Recovery Periods 429
  - Part 2 Review Questions 430
  - Part 2 Review Questions Answers 431
- Takeaways 432

Part 1 Defining Depreciation and Depreciation Methods

Depreciation is an annual allowance for the wear and tear of certain property that includes the process of allocating the cost of a tangible asset to expense over its estimated useful life. To be depreciable, tangible property must have a limited life. Tangible property can be divided into two categories: real property and personal property. Real property is land, land improvements, buildings, and building improvements. Land does not have a limited life; therefore, it does not qualify for depreciation. Personal property is usually business machinery and equipment, office furniture, and fixtures. The term "personal property" should not be confused with property owned by an individual for personal use.

Depreciation

Depreciation is a way of accounting for the costs associated with durable goods used in a business, for investment, or for a hobby. The recovery period is determined by the IRS and the taxpayer deducts the cost of the item over the property class life. Only the percentage of the cost corresponding to the percentage of use attributable to deductible purposes can be depreciated; costs attributed to personal use can never be depreciated. Depreciation starts when the asset is placed into service and ends when the property is disposed or worn out.

Basis is a way of determining the cost of an investment in property and is decided by how it was acquired. If the property was purchased, the purchase price is the basis. Any improvements made to the property are then added to that basis. The purchase price plus improvements constitutes the adjusted basis. Other items that add to the basis are the expenses of acquiring the property (commissions, sales tax, and freight charges). There are also items that reduce the basis, which include depreciation, nontaxable distributions, and postponed gain on home sales. This is also referred to as "cost basis".

Section 179

Section 179 is an internal revenue code that allows the taxpayer an immediate deduction on certain business assets. Business owners can take the purchase price of business equipment in the year of purchase and depreciate the asset 100%. Federal law allows an expense election up to $1,050,000 of the cost of certain business property. Section 179 property cost phase out begins at $2,620,000 for tax year 2021. For tax year 2022 the limits are $1,080,000 with a total purchase of $2,700,000.

Taxpayer can choose to take a portion of Section 179 instead of the entire amount of the asset. For example, Solomon purchased a tractor for his farming business. The tractor cost $45,000, and Solomon decided to use 50% of the cost as Section 179. The remaining $22,500 would be used as a yearly depreciation deduction.

Bonus Depreciation

Bonus depreciation was designed to stimulate investment in business property that is not land or buildings. IRC section 168(k) is the code that provides the explanation of the accelerated depreciation. The IRS sometimes refers to bonus depreciation as a "special depreciation allowance". For tax year 2021, the allowable depreciation is 100% of qualified business property. The immediate deduction is eligible for property that has been placed in service between September 27, 2017 and January 1, 2023. Here is the phase out after January 1, 2023:

2023: 80%
2024: 60%
2025: 40%
2026: 20%

Property that qualifies for bonus depreciation must have a useful life of 20 years or less. The property must also be new for the taxpayer. If the taxpayer leased the equipment, prior to purchase, the property is disqualified for bonus depreciation.

The Beginning and End of Depreciation

Depreciation begins when the property is placed in service for use in the trade or business or for the production of income. Depreciation ends when the cost and added basis, if any, have been fully recovered or when the property is retired from service, whichever comes first.

Property is placed in service when it is ready and available for a specific use for a business activity, an income-producing activity, a tax-exempt activity, or a personal activity. Even if the property is not being used, it is still placed in service when it is ready, available, and capable of performing its specific use.

When a taxpayer places an improvement or addition in service after the original asset was placed in service, the improvements or addition is a separate asset. For example, Gabriela placed her rental in service and then made some major improvements. The improvements were more than the purchase price of the rental. The improvements will be a separate line item to be depreciated and could have a different class life. See §1.263(a)-3T(e)(3) or (e)(5) for more information.

Example 1: Joel purchased a copy machine in December of last year for his printing business. The machine was delivered in January but not installed. Joel had the machine installed and ready for use in February of the current tax year. The machine would be considered to be placed in service in February of the current year, and not December or January, because it wasn't until it was installed in February that the machine became ready to be placed in service.

If the property has been converted from personal to business use, the "placed in service" date is the date it was converted to business use or to an income-producing activity. In other words, depreciation begins when the property has been placed in service.

Example 2: Nicolas purchased a home as his primary residence in 2010, and on February 10, 2019, he converted it to a rental property. Therefore, depreciation begins the day it was placed into service as an income-producing property.

Property That Can Be Depreciated

Most types of tangible property can be depreciated. Examples of tangible property are:

- ➢ Buildings
- ➢ Vehicles
- ➢ Machinery
- ➢ Furniture
- ➢ Equipment
- ➢ Storage facilities

Some intangible items that can be depreciated include:

- Copyrights
- Patents
- Computer software (if the software life value is more than one year)

Property that can be depreciated must meet the following requirements:

- Must be the taxpayer's own property.
- Must be used in the taxpayer's business or income-producing activity.
- Property must have a determinable useful life.
- The property is expected to last more than one year.

Property Owned

To claim depreciation, one must be the owner of the property, even if the property has debt. Leased property can be claimed only if ownership of the property includes the following:

- The legal title to the property.
- The legal obligation to pay for the property.
- The responsibility to pay maintenance and operating expenses.
- The duty to pay any taxes on the property.
- The risk of loss if the property is destroyed, condemned, or diminished in value through obsolescence or exhaustion.

Example: Amanda made a down payment on a rental property and took over Tom's mortgage payments. Amanda owns the property and can depreciate it.

If the property is held as a business or as an investment property as a life tenant, the taxpayer may depreciate the property.

Property Having a Determinable Useful Life

Property must have a determinable useful life to be depreciated. It must be something that wears out, decays, gets used up, becomes obsolete, or loses its value from natural causes.

Property Lasting More than One Year

To be able to depreciate property, the useful life should extend significantly beyond the year the property was placed in service.

Example: Ms. Wilson maintains a library for her tax business and purchases yearly technical journals for its use. The library would be depreciated because the technical journals do not have a useful life of more than one year before the information contained will become outdated. The technical journals can be taken as a yearly business expense.

Property Used in Business or an Income-Producing Activity

To claim depreciation on property, the income-producing activity must be used in business. If the taxpayer uses the property to produce an investment use, then the income is taxable. Personal property cannot be depreciated.

Depreciation

If the property is used for business and personal use, the portion used as business may be depreciated. For instance, you cannot deduct depreciation on a car used only for commuting to and from work or for personal shopping trips and family vacations. You must keep records showing business and personal use of the property.

Containers used for the products one sells are considered inventory and cannot be depreciated. Containers used to ship products can be depreciated if they have a life expectancy of more than one year and meet the following requirements:

> - Qualify as property used in business.
> - Title to the containers does not pass to the buyer.

To determine if the above requirements are met, the following things need to be considered:

> - Does the sales contract, sales invoice, or some other type of order acknowledgement indicate whether the taxpayer has retained the title of the containers?
> - Does the invoice treat the containers as a separate item?
> - Do the taxpayer's records indicate the basis of the containers?

Property That Cannot Be Depreciated

Land does not wear out; therefore, it cannot be depreciated. The cost of land generally includes clearing, grading, planting, and landscaping. Although land is never depreciated, certain improvements to the land can be depreciated, such as landscaping and improvements to a building.

The following exceptions are property that cannot be depreciated even if the requirements are met:

> - Property placed in service and disposed of in the same year.
> - Equipment used to build capital improvements.
> - Section 197 intangibles that must be amortized.
> - Certain term interests.

Inventory is not depreciated. Inventory is any property that is held primarily for sale to customers in the ordinary course of business. If the taxpayer is in the rent-to-own business, certain property held for business may be considered as depreciable instead of inventory. See Publication 946.

Property Acquired by Like-kind Exchanges

Like-kind property is property of the same nature, character, or class. Quality or grade does not matter. For example, real property that is improved with a residential rental house is like-kind to vacant land. Most common like-kind exchanges are real property, or better known as a 1031 exchange.

A 1031 exchange gets its name from Section 1031 of the U.S. Internal Revenue Code, which allows you to postpone paying capital gains taxes when you sell an investment property and reinvest the proceeds from the sale within certain time limits in a property or properties of like kind and equal or greater value.

De minimis Safe Harbor Election

The taxpayer can elect to deduct small dollar amounts for expenditures for acquiring or manufacturing of property that generally needs to be capitalized under the general rules. The amount spent needs to be ordinary and necessary expenses to carry on the trade or business for the taxpayer. Costs include materials, supplies, repairs, and maintenance usually under $2,500. See IRC Section 1.263.

Depreciation Methods

Modified Accelerated Cost Recovery System (MACRS)

The Modified Accelerated Cost Recovery System (MACRS) is the current depreciation method used in the United States to calculate depreciable assets. MACRS should be used to depreciate property. MACRS is not used in the following circumstances:

- Property placed in service before 1987.
- Property owned or used in 1986.
- Intangible property.
- Films, video tapes, and recordings.
- Certain corporate or partnership property that was acquired in a nontaxable transfer.
- Property that has been elected to be excluded from MACRS.

Property Placed in Service Before 1987

If property was placed in service before 1987 (unless the taxpayer elected to use MACRS after July 31, 1986) it must use ACRS or Straight Line. See Publication 534.

MACRS is generally used to depreciate property that was acquired for personal use before 1987 but placed in service after 1986. Improvements made to the property placed in service before 1986 is depreciated as a separate entry using MACRS depreciation.

Certain property that was acquired and placed in service after 1986 may not be able to use MACRS. In any of the following personal property situations MACRS cannot be used:

- The taxpayer or someone related to the taxpayer owned or used the property in 1986.
- The taxpayer acquired the property from a person who owned it in 1986; and, as a part of the transaction, the user of the property did not change.
- The taxpayer leased the property to a person (or someone related to them) who owned or used the property in 1986.
- The taxpayer acquired the property in a transaction in which the following took place:
  - The user of the property did not change.
  - The property was not a MACRS property in the hands of the person from whom the taxpayer acquired it due to one of the reasons above.

When a taxpayer cannot depreciate Section 1250 property using MACRS in any of the following situations:

- The taxpayer or someone related to the taxpayer owned the property in 1986.

- The taxpayer leased the property to a person who owned the property or to someone related to that person in 1986.
- The taxpayer acquired the property in a like-kind exchange, involuntary conversion, or repossession of property that was owned by the taxpayer or someone related to the taxpayer in 1986.

MACRS only applies to the part of basis in the acquired property that represents cash paid or unlike property exchanged. It does not apply to the carried-over part of the basis.

Exceptions to the above include the following:

- Residential rental property or nonresidential real property.
- Any property if, in the first tax year that it is placed in service, the deduction under Accelerated Cost Recovery System (ACRS) is more than the deduction under MACRS using the half year convention. See Publication 534.

The following are related persons who cannot depreciate Section 1250 property:

- An individual and a member of their family, including only a spouse, child, parent, brother, sister, half-brother, half-sister, ancestor, and lineal descendant.
- A corporation or an individual who directly or indirectly owns more than 10% of the value of the outstanding stock of that corporation.
- Two corporations that are members of the same controlled group.
- A trust fiduciary and a corporation if more than 10% of the value of the outstanding stock is directly or indirectly owned by or for the trust or grantor of the trust.
- The grantor and fiduciary; and the fiduciary and beneficiary of any trust.
- The fiduciaries of two different trusts and the fiduciaries and beneficiaries of two different trusts if the same person is the grantor of both trusts.
- A tax-exempt educational or charitable organization and any person (or a member of that person's family) who directly or indirectly controls the organization.
- Two S corporations, an S corporation and a regular corporation, if the same individual owns more than 10% of the value of the outstanding stock of each corporation.
- A corporation and a partnership if the same persons own both of the following:
  - More than 10% of the value of the outstanding stock of the corporation.
  - More than 10% of the interest gained from the capital or profits of the partnership.
- The executor and beneficiary of any estate.
- Two partnerships, if the same person directly or indirectly owns more than 10% of the capital or profits of each.
- The related person and a person who is engaged in trades or businesses under common control. See IRC section 52(a) and 52(b).

The buyer should determine the nature of a relationship before the property is acquired.

Intangible Property

Intangible property is anything of value that can be owned that has no corresponding physical object (e.g., a patent, copyright, or partnership interests). These are generally depreciated using the straight-line method. The taxpayer may choose to depreciate intangible property by using the income forecast method, which is not covered in this course. See Publication 946.

Straight Line Method

The straight line method of depreciation allows the taxpayer to deduct the same amount each year over the useful life of the property. To determine the deduction, first determine the adjusted basis, salvage value, and estimated useful life of the property. Subtract the salvage value, if any, from the adjusted basis. The balance is the depreciation that can be taken for the property. Divide the balance by the number of years in the useful life. This is the yearly depreciation deduction. To use the straight line method, prorate the depreciation deduction by dividing the value proportionally based on a unit of time or number of months in use.

Example: Francisco purchased a patent in August for $5,100 that is defined in Section 197. Francisco will depreciate the patent using the straight line method. The useful life for a patent is 17 years with no salvage value. Francisco would divide the $5,100 basis by 17 years to get the yearly depreciation of $300. In the first year of business, Francisco only used the patent for 9 months so he would have to multiply the $300 x 9/12 to get his deduction of $225 for the first year. Over the next full year, Francisco would claim the $300 depreciation deduction.

Computer software is generally a Section 197 tangible and cannot be depreciated if the taxpayer acquired it in connection with the acquisition of assets constituting a business. However, when it meets the following tests, computer software that is not a Section 197 intangible can be depreciated even if it's acquired in a business acquisition:

- It is readily available for purchase by the general public.
- It is subject to a nonexclusive license.
- It has not been substantially modified.

If the software meets the above test, it may also qualify for Section 179. If computer software can be depreciated, use the straight line method over a useful life of 36 months.

Part 1 Review Questions

To obtain the maximum benefit from this chapter, LTP recommends that you complete each of the following questions, and then compare them to the answers with feedback that immediately follow. Under governing self-study standards, vendors are required to present review questions intermittently throughout each self-study course.

These questions and explanations are not part of the final examination and will not be graded by LTP.

DP1.1
Which of the following is the current tax depreciation system in the United States?

a. MACRS
b. ACRS
c. Half-year convention (HY)
d. Mid-month convention (MM)

Depreciation

DP1.2

Depreciation is a(n)____ allowance for the wear and tear of certain property.

 a. recovery period
 b. annual
 c. monthly
 d. quarterly

DP1.3

Which of the following is not tangible property?

 a. Buildings
 b. Machinery
 c. Furniture
 d. Cell phones

Part 1 Review Questions Answers

DP1.1

Which of the following is the current tax depreciation system in the United States?

 a. MACRS
 b. ACRS
 c. Half-year convention (HY)
 d. Mid-month convention (MM)

Feedback: Review section *Modified Accelerated Cost Recovery System (MACRS)*.

DP1.2

Depreciation is a(n)____ allowance for the wear and tear of certain property.

 a. recovery period
 b. annual
 c. monthly
 d. quarterly

Feedback: Review section *Depreciation*.

DP1.3

Which of the following is not tangible property?

 a. Buildings
 b. Machinery
 c. Furniture
 d. Cell phones

Feedback: Review section *Property That Can Be Depreciated*.

Part 2 Depreciation Basis and Depreciation under MACRS

To the beginner tax professional depreciation and basis can be overwhelming, but when one understands the basics, then depreciation and basis are easy to determine.

Basis of Depreciable Property

To calculate the depreciation deduction, you must know the basis of the property. To determine the basis of the property, you must know the cost of the property.

Cost Basis

The basis of property that has been purchased is the cost plus the amounts paid for certain items. The cost includes the amount paid in cash, debt obligations, other property, or services. Some items that might be added to basis are:

- Sales tax
- Freight charges
- Installation fees
- Testing fees
- Settlement costs
- Legal and recording fees
- Abstract fees
- Survey charges
- Owner's title insurance
- Amounts the seller owes that the buyer agrees to pay, such as back taxes, interest, recording or mortgage fees, charges for improvements or repairs, and sales commissions.

Other Basis

Other basis refers to the way the owner of the property received the property. Was the property acquired by a like-kind exchange, as payment for services performed, as a gift, inheritance, or some other way? See Publication 551.

Adjusted Basis

Certain adjustments, whether an increase or a decrease, may have to be made to determine the adjusted basis in property. These events occur between the time that the property was acquired and placed into service. The events could include any of the following:

- Installing utility lines
- Paying legal fees
- Setting zoning issues
- Receiving rebates
- Incurring a casualty or theft loss

Reduce the basis of property by the depreciation allowed or allowable, whichever is greater. "Depreciation allowed" is depreciation that the taxpayer was entitled to and has already deducted as a tax benefit. "Depreciation allowable" is depreciation that the taxpayer was entitled to but did not yet deduct. See Publication 551.

Figuring Depreciation Under MACRS

The Modified Accelerated Cost Recovery System (MACRS) is used to recover the basis of most business and investment property placed in service after 1986. MACRS consists of two depreciation systems: the General Depreciation System (GDS) and the Alternative Depreciation System (ADS). These two systems provide different methods and recovery periods to figure deductions. Generally, the method used is GDS unless the law requires the ADS method to be used, or the taxpayer has elected to use ADS.

If the taxpayer is required to use ADS to depreciate the property, no special depreciation allowance can be claimed on the property. Although the property may qualify for GDS, the taxpayer can elect to use ADS. The election must cover all property in the same property class that was placed in service during the year.

GDS Property Classifications

There are nine property classifications under GDS. The classifications are divided by the length of the depreciation period and by the type of property being depreciated. Most of the classifications have the same recovery period as the title of the year. See Publication 946.

Classification One, 3-year property:

- Tractor units for over-the-road use.
- Racehorses that were over 2-years-old when placed in service.
- Any other horses that were over 12-years-old when placed in service.

Classification Two, 5-year property:

- Automobiles, taxis, buses, and trucks.
- Office machinery such as calculators, copiers, and computers.
- Dairy cattle and breeding cattle.

Classification Three, 7-year property:

- Office furniture and fixtures such as desks, chairs, and a safe.
- Railroad tracks.
- Any property that does not have a class life and has not been designated by law as being in any other class.

Classification Four, 10-year property:

- Any tree or vine bearing fruit or nuts.
- Any single-purpose agricultural or horticultural structure.
- Vessels, barges, tugs, and similar water transportation equipment.

Classification Five, 15-year property:

- Certain improvements made directly to land or added to land, such as shrubbery, fences, roads, sidewalks, and bridges.
- Any municipal wastewater treatment plant.
- The initial clearing and grading for land improvements for gas utilities.

Classification Six, 20-year property:

- Farm buildings, other than single-purpose agricultural or horticultural structures.
- Initial clearing and grading land improvements for electric utility transmission and distribution plants.

Classification Seven, 25-year property:

- Property that is an integral part of the gathering, treatment, or commercial distribution of water, all other property regarding water would be 20-year property.
- Municipal sewers other than property placed in service under a binding contract in effect at all times since June 9, 1996.

Classification Eight, Residential rental property:

Rental property includes any building or structure such as rental income, which includes dwelling units and mobile homes. A dwelling unit is considered to be an apartment or house that is used to provide living accommodations in a building or structure. Motels, hotels, and other similar establishments that use more than 50% of the rooms for transients are not included; for these, the property class-life is 27.5 years.

Classification Nine, Nonresidential real property:

This is Section 1250 property, such as an office building, store, or warehouse that is not a residential rental property or a property with a class life of less than 27.5 years.

There are always exceptions to the rules. If this is the case, one must do research related to the particular situation. Any other GDS recovery periods that are not listed above can be found in Appendix B of Publication 946.

Which Convention Applies?

A convention method is established under MACRS to determine the portion of the year to depreciate property both in the year the property was placed in service and in the year of disposition. The convention used determines the number of months for which one can claim depreciation. The three methods are: Mid-month, Mid-quarter, and Half-year. Mid-month convention is used for nonresidential real property, residential real property, and any railroad grading or tunnel bore. Under this convention, one-half month of depreciation is allowed for the month the property was placed in service or disposed of.

Example: Josue uses the calendar year accounting method and placed nonresidential real property in service in August. The property is in service for 4 months (September, October, November, and December). Josue's numerator is 4.5 (4 months plus 0.5). Josue would multiply the depreciation for a full year by 4.5/12, or 0.375.

If the taxpayer does not use the asset solely for business, then the asset must be multiplied by the business percentage for the year, and then multiply the result by the fraction found in the MACRS depreciation tables.

Depreciation

Example: In February 2021, Jennifer purchased office furniture for $2,600. She used the office furniture for her business only 50% of the time. Furniture is a 7-year property. The depreciation percentage is taken from Table A-2 found in Publication 946. Since Jennifer purchased the furniture in the first quarter of the year, she would use the mid-quarter convention placed in service in the first quarter. The amount Jennifer could depreciate her first year would be the cost of the furniture ($2,600) times the percentage of its use for business (50%) times the percentage provided from the depreciation table (25%), which amounts to $325.00.

The Mid-quarter convention is used if the Mid-month convention does not apply, and the total depreciable basis of MACRS property placed in service is in the last 3 months of the tax year.

If the Mid-quarter convention is used for a particular year, each item of depreciable personal property placed in service during that year must be depreciated using the Mid-quarter convention for its entire recovery period.

Nonresidential real property, residential rental property, railroad grading or tunnel bore property placed in service and disposed of in the same year, and property that is being depreciated under a method other than MACRS are all excluded from using the Mid-quarter convention. Under this convention, treat all property placed in service or disposed during any quarter of the tax year as placed in service. This means that 1½ months of depreciation is allowed for the quarter the property is placed in service or disposed.

The Half-year convention is used if neither the Mid-quarter nor the Mid-month convention applies. Under this convention, treat all property placed in service or disposed of during a tax year as placed in service or disposed of at the midpoint of the year. This means that one-half year of depreciation is allowed for the year the property is placed in service or disposed.

When the taxpayer elects to use the half-year convention, a half-year of depreciation is allowed in the first year their property is placed in service, regardless of when the property is placed in service during the tax year. For each of the remaining years of the recovery period, the taxpayer can claim a full year of depreciation. If the property is held for the entire recovery period, a half-year of depreciation is claimed for the year following the end of the recovery period. If the property is disposed before the recovery period ends, a half-year of depreciation is allowable for the year of disposition.

Changing Accounting Methods

To change the accounting method used for depreciation, the taxpayer needs to file Form 3115, *Application for Change in Accounting Method,* to be approved by the IRS.

The following are examples of a change in the method of accounting used for depreciation:

- A change from an impermissible method of determining depreciation for property if it was used in two or more consecutively filed tax returns.
- A change in the treatment of an asset from non-depreciable to depreciable, or vice versa.
- A change in the depreciation method, period of recovery, or convention of a depreciable asset.
- A change from not claiming to claiming the special depreciation allowance if the election was made to not claim the special allowance.

➤ A change from claiming a 50% special depreciation allowance to claiming a 100% special depreciation allowance for qualified property acquired and placed in service after September 27, 2017, if the election was not made under IRC section 168(k)(10) to claim the 50% special allowable depreciation.

Changes in depreciation that are not a change in method of accounting are as follows:

➤ An adjustment in the useful life of a depreciable asset for which depreciation is determined under Section 167.
➤ A change in use of an asset in the hands of the same taxpayer.
➤ Making a late depreciation election or revoking a timely valid depreciation election, including the election not to deduct the special depreciation allowance.
➤ Any change in date of when a depreciable asset was placed in service.

If the taxpayer does not qualify to use the automatic procedure by filing Form 3115, then he or she must use the advance consent request procedures. See Instructions Form 3115.

Idle Property

Depreciation can still be claimed on property that is placed in service, even if a property is temporarily idle and not being used. For instance, if Emilio owns a printing press but has not used it for six months of the current tax year because he has not had any jobs that require the machine, then he can continue claiming depreciation on his printing press.

Cost or Other Basis Fully Recovered

Stop depreciating property when the property has fully recovered its cost or other basis.

Retired from Service

When the property has been retired from service, depreciation stops. Property is retired from service when it has been permanently withdrawn from use in trade or business; in production of income; or if the property has been sold or exchanged, converted to personal use, abandoned, transferred to a supply, or destroyed. Disposition of an asset includes the sale, exchange, retirement, physical abandonment, or destruction of an asset.

Understanding the Table of Class Lives and Recovery Periods

There are two sections in the *Table of Class Lives and Recovery Periods* for depreciation. Table B-1 is *Specific Depreciable Assets Used in All Business Activities, Except as Noted*; this table lists the assets used in all business activities. Some items included could be office furniture; information systems such as computers; and secondary equipment, like printers or computer screens.

Table B-2 is used for all other activities, such as those involving agriculture, horse racing, farm buildings, and single purpose agricultural or horticultural structures.

Use the tables in numerical order. Look on Table B-1 first; if you do not find the asset you are looking for, then check Table B-2. Once the asset has been located, use the recovery period shown in the table. However, if the activity is specifically listed in Table B-2 under the type of activity in which it is used, then use the recovery period for that activity in that table.

Depreciation

Each table gives the asset class, the class life, and the recovery period in years. Understanding these tables is paramount for the beginning tax professional. You do not have to memorize the tables – just know where to find the information and how to use it correctly.

If the property is not listed in either table, check the end of Table B-2 to find *Certain Property for Which Recovery Periods Assigned*. Generally, the property has a recovery period of 7 years GDS or 12 years ADS.

Example: Peter Martinez owns a retail clothing store. During the year, he purchased a desk and cash register for business use. Peter finds "office furniture" in Table B-1, under asset class 00.11. Cash register is not listed in Table B-1. Peter then looks in Table B-2 and finds the activity "retail store" under asset class 57.0, *Distributive Trades and Services*, which includes assets used in wholesale and retail trade. The asset class does not specifically list office furniture or a cash register. Peter uses asset class 00.11 for the desk. The desk has a 10-year class life and a 7-year recovery period for GDS. Peter elects to use ADS; the recovery period is 10 years. For the cash register, Peter uses asset class 57.0 because a cash register is not listed in Table B-1, but it is an asset used in the retail business. The cash register has a 9-year class life and a 5-year recovery period for GDS. If Peter elects to use the ADS method, the recovery period is 9 years.

Part 2 Review Questions

To obtain the maximum benefit from this chapter, LTP recommends that you complete each of the following questions, and then compare them to the answers with feedback that immediately follow. Under governing self-study standards, vendors are required to present review questions intermittently throughout each self-study course.

These questions and explanations are not part of the final examination and will not be graded by LTP.

DP2.1
To determine the basis of property, which of the following should be added to the cost?

1. Sales tax
2. Testing fees
3. Survey charges
4. Settlement costs

   a. 1 and 2
   b. 2, 3, and 4
   c. 3 and 4
   d. 1, 2, 3, and 4

DP2.2
The General Depreciation System (GDS) has _____ property classifications.

   a. 5
   b. 7
   c. 9
   d. 12

DP2.3

Andres would like to change his accounting method. Which form would he submit to receive the IRS approval?

   a. Form 8829
   b. Form 3115
   c. Form 8867
   d. Form 8849

Part 2 Review Questions Answers

DP2.1

To determine the basis of property, which of the following should be added to the cost?

   1. Sales tax
   2. Testing fees
   3. Survey charges
   4. Settlement costs

   a. 1 and 2
   b. 2, 3, and 4
   c. 3 and 4
   d. 1, 2, 3, and 4

Feedback: Review section *Basis of Depreciable Property.*

DP2.2

The General Depreciation System (GDS) has _____ property classifications.

   a. 5
   b. 7
   c. 9
   d. 12

Feedback: Review section *GDS Property Classifications.*

DP2.3

Andres would like to change his accounting method. Which form would he submit to receive the IRS approval?

   a. Form 8829
   b. Form 3115
   c. Form 8867
   d. Form 8849

Feedback: Review section *Changing Accounting Methods.*

Takeaways

Although depreciation may seem overwhelming, this subject must be understood to prepare accurate business tax returns. Depreciation is used to benefit the taxpayer; the IRS has defined the convention and class type and has figured the percentage amount. All the tax professional needs to do is find the correct class type and percentage amount to calculate the correct depreciation amount for the taxpayer. A tax professional should not rely on software to do the calculation but understand depreciation to make sure the software is calculating the depreciation correctly.

TEST YOUR KNOWLEDGE!
Go online to take a practice quiz.

Chapter 13 Capital Gains and Losses

Introduction

Almost everything a taxpayer owns and uses for personal or investment purposes is a capital asset. When a capital asset is sold, the difference between the basis in the asset and the amount the item is sold for is either a capital gain or a capital loss. A capital gain is the profit that results from selling an investment (stocks, bonds, or real estate) for a higher price than it was purchased. Capital gains may refer to investment income that arises in relation to real assets (such as property), financial assets (such as shares of stocks or bonds), and intangible assets (such as goodwill). A capital loss arises if the proceeds from the sale of a capital asset are less than the purchase price. The taxpayer can deduct up to a $3,000 loss ($1,500 if filing MFS). The capital loss that exceeds the limit amount may be taken in future years.

Objectives

At the end of this lesson, the student will:

- Explain the holding periods for different types of property.
- Understand the difference between short-term and long-term capital gains.
- Identify capital assets.
- Determine basis before selling an asset.
- Establish when the primary residence is excluded from capital gain.

Resources

Form 1040	Publication 17	Instructions Form 1040
Form 1099-B	Publication 523	Instructions Form 1099-B
Form 4797	Publication 544	Instructions Form 4797
Form 6252	Publication 551	Instructions Form 6252
Form 8949	Tax Topic 409, 703	Instructions Form 8949
Schedule D		Instructions for Schedule D

Capital Gains and Loss

Table of Contents

Introduction	433
Part 1 Capital Assets	435
Basis of Property	436
Holding Period	436
Capital Gains Distributions	436
Adjusted Basis	436
Increases to Basis	437
Decreases to Basis	437
Determining Capital Gains and Losses	437
Sale of Stocks and Mutual Funds	438
Sale of Personal Residence	438
Exclusion	438
Partial Exclusion	439
Calculating the Sales Price	440
Widowed Taxpayers	440
Incapacitated Taxpayers	440
Divorced Taxpayers	440
Installment Sales	441
Inherited Property	441
Gift of Property	441
Form 8949: Reporting Capital Gains and Losses	442
Codes for Form 8949	443
Capital Assets Held for Personal Use	444
Virtual Currency	445
Part 1 Review Questions	445
Part 1 Review Questions Answers	446
Takeaways	447

Part 1 Capital Assets

Capital assets are items held for personal use, pleasure, or investment purposes. Some examples of capital assets are:

- Stocks or bonds held in a personal account.
- A house owned and used by the taxpayer and family.
- Household furnishings.
- A car used for pleasure and/or work.
- Coin or stamp collections.
- Gems and jewelry.
- Gold, silver, or other metal types.
- Timber grown on taxpayer personal property or investment property.

A capital asset can be any property held by the taxpayer; however, the following would be considered noncapital assets:

- Property held mainly for sale to customers or property that will physically become a part of merchandise for sale to customers (e.g., inventory).
- Depreciable property used in trade or business, even if 100% depreciated.
- Real property used in trade or business.
- Accounts or notes receivable acquired in the ordinary course of a trade or business for services rendered, or the sale of stock in trade or other property included in inventory.
- A copyright, a literary, musical, or artistic composition, a letter or memorandum, or a similar property that is as follows:
    - Created by personal efforts.
    - Prepared or produced for the taxpayer in the case of a letter, memorandum, or similar property.
    - Received from an individual who created the property or for whom the property was prepared under circumstances entitling the taxpayer to the basis of the person who created the property, or for whom it was prepared or produced.
- U.S. government publications received from the government for free or for less than the normal sales price.
- Any financial instruments for commodities derivative held by a commodities derivatives dealer.
- Hedge fund transactions, but only if the transaction is clearly identified as a hedging transaction before the close of the day on which it was acquired or originated.
- Supplies of a type regularly used or consumed in the ordinary course of trade or business.
- Property deducted under the de minimis safe harbor for tangible property.

The rate at which the gain on the sale of a capital asset will be taxed depends on the type of capital asset, the holding period, and the taxpayer's tax bracket. If the taxpayer has a capital loss, the loss will be netted against any realized gain. If the taxpayer has a net loss in excess of $3,000, he or she will be able to deduct up to $3,000 of the loss against the taxpayer's ordinary income in the year of the sale. The unused capital loss would then be carried forward to subsequent years and used to help offset net capital gains or ordinary income up to $3,000 a year until the loss is depleted. If the taxpayer is filing as Married filing separately, the limit is $1,500.

Basis of Property

Basis is a way of determining the cost of an investment in property and is decided by how it was acquired. If the property was purchased, the purchase price is the basis. Any improvements made to the property are then added to that basis. The purchase price plus improvements constitutes the adjusted basis. Other items that add to the basis are the expenses of acquiring the property (commissions, sales tax, and freight charges). There are also items that reduce the basis, which include depreciation, nontaxable distributions, and postponed gain on home sales. This is also referred to as cost basis.

Basis is the amount of the investment in the asset for tax purposes. To calculate the gain or loss, basis is needed on the sale or disposition of the asset. Recordkeeping must be accurate to adjust the basis of the property when it is sold.

If a single transaction includes multiple properties, the total cost must be allocated among the separate properties according to the fair market value established by each property's basis. As a result of the allocation, the basis that each property takes is the original unadjusted basis for tax purposes. This rule applies in determining basis for depreciation purposes or a gain or loss, on a transaction.

Holding Period

The holding period (the length of time an individual "held" or owned a property) determines whether the capital gain or loss is short-term or long-term. To determine the holding period, start counting on the day after the date the taxpayer acquired the property. Holding periods end on the day the taxpayer sold the property. Short-term property is property held for one year (365 days) or less. Long-term property is property held for more than one year. For example, if the taxpayer purchased property on September 20, 2020, and sold it on September 20, 2021, the taxpayer would have a short-term capital gain or loss. However, if the taxpayer waited one more day and sold the property on September 21, 2021, the transaction would be a long-term capital gain or loss. It is important to correctly determine the holding period because the maximum tax rate is based on the holding period. To calculate the total net gain or loss, combine the net short-term gains or losses with the net long-term gains or losses.

Capital Gains Distributions

Capital gains distributions are paid to the taxpayer by brokerage firms, mutual funds, and investment trusts. The capital gains distributions from mutual funds are long-term capital gains regardless of how long the taxpayer owned the stock. Distributions of net-realized short-term capital gains are reported on Form 1099-DIV as ordinary dividends.

Adjusted Basis

To arrive at the adjusted basis, the taxpayer must make allowable adjustments to the basis of the property. The taxpayer would figure the gain or loss on a sale, exchange, or other disposition of property, or would figure the allowable depreciation, depletion, or amortization. The result is the property's adjusted basis.

Increases to Basis

To increase the property basis, the improvements must have a useful life of more than 1 year. Examples of capital improvements that would increase the property basis are an addition to the primary home, replacing the entire roof, and paving the driveway. Each one of these items may have a different class life for depreciation. Each would have to be depreciated by the rules for their property. Each depreciation class should have a separate set of recordkeeping.

Decreases to Basis

There are certain items that will cause the property to decrease its basis. Those items include certain vehicle credits, IRC section 179 deductions, residential energy credits, casualty and theft losses, and insurance reimbursement. See Publication 551.

Determining Capital Gains and Losses

Capital gains or losses are either short-term or long-term. If the property was disposed of and it was inherited, the basis is generally the fair market value of the property at the date of the owner's death. Nonbusiness bad debt is treated as a short-term capital loss.

Form 1099-DIV

The reported amount is found on Form 1099-DIV, box 2a, and entered on Schedule D, line 13, no matter how long the investment was held. The amount in box 2b is reported on line 11 of the *Unrecaptured Section 1250 Gain Worksheet*. The amount in 2c is reported on *Exclusion of Gain on Qualified Small Business Stock* (QSB). The amount in 2d is reported on line 4 of the *28% Rate Gain Worksheet*.

Capital Gains and Loss

If the taxpayer earns dividends from an account that is held by a commercial company even though the account is held in the taxpayer's name, the commercial account will distribute Form 1099-DIV to the taxpayer in the amount of their capital gains distributions. This transaction is reported on Schedule D, line 13.

Sale of Stocks and Mutual Funds

The taxpayer should receive Form 1099-B, which reports the total proceeds from the sale of stock or mutual funds. The proceeds are reported on Form 8949.

To determine the capital gain on stocks or mutual funds, the taxpayer must know the cost basis. The cost basis is the purchase price plus any costs related to its purchase and/or to any paid commissions. The cost basis is subtracted from the selling price to determine the capital gains. This information, along with the purchase date and sales date, is included on Form 8949. The trade date—not the settlement date—is used to determine whether the transaction is long-term or short-term

The cost basis of a mutual fund is the cash investment amount plus any reinvested dividends and capital gains minus any returns of capital that were received. If it is less than the entire value of the funds sold, then one must figure the cost basis of the shares sold. To use the average cost per share, the taxpayer must have acquired the shares at various times and various prices and must have left the shares on deposit in an account that is handled by a custodian or agent who acquires or redeems those shares.

Sale of Personal Residence

The Taxpayer Relief Act of 1997 repealed IRC section 1034, *Deferral of Gain on Sale of Residence*, and amended section 121, *The Once-in-a-Lifetime Exclusion of Gain*. Previously, IRC section 1034 allowed taxpayers to defer the gain on the sale of a principal residence if a replacement residence was purchased within two years and if the replacement residence's price was equal to or exceeded the adjusted selling price of the former residence. Now, however, the current law under IRC section 121 is considerably more generous. The sale of the primary residence is reported on the taxpayer's tax return only if there is a taxable gain or if the property was used for business.

To qualify for the exclusion, the taxpayer must meet the following "ownership and use" tests during the last five-year period ending on the date of the sale:

- Owned the home for at least two years (the ownership test).
- Lived in the home as the main home for at least two years (the use test).

A taxpayer can meet the ownership and use test during different two-year periods if they meet both tests during the five years before the date of the sale.

Exclusion

If all the following are true, a taxpayer can exclude the entire gain of the sale of their main home up to $250,000 or up to $500,000 if Married Filing Jointly or as a Qualifying widow(er):

Capital Gains and Losses

> ➢ The taxpayer is married and filing a joint return for the year.
> ➢ Either the taxpayer or the spouse meets the ownership test.
> ➢ Both the taxpayer and the spouse meet the use test.

If the taxpayer's divorce decree allows the taxpayer's former spouse to live in the home the taxpayer owns, the taxpayer is considered to have also lived there for the purposes of claiming the exclusion. The exclusion is limited to one sale every two years on sales after May 6, 1997.

Partial Exclusion

The amount of gain a taxpayer can exclude must be prorated if the sale of a home is due to a job relocation, health reasons, or other unforeseen circumstances of the homeowner (or the homeowner's spouse if they file a joint return), and if any the following are also true:

> ➢ The taxpayer did not meet the ownership and use test.
> ➢ The taxpayer is excluding gain on the sale of another home after May 6, 1997.
> ➢ The homeowner (or the homeowner's spouse if they file a joint return) sells more than one home in a two-year period.
> ➢ The taxpayer owned a home on August 5, 2020, sold it before August 5, 2021, and did not meet the ownership or use tests.
> ➢ The taxpayer used part of the home for business or rental purposes.
> ➢ The sale or other disposition of one's home includes disposition by sale, exchange, involuntary conversion (condemnation), foreclosure, or other dispositions. If the home was abandoned, foreclosed, or repossessed, the taxpayer should receive Form 1099-A, *Acquisition or Abandonment of Secured Property*, from the lender who acquired the property. This form should be used to calculate whether there is a gain or loss on the property.

Sales of residences other than the taxpayer's main residence are treated differently than sales of primary residences for tax purposes. If the taxpayer sells a residence that is not their principal residence, a capital gain or loss would be reported on Form 8949 and then on Form 797. While a loss on a main residence is not deductible, a loss on a residential rental house may be deductible.

Because the exclusion only pertains to residences, if the taxpayer used part of their home for business or rental purposes, some of the gain may not qualify for the exclusion. Any gain due to depreciation claimed after May 6, 1997, cannot be excluded.

Example: Bill Burns had taken depreciation in prior years for an office in the home before changing it back to a bedroom and using it for personal purposes for two out of the five years prior to the sale. In this instance, Mr. Burns can exclude all the gain from the sale of the house, except for gain from depreciation after May 6, 1997.

If the taxpayer cannot exclude all of the gain, you would treat the sale as two transactions: one business and one personal.

Example: On February 1, 2018, Amy bought a house. She moved in on that date and lived in it until May 31, 2019, when she moved out of the house and put it up for rent. The house was rented from June 1, 2019 to March 31, 2020. Amy moved back into the house on April 1, 2020, and lived there until she sold it on January 31, 2021. During the five-year period ending on the date of the sale (February 1, 2018 to January 31, 2021), Amy owned and lived in the house for more than two years.

Five-Year Period	Used as Home		Used as Rental
2/1/18 – 5/31/19	16 months		
6/1/19 – 3/31/20			10 months
4/1/20 – 1/31/21	22 months		
	38 months		10 months

Because she lived in the home for more than two years, Amy can exclude gain up to $250,000. However, as mentioned above, she cannot exclude the part of the gain equal to the depreciation she claimed for renting the house after May 6, 1997.

Calculating the Sales Price

Anytime the taxpayer sells a home, land, stock, or other security, he or she will receive either Form 1099-S, *Proceeds from Real Estate Transactions*, or Form 1099-B, *Proceeds from Broker and Barter Exchange Transactions*.

Forms 1099-S and 1099-B are "reporting documents" that provide the gross proceeds or sales price. If the taxpayer sold one stock several times, Form 1099-B might only report the gross proceeds together. The taxpayer can divide the gross proceeds by the total number of shares sold to arrive at an average price per share. The taxpayer can then multiply the price per share by the number of shares sold on each occasion to arrive at the sales price.

Widowed Taxpayers

The Mortgage Forgiveness Debt Relief Act of 2007 allows a surviving spouse to exclude up to $500,000 of the gain from the sale of a principal residence owned jointly. The sale needs to occur within two years from the death of the spouse. Exceptions apply.

Incapacitated Taxpayers

Taxpayers who own a residence are still considered to reside in that residence even if they become physically or mentally incapable of self-care and are placed in a care facility licensed by a state or governmental subdivision such as a nursing home. However, the taxpayer must have owned and used the residence as a principal residence for a period of at least one year during the five years preceding the sale to qualify for IRC section 121 exclusion.

Divorced Taxpayers

If the taxpayer is divorced, and the primary residence is transferred to the taxpayer, the time during which the taxpayer's former spouse owned the residence is added to the taxpayer's period of ownership. A taxpayer who owns a residence is considered to have used it as a principal residence while the taxpayer's spouse or former spouse is granted use of the residence under the terms of the divorce or separation instrument.

Installment Sales

An installment sale is a sale of property in which the taxpayer receives a payment after one year of the sale. An installment sale is an arrangement where some or the entire selling price is paid in a later year. Owners who sell homes and finance the purchase themselves often do so as an installment sale. This is beneficial because the taxpayer does not have to pay taxes on the entire gain in the year of sale. It can also benefit the taxpayer by keeping the gain from pushing them into a higher tax bracket. For taxpayers looking for a steady stream of income over a period of time, the installment sale can provide this income.

The gain from an installment sale is usually reported in the year it is received. However, the taxpayer can elect to report all of the gain in the year of sale, which can be beneficial if the taxpayer had other capital losses to offset the gain. The income from the sale is reported on Form 6252, *Installment Sale Income.* Interest income is reported on Schedule B as it is received. The gain is reported on Form 4797 if it is a business gain. Personal gain is reported on Form 8949.

If a taxpayer has a loss, it cannot be reported as an installment sale. Personal losses are not deductible. If it is a business loss, the entire loss will be reported on Form 4797 in the year of the sale. The interest earned is still reported on Schedule B.

Inherited Property

The basis of inherited property is the property's fair market value (FMV) at the date of death or at an alternate valuation date if chosen by the executor of the estate. The election to use the alternate valuation date is irrevocable. The alternate date is generally six months after the decedent's death or some earlier date of sale or distribution. Alternate valuation can be elected only if the property use decreased both the value of the gross estate and the combined estate and a generation-skipping transfer of tax liability. The holding period is always considered long-term regardless of how long the taxpayer actually owned the property because it includes the holding period of the deceased.

Gift of Property

To determine the basis of property received as a gift, it is necessary to know the donor's adjusted basis of the gift when given to the taxpayer, the fair market value at the time it was given to the taxpayer, and the amount of gift tax that was paid. The taxpayer's basis for figuring gain at the time of the sale or for figuring the disposition of the asset at the time of the sale is the donor's adjusted basis, plus or minus any changes during the period the taxpayer held the property. The taxpayer's basis for figuring loss is the fair market value when received, plus or minus any required adjustments to the basis made during the period the taxpayer held the asset.

The amount of paid gift tax to be included in the basis of the asset depends on the date the gift was received.

Capital Gains and Loss

Example: The taxpayer received an acre of land as a gift. At the time the gift was given, the land had a fair market value of $8,000. The donor had purchased the land for $10,000, making the property's adjusted basis. After the taxpayer received the property, no events occurred to increase or decrease the basis. If the taxpayer later sells the property for $12,000, he will have a $2,000 gain. The taxpayer must use the donor's adjusted basis ($10,000) at the time of the gift as the basis to figure gain. If he sells the property for $7,000, he will have a $1,000 loss because he must use the fair market value ($8,000) at the time of the gift to figure loss. If the sales price is between $8,000 and $10,000, he will have neither a gain nor a loss.

Form 8949: Reporting Capital Gains and Losses

Portion of 2021 Form 8949

Form 8949 is used to report the sales and exchanges of capital assets. It also allows the taxpayer and the IRS to reconcile what has been reported to the IRS on Forms 1099-B or 1099-S.

Individual taxpayers report the following information on Form 8949:

> The sale or exchange of a capital asset.
> Gains from involuntary conversions.
> Nonbusiness bad debts.
> Worthless stocks or bonds.

When using Form 8949, the taxpayer separates the short-term and long-term capital gains and losses. If the disposed property was inherited, it is treated as a long-term asset. Remember, when figuring the holding period, the calculation starts one day after the property has been received. Short-term losses and gains are reported on Form 8949, Part I. Long-term losses and gains are reported in Form 8949, Part II.

Example: Rachel purchased 300 shares of Imperial Soap for $1,000. She sold the stock this year for $1,200. Rachel realized a gain of $200, not the $1,200 in proceeds she received from the sale. Only the $200 is included in gross income since the $1,000 is Rachel's return of capital.

Codes for Form 8949

Below are the definitions that tell the IRS if the sale was a short-term or long-term. The codes also determine if the asset basis was reported to the IRS or not. The taxpayer received either Form 1099-B or a substitute statement with the codes. These codes are used for Box A-F on Form 8949.

A	Short-term basis reported to the IRS.
B	Short-term basis not reported to the IRS.
C	Short-term basis not reported on Form 1099-B.
D	Long-term basis reported to the IRS.
E	Long-term basis not reported to the IRS.
F	Long-term transaction not reported on Form 1099-B.

The following codes are used for Form 8949, Columns F and G, that are reported on Form 1099-B or a substitute statement

B	Basis on Form 1099-B is incorrect.
C	The taxpayer disposed of collectibles.
D	Form 1099-B showed an accrued market discount.
E	The taxpayer received Form 1099-B, 1099-S, or some substitute statement for a transaction, and there are selling expenses or option premiums that are not reflected on the form or statement by an adjustment to either the proceeds or basis shown.
H	The taxpayer sold or exchanged their primary residence for a gain that wasn't reported on Form 8949, Part II.
L	The taxpayer has a nondeductible loss other than a loss indicated by code *W* that was not reported.
M	Select this code to tell the IRS that the taxpayer reported multiple transactions on a single row.
N	The taxpayer received Forms 1099-B as a nominee instead of the actual owner of the property.
O	The taxpayer has an adjustment not designated by the other codes.
Q	Select this code to tell the IRS that the taxpayer sold or exchanged qualified small business stock and excluded part of the gain.
R	Select this code to tell the IRS that the taxpayer is electing to postpone all or part of the gain under the rules explained in the Schedule D instructions for rollover of gain.

Capital Gains and Loss

S	The taxpayer had a loss from the sale, exchange, or worthlessness of small business stock, and the total loss is more than the maximum amount that can be treated as an ordinary loss. See IRC section 1244 for more information.
T	The taxpayer received Form 1099-B or some substitute statement and the type of gain or loss (short-term or long-term) in box 2 is incorrect.
W	Select this code to tell the IRS that the taxpayer has a nondeductible loss from a wash sale.
X	The taxpayer can exclude all or part of the capital gain under the "DC Zone and Community Assets Exclusion".
Y	Reporting a gain from a QOF investment that was deferred in a prior year.
Z	*Qualified Opportunity Zone (QO) Fund Eligible Gain Deferral.* Until December 31, 2026, if the taxpayer has an eligible gain, he or she may make a deferral on part or all of the gain that would normally be included as income.

If none of the statements in column F apply, leave columns F and G blank. If more than one code is entered in column F on the same row, enter the net adjustments in column G. For example, if one adjustment is $5,000 and another is $1,000, enter $4,000 ($5,000 − $1,000). Enter all the codes that apply in alphabetical order; do not use commas to separate the codes. For example, write "BOQ", not "B.O.Q." or "B, O, Q".

Capital Assets Held for Personal Use

When a taxpayer sells their primary residence, it could be a reportable transaction. Factors that could trigger the transaction is:

1. Sales amount
2. Filing status
3. Depreciated a portion of the house

If the taxpayer and spouse sold their primary residence and the gain was over $500,000 ($250,000 all other filing status) the amount is reported on Schedule D. If the gain is less than $500,000 ($250,000 all other filing status) it may not be taxable. See IRC section 121.

If the taxpayer converted the depreciable property to personal use, all or part of the gain on the sale or exchange would be recaptured as ordinary income. Recaptured means the gain realized by the sale of capital property that is depreciable and must be reported. A loss from the sale or exchange of personal use asset is not deductible.

Example: Sally sold her main home in 2020 for $320,000 and received Form 1099-S showing the $320,000 gross proceeds. The selling expense was $20,000 and her home basis was $100,000. Sally would be able to exclude the entire $200,000 gain from her income.

$ 320,000	Sales price
− $ 100,000	Basis
− $ 20,000	Selling expenses
$ 200,000	**Capital gain (excluded from income)**

Virtual Currency

The IRS defines "virtual currency" as a digital representation of value that functions as a medium of exchange, a unit of account and a store of value other than a representation of the United States dollar or a foreign currency. Convertible virtual currency is virtual currency (VC) that has an equivalent value in real currency, or that acts as a substitute for real currency. Cryptocurrency, is generally referred to as coins or tokens, is a type of virtual currency that utilizes cryptography to secure transactions that are digitally recorded on a distributed ledger, such as a blockchain. A taxpayer has gross income when he receives the cryptocurrency (i.e., recorded on the distributed ledger) and has dominion and control over it.

Virtual currency received as payment for goods or services is considered income equal to the fair market value (FMV) on the date received. Payment by virtual currency is included as income, the FMV is determined by the United States dollar (USD). Employers paying VC as compensation for services constitute wages for employment tax purposes and is subject to Federal tax withholding. VC Payments are subject to the same information reporting as other payments (e.g., Forms W-2, 1099, 1042 – Misc., etc.). See Notice 2014-21, 2014-16, and IRB 938.

Payments made by VC are subject to back-up withholding rules to the same extent as other payments. A taxpayer who successfully "mines" virtual currency has gross income equal to the fair market value of the virtual currency as of the date of receipt.

Form 1040 has a question that is to be asked of all taxpayers: "did you receive, sell, exchange, or otherwise dispose of any financial interest in any virtual currency?".

> At any time during 2021, did you receive, sell, exchange, or otherwise dispose of any financial interest in any virtual currency? ☐ Yes ☐ No

As the professional do not assume the answer is no; ask the taxpayer and mark the appropriate box, based on their answer.

Not reporting the sale or exchange of virtual currencies could resort in a tax consequence. See Publication 544.

Part 1 Review Questions

To obtain the maximum benefit from this chapter, LTP recommends that you complete each of the following questions, and then compare them to the answers with feedback that immediately follow. Under governing self-study standards, vendors are required to present review questions intermittently throughout each self-study course.

These questions and explanations are not part of the final examination and will not be graded by LTP.

CGLP1.1
Which scenario could make a taxpayer pay a capital gains tax on their primary residence?

a. The taxpayer lived in the main house for two of the last five years.
b. The taxpayer's gain on his primary residence is less than $250,000.
c. The taxpayer and his or her spouse have lived in the house for two of the last five years.
d. The taxpayer sold the house in 18 months because they found a house they liked more.

Capital Gains and Loss

CGLP1.2

Which of the following best describes basis?

a. Basis is the amount of investment in the asset for tax purposes.
b. Basis includes inventory.
c. Basis includes land.
d. Basis is a capital asset.

CGLP1.3

Is virtual currency subject to back-up withholding?

a. True
b. False

CGLP1.4

James was paid in virtual currency by his employer. How does he report the income?

a. James does not have to claim virtual currency as income.
b. James needs to report the payment as the fair market value on the date received.

Part 1 Review Questions Answers

CGLP1.1

Which scenario could make a taxpayer pay a capital gains tax on their primary residence?

a. The taxpayer lived in the main house for two of the last five years.
b. The taxpayer's gain on his primary residence is less than $250,000.
c. The taxpayer and his or her spouse have lived in the house for two of the last five years.
d. **The taxpayer sold the house in 18 months because they found a house they liked more.**

Feedback: Review section *Sale of Personal Residence.*

CGLP1.2

Which of the following best describes basis?

a. **Basis is the amount of investment in the asset for tax purposes.**
b. Basis includes inventory.
c. Basis includes land.
d. Basis is a capital asset.

Feedback: Review section *Basis of Property.*

CGLP1.3

Is virtual currency subject to back-up withholding?

a. **True**
b. False

Feedback: Review section *Virtual Currency.*

CGLP1.4
James was paid in virtual currency by his employer. How does he report the income?

    a. James does not have to claim virtual currency as income.
    b. James needs to report the payment as the fair market value on the date received.

Feedback: Review section *Virtual Currency.*

Takeaways

The original basis for property is its cost, except as otherwise provided by law. The cost is the amount paid for such property in cash or other property. The basis includes acquisition costs such as commissions, legal fees, recording fees, and sales taxes, as well as installation and delivery costs. The cost of property includes not only the amount of money or other property paid, but also the amount of paid mortgage or liability costs in connection with the purchase. It makes no difference whether the taxpayer assumes the liability by taking over the payments or merely purchases the property at the asking price. When the property is disposed, any remaining amount of mortgage or liability of which the seller is relieved is treated as part of the amount realized. Real estate taxes are included as part of the property's basis if the buyer assumes the seller's obligation to pay them.

Capital gains and losses are classified as long-term or short-term. If the asset has been held for more than one year before the asset was disposed, it is considered to be a long-term capital gain or loss. If the asset is held for less than one year, it is considered a short-term capital gain or loss.

TEST YOUR KNOWLEDGE!
Go online to take a practice quiz.

Chapter 14 Electronic Filing

Introduction

Electronic filing (also referred to as e-file and e-filing) is the process of submitting tax returns over the internet via approved tax software. The e-file system has made tax preparation significantly easier, and the IRS notifies software users within 24-48 hours if the tax return was accepted or rejected. E-filing is not available year-round but begins in January and ends in October; the IRS determines when e-filing begins and ends each year, and states follow the IRS dates. An electronic return originator (ERO) is the individual who originates the electronic submission of the tax return. To file a return electronically, the individual needs to be an Authorized IRS e-file Provider.

Objectives

At the end of this lesson, the student will be able to do the following:

➢ Understand the different e-filing options.
➢ Know which form(s) to use when the taxpayer opts-out of e-filing.
➢ Identify which forms are unable to be e-filed.

Resources

Form 8453	Publication 17	Instructions Form 8453
Form 8878	Publication 1345	Instructions Form 8878
Form 8878-A	Publication 3112	Instructions Form 8878-A
Form 8879		Instructions Form 8879
Form 9325		Instructions Form 9325

Table of Contents

Introduction 448
Part 1 Electronic Return Originator (ERO) 450
    Obtaining, Handling, and Processing Return Information from Taxpayers 450
    e-File Providers 450
    Becoming an e-File Provider 450
    Who are Principals and Responsible Officials? 451
    Step One: Creating an IRS e-Services Account 451
    Step Two: Submitting the Application 452
    Step Three: Passing the Suitability Check 452
    Denial to Participate in IRS e-File 453
    Acceptance to Participate in IRS e-File 453
    e-File Provider Penalties 453
    Verifying Taxpayer Identification Numbers (TINs) 454
    Nonstandard Document Awareness 455
    Safeguarding Taxpayer Information 455
    Client Protection 456
    The Gramm-Leach-Bliley Act 456
    Reporting Security Incidents 457
    Part 1 Review Questions 457
    Part 1 Review Questions Answers 458
Part 2 Transmitting Returns 460
    Filing the Completed Return 460
    Submission of Paper Documents 460
    Providing Information to the Taxpayer 461
    Processing Return Information from Taxpayers 461
    What the Taxpayer Should Receive 461
    File Accurate Tax Return to Receive Timely Refund 462
    Resubmitting Rejected Tax Returns 462
    Electronic Postmark 462
    Acknowledgment of Transmitted Returns 462
    Balance Due Returns 463
    Pay by Check 463
    Electronic Funds Withdrawal 464
    Credit or Debit Card Payments 464
    Electronic Federal Tax Payment System (EFTPS) 464
    Returns Not Eligible for IRS e-File 464
    Refund Delays 464
    Refund Offsets 465
    Where's My Refund? 465
    Bank Products 466
    E-File Guidelines for Fraud and Abuse 466
    Double Check the Taxpayer's Address 466
    Avoiding Refund Delays 467
    Signing an Electronic Tax Return 467
    Electronic Signature Methods 467
    IRS e-File Signature Authorization 467
    Guidance for Electronic Signatures 468
    IRS e-File Security and Privacy Standards 468
    Part 2 Review Questions 469
    Part 2 Review Questions Answers 470
Takeaways 471

Part 1 Electronic Return Originator (ERO)

An electronic return originator (ERO) is an authorized IRS e-file provider that originates submissions of returns he or she either prepares or collects from taxpayers who want to e-file their returns. An ERO originates the electronic submission of a return after the taxpayer authorizes the e-filing of the tax return. The ERO must have either prepared the return or collected it from a taxpayer. An ERO originates the electronic submission by one of the following methods:

- Electronically sending the return to a transmitter that will transmit the return to the IRS.
- Directly transmitting the return to the IRS.
- Providing the return to an intermediate service provider to transmit it to the IRS.

Obtaining, Handling, and Processing Return Information from Taxpayers

If the return was prepared by a paid preparer, the ERO must always identify the paid preparer in the proper field of the electronic record and include the paid preparer's following information:

- Name
- Address
- EIN (if a member of a firm)
- PTIN

An ERO who chooses to originate returns that have not been prepared by the firm becomes the tax preparer when, entering the data, the ERO discovers errors that require substantive changes and makes the changes. A non-substantive change is a correction limited to a transposition error, a misplaced entry, a spelling error, or an arithmetic correction. The IRS considers all other changes substantive, and the ERO becomes the tax preparer if corrections are made.

e-File Providers

An authorized IRS e-file provider is a business or organization authorized by the IRS to participate in their e-file program. A Provider may be an Electronic Return Originator (ERO), an Intermediate Service Provider, a Transmitter, a Software Developer, a Reporting Agent, or an Affordable Care Act (ACA) Provider. These different roles are not mutually exclusive, and one person or entity can have more than one. For example, a Provider may be an ERO while also being a Transmitter or a tax return preparer. Even though the activities and responsibilities for IRS e-file and return preparation are distinct and different from each other, one person can possess both titles, duties, and responsibilities at the same time.

A Transmitter is the person, entity, or software that literally sends the return data electronically directly to the IRS. A Provider is one who has been authorized by the IRS to file tax returns electronically, typically through a third-party transmitter such as a tax software provider; filing a return is not the same thing as sending it.

Becoming an e-File Provider

To become an e-file provider, an individual must submit a completed application to the IRS requesting the proper authorization, a process that usually takes 45 days. To complete the application quickly, the individual should have the following information prepared:

- ➤ Know which Provider options can be furnished to taxpayers.
- ➤ Enter identification information for the company.
  - Employer Identification Number.
  - Name of the company.
  - Enter the name, date of birth, Social Security number, current professional information, and citizenship status of the organization's Principal and Responsible Official. Mark if either or both are an attorney, certified public accountant, enrolled agent, officer of a publicly traded corporation, or a bonded bank official.

Who are Principals and Responsible Officials?

The Principal is the individual who is ultimately responsible for anything and everything that occurs regarding e-filing at the firm. Although a firm can have more than one "Responsible Official", there can be only one Principal, and the individual designated as the Principal must be on the application. Any of the following individuals that participate in the e-file operations of the company are eligible to be designated as the Principal:

- ➤ A sole proprietor of the business. For sole proprietorships, the sole proprietor must be the Principal.
- ➤ A partner who has at least 5% or more interest in the partnership. If no partner has 5% or more, the Principal needs to be an individual who is authorized to act for the partnership in legal or tax matters.
- ➤ The President, Vice-President, Secretary, or Treasurer of a corporation are all eligible to be a Principal.
- ➤ The Principal for an entity that is not any of the above needs to be an individual with the authority within the company to act on behalf of the entity in legal or tax matters.

If any of the above individuals are not involved in the e-file operation of the company, then a large firm with multilayered management can substitute a "Key Person" who participates substantially in the firm's electronic filing operations as the principal for the e-file application.

Unlike the Principal, who is a single person responsible for e-file matters across the whole company, Responsible Officials are the people in charge of the day-to-day e-file operations at specific locations such as offices. They are the first point of contact with the IRS and have the authority to sign and revise IRS e-file applications. Responsible Officials must set the revenue procedures for e-filing and for all publications and notices thereof and ensure that employees follow them. Responsible Officials can oversee the operations at more than one office, and though there can be more, each firm must have at least one Responsible Official, although it can always add more later; the Principal can also be the Responsible Official.

Step One: Creating an IRS e-Services Account

Before starting the e-file application process, the individual must create an account with IRS Secure Access. To do this, the individual will register using a two-factor authentication process at irs.gov. After this, the taxpayer will be asked to provide the following information to create the account:

- ➤ Full legal name
- ➤ Home address

- Social Security number
- Date of birth
- Phone number
- Email address

Any other individuals that the firm wishes to appoint as either the Principal or as Responsible Officials must also create e-services accounts. Account creators must return to the e-Services site within 28 days of receiving the confirmation code to confirm the registration and thus allow the firm to continue the application process.

Step Two: Submitting the Application

Once all relevant individuals have confirmed their e-Services accounts, the firm can apply to become an authorized IRS e-file provider. The next steps of the application process are as follows:

1. Log in to e-Services and access the online application to become an IRS e-file provider.
2. Select the e-file provider type (Transmitter, ERO, etc.).
3. Enter the identification information of the firm and services provided.
4. Enter the name, home address, SSN, DOB, and citizenship status for each principal and responsible party for the firm.
5. Enter the Principal and Responsible Official(s) current professional status (attorney, certified public accountant, enrolled agent, etc.) and any other requested information.
6. Each Principal and Responsible Official must answer several personal questions and sign the Terms of Agreement (TOA) using the PIN they selected when creating their e-services accounts.
7. Each Principal and Responsible Official must declare under penalty of perjury that all the personal information they entered is true.

Submit the IRS e-file application and retain the tracking number provided after the submission of the application was successful.

Any individuals appointed to become the Principal or a Responsible Official who are not an EA, CPA, or attorney must pass a background check before the application can continue. To do this, first request a fingerprint card from the IRS by calling their toll-free number (1-866-255-0654). Once the IRS has mailed the cards, take them to a trained professional at your local police department or to a company certified to provide that service. They will perform the fingerprinting of each Principal and Responsible Official, who must each sign the card that contains their fingerprints.

Step Three: Passing the Suitability Check

Once the IRS has received, processed, and reviewed the application, they will conduct a "suitability check" to determine if the firm qualifies to become an e-file provider. The "suitability check" consists of the following checks on the firm, on each person listed as a principal or responsible official on the application, and on all documents related to the application:

- A credit check.
- A tax compliance check.

- A criminal background check.
- A check for prior noncompliance with IRS e-file requirements.

If the firm passes the suitability check they will receive their acceptance letter from the IRS with the electronic filing identification number (EFIN), which should not be confused with the firm's EIN.

Denial to Participate in IRS e-File

If the firm, a Principal, or a Responsible Official fails the suitability check, the IRS will notify the applicant of denial to participate in the program, the date they may reapply, and if they may reapply sooner if the suitability issues are resolved.

Acceptance to Participate in IRS e-File

After an applicant passes the suitability check and the IRS completes the processing of the application, the IRS will notify the applicant of their acceptance or rejection to participate in the program. A provider does not have to reapply unless the IRS suspends the provider from participation in the program for a violation. If any of the information on the original application changes, the provider will have 30 days to update the information by resubmitting the application with the assorted changes.

If the professional status of a Principal or Responsible Official changes, the firm must update its e-file application and resubmit the individual's fingerprints for a new background check. If a Principal or a Responsible Official dies, the Provider must remove or replace the deceased within 30 days by resubmitting the application. If this is not done, the IRS will remove the deceased individual(s) from the e-file application themselves, which may result in rejected returns because of leaving one of the firm's offices uncovered. The IRS will also remove Providers if they are unable to contact the provider or if the IRS' mail is returned to them as undeliverable because the Provider failed to update their physical mailing address, in which case the IRS will reject all returns submitted by the Provider until the Provider updates their information.

e-File Provider Penalties

Monitoring

The IRS monitors Providers by visiting the locations where one performs IRS e-file activities and by reviewing the e-file records the IRS requires them to keep. Monitoring may include, but is not limited to, the following:

- Reviewing the quality of e-file submissions for rejects and other defects.
- Checking adherence to signature requirements on returns.
- Scrutinizing advertising material.
- Examining records.
- Observing office procedures.
- Conducting periodic suitability checks.

The IRS monitors the regulations put in place by the Providers to ensure they are in compliance with IRC §6695(g).

Revocation

The IRS will revoke participation from an authorized Provider, Principal, or Responsible Official if so ordered by a federal court or a federal or state legal action. If the legal action expires or is reversed, the revoked Provider may reapply to participate in IRS e-file after the legal action expires or is reversed.

Sanctioning

IRS e-file violations may result in warning or sanctioning an authorized IRS e-file Provider, a Principal, or a Responsible Official. Sanctioning may take the form of a written reprimand, a suspension, or an expulsion from participating in the e-file program. In most circumstances, a sanction is effective 30 days after the date of the letter informing individuals of a sanction against them or the date that the reviewing officers or the Office of Appeals affirms the sanction, whichever is later. If a Provider, Principal, or Responsible Official is suspended or expelled from participation in e-filing, every entity that listed the suspended or expelled Principal or Responsible Official on their e-file application may also be suspended or expelled. Although notice must eventually be given, the IRS has full authority to immediately suspend or expel anyone without a prior warning or notice.

Infractions

The IRS categorizes the seriousness of infractions in three different levels.

Level One Infractions are infringements of IRS e-file rules and requirements that have little-to-no harmful effect on the quality of the returns or on the IRS e-file program. This infraction could result in a written reprimand but may not lead to a suspension or expulsion.

Level Two Infractions are violations of IRS e-file rules and requirements that have an unfavorable impact upon the quality of the returns or on the IRS e-file program. The repeating Level One Infractions after the IRS has notified the person about the current violation could cause an increase to Level Two Infraction. Depending on the nature of the infraction, the IRS may limit participation in IRS e-file or suspend the authorized IRS e-file Provider from participation in IRS e-file for a period of one year.

Level Three Infractions are violations of IRS e-file rules and requirements that have a significant adverse impact on the quality of tax returns. Level Three Infractions include continued Level Two Infractions after the IRS has brought the Level Two Infraction to the attention of the Provider. A Level Three Infraction may result in suspension from participation in IRS e-file for two years or, depending on the severity of the infraction (such as fraud, identity theft, or criminal conduct), in removal without the opportunity for future participation. The IRS reserves the right to suspend or expel a Provider prior to administrative review for Level Three Infractions. See Publication 3112.

Verifying Taxpayer Identification Numbers (TINs)

To help safeguard taxpayers from fraud and abuse, the tax preparer should confirm the identity and identification number of taxpayers, spouses, and dependents listed on every tax return prepared. Taxpayer Identification Numbers include SSNs, EINs, adopted taxpayer identification numbers (ATINs), and individual taxpayer identification numbers (ITINs). To confirm identities, the paid preparer should request to see both a current government-issued photo ID and the taxpayer's original identification number.

If the identification card does not have the same address as the one on the tax return, ask additional questions to verify the taxpayer's identity. Although the addresses are not required to match, confirming the identity of the taxpayer is a fundamental part of a tax professional's due diligence. Using an incorrect identification number or the same number on multiple returns or an incorrect name with the wrong identification number are some of the most common reject causes of e-filed returns. To minimize rejections, the preparer should verify the taxpayer's name and identification number prior to submitting the tax return electronically to the IRS.

Nonstandard Document Awareness

The IRS has identified key indicators of potential abuse and fraud such as altered, forged, or fabricated Forms W-2, W-2G, and 1099-R, especially when prepared by hand. Information on the reporting forms should never be altered. If the employer must make any changes, the employer should provide the employee with a corrected document, and a corrected reporting form should be sent to the IRS and the SSA. Any time the tax professional has a questionable income document, report it to the IRS.

Safeguarding Taxpayer Information

"Taxpayer information" is any piece of information that has been furnished for or by the taxpayer in any form or manner such as in person, over the phone, by mail, or by fax for the purpose of preparing the taxpayer's tax return. It includes, but is not limited to, the following pieces of information:

- Name
- Address
- Identification number
- Income
- Receipts
- Deductions
- Dependents
- Tax liability

Criminal and monetary penalties may be imposed on individuals preparing taxes or providing tax preparation services. This includes tax preparers that knowingly or recklessly make unauthorized disclosures with the preparation of income tax returns. See Title 26 IRC §301.7216.1 and §6713. Some common safeguarding strategies are:

- Lock doors to restrict access to files.
- Passwords to access computer files.
- Encrypting electronically-stored taxpayer data.
- Keep a backup of electronic data for recovery purposes. Backup files regularly.
- Shred taxpayer information.

For more information about safeguarding personal information, go to the official website of the Federal Trade Commission at www.ftc.gov.

Client Protection

The IRS has created several basic security guidelines for tax preparers to follow while preparing returns, which will make clients' data and their businesses safer:

- ➢ Learn to recognize phishing emails, especially those that look like they originated from the IRS. Never open an embedded link or attachment from an email that looks suspicious.
- ➢ Create a data security plan using the guidelines found in the Publication 4557, Safeguarding Taxpayer Data.
- ➢ Review your internal controls:
    - o Install anti-malware and anti-virus security software on all devices (laptops, desktops, routers, tablets, phones, etc.) and keep the software up to date.
    - o Use strong passwords of 8 or more characters with a mixture of upper and lowercase letters, numbers, and special symbols that do not start or end with a space or include common phrases or the names of loved ones or pets.
    - o Encrypt all sensitive files and emails and use strong password protections.
    - o Back up sensitive data to a safe and secure external source that is not connected to a network full-time.
    - o Wipe, clean, or destroy old hard drives or printers containing sensitive data.
    - o Limit access to taxpayer data exclusively to individuals who need to know.
    - o Perform weekly checks on the number of returns filed with your firm's EFIN through your eServices account, and compare that number with the number of returns your firm has actually prepared to make sure no one is fraudulently using your EFIN to e-file returns without your knowledge. Individuals can do the same thing via their PTIN account.
- ➢ Report any data theft or data loss to the appropriate IRS Stakeholder Liaison.
- ➢ Sign up on the IRS website to receive email notices from e-News for Tax Professionals, Quick Alerts, and Social Media.

The Gramm-Leach-Bliley Act

Enacted by Congress in 1999, the Gramm-Leach-Bliley Act implemented various safeguard rules and the financial privacy rule to protect taxpayers' private information. Safeguard rules require tax return preparers, data processors, transmitters (ERO), affiliates, service providers, and others to ensure the security and confidentiality of customer records and information. The financial privacy rule requires the following to give their customers privacy notices that explain the financial institution's information collection and sharing practices:

- ➢ Tax return preparers
- ➢ Data processors
- ➢ Transmitters
- ➢ Affiliates
- ➢ Service providers
- ➢ Anyone significantly engaged in providing financial products or services that include the preparation or filing of tax returns

Reporting Security Incidents

Online Providers of individual tax returns shall report any adverse event or threat of an event that could result in an unauthorized disclosure, misuse, modification, or destruction of information. These types of incidents can affect the confidentiality, integrity, and availability of taxpayer information or the ability for a taxpayer to prepare or file a return. Types of incidents include theft of information, loss of information, natural disasters (such as floods, earthquakes, or fires that destroy unrecoverable information), and computer system or network attacks using such tools as malicious code or denials of service. If the tax professional experiences a security incident or is hacked, report it to the IRS immediately.

Part 1 Review Questions

To obtain the maximum benefit from this chapter, LTP recommends that you complete each of the following questions, and then compare them to the answers with feedback that immediately follows. Under governing self-study standards, vendors are required to present review questions intermittently throughout each self-study course.

These questions and explanations are not part of the final examination and will not be graded by LTP.

EFP1.1
What does the acronym ERO stand for?

　　a. Electronic Return Originator
　　b. Electric Refund Option
　　c. Electronic Return Operator
　　d. Electronic Refund Originator

EFP1.2
A provider, as defined by the IRS, includes all of the following, **except?**

　　a. Electronic Return Originator (ERO)
　　b. A Software Developer
　　c. A Reporting Agent
　　d. An Enrolled Agent

EFP1.3
Which of the following best describes an Electronic Return Originator (ERO)?

　　a. Originates the electronic submission of tax returns to the IRS
　　b. Issues the tax refund
　　c. Accepts tax liability payments
　　d. Issues an extension on the taxpayer's behalf

Electronic Filing

EFP1.4
Which of the following best describes the Principal?

a. Javier, who works for XYZ Company and e-files all returns.
b. Alyssa, who handles all e-filing responsibilities.
c. Lexa, who is a receptionist.
d. Spencer, who does not prepare or e-file tax returns.

EFP1.5
Who is most likely to be the Responsible Official?

a. Taylor, who runs the electronic day-by-day operations.
b. Abigail, who is the receptionist.
c. Jess, who prepares and e-files his returns electronically.
d. Landon, who is the electronic filing marketing manager.

EFP1.6
If the individual who is appointed as the Principal or the Responsible Official is not an EA, CPA, or attorney, which of the following must the individual pass before the application moves forward?

1. Background check
2. Fingerprint card
3. Credit check
4. Tax compliance check

a. 1 only
b. 1 & 4
c. 2 only
d. 1, 3, & 4

Part 1 Review Questions Answers

EFP1.1
What does the acronym ERO stand for?

a. Electronic Return Originator
b. Electric Refund Option
c. Electronic Return Operator
d. Electronic Refund Originator

Feedback: Review section *Part 1: Electronic Return Originator.*

EFP1.2
A provider, as defined by the IRS, includes all of the following, **except?**

a. Electronic Return Originator (ERO)
b. A Software Developer
c. A Reporting Agent
d. An Enrolled Agent

Feedback: Review section *Part 1: Electronic Return Originator.*

EFP1.3
Which of the following best describes an Electronic Return Originator (ERO)?

    a. Originates the electronic submission of tax returns to the IRS
    b. Issues the tax refund
    c. Accepts tax liability payments
    d. Issues an extension on the taxpayer's behalf

Feedback: Review section *Part 1: Electronic Return Originator.*

EFP1.4
Which of the following best describes the Principal?

    a. Javier, who works for XYZ Company and e-files all returns.
    b. Alyssa, who handles all e-filing responsibilities.
    c. Lexa, who is a receptionist.
    d. Spencer, who does not prepare or e-file tax returns.

Feedback: Review section *Who are the Principals and Responsible Officials.*

EFP1.5
Who is most likely to be the Responsible Officials?

    a. Taylor, who runs the electronic day-by-day operations.
    b. Abigail, who is the receptionist.
    c. Jess, who prepares and e-files his returns electronically.
    d. Landon, who is the electronic filing marketing manager.

Feedback: Review section *Who are the Principals and Responsible Officials.*

EFP1.6
If the individual who is appointed as the Principal or the Responsible Official is not an EA, CPA, or attorney, which of the following must the individual pass before the application moves forward?

    1. Background check
    2. Fingerprint card
    3. Credit check
    4. Tax compliance check

    a. 1 only
    b. 1 & 4
    c. 2 only
    d. 1, 3, & 4

Feedback: Review section *Who are the Principals and Responsible Officials.*

Part 2 Transmitting Returns

Electronic filing is mandatory for tax preparers who file 11 or more Form 1040 returns during any calendar year. If the firm has more than one preparer, all individual returns prepared by the firm contribute to that number. For example, Javier is the owner of a tax preparation company and does not prepare returns. His employee, Rosemarie, prepares five tax returns that contain a Schedule C. Oscar prepares 10 returns, and Mario prepares 100 individual tax returns. Javier's company needs to file the returns electronically because the firm as a whole prepared more than 11 returns.

All authorized IRS e-file providers must ensure that returns are promptly processed on or before due date of the return (including extensions). An ERO must ensure that stockpiling returns does not occur at the company. "Stockpiling" is both collecting returns from taxpayers prior to official acceptance in the IRS e-file program and waiting more than three calendar days to submit a return to the IRS once the ERO has all the necessary information for an e-file submission. Tax professionals who are EROs must advise their clients that they cannot transmit returns to the IRS until the IRS begins accepting transmissions. Tax returns held prior to that date are not considered "stockpiled".

Filing the Completed Return

Once the return has been completed and signed by all the necessary parties (taxpayer, preparer, etc.), it is time to file the return to the IRS. If sending the return by mail, one must acquire an envelope and postage of sufficient size and amount and mail it to the address designated by the IRS. If mailing the tax return or payment voucher, use the link to find the correct address. https://www.irs.gov/filing/where-to-file-paper-tax-returns-with-or-without-a-payment.

Electronic filing was introduced by the IRS in 1986. Filing electronically, and having a refund deposited directly into a bank account, is the fastest and greenest way of filing the return. If the taxpayer has a balance due, the amount owed could be withdrawn from a bank account as well. Electronic filing saves the snail mail waiting time for sending or receiving a paper check.

Submission of Paper Documents

As been discussed throughout this course, there are a multitude of forms that may need to be completed and attached to a taxpayer's return for submission to the IRS. Some software companies allow forms to be attached as PDFs to the tax return prior to submission. If the software company does not support this feature, the documents need to be attached to Form 8453 (which does not need to be signed) and mailed to the IRS using the address on page 2 of Form 8453. The following is a list of the supporting documents that will need to be mailed with Form 8453 if the software does not allow PDF attachments to the return:

- Form 1098-C: Contributions of Motor Vehicles, Boats, and Airplanes
- Form 2848: Power of Attorney
- Form 3115: Application of Change in Accounting Method
- Form 3468: Investment Credit, Historical Structure Certificate
- Form 4136: Certificate for Biodiesel and Statement of Biodiesel Reseller
- Form 5713: International Boycott Report

- Form 8283: Noncash Charitable Contributions, Section B Appraisal Summary
- Form 8332: Release of Claim to Exemption for Children of Divorced or Separated Parents
- Form 8858: Information Return of U.S. Persons with Respect to Foreign Disregarded Entities
- Form 8885: Health Coverage Tax Credit
- Form 8864: Certificate for Biodiesel and Statement of Biodiesel Reseller
- Form 8949: Sales and Other Dispositions of Capital Assets, or a statement with the same information

Providing Information to the Taxpayer

The ERO must provide a complete copy of the return to the taxpayer. EROs may provide this copy in any medium—electronic or another form that is acceptable to both the taxpayer and the ERO. The copy does not need the Social Security number of the paid preparer, but the preparer's PTIN is required. A complete copy of a taxpayer's return includes, when applicable, Form 8453 and any other documents that the ERO cannot electronically transmit in addition to the electronic portion of the return.

The electronic portion of the return can be printed onto a copy of an official form or in some unofficial form. However, on an unofficial form, the ERO must match data entries with the relevant line numbers or with the descriptions found on official forms. If the taxpayer provided a completed paper return for electronic filing, and the information on the electronic portion of the return is identical to the information provided by the taxpayer, the ERO does not have to provide a printout of the electronic portion of the return to the taxpayer. The ERO should advise the taxpayer to retain a complete copy of their return and all supporting material. The ERO should also advise taxpayers that amended returns beginning 2019 can be e-filed. All others prior to 2019 must be filed as paper returns and mailed to the IRS submission processing center.

Processing Return Information from Taxpayers

Before an ERO can originate the electronic submission of a return, they must first either prepare the return or collect the already completed return and its various documents from the person who prepared it. If the return was prepared by someone else, the ERO must always identify the paid preparer in the appropriate field. EROs may either transmit the return directly to the IRS or transmit it through another provider. An authorized IRS e-file provider may disclose tax return information to other providers for the purpose of preparing a tax return under Reg. 301.7216. For example, an ERO may pass on return information to an intermediate service provider or a transmitter for the purpose of having an electronic return formatted or transmitted to the IRS.

What the Taxpayer Should Receive

Taxpayers should keep copies of the following documents received from the preparer:

- Form 8879 (PIN program)
- Any Form W-2, Form 1099, etc., and any other backup material for the return
- A copy of the electronically filed return
- A copy of Form 9325, *General Information for Taxpayers Who File Electronically*, which tells taxpayers the procedure to follow if they do not receive their refund

File Accurate Tax Return to Receive Timely Refund

An electronically filed tax return is the best way for the tax professional to file an accurate tax return. To ensure the tax return is processed quickly, the ERO should take the following steps:

- File electronically.
- Submit an accurate, complete, error-free return.
- Verify that the Social Security number(s) or Taxpayer Identification Number(s) are accurate for all individuals included on the tax return.
- Provide the taxpayer's correct mailing address in case the IRS mails a refund check.
- Use correct bank account and routing number for a direct deposit.

Resubmitting Rejected Tax Returns

If the taxpayer's tax return is rejected by the IRS, the ERO has 24 hours to explain to the taxpayer the reason for the rejection. If the return can be fixed and resubmitted, then the return can be retransmitted. The taxpayer could decide to mail the tax return instead of retransmitting the return. If the taxpayer chooses to mail the return, they would need a paper copy to send to the IRS. If the taxpayer chooses not to have the electronic portion of the return corrected and transmitted to the IRS or if it cannot be accepted for processing by the IRS, the taxpayer must file a new paper return. This must be filed by the due date of the return or within 10 calendar days after the date the IRS gave notice of the return's rejection, whichever of the two is later. The paper return should include an explanation of why the return is being filed after the due date.

Electronic Postmark

When a tax return is e-filed, a transmitter will electronically postmark it to show when it was filed. The postmark is created at the time the tax return is submitted and includes the date and time of the transmitter's time zone. An e-filed tax return is a timely filed return if the electronic postmark is on or before the filing deadline.

Acknowledgment of Transmitted Returns

The IRS electronically acknowledges the receipt of all transmissions and will either accept or reject the transmitted returns for specific reasons. Accepted returns meet the processing criteria and are considered "filed" as soon as the return is signed electronically or by hand. Rejected returns fail to meet processing criteria and are considered "not filed." See Publication 1345, *Handbook for Authorized IRS e-File Providers of Individuals Tax Returns*.

The acknowledgment record of accepted returns contains other useful information for originators, such as: if the IRS accepted a PIN, if the taxpayer's refund will be applied to a debt, if an elected electronic funds withdrawal was paid, and if the IRS approved a request for extension on Form 4868. EROs should check the acknowledgment records stored by their tax software regularly to identify returns that require follow-up action and then take reasonable steps to address the issues specified in those records. For example, if the IRS does not accept a PIN on an individual income tax return, the ERO must provide a completed and signed Form 8453 for the return.

Rejected returns can be corrected and retransmitted without new signatures or authorizations if changes do not differ from the amount in the electronic portion of the electronic return by more than $50 to "total income" or AGI of more than $14 to "total tax," "federal income tax withheld," "refund," or "amount owed." The taxpayer must be given copies of the new electronic return data if changes are made. If the required changes are greater than the amounts discussed above, new signatures will be required, and the taxpayer must be given copies of their new signatures.

Balance Due Returns

Taxpayers who owe additional tax must pay their balances due by the original due date of the return or be subject to interest and penalties. An extension of time to file may be filed electronically by the original due date of the return, but it is an extension of time to file the return, not an extension of time to pay a balance due. Tax professionals should inform taxpayers of their obligations and options for paying balances due. Taxpayers have several choices when paying taxes owed on their returns as well as paying estimated tax payments.

As discussed previously, tax returns with amounts due can still be filed electronically, and the payment can also be made directly to the IRS via ACH withdrawals. The taxpayer can schedule a payment on or before the tax payment deadline. If a balance due return was submitted after the due date, the payment date must be the same day the Provider transmitted the return. Taxpayers can make payments by Electronic Fund Withdrawal for amounts due from the following forms:

- Current year Form 1040.
- Form 1040-ES, *Estimated Tax for Individuals*. When filing the tax return, the taxpayer can select all four dates to electronically make the payment.
- Form 4868, *Application for Automatic Extension of Time to File U.S. Individual Income Tax Return*.
- Form 2350, *Application for Extension of Time to File U.S. Income Tax Return for Citizens and Resident Aliens Abroad Who Expect to Qualify for Special Tax Treatment*.

The tax professional needs to make sure the client's banking information is accurate and includes the routing transit number (RTN), the bank account number, the account type (checking or savings), the date the payment will be withdrawn (year, month, and day), and the amount of the payment. If the payment is being made after the due date, this should include interest and penalties as well.

As discussed previously, there are other ways to pay the balance due, such as IRS Direct Pay, via credit or debit card (though some credit card companies may charge an additional fee called a "cash advance" to use this method), using the Electronic Federal Tax Payment System (EFTPS), by check or money order, or through an installment agreement.

Pay by Check

Taxpayers may still mail their payment due to the IRS, but the payment should be accompanied with Form 1040-V. The paid preparer must supply taxpayers with copies if they mail Form 1040-V with their check or money order. Taxpayers must mail the payment due by April 15, even if their return was electronically filed earlier.

Form 1040-V is a statement that is sent with a check or money order for any balance due on the taxpayer's current tax year. If the taxpayer files electronically, the voucher and payment are sent together. Most tax preparation software will generate Form 1040-V automatically.

Electronic Funds Withdrawal

Taxpayers can authorize an electronic funds withdrawal (EFW) when they e-file their return if they have a balance due on the return. Taxpayers who choose this option must provide the tax professional with the account number and routing transit number for a savings or checking account. If the financial institution is unable to locate or match the numbers entered in a payment record with account information given on the tax return for the taxpayer, the institution will reject the direct debit request and return the money back to the sender.

Credit or Debit Card Payments

Taxpayers may also pay electronically using a credit or debit card. Taxpayers can make credit or debit card payments when e-filing, or by telephone, or the Internet. A third-party provider may charge a service fee to process the payment.

Electronic Federal Tax Payment System (EFTPS)

Individual taxpayers who make more than one payment per year should enroll in EFTPS. After the taxpayer has been enrolled, they will receive two separate mailings. One is the confirmation or update form; the second is a letter that includes the taxpayer's enrollment trace number, PIN, and instructions on how to obtain an Internet password. Payments on EFTPS can be made 24 hours, 7 days a week; however, to make a timely payment, it must be submitted before 8:00 p.m. EST at least one calendar day prior to the tax due date. Taxpayers can schedule payments up to 365 days in advance.

Returns Not Eligible for IRS e-File

The following individual income tax returns and related return conditions must be paper filed and they cannot be processed using IRS e-file:

- Tax returns with fiscal-year tax periods.
- Amended tax returns prior to 2019.
- Returns containing forms or schedules that cannot be processed by IRS e-file.

Refund Delays

Before giving a taxpayer a refund, the IRS will verify that the taxpayer does not owe any past taxes or other debts such as child support, student loans, unemployment compensation, or any state income tax obligation. If the taxpayer or spouse owes, the refund amount will be applied to their amount owed before any refund amount is paid to the taxpayer. If the amount owed is greater than the amount of refund, then the entire amount of that refund and any future refunds will be applied to offset the amount owed until it has been paid in full.

The following are other reasons a refund could be delayed:

- The return has errors, is incomplete, or needs further review.
- The return includes a claim for refundable credits and was held until Feb 15.
- The return is impacted by identity theft or fraud.
- The tax return includes Form 8379, Injured Spouse Allocation, which can take up to 14 weeks to process and review.

- Errors in the direct deposit information that cause the refund to be sent by check.
- Financial institution's refusal of direct deposit, which will result in the refund being sent by check.
- The estimated tax payments differ from the amounts reported on a tax return.
- Bankruptcy.
- Inappropriate claims for EITC.
- Recertification to claim EITC.

When the refund is delayed, the IRS will send a letter to the taxpayer explaining the issue(s) and how to resolve them. The letter or notice contains the telephone number and address for the taxpayer to use or to acquire further assistance. If there is a delay, the taxpayer can search for the needed information on the IRS website discussed in the "Where's My Refund?" section.

Refund Offsets

When taxpayers owe a prior-year balance, the IRS will offset their current-year refund to pay the balance due on the following items:

- Back taxes.
- Child support.
- Federal agency non-tax debts such as student loans.
- State income tax obligations.

If taxpayers owe any of these debts, their refund will be offset until the debt has been paid off or the refund has been spent, whichever occurs first.

Where's My Refund?

"Where's My Refund?" is a portal on the IRS website that provides information about a taxpayer's refund status. This system is updated once every 24 hours (usually at night), and the taxpayer can begin checking where their refund is within 24 hours after the IRS has acknowledged the tax return—not the date that the provider transmitted the tax return.

Taxpayers will need the following information to track their refund:

- SSN.
- Filing status.
- The full refund amount.

To receive assistance from the IRS or a Taxpayer Assistance Center (TAC) over the phone or in person, a return must have been filed electronically and also have a refund. Otherwise, they will not be able to help. IRS personnel can only research tax returns that were filed at least 21 days before. If the return was mailed, the taxpayer must wait at least 6 weeks for the return to be processed.

The Protecting Americans from Tax Hikes Act, or PATH Act, of 2015 allowed Congress to hold refunds from tax returns with refundable credits until February 15 to reduce the potential for fraud by giving the IRS more time to process and check those returns. Any refunds from tax returns with refundable credits that were held will be released after February 15 in the order that they were received and electronically approved. If the taxpayer is claiming a refundable credit, they should only call the IRS when the "Where's My Refund?" portal directs them to call.

Bank Products

Tax-related bank products are another way for a taxpayer to receive their refund and can be offered to clients to defray the cost of tax preparation fees. The most common types of bank products are as follows:

- Bank Cards: When the deposit is loaded on a bank card to be used like a debit card. Additional fees may apply to the taxpayer.
- Cashier's Check: A paper check that the taxpayer can either cash at a check cashing service or deposit into their personal checking or savings account.
- Refund Advance Loans: A loan from the bank that is based on the taxpayer's refund or a flat amount.

The advantage of using a third-party bank is that the tax preparer's fee can be deducted from the taxpayer's refund. While tax-related bank products are a convenient option for many taxpayers, there are additional fees associated with each bank product, which can vary from bank to bank. If the tax professional marks a tax return for electronic filing when preparing a tax return using software, he or she will be prompted to choose how they would like to receive their refund. There are additional fees charged by the bank and the filing software for each type of bank product. The remaining balance will be distributed to the taxpayer by direct deposit, prepaid debit card, or check. Each bank offers different products, so determine which products are best for your clients. The downside to using a bank product is that if the taxpayer owes child support, back taxes, student loans, or other debts, these debts will be paid before the tax professional receives their preparation fees, which could create an additional fee for taxpayers from their preparers who will now have to collect the fees themselves.

E-File Guidelines for Fraud and Abuse

A "fraudulent return" is a return in which an individual is attempting to file using someone else's name or SSN or in which the taxpayer is presenting documents or information that have no basis in fact. A potentially abusive return is a return that the taxpayer is required to file but which contains inaccurate information that may lead to an understatement of a liability or the overstatement of a credit that could result in a refund to which the taxpayer may not be entitled.

Providers must be on the lookout for fraud and abuse. Electronic return originators (ERO) must be particularly diligent, because they are the first point of contact with taxpayers' personal information, and they are the ones who compile their information to prepare and file the returns. An ERO must be diligent in recognizing fraud and abuse, reporting it to the IRS and preventing it whenever possible. Providers must cooperate with the IRS's investigations by making information and documents related to returns with potential fraud or abuse available to the IRS upon request. An ERO who is also the paid preparer should exercise due diligence in the preparation of all returns involving refundable tax credits, as those credits are the popular target for fraud and abuse. Internal Revenue Code requires paid preparers to exercise due diligence in determining a taxpayer's eligibility for the credit.

Double Check the Taxpayer's Address

Tax professionals should inform taxpayers that the address on the first page of the return, once processed by the IRS, will be used to update the taxpayer's recorded address. The IRS will use the taxpayer's address of record for notices and refunds.

Avoiding Refund Delays

Tax professionals should make sure that all the information is current when they e-file a tax return to avoid refund delays. The tax professional should also inform clients how to avoid delays by having their information correct – encouraging them to double-check the info they provide. Tax preparer should be aware of the following to help avoid delays:

- Make sure to see the actual Social Security card and other forms of identification for all taxpayers and dependents.
- Double-check the data entry of all information prior to submission for e-file.
- Don't allow the taxpayer to insist upon filing erroneous tax returns (if the taxpayer does, return their documents and do not complete the return).
- If the client is new, ask if they filed electronically in the past.
- Keep track of the issues that result in a client's refund delays, document the delays, and add the documentation to the client's files.

Signing an Electronic Tax Return

As with an income tax return submitted to the IRS in paper form, an electronic income tax return is signed by both the taxpayer and the paid preparer. The taxpayer would sign electronically. The taxpayer must sign and date the "Declaration of Taxpayer" to authorize the origination of the electronic submission of the return to the IRS prior to its transmission. The taxpayer must sign a new declaration if the electronic return data on an individual's income tax return is changed after the taxpayer signed the Declaration of Taxpayer and if the amounts differ by more than $50 to "total income" (or AGI) or $14 to "total tax," "federal income tax withheld," "refund," or "amount you owe."

Electronic Signature Methods

Individual income tax returns are signed using PIN numbers generated in one of two ways: the taxpayers can pick it themselves, or the paid tax preparer can generate one for them. Both methods allow the taxpayer to use a personal identification number (PIN) to sign the various forms, although self-selecting a PIN requires the taxpayer to provide his or her prior year adjusted gross income (AGI) amount so the IRS can confirm the taxpayer's identity, link it with the taxpayer's other returns from across the years, and detect any returns fraudulently filed under the taxpayer's name in the future. Signature documents are not required when the taxpayer signs using the self-select method and enters their PIN directly into the electronic return. This does not apply to the practitioner-generated PIN. In all instances, the taxpayer must sign Form 8879, Signature Authorization Form, even if a practitioner-generated PIN was used.

IRS e-File Signature Authorization

When taxpayers are unable to enter their PINs directly into the electronic return, taxpayers must authorize the ERO to enter their PINs by completing Form 8879, *IRS e-file Signature Authorization*.

The ERO may enter the taxpayer's PIN in the electronic return record before the taxpayer signs Form 8879 or 8878, but the taxpayer must sign and date the appropriate form before the ERO originates the electronic submission of the return. In most instances, the taxpayer must sign and date Form 8879 or Form 8878 after reviewing the return and ensuring that the information on the form matches the information on the return.

Electronic Filing

The taxpayer who provides a completed tax return to an ERO for electronic filing may complete the IRS e-file signature authorization without reviewing the return originated by the ERO. The line items from the paper return must be entered on the application Form 8879 or Form 8878 prior to the taxpayer's signing and dating of the form. The ERO may use pre-signed authorizations as authority to input the taxpayer's PIN only if the information on the electronic version of the tax return agrees with the entries from the paper return.

The taxpayer and the ERO must always complete and sign Forms 8879 or 8878 for the practitioner PIN method for electronic signatures. The taxpayer may use the practitioner PIN method to electronically sign Form 4868, *Application for Automatic Extension of Time to File US Individual Income Tax Return*, if a signature is required. A signature is only required for Form 4868 when an electronic funds withdrawal is also being requested. The ERO must retain Form 8879 and Form 8878 for 3 years from the return's due date or the date received by the IRS, whichever is later. EROs must not send Form 8879 and Form 8878 to the IRS unless the IRS requests that they do so.

Guidance for Electronic Signatures

If the tax professional's software allows electronic signatures for Forms 8878 and 8879, the taxpayer can choose to sign it that way instead of using a PIN. Technology has created many different types of e-signatures. For tax preparation, it is not the specific technology that is important but rather that the acceptable signature method is used to capture the taxpayer's information. The following are examples of currently accepted methods by the IRS:

- A handwritten signature that is inputted on an electronic signature pad.
- A handwritten signature, mark, or command inputted on a display screen by means of a stylus device.
- A digitized image of a handwritten signature that is attached to an electronic record.
- A name typed in by the signer (for example, typed at the end of an electronic record or typed into a signature block on a website form).
- A digital signature.
- A mark captured as a scalable graphic.
- A secret code, password, or PIN used to sign the electronic record.

The software must record the following data for the e-signature to be valid:

- Digital image of the signed form.
- Date and time of the signature.
- Taxpayer's computer IP address; used for remote transactions only.
- Taxpayer's login identification (username); used for remote transactions only.
- Method used to sign the record (typed name) or a system log or some other audit trail that reflects the completion of the electronic signature process by the signer.
- Identity verification; taxpayer's knowledge-based authentication past results for in-person transactions and confirmation that government photo identification has been verified.

IRS e-File Security and Privacy Standards

The IRS has mandated six security, privacy, and business standards to better serve taxpayers and protect the information collected, processed, and stored by Online Providers of individual income tax returns.

1. Extended validation of SSL Certificate and minimum encryption standards.
2. Periodic external vulnerability scan.
3. Protecting against bulk filing of fraudulent tax returns.
4. Public Domain Name Registration
5. Reporting of Security Incidents
6. Information Privacy and Safeguard Policies

Part 2 Review Questions

To obtain the maximum benefit from this chapter, LTP recommends that you complete each of the following questions, and then compare them to the answers with feedback that immediately follows. Under governing self-study standards, vendors are required to present review questions intermittently throughout each self-study course.

These questions and explanations are not part of the final examination and will not be graded by LTP.

EFP2.1
Which of the following would the taxpayer not receive from the ERO?

a. Form 8879
b. Form W-2
c. Copy of the return that was electronically filed
d. Tickets to the Super Bowl

EFP2.2
When a tax return is prepared, the tax professional needs to verify the accuracy of which identification numbers?

a. SSN, ITIN, and PTIN
b. SSN, ITIN, and ATIN
c. ITIN, EFIN, and PTIN
d. ATIN, EFIN, and CTIN

EFP2.3
Which of the following copies should the taxpayer keep?

1. Form 8879
2. Income documents related to the tax return
3. Copy of their driver's license
4. The copy of the tax return that the preparer gave to them

a. 1 & 3
b. 3 only
c. 1 & 2
d. 1, 2, & 4

Electronic Filing

EFP2.4

If a tax return has been rejected and the ERO cannot rectify the issue, how soon does he need to notify the taxpayer?

   a. Does not need to notify, just resubmit the tax return.
   b. 24 hours of receiving the rejection notice.
   c. 10 calendar days after the rejection notice.
   d. 72 hours of receiving the rejection notice.

Part 2 Review Questions Answers

EFP2.1

Which of the following would the taxpayer not receive from the ERO?

   a. Form 8879
   b. Form W-2
   c. Copy of the return that was electronically filed
   d. Tickets to the Super Bowl

Feedback: Review section *What the Taxpayer Should Receive.*

EFP2.2

When a tax return is prepared, the tax professional needs to verify the accuracy of which identification numbers?

   a. SSN, ITIN, and PTIN
   b. SSN, ITIN, and ATIN
   c. ITIN, EFIN, and PTIN
   d. ATIN, EFIN, and CTIN

Feedback: Review section *Verifying Taxpayer Identification Numbers (TINs).*

EFP2.3

Which of the following copies should the taxpayer keep?

   1. Form 8879
   2. Income documents related to the tax return
   3. Copy of their driver's license
   4. The copy of the tax return that the preparer gave to them

   a. 1 & 3
   b. 3 only
   c. 1 & 2
   d. 1, 2, & 4

Feedback: Review section *What the Taxpayer Should Receive.*

EFP2.4

If a tax return has been rejected and the ERO cannot rectify the issue, how soon does he need to notify the taxpayer?

   a. Does not need to notify, just resubmit the tax return.
   b. 24 hours of receiving the rejection notice.
   c. 10 calendar days after the rejection notice.
   d. 72 hours of receiving the rejection notice.

Feedback: Review section *Resubmitting Rejected Tax Returns*.

Takeaways

Electronic filing is one of the safest ways to file a tax return, and paid tax preparers are mandated to e-file federal tax returns if they prepare more than 11 returns. Title 26 can impose criminal and monetary penalties on any person who fraudulently engages in preparing or providing services in connection with the tax preparation business. A paid tax professional must guard their clients' information to avoid such penalties. The adoption of e-filing has saved preparers time and resources. Although there are individuals who still prepare returns by hand, the vast majority use software and reap the benefits of all the advantages that come with being automated.

TEST YOUR KNOWLEDGE!
Go online to take a practice quiz.

Chapter 15 Extensions and Amendments

Introduction

If taxpayers are unable to file their federal individual tax returns by the due date, they may be able to qualify for an automatic six-month extension of time to file. The taxpayer can either electronically file or mail Form 4868 to the IRS to file for the extension. If the taxpayer has filed a return and realizes that a mistake was made, they would file an amended return by using Form 1040-X.

Objectives

At the end of this lesson, the student will:

- Understand when an amendment must be filed.
- Realize when to use Form 4868.
- Identify when the installment agreement should be used.

Resources

Form 1040	Publication 17	Instructions Form 1040
Form 1040-X	Publication 54	Instructions Form 1040-X
Form 4868	Tax Topic 308	Instructions Form 4868

Table of Contents

Introduction	472
Part 1 Form 4868: Extension of Time to File	473
Late Payment Penalty	473
Making Extension Payments	474
Installment Agreement Request (Form 9465)	474
Part 1 Review Questions	475
Part 1 Review Questions Answers	476
Part 2 Amended Returns	477
Complete Form 1040-X	479
State Tax Liability	480
Part 2 Review Questions	480
Part 2 Review Questions Answers	482
Takeaways	483

Part 1 Form 4868: Extension of Time to File

File Form 4868, *Application for Automatic Extension*, to file for an automatic six-month extension for filing a federal return. The extension is for filing the tax return only. If the taxpayer has a balance due, the payment must be paid by April 15 or the due date of the return. There are three ways to request an automatic extension:

> File Form 4868 electronically.
> Pay all or part of the estimated income tax due using the Electronic Federal Tax Payment System (EFTPS) or a credit or debit card.
> Mail Form 4868 to the IRS and enclose the tax payment.

To qualify for the extension for extra time, taxpayers must estimate their tax liability as accurately as possible and enter it on Form 4868, line 4, before filing Form 4868 by the regular due date of the return. If the IRS does not accept the extension of time, the taxpayer will receive a letter of denial stating the need to file his or her tax return and how much time they have to file. If the application was accepted, the taxpayer can file any time prior to the extension's due date. For example, if Nolan filed an extension on April 15, 2021, for his 2020 tax return and had no balance due but was missing a W-2 that he didn't receive until July 1, 2021, he could have waited until July 2, 2021, to complete and file his return.

Portion of 2021 Form 4868

If the taxpayer, who is a U.S. citizen or resident, is out of the country, the extension is valid for four months. Part I of Form 4868 is used to identify the taxpayer. Part II is for information about how the tax return should be filed.

Late Payment Penalty

The taxpayer may be charged a late payment penalty of $\frac{1}{2}$% of 1% of any tax (except estimated tax) not paid by the regular filing deadline. An additional monthly penalty with a maximum rate of 25% of the unpaid amount is charged on any unpaid tax. If the taxpayer can show reasonable cause for not paying on time, a statement should be attached to the return (not to Form 4868), and the late penalty payment will not be charged. Both of the following requirements need to be met to be considered reasonable cause:

Extensions and Amendments

> ➤ Paid at least 90% of the tax liability before the regular due date of the return via withholding, estimated payments, or payments made with Form 4868.
> ➤ The remaining balance is paid with tax return on the extended due date.

If the taxpayer has a balance due, interest is accrued on the unpaid balance. The penalty is 5% of the amount due for each month or part of a month the return is late. If the return is more than 60 days late, the minimum penalty is $435 or the balance of the tax due on the return, whichever is smaller. The maximum penalty is 25%.

Making Extension Payments

For extensions, payments can be made electronically by credit card, debit card, money order, the EFTPS system, a direct transfer from a bank account using Direct Pay, or an ACH from the taxpayer's checking or savings account. When making a payment with the extension, remember to include the payment amount on Form 1040, Schedule 3, line 9. EFTPS can also be paid via phone. The taxpayer must write down the confirmation number he or she received when making an electronic payment. If the electronic payment has been designated as an extension payment, then do not file Form 4868.

> *Señor 1040 Says:* If the taxpayer and spouse filed separate Form 4868s with payments and then chose to file the tax return as married filing jointly, make sure to include both payment amounts on Form 4868, line 5.

When paying by check or cashier's check, Form 4868 should be included and mailed to the address on Form 4868. Make sure the check or money order is made payable to United States Treasury. The taxpayer should include their SSN and write Form 4868 in the memo on the check. Do not send cash. Checks over $100 million or more are not accepted, so any payments exceeding that amount will have to be split into two or more payments. The $100 million limit does not apply to other payment methods (such as electronic payments). As with Form 1040, there are specific mailing addresses to mail extension payments. To find which mailing address should be used, see Instructions Form 4868, page 4.

Installment Agreement Request (Form 9465)

If a taxpayer owes the federal government more than can be paid at one time, the taxpayer can file Form 9465, *Installment Agreement Request*, which asks permission to pay the taxes on a monthly basis. The IRS charges a late-payment penalty of 25% per month. If the return was not filed in a timely manner, the late payment penalty is 5% per month. The IRS usually notifies the taxpayer within 30 days of approval or denial of the proposed payment plan.

The user fee for new installment agreements is $225. The taxpayer can also set up a payroll deduction installment agreement, and that fee is $225. If the taxpayer uses an online payment portal, the user fee would be $31.00, if using credit card, check or money order the payment set-up fee is $149.00. If the taxpayer's income is below a certain level (250% of the annual poverty level), the installment agreement may be reduced to $43. Form 13844 must be completed to qualify.

If the taxpayer elects to use the installment agreement, interest and a late-payment penalty will still apply on the unpaid amount by the due date. In agreeing to an installment payment, the taxpayer also agrees to meet all future tax liabilities. If the taxpayer does not have adequate withholding or make estimated payments so their tax liability will be paid in full of a timely filed return, they will be considered in default of the agreement, and the IRS can take immediate action to collect for the entire amount. Form 9465 can be filed electronically with the taxpayer's tax return. The penalties and interest can be avoided if the tax bill is paid in full on the due date.

If the taxpayer can make the payment in full in 120 days, to avoid the installment agreement fee, the taxpayer can call the IRS or apply online and ask for a payment agreement. See Instructions Form 9465, *Installment Agreement Request*.

By completing Form 9465 the taxpayer agrees to the following terms. The terms of the installment agreement are:

- The Installment agreement will remain in effect until all liabilities (including penalties and interest) are paid in full.
- Taxpayer will make each payment monthly by the due date that was chosen on Form 9465. If unable to make a monthly payment, the taxpayer will notify the IRS immediately.
- The agreement is based on current financial condition. IRS may modify or terminate the agreement if the taxpayer's information changes. When requested, taxpayer will provide current financial information.
- Must file all federal tax returns and pay on time any federal taxes owed.
- IRS will apply federal refunds or overpayments to the entire amount owed, including the shared responsibility payment under the ACA, until paid in full.
- If the taxpayer defaults on the installment agreement, an additional $89 reinstatement fee will be charged to reinstate the installment agreement. IRS has the authority to deduct this fee from the first payment after the agreement was reinstated.
- IRS will apply all payments made on this agreement in the best interest of the United States. Generally, IRS will apply the payment to the oldest collection period.

IRS can terminate the installment agreement if the taxpayer does not make the monthly payment as agreed. If the agreement is terminated, the IRS could collect the entire amount owed, except the Individual Shared Responsibility Payment under the ACA, by levying the taxpayers' income, bank accounts, or other assets, and even seizing property. If the tax collection is in jeopardy, the IRS may terminate the agreement. The IRS may file a Notice of Federal Tax Lien, if not already been filed.

Part 1 Review Questions

To obtain the maximum benefit from this chapter, LTP recommends that you complete each of the following questions, and then compare them to the answers with feedback that immediately follows. Under governing self-study standards, vendors are required to present review questions intermittently throughout each self-study course.

These questions and explanations are not part of the final examination and will not be graded by LTP.

Extensions and Amendments

EAP1.1
Which of the following is true when filing Form 4868?

a. Interest is charged on the tax that was not paid by the due date of the return, even if an extension was filed.
b. Electronic filing cannot be used to file an extension of time to file.
c. Any U.S. citizen who is out of the country on April 18, 2022, is allowed an automatic six-month extension of time to file his or her return and pay any federal balance due.
d. Filing Form 4868 provides an automatic two-month extension to file and pay income tax.

EAP1.2
Which scenario is correct?

a. Marie filed Form 4868 on April 18, 2022, but did not pay the amount due. Marie may be charged a late penalty.
b. Paul died on April 1, 2022, and did not file a return. Paul will be charged death taxes on his 2021 tax return.
c. Pedro did not file Form 4868 and will receive a refund. Pedro will be charged a late penalty on the refund amount.
d. Reed filed his tax return timely and will be charged a penalty for filing on time.

EAP1.3
Faith has a balance due on her 2021 federal tax return and needs to make monthly payments to the IRS. Which of the following would she use?

a. Form 4868
b. Form 1040X
c. Form 9465
d. Form 1040

Part 1 Review Questions Answers

EAP1.1
Which of the following is true when filing Form 4868?

a. **Interest is charged on the tax that was not paid by the due date of the return, even if an extension was filed.**
b. Electronic filing cannot be used to file an extension of time to file.
c. Any U.S. citizen who is out of the country on April 18, 2022, is allowed an automatic six-month extension of time to file his or her return and pay any federal balance due.
d. Filing Form 4868 provides an automatic two-month extension to file and pay income tax.

Feedback: Review section *Form 4869: Extension of Time to File.*

EAP1.2

Which scenario is correct?

  a. **Marie filed Form 4868 on April 18, 2021, but did not pay the amount due. Marie may be charged a late penalty.**
  b. Paul died on April 1, 2022, and did not file a return. Paul will be charged death taxes on his 2021 tax return.
  c. Pedro did not file Form 4868 and will receive a refund. Pedro will be charged a late penalty on the refund amount.
  d. Reed filed his tax return timely and will be charged a penalty for filing on time.

Feedback: Review section *Late Payment Penalty*.

EAP1.3

Faith has a balance due on her 2021 federal tax return and needs to make monthly payments to the IRS. Which of the following would she use?

  a. Form 4868
  b. Form 1040X
  c. Form 9465
  d. Form 1040

Feedback: Review section *Installment Agreement*.

Part 2 Amended Returns

Form 1040-X is available to be e-filed as long as the original return was filed electronically. In 2021 there are new mailing addresses for where to send an original and amended tax return. Be aware of where to send the information so the taxpayer's information is not lost by sending to an incorrect address.

Form 1040-X

Extensions and Amendments

When an original return must be corrected and the corrections will alter the current tax calculations, an amended tax return must be filed. An amended return cannot be filed unless the original return has been completed, but once it has been filed, an amended return becomes the new tax return for the taxpayer. The amended return is used to change items that were previously claimed and now need adjusting because they were originally over- or understated.

For example, if the taxpayer needs to report additional income from a W-2 that arrived after the taxpayer filed the original return or if the taxpayer needs to remove a dependent because they were not eligible to claim them, the taxpayer would file an amended return. Taxpayers who wish to receive a refund from an amended return must file the amendment within three years (including extensions) of the date the original return was filed or within two years of the date the tax was paid, whichever was later.

Example: Isabella filed her original return on March 1 of the current tax year, and her return was due April 15 of the same year. Isabella is considered to have filed her return by April 15. However, if Isabella had filed for an extension until October 15 and filed her return on July 1, her return is considered to be filed on July 1.

Other reasons a taxpayer might need to file an amendment are:

- To add or remove dependents.
- To report the proper filing status.
- To report additional income from a W-2, Form 1099, or some other income statement.
- To make changes in above-the-line deductions, standard deductions, or itemized deductions.
- To add or remove tax credits.
- To report bad debt or worthless security.
- To report foreign tax credit or deduction.

The status of an amended return can be tracked using the web portal "Where's My Amended Return?" on the IRS website after providing one's identification number (SSN, ITIN, etc.), date of birth, and zip code.

Do not file Form 1040-X in the following situations:

- The taxpayer is requesting a refund of penalties and interest or an addition to tax that has already been paid. Instead, use Form 843, *Claim for Refund and Request for Abatement*.
- The taxpayer is requesting a refund for his or her share of a joint overpayment that was offset against a past-due obligation of his or her spouse. Instead, file Form 8379, *Injured Spouse Allocation*.

Interest and penalties will also be charged from the due date of the return for failure to file, negligence, fraud, substantial valuation misstatements, substantial understatements of tax, and reportable transaction understatements.

Complete Form 1040-X

The following content is how to file the 1040-X when not using software. Most software will have the preparer add Form 1040-X, and then save the form to the return, then make changes on the form that was added or removed from the original return. For example, Jimmy received an additional W-2. Tax preparer would enter the W-2 as an additional form, and software will flow the information to Form 1040- X. Filing the form electronically helps since one does not need to mail the return and information.

Portion of Form 1040-X

Part I of the 1040-X is where the taxpayer would make changes that affect lines 1-31 of the original tax return. Part II is where the taxpayer can choose to have $3 go to the Presidential Election Campaign Fund. This must be done within 20.5 months after the original due date of the return. Part III is for the explanation of changes. The IRS wants to know what was changed on the return and why the taxpayer is filing Form 1040-X.

The three columns on Form 1040-X are as follows:

➢ Column A: The original return amount.
➢ Column B: The Net Change. Enter the change in amount for each line that is altered.
➢ Column C: The correct amount. Add or subtract column B (if there is an entry) from column A and enter amount in column C.

Example: Robert reported $41,000 as his adjusted gross income on his 2021 Form 1040. He then received another Form W-2 for $500 after he had already filed his return. He should complete line 1 of Form 1040-X as follows:

	Column A	Column B	Column C
Line 1	$41,000	$500	$41,500

Extensions and Amendments

On Form 1040-X, input the income, deductions, and credits as originally reported on the return in Column A, input the changes being made in Column B, and place the difference or sum in Column C. Next, figure the tax on the corrected amount of taxable income and calculate the amount owed or to be refunded. If the taxpayer owes taxes, the taxpayer should pay the full amount with Form 1040-X. The tax owed will not be subtracted from any amount credited to estimated tax.

If the taxpayer cannot pay the full amount due on the amended return, he or she can ask to make monthly installment payments using Form 9465. If the taxpayer overpaid taxes, they will receive a refund. The overpayment refunded based on the amended return is different and separate from any refund gained from the original return.

When assembling an amended return to be mailed, make sure that the schedules and forms are behind Form 1040-X and that the taxpayer (and spouse if filing jointly) sign the 1040-X. If the amendment was prepared by a paid tax preparer, the tax preparer must sign as well.

> *Señor* 1040 Says: Make sure to use the correct form for the year that is being amended. To find the forms you need, go to www.irs.gov, and choose the correct form(s) to amend the tax return.

Attach these forms to the front of Form 1040-X if they support changes made on the return:

- Forms W-2, W-2c, and Form 2439.
- Forms W-2G and 1099-R.
- Forms 1042-S, SSA-1042S, RRB-1042S, and 8288-A.

Attach to the back of Form 1040-X any Form 8805, *Foreign Partner's Information Statement of Section 1446 Withholding Tax*, that supports the changes made.

When sending a check or money order to the IRS for payments of taxes due, do not attach the check to the return. Instead, enclose it in the envelope and make sure the check is made out to "United States Treasury."

State Tax Liability

If a return is changed for any reason, it may affect the state income tax liability. This includes changes made as a result of an examination of the return by the IRS. The IRS will inform the taxpayer's state if adjustments are made on his or her federal tax return.

Part 2 Review Questions

To obtain the maximum benefit from this chapter, LTP recommends that you complete each of the following questions, and then compare them to the answers with feedback that immediately follows. Under governing self-study standards, vendors are required to present review questions intermittently throughout each self-study course.

These questions and explanations are not part of the final examination and will not be graded by LTP.

EAP2.1
Which scenario is true?

a. The taxpayer has two years to make any corrections that result in additional tax refunds, including extensions after the date the original return was filed or within 3 years after the date the tax was paid, whichever was later.
b. The taxpayer has four years to make any corrections that result in additional tax refunds, including extensions after the date the original return was filed or within 2 years after the date the tax was paid, whichever was later.
c. The taxpayer has three years to make any corrections that result in additional tax refunds, including extensions after the date the original return was filed or within 2 years after the date the tax was paid, whichever was later.
d. The taxpayer is not allowed to make any corrections on previous year tax returns.

EAP2.2
Which of the following is used to file a federal amended return?

a. Form 1040
b. Form 1040-X
c. Form 4868
d. Form 2241

EAP2.3
Which of the following would not be a valid reason to file an amendment?

a. Taxpayer changing personal exemptions.
b. Taxpayer claiming their cousins' dependents.
c. Taxpayer reporting additional income.
d. Taxpayer claiming additional tax credits.

EAP2.4
Lorena filed her original tax return on April 15 and was scheduled to receive a tax refund on May 9. Lorena realized she forgot income from her summer job. She files an amended return on May 3. The amended tax return resulted in Lorena having a balance due. Lorena paid her balance due on May 3. Which scenario is true?

a. Lorena is not subject to a penalty because she paid her tax due on May 3.
b. Lorena is subject to a penalty for not paying her tax due by April 15.
c. Lorena is subject to a penalty for amending her tax return.
d. Lorena does not have to report the income from her summer job.

Extensions and Amendments

Part 2 Review Questions Answers

EAP2.1
Which scenario is true?

a. The taxpayer has two years to make any corrections that result in additional tax refunds, including extensions after the date the original return was filed or within 3 years after the date the tax was paid, whichever was later.
b. The taxpayer has four years to make any corrections that result in additional tax refunds, including extensions after the date the original return was filed or within 2 years after the date the tax was paid, whichever was later.
c. The taxpayer has three years to make any corrections that result in additional tax refunds, including extensions after the date the original return was filed or within 2 years after the date the tax was paid, whichever was later.
d. The taxpayer is not allowed to make any corrections on previous year tax returns.

Feedback: Review section *Part 2: Amended Returns.*

EAP2.2
Which of the following is used to file a federal amended return?

a. Form 1040
b. Form 1040-X
c. Form 4868
d. Form 2241

Feedback: Review section *Part 2: Amended Returns.*

EAP2.3
Which of the following would not be a valid reason to file an amendment?

a. Taxpayer changing personal exemptions.
b. Taxpayer claiming their cousins' dependents.
c. Taxpayer reporting additional income.
d. Taxpayer claiming additional tax credits.

Feedback: Review section *Part 2: Amended Returns.*

EAP2.4
Lorena filed her original tax return on April 15 and was scheduled to receive a tax refund on May 9. Lorena realized she forgot income from her summer job. She files an amended return on May 3. The amended tax return resulted in Lorena having a balance due. Lorena paid her balance due on May 3. Which scenario is true?

a. Lorena is not subject to a penalty because she paid her tax due on May 3.
b. Lorena is subject to a penalty for not paying her tax due by April 15.
c. Lorena is subject to a penalty for amending her tax return.
d. Lorena does not have to report the income from her summer job.

Feedback: Review section *Part 2: Amended Returns.*

Takeaways

This chapter gives a brief understanding of extensions and amendments. The paid tax professional must understand who should file for an extension and when to file an amendment as these are two separate processes.

If more time is needed to file the tax return, the individual should file for an extension. However, an extension of time to file *is not an extension of time to pay*. Payment is still owed by the April 15th deadline or the taxpayer will pay late payment penalties. An extension of time to file does not change this. Although an extension of time to pay and various payment plans do exist, these should not be confused with extensions of time to file.

TEST YOUR KNOWLEDGE!
Go online to take a practice quiz.

The Latino Tax Professionals Association (LTPA) is a professional association dedicated to excellence in serving tax professionals who work in all areas of tax practice, including individual practitioners, accounting and bookkeeping services, enrolled agents, certified public accountants, and immigration attorneys. Our unique, interactive e-book and online training system provides the only tax and bookkeeping training in both English y en español. Our mission is to provide knowledge, professionalism, and community to those who serve the Latino taxpayer, to help you grow your practice and increase your profits by attracting more Latino clients, and to provide the best tax preparation training available.

Latino Tax Professionals Association, LLC
1588 Moffett Street, Suite F
Salinas, California 93905
866-936-2587
www.latinotaxpro.com

For support: edsupport@latinotaxpro.org

Made in the USA
Columbia, SC
20 June 2022